AF361598

A Political Companion to James Baldwin

A POLITICAL COMPANION TO

James Baldwin

EDITED BY Susan J. McWilliams

UNIVERSITY PRESS OF KENTUCKY

Editorial and Sales Offices: The University Press of Kentucky
663 South Limestone Street, Lexington, Kentucky 40508-4008
www.kentuckypress.com

Library of Congress Cataloging-in-Publication Data

Names: McWilliams, Susan Jane, 1977– editor.
Title: A political companion to James Baldwin / edited by Susan J. McWilliams.
Description: Lexington : University Press of Kentucky, [2017] | Series:
  Political companions to great American authors | Includes bibliographical
  references and index.
Identifiers: LCCN 2017038157| ISBN 9780813169910 (hardcover : alk. paper) |
  ISBN 9780813169927 (pdf) | ISBN 9780813169934 (epub)
Subjects: LCSH: Baldwin, James, 1924–1987—Political and social views. |
  Politics and literature—United States—History—20th century. | Politics
  in literature.
Classification: LCC PS3552.A45 Z849 2017 | DDC 818/.5409—dc23
LC record available at https://lccn.loc.gov/2017038157

This book is printed on acid-free paper meeting the requirements of the
American National Standard for Permanence in Paper for Printed Library
Materials.

Manufactured in the United States of America.

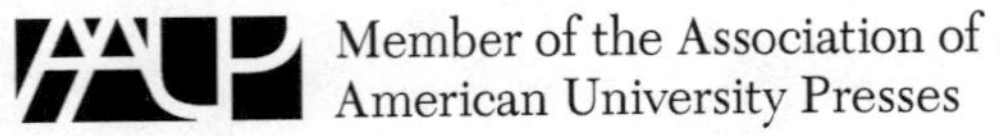

Contents

Series Foreword

Those who undertake a study of American political thought must attend to the great theorists, philosophers, and essayists. Such a study is incomplete, however, if it neglects American literature, one of the greatest repositories of the nation's political thought and teachings.

America's literature is distinctive because it is, above all, intended for a democratic citizenry. In contrast to eras when an author would aim to inform or influence a select aristocratic audience, in democratic times, public influence and education must resonate with a more expansive, less leisured, and diverse audience to be effective. The great works of America's literary tradition are the natural locus of democratic political teaching. Invoking the interest and attention of citizens through the pleasures afforded by the literary form, many of America's great thinkers sought to forge a democratic public philosophy with subtle and often challenging teachings that unfolded in narrative, plot, and character development. Perhaps more than any other nation's literary tradition, American literature is ineluctably political—shaped by democracy as much as it has in turn shaped democracy.

The Political Companions to Great American Authors series highlights the teachings of the great authors in America's literary and belletristic tradition. An astute political interpretation of America's literary tradition requires careful, patient, and attentive readers who approach the text with a view to understanding its underlying messages about citizenship and democracy. Essayists in this series approach the classic texts not with a "hermeneutics of suspicion" but with the curiosity of fellow citizens who believe that the great authors have something of value to teach their readers. The series brings together essays from varied approaches and viewpoints for the common purpose of elucidating the political teachings of the nation's greatest authors for those seeking a better understanding of American democracy.

Patrick J. Deneen
Series Editor

Introduction

Susan J. McWilliams

"It is a Baldwinian moment," a colleague says to me in the spring of 2016. He says this at the end of an academic year in which college students across the United States have—with a speed that seems to surprise even themselves—organized protests and occupied buildings and issued demands for greater racial diversity, equity, and sensitivity on their campuses. Those students are reading Baldwin, quoting Baldwin, rediscovering Baldwin. The measure of a certain kind of public conversation, my Facebook feed flashes regularly with snippets of *The Fire Next Time,* a book that seems so newly relevant to so many (including to Ta-Nehisi Coates, who took the form for his 2015 best seller *Between the World and Me* from Baldwin's tome).[1] So to my colleague, I nod. It is a Baldwinian moment.

But it is hardly the first Baldwinian moment, hardly the first moment in which Baldwin's prophetic words about the pain and peril of America's race problem have washed to the forefront of our public life, even in recent years. Consider the year 2013, when George Zimmerman was acquitted for the murder of black teenager Trayvon Martin, and the hashtag #BlackLivesMatter first appeared on the Internet, then grew into an activist movement that drew new and unflinching attention to the regularity of violence, particularly state violence, against African Americans. As Lisa Beard and Eddie Glaude argue later in this volume, Baldwin's imprint on and resonance in the Black Lives Matter movement is unmistakable.

And before Black Lives Matter, the ascendancy and presidency of Barack Obama had seemed to many—see P. J. Brendese's essay in this volume—like Baldwinian moments. After all, Obama's early encounters with Baldwin's writings helped shape the future president's earliest thoughts about American political life and identity—helping, as one writer put it, to turn "Barry" into Barack.[2] "One is struck by the connection between them," Colm Tóibín observes, "two men remaking the world against all the odds in their own likeness, not afraid to ask, when faced with the future of America as represented by its children, using James Baldwin's wonderful phrase, questions that are alien to most politicians: 'What will happen to all that beauty?'"[3] And yet others noted that Baldwin understood, well before a black president seemed an immediate potentiality, that the symbolic placement of a black body in the White House might easily be used to downplay or discredit systematic racial inequalities.[4] Against those who longed for Obama's election to mean a finally "postracial" America, Baldwin's writings cautioned, appropriately and presciently, otherwise.

I can keep going back through the storehouse of Baldwinian moments: keep going back to the *Parents v. Seattle* and *Meredith v. Jefferson* decisions of 2006, back through the decades-long debates about gay rights and gay marriage, back to the self-immolation of south central Los Angeles in the "Rodney King riots" in 1992, back to the Willie Horton ad that defined the 1988 presidential campaign, back to the early 1980s, when Baldwin was still very much alive and very much writing and very much in a moment that was his, not just in spirit, but in body, too.

They are all Baldwinian moments, these moments in American life, I think. This is still Baldwin's America. It's just that at some moments, we happen to notice it more than others.

America is still that "exceedingly monotonous minstrel show," running over and again through "the same dances, same music, same jokes," and in which Baldwin played participant, viewer, and critic. "One has done (or been) the show so long that one can do it in one's sleep," he said; he had the script down.[5] Before and since Baldwin's death almost thirty years ago, the American political experience, and particularly the racial politics that lie in the bloody and battered heart of that experience, keeps turning us back and back to the importance of turning back to Baldwin.

Baldwin and the American Experience

I use the language of "experience" intentionally, since for Baldwin, experience is a bedrock problem for Americans. In fact, in the next-to-last paragraph of "The Black Boy Looks at the White Boy," itself the last essay in

Nobody Knows My Name, he writes that "the general fear of experience is one of the reasons that the American writer has so peculiarly difficult and dangerous a time."[6]

Before I explore that claim, I need to say that there is no doubt that James Baldwin considered all American writing—including his own—to be bound up in American political and social history, bound up in ways that are reflective of and instructive about American politics. He could write about "the American writer" in the singular for this reason; in Baldwin's account, anyone marking up a page in the United States is someone who bears the marks of some national past and present. Even though we might not be trapped in our nation, our nation is trapped in us.

But although Baldwin saw American writers as the products of some grand American machinery—a machinery that all Americans "had been made and mangled by"—he thought of them also as something more.[7] For Baldwin, if American writers are inescapably products of American politics, they can also be prophets within American politics. If they do not set the terms or topics or even the language of conversation, they have the capacity to redirect where that conversation goes and to alter the language in which that conversation takes place. In Baldwin's imagination, writers are America's students and teachers. They are both cogs and wrenches in the works. They exist in a state of perpetual lovers' quarrel: hitched to the republic but often humiliated by it, entranced by but distrustful of its highest promises, and full of all the rapture and terror that any real love brings. American writers are struggling, always struggling, for the heart of America. At the core of that struggle is the struggle to witness: to see and feel and accept and articulate the truth of what is and has been, to let oneself be terrorized by that truth, then to transmit that truth to the page.

Consider again, Baldwin's bold but elusive claim about American experience: "The general fear of experience is one of the reasons that the American writer has so peculiarly difficult and dangerous a time." A careful reader will notice that this line can be faithfully interpreted in at least two ways. Each interpretation brings Baldwin into a different level of relief, and the mutual, tense coexistence of these interpretive views microcosmically represents the tightness and tension of Baldwin's mind as well as the unifying force of Baldwin's political vision.

At first pass, you could interpret this line as ascribing "the general fear of experience" to Americans and American culture at large. Therefore, the

American writer—whose currency and responsibility is faithfulness to experience, Baldwin often says—lives at odds with his audience. The American writer is engaging in a conversation with people and a polity who refuse to listen, with people and a polity who don't really want to engage in conversation. Since conversation has to be dialogic—to be *con*-versing, etymologically, you must be speaking *with,* and not just to—the problem of the American writer is obvious.

This possibility runs throughout Baldwin's writing, both fiction and nonfiction, both early and late in his life. Baldwin's America is one in which real intellectual effort is discounted and distrusted, in which people prefer whatever illusions they can get their hands on to the ultimate truth of their own mortality. It is a land of willful ignorance and violent innocence. His Americans are anxious, vertiginous, terrified—and desperate to do what they need to do to pretend otherwise, lest they have to interrogate what it is that underlies that terror, and risk exposing it. For Baldwin, Americans are beset by paranoia. It is a paranoia fed on fear—"some nameless fear," Baldwin says, "that has nothing to do with Negros."[8] But then again, the nameless fear has everything to do with them. For white Americans in particular, as Baldwin says:

> The prevailing notion of American life seems to involve a kind of rung-by-rung ascension to some hideously desirable state. If this is one's concept of life, obviously one cannot afford to slip back one rung. When one slips, one slips back not a rung but back into chaos and no longer knows who he is. And this reason, this fear, suggests to me one of the real reasons for the status of the Negro in this country. In a way, the Negro tells us where the bottom is: *because he is there,* and *where* he is, beneath us, we know where the limits are and how far we must not fall.[9]

The grand American illusions—that there is mobility, and there is progress, and there is advancement, and that these things all have meaning, and that there is order—need, to achieve more than illusory status (for nonblack people, anyway), the support of another illusion: the illusion of racial hierarchy and black inferiority. That illusion, of course, authorizes both systematic violence against black individuals and communities and a willful blindness to the fact and nature of that violence.

Racism and racialized violence, tied as they are to the maintenance of the grandest American illusions, have such intractable power because the alternative for white Americans in particular is to abandon the neat promises of fantasy progress ladders and to dive into the messy truth: the truth that, in Baldwin's words, "everyone born is going to have a rather difficult time getting through his life" and that "people fall in love according to some principle that we have not as yet been able to define, to defend or isolate."[10] Life is hard, and love is a mystery, and then we die, and none of us is the favorite child. These are truths, perhaps *the* truths of human life. There is nothing more basic, and yet nothing more at odds with the most basic of American pretensions, the basic American conceit that we are each masters of our own destiny whose work and effort are rightly ordered and rewarded in this world, and the concomitant American conceit of white supremacy that whiteness is favored, favorite, special. Almost without exception, Baldwin's American characters—think of David in *Giovanni's Room,* John in *Go Tell It on the Mountain,* Leo Proudhammer in *Tell Me How Long the Train's Been Gone*—are characters who are terrified about the basic truths of who they are, about what it means to be human, about what it means to live and love and be certain of your own eventual death.

To write truthfully about blacks in America is to reveal the deceptive nature of claims of black inferiority. And to reveal the deceptive nature of those claims is to open your audience to the deceptive nature of the grander, fundamental American illusions—that so many of the underlying ambitions of American life *are* illusions. Baldwin often exhorts his readers, and his listeners, to self-examination (in a Socratic key, as Joel Schlosser argues in this volume); that is the concluding cadence, the refrain throughout his entire corpus. In that sense, he seems to stand outside his audience, the writer who is shouting in the ear of someone who is not quite deaf, but affects to be.

And yet Baldwin knew that within this morass of self-resistance and self-deceit, this is the nation whose slaveholding founders got stuck in our minds the deepest, democratic truth of human existence: the truth that all people are created equal. There is perversity in that, but there is hope there, too—at least enough reason to try for a conversation.

The Depths of Democracy

To endeavor to hear James Baldwin properly, then, it is important to go beyond his conventional reputation as a writer concerned mostly with questions of race in America. That account of things is correct as far as it goes, but it does not go nearly far enough. "Baldwin is large; he contains multitudes!" as Dwight A. McBride reminds us, cautioning us against what Baldwin recognized as the dangers of privileging—in our thinking about African Americans—the category of race over all other forms of difference.[11] And that's not to mention the ways in which Baldwin might well resist the idea that we should understand him primarily in terms of categories of difference in the first place.

For as the essays in this volume make clear, Baldwin is not just one of the nation's most important thinkers on matters of racial consciousness and injustice but also one of our most articulate theorists of democratic life. His ability to plumb the depths of the national psyche, to see beneath the appearances of our conventional apparatus, makes him one of the most prescient and prophetic political thinkers in the history of the American experiment.

For Baldwin, understanding the surface dilemma of racial injustice in the United States was never enough. For him, it was necessary to go deeper, to tend to the cringing ambivalences, the terrors of belonging, the screaming and anxious clamor of the American soul. In Baldwin's telling, the machinery of our history has mangled us all; even if we could take apart the machinery, we could not repair all the damage that has been done to our selves. Against the idea that ending formal or legal manifestations of racism would end America's color problem, Baldwin insists on a fuller acknowledgment of human limitation and the ways in which racialized experience permeates our everyday life and language. Against the common refrain that "raising awareness" of racist practices is enough to overcome them, Baldwin argues that a much more radical spiritual transformation is in order. Confronting racial injustice requires attention to a basic political fact: that "the interior life is a real life, and the intangible dreams of people have a tangible effect on the world."[12]

Taking that fact seriously demands relentless inward witnessing—a fact that also finds expression in Baldwin's notion that "the general fear of experience is one of the reasons that the American writer has so peculiarly difficult and dangerous a time." For that line could be read as ascribing "the general fear of experience" to the American writer himself. The fear of experience could be Baldwin's own. Of course, the writer who fears experience would have a "peculiarly difficult and dangerous" time of it. He would be at odds with himself, a man set against his craft, his heart set against his hand. Writers must fight, for themselves and for us, against our all-too-human resistance to the truth, and to ourselves.

One of the prevailing themes of Baldwin's work involves the difficult necessity of looking into the past to understand the truth of the present. We must look back to see how we got here, and really where we are. For any black American, that seems especially gruesome a task. It is often in this vein that Baldwin does draw for us, on numerous occasions, an autobiographical picture of a writer who is fighting his own fear. In multiple essays, for instance, Baldwin describes his own fear of visiting the South. "The South had always frightened me," he writes. "How deeply it had frightened me—though I had never seen it."[13] Elsewhere, Baldwin describes his envy of Ingmar Bergman in "The Northern Protestant" in this way: "It did not seem likely, after all, that I would ever be able to make of my past, on film, what Bergman had been able to make of his. In some ways, his past is easier to deal with: it was, at once, more remote and more present." Baldwin then hopes he could "*dare* to envision" his own tragic hero—himself.[14] I take the verb he uses to be significant: You only need to *dare* to do something when you are deeply afraid of doing it.

In his own telling, perhaps Baldwin's greatest act of daring—and the confrontation with his own greatest fear—was to come to terms with his own Americanness. In one of his most memorable essays, "The Discovery of What It Means to Be an American" (an essay whose journey is reflected in his novel *Giovanni's Room*), Baldwin writes that he had assumed, before he went to France, that he knew something of his own identity—which he defined against the prevailing American culture. But in Europe, he writes, "I proved, to my astonishment, to be as American as any Texas G.I."[15] Much of Baldwin's writing, I think, has to be read as the story of his experience wrestling with the fear born of that revelation. He says in "East River, Downtown" that "the American Negro deludes himself if he imagines himself capable of any loyalty other than his loyalty to the United States."[16] If we apply here Baldwin's contention about the nature of illusions in human life, he is here trying to face down the fear that comes with taking down that particular delusion. (If "nobody knows my name," it is true that you do not know my name, but then again, neither do I.) Baldwin is describing, in so much of his writing, the process of his own disillusionment. And disillusionment is tragic as well as liberatory.

Moreover, the ultimate fear of experience with a writer is the fear of writing itself, the fear of addressing an audience and of being misunderstood or not understood. And that's where, I think, the two interpretive possibilities for the line with which I began—the general fear pertaining to the culture, and the general fear pertaining to the writer—are joined. For I take one of Baldwin's great strengths to be a kind of Hegelian point: that our greatest challenge and our greatest resistance is seeing the other in the self, and recognizing that you're part of some universal thing called the human.

For the writer, that can be a terrible challenge—he has to see himself in the audience, and if it is a difficult or hostile audience, like the American audience, that's especially hard. If Americans are, as Baldwin describes them in "Notes for a Hypothetical Novel," "a handful of incoherent people in an incoherent country," then Baldwin has to come to terms with his own incoherence. And as a writer, Baldwin also has to get the audience to see themselves in him, to see their own incoherence through his. As Baldwin says, "I'm certain that there is something which unites all the Americans in this room, though I can't say what it is."[17]

He does say it, though, when he offers a vision of the truth with which all Americans—and which all accounts of American politics—have to wrestle. In "Alas, Poor Richard," Baldwin writes: "The past of a Negro is blood dripping down through leaves, gouged-out eyeballs, the sex torn from its socket and severed with a knife. But this past is not special to the Negro. The horror is also the past, and the everlasting potential, or temptation, of the human race."

Horror is the fact, and safety is the illusion. For Baldwin, accepting that truth is "the source of all our power," not just in the generally human but in the politically democratic sense. For the fact of our horror and depravity is our *common* fact. It is, along with our births and deaths and capacities for love and laughter, what makes us human and what gives truth to that old proposition that all people are created equal. "If we do not know this, it seems to me," Baldwin writes, "we know nothing about ourselves, nothing about each other." So "one must first accept this paradox, with joy."[18] Rather than fear the horror generally, Baldwin wants us to name it explicitly. We cannot predicate our lives on "some nameless fear" without doing a basic kind of violence to ourselves, and to others—as the story of blacks in America reminds us. This is the lesson of the American political experience and the lesson that precedes any true democratic achievement: We must know and name the fear in order to know and name ourselves.

Our Other's Keepers

For Baldwin, perhaps the most essential moral task confronting Americans—the essential political task facing the American republic—is to recognize the interconnectedness of all our lives. "One has got to arrive at the point," he argues, "where one realizes that if one man is hungry everyone is hungry."[19] At minimum, his is a call for mutual recognition and understanding. Yet as I said before, Baldwin understood that among the greatest difficulties in human life is the attempt to understand others and the attempt to make oneself understood. Such attempts always have imperfect results, and often great *mis*understanding results. Even as we are all interconnected, we are all embodied separately, and the latter fact provides an obstacle to understanding the former.

In the same vein, Baldwin saw that part of the great democratic duty involved trying to find the right words to articulate experience.[20] He labored mightily to convey the truth of his own experiences, and he worked just as hard to imagine and be faithful to the experiences of others. This is perhaps best illustrated by the fact that, unlike many if not most writers of fiction, Baldwin's main characters cross not only the color line but also demarcations of gender and sexuality. His writing reflects an essential commitment to the idea that bearing witness to other human beings is a central political responsibility, and in striving to meet that responsibility we give ourselves the best chance of transformation or even salvation.

Baldwin's own deep witnessing of Americans and American political life is so powerful, so spot-on, that it can be almost eerie to read in the present day. To offer only one example: almost fifty years ago Baldwin predicted the American West was headed toward a crisis because people there have always seemed intent on buying houses they cannot afford; "ain't a damn thing paid for out there," he said. This prophecy of a housing crisis would be astounding enough on its own. But Baldwin goes further and makes an even more haunting claim. The crisis of the overmortgaged American, Baldwin predicted, presaged a renewed racial crisis in the United States. "If your Cadillac and your swimming pool aren't paid for and you know you can't go any further West," he said, "then, of course, any black boy or Mexican coming anywhere *near* your monstrously mortgaged joint, which is *all you have,* is an intolerable threat."[21]

Today, when an energized nativism has radiated from the American Southwest to all corners, propelling a shoddy real estate developer into the White House, Baldwin's prophecy is almost painful in its prescience. His ability to link what to many seem unconnected political phenomena in the present day—the subprime mortgage explosion and renewed hostility to foreigners, "illegals," and nonwhites—testifies to the depth of his political seeing. Half a century ago Baldwin understood the true dimensions of the twenty-first-century "housing crisis" better than most contemporary commentators (and better than all contemporary economists), as he so well understood the broad outlines of the American nation and much of the modern world beyond its borders.

Mapping Baldwin

In this spirit, the essays in this volume work to elaborate James Baldwin's political teachings on matters both general and specific. They address Baldwin as a democratic theorist, activist, and citizen, delving into topics such as the civil rights movement, religion, homosexuality, and women's liberation. In covering all that ground, these essays—a combination of essays reprinted, revised, and entirely new—try to make clear the breadth and depth of Baldwin's thought and showcase his continuing relevance to American political life and thought in the present day.

Part 1 of the book, "Collective Consciousness and Community," aims to explore the ways in which Baldwin's work speaks to and galvanizes a collective American polity. Chapter 1, "'A Most Disagreeable Mirror': Race Consciousness as Double Consciousness" by Lawrie Balfour, both positions Baldwin in relation to W. E. B. Du Bois and also expands notions of consciousness to discuss Baldwin's ability to reach across and beyond the color line. Balfour's essay draws upon the Du Boisian notion of double consciousness in order to establish a sense of general race consciousness. In doing so, Balfour, and in turn Baldwin, challenge the notion that white supremacy was extinguished with the extinction of slavery. Balfour's Baldwin often acts as a trickster figure, using a polyphonic voice to speak to both white and black Americans, placing emphasis on a joint sense of community, and in turn, burden. Balfour's essay is significant in establishing Baldwin's simultaneous appreciation yet careful delineating of community.

Chapter 2, "The Race of a More Perfect Union: James Baldwin, Segregated Memory, and the Presidential Race," draws upon Balfour's race consciousness but shifts the focus from split consciousness to split memory. Brendese's essay uses the 2008 election of President Barack Obama to examine racial tensions and divisions present in memory, both between and within black and white Americans. Brendese's study of Baldwin addresses the political implications of segregated memory in order to dismantle those unconscious barriers preventing the desegregation of history, narrative, and myth. Brendese's essay goes on to expand Baldwin's views of history; namely, that the past and present are inextricably and forever bound to one another. Utmost emphasis is placed on understanding both individual and societal histories. In order to move forward, a greater collective memory must be rectified, or else the stark divisions present in America's remembering speak ill of the potential for future progress.

This segregated memory may also be linked to an American affinity for disconnection; in this case, to disconnect from one's past and/or fellow Americans. This civic atrophy of community is explored in chapter 3, "James Baldwin and the Politics of Disconnection." There, I examine those works of Baldwin's, both fiction and essay, concerned with American citizenship and its complicity with a growing sense of a fractured nationality, reaching beyond explicit white and black racial tension. This work also incorporates Baldwin's internationalism, exploring his frequent choice to reside in other countries. As the essay suggests, Baldwin's own disconnection from America allowed him to see its internal disconnection all the clearer.

Nicholas Buccola's essay, "What William F. Buckley Jr. Did Not Understand about James Baldwin: On Baldwin's Politics of Freedom" examines similar tenets of individualism, history, and myth while adding critical exposition of Baldwin's views on freedom and liberty. In chapter 4, Buccola uses dialectic between Baldwin and Buckley in order to trace Baldwin's views on freedom and the limits of politics, supported by Baldwin's own essays. Buccola's analysis of Buckley's misunderstanding of Baldwin serves in its own way as a mirror in reflecting what can thus be gleaned from Baldwin's work.

Part 2 of the volume, "Prophecy, Religion, and Truth," aims to explore the religious side of Baldwin, both in his application of religious rhetoric and the theological underpinnings of his work. Chapter 5 is George Shulman's "Baldwin, Prophecy, and Politics." Shulman's work deftly moves from placing Baldwin in the prophetic tradition to discussion of how Baldwin's position as prophet works toward a better understanding of American liberalism and modernity. Shulman explores the ontological categories of whiteness and blackness as discussed by Baldwin, as well as their greater implications for both innocence and domination. Shulman's piece is important for understanding Baldwin in its ability to marry Baldwin's religiosity with his personal political practice.

Chapter 6, Vincent Lloyd's "The Negative Political Theology of James Baldwin," builds upon Shulman's theory of Baldwin as prophet but expands discourse on Baldwin's religiosity by exploring components of Christianity and their various transformations. Lloyd charts out the "transformed theology" present in Baldwin's work, a theology that is Christian in nature but tailored by Baldwin to support those political concepts he values most; namely community and love. Lloyd's work effectively demonstrates how Baldwin's manipulation of Christianity, often viewed as symbiotic with American politics, thus uniquely translates into a political ideology of liberation and identity formation.

Chapter 7, Wilson Carey McWilliams's *Go Tell It on the Mountain: James Baldwin and the Politics of Faith,*" treats Baldwin's religiosity as a means of exploring both relevant cultural factors shaping Baldwin's writing as well as examining the foundational, evangelist tenets of Baldwin's faith that informed his political standing. McWilliams's close reading of *Mountain* not only unpacks the characters of the novel as various disquisitions on faith but also uses these instances of faith to reveal what Baldwin has to say on identity, multiculturalism, and the universal power of love. The chapter is both an important synthesis of the two approaches to Baldwin's religion and original in thought and examination.

Joel Schlosser's chapter, the eighth in the book, establishes the theme for part 3 of this book, "The Individual Life, the Interior Life, the Unexamined Life," perhaps best articulated by Baldwin himself when he claims that the interior life is real. In "Socrates in a Different Key: James Baldwin and Race in America," Schlosser takes Baldwin up on his assertion and argues that Baldwin's belief is a transformation of Socratic thought, namely that the unexamined life is not one worth living. Schlosser's work examines both Baldwin's fiction and essays as methods of understanding Baldwin's argument that self-examination is perhaps the championing tenet of American individualism. In order to confront historical atrocities and violence in and of communities, examination of oneself and one's role in the Great American Drama is irreplaceable. This essay sets up an examination of Baldwin's take on individualism and the citizen's responsibility, duty, and obligation to examine oneself by means of addressing societal ills.

Although Brian Norman's essay, chapter 9, "Crossing Identitarian Lines: Women's Liberation and James Baldwin's Early Essays," may seem an abrupt gear switch, the content proves relevant in its advocacy for the political implications of individual experience. Norman's Baldwin is an author very much concerned with gender; namely, Norman demonstrates how Baldwin's writings can be read as protofeminist pieces whose focus on the importance of individual experiences dovetails with suffrage, exclusion, and gender violence in America. Although Baldwin never explicitly announces his feminism, his treatments of race and sexuality, when read through a feminist lens, prove to be intersectional insofar as they can inform gendered experiences of oppression and suffering. Norman is careful to establish that oppression faced by African Americans and women are not interchangeable; rather, the early examination of one can shed light on the progress of the other. Norman's reading of Baldwin further aids our understanding of Baldwin's tying together of democracy and identity in that democracy is dependent upon the liberation of all rather than a few.

Chapter 10, Ulf Schulenberg's "'Where the People Can Sing, the Poet Can Live': James Baldwin, Pragmatism, and Cosmopolitan Humanism," places Baldwin within a larger intellectual tradition of both Western political philosophy and the African American intersections with(in) it. Schulenberg's work then narrows its focus to develop and trace Baldwin's humanism, a humanism that argues for individual responsibility in a democratic society. Schulenberg's essay challenges public-private dichotomies, drawing off of Baldwin's collapsing of the interior and exterior lives, and ultimately brings to discussion Baldwin's view of the potential of democracy should individuals all recognize their collective and individual responsibilities.

Jack Turner's "Baldwin's Individualism and Critique of Property," the eleventh chapter, serves as the final essay in the section and brings several threads together in discussion of Baldwin's individualism and democratic divestment. He further cements the notion that Baldwin's primary tool in combating white supremacy is recognizing the power of the individual to self-create and reshape systems and institutions. Turner's work is consistent with Baldwin's challenging of the myths of American liberalism and brings Baldwin into conversation with some of the American Founders. Turner argues that Baldwin is in favor of individuals divesting from white-supremacist institutions and ideology because participating in a racist economy implicates one in an unjust society. Voluntary dispossession is a political move par excellence according to Turner, signifying a refusal to participate in the impoverishment of African Americans. Turner's work ties together Baldwin's views on political action, religious thought, and individualism in an effective closing that also draws on several of the previous authors.

Part 4, "Violence and Vision," the final section of this volume, adds to that contemplation of the interior the exterior of American politics, to the very real forms of violence, often state-sanctioned, that are brought to bear on black bodies and the vision that Baldwin tries to cultivate against those forms of violence. In chapter 12, the first essay in this section, Lisa Beard's "James Baldwin on Violence and Disavowal," notes that it is fitting that in national discourse surrounding police killings and related Black Lives Matter protests, so many reporters and activists have turned to James Baldwin to interpret contemporary racial politics and summon people toward political action. Baldwin, so relentless at confronting "white innocence" in his time, offers a vocabulary about violence and disavowal that aligns with and enunciates Black Lives Matter interventions in important ways. That's because in Baldwin's account, white violence is not only monstrous but also denied, hidden behind national stories of civic virtue and myths of black criminality. The contemporary moment—from protests in the wake of Trayvon Martin's death to protests in Ferguson and Baltimore—thus demands that we revisit Baldwin's own way of encountering violence and disavowal in American politics.

In chapter 13, "James Baldwin and Black Lives Matter," Eddie S. Glaude Jr. picks up on several of the themes in Beard's essay and writes that the Black Lives Matter movement reflects a particular strain of perfectionism that takes shape under conditions of domination, a tradition of which Baldwin is an exemplar. In that tradition, which Glaude describes as black democratic perfectionism, contemporary activists follow Baldwin in a radical cultivation of democratic individuality in the service of racial justice. That radical cultivation requires an unflinching encounter with the ugliness of who we are and a rejection of all the comforting illusions that mask the reality of American life.

In chapter 14, the final essay in this volume, "'Tell Him I'm Gone': On the Margins in High-Tech City," Rachel Brahinsky illustrates how Baldwin unmasked reality in one important case; she uses James Baldwin's commentary on 1960s San Francisco to consider racial capitalism's urban consequences years later. Arguing that urban space plays a key role in shaping the bounds of racial justice, both in Baldwin's time and beyond, Brahinsky uses Baldwin to foreground a politics of place that seeks to move toward urban justice. Brahinsky's essay further reflects on how urban policy has intersected with the everyday black geographies that Baldwin investigated, with a call for a revisioning of those same geographies. Through reseeing place, she argues, we may also reimagine racial marginalization in American cities.

Together, the fourteen essays in this volume argue for new reading, a reading that celebrates Baldwin as an important contributor to political and democratic theory. Baldwin's works cut across lines of race, gender, and sexuality, providing a pivotal cross section of American life and love that, although born of a certain age and era, offer critical insights into America's past and political present. Perhaps, and almost certainly, Baldwin said it best when he said that "the story of the Negro in America is the story of America—or, more precisely, it is the story of Americans."[22] Only when we feel the terror of belonging can we understand what belonging is, and only by understanding the horror can we claim to have any true measure of loyalty or even love.

Notes

1. Ta-Nehisi Coates, *Between the World and Me* (New York: Random House, 2015).

2. Richard Wolfe et al., "When Barry Became Barack," *Newsweek*, March 31, 2008.

3. Colm Tóibín, "James Baldwin and Barack Obama." *New York Review of Books* 55, no. 16 (October 23, 2008).

4. Lavelle Porter, "James Baldwin in Obama's America," *GC Advocate*, October 2010, http://gcadvocate.com.

5. James Baldwin, "Black Power," in *The Cross of Redemption: Uncollected Writings*, ed. Randall Kenan (New York: Pantheon, 2010), 81.

6. James Baldwin, "The Black Boy Looks at the White Boy," in *The Price of the Ticket: Collected Nonfiction, 1948–1985* (New York: St. Martin's, 1985), 303.

7. James Baldwin, "Princes and Powers," in *The Price of the Ticket*, 45.

8. James Baldwin, "In Search of a Majority," in *The Price of the Ticket*, 233.

9. Ibid., 232.

10. Ibid., 234.

11. Dwight A. McBride, "How Much Time Do You Want for Your Progress? New Approaches to James Baldwin," in *James Baldwin Now*, ed. McBride (New York: New York University Press, 1999), 2.

12. James Baldwin, "The Discovery of What It Means to Be an American," in *The Price of the Ticket*, 176.

13. James Baldwin, "A Fly in Buttermilk," in *The Price of the Ticket*, 161.

14. James Baldwin, "The Northern Protestant," in *The Price of the Ticket*, 204.

15. Baldwin, "The Discovery of What It Means to Be an American," 172.

16. James Baldwin, "East River, Downtown," in *The Price of the Ticket*, 266.

17. James Baldwin, "Notes for a Hypothetical Novel," in *The Price of the Ticket*, 237–38.

18. Baldwin, "East River, Downtown," 286.

19. James Baldwin and Margaret Mead, *A Rap on Race* (Philadelphia: Lippincott, 1971), 148.

20. Lawrie Balfour, *The Evidence of Things Not Said* (Ithaca, NY: Cornell University Press, 2001), 134.

21. James Baldwin and Budd Schulberg, "Dialogue in Black and White (1964–1965)," in *James Baldwin: The Legacy*, ed. Quincy Troupe (New York: Simon and Schuster, 1989): 135–60, 153.

22. James Baldwin, "Alas, Poor Richard," in *The Price of the Ticket*, 286.

I

Collective Consciousness and Community

1

"A Most Disagreeable Mirror"

Race Consciousness as Double Consciousness

Lawrie Balfour

"As is the inevitable result of things unsaid, we find ourselves until today oppressed with a dangerous and reverberating silence."[1] The writer of these words is James Baldwin (1924–1987), and "the dangerous and reverberating silence" is the unspoken story of racial brutality that qualifies any claim for the achievements of American democracy. Although Baldwin issued his warning before the undoing of legal segregation, his assessment of the United States as a nation haunted by its racial heritage goes to the core of the post–civil rights predicament. For Baldwin foresees the limits of formal equality and pushes beyond them to inquire why African Americans continue to be excluded from the full enjoyment of American democratic promises.[2] He exposes the difficulty of attacking the roots of racial inequality once the trunk and limbs of legal subordination have been destroyed.

This essay explores Baldwin's work as a rich resource for approaching the puzzle of race consciousness—the ongoing power of racial identity in a society where white supremacy is supposed to have been permanently discredited and blackness is no longer an acceptable justification for dehumanizing treatment.[3] By insisting that appeals to race-blindness not only fail as a solution to racial inequalities but also condemn to silence those Americans whose race gets noticed, Baldwin rejects the possibility of bracketing racial identity. By exposing the complexity of his experiences and the tensions inherent in his own identity, however, he intimates just how difficult the task of race-conscious theorizing must be.

Illuminating the power of racial identity, Baldwin realizes, is as risky as it is necessary. On one hand, the line between white and black citizens is taken for granted in countless daily interactions. To ignore the ways in which American lives remain circumscribed by that line is to mute claims about the racial dimension of American experiences—including experiences of injustice. On the other hand, focusing on the distinction between "whiteness" and "blackness" obscures the multiplicity of those experiences and excludes those that it cannot subsume. "An obvious and complex phenomenon," race functions as a way of ordering the world according to distinctions that have no simple, natural, cultural, or socioeconomic justification.[4] Although the black-white line is not the only racial division in the United States, and racial divisions are not the only cleavages, American preoccupation with this line merits specific attention. Baldwin's essays are thus particularly valuable insofar as they illuminate the tenacity of the distinction between "black" and "white," *despite* the hybridity that is disguised by these terms, and *despite* the significance of intraracial and societal divisions by gender and class.

I call this phenomenon that Baldwin's essays evoke so effectively *race consciousness*. As a descriptive term, race consciousness conveys the ways in which "whiteness" and "blackness" are noticed (or not noticed). Because the term implies no moral judgment, it defuses the accusatory ring of racism, which too often elicits a defensive reaction and impedes inquiry. By going to the level of assumptions and unacknowledged beliefs, moreover, race consciousness provides a way of capturing those effects of racial identity that are untouched by the idea of racial discrimination understood as a category of discrete, intentional acts. Probing the sources of race consciousness and tracing its effects, Baldwin reveals how even the most enlightened citizens are affected by life in a democratic society in which the persistence of racial hierarchy is simultaneously condemned and taken for granted.

Beyond this descriptive meaning, race consciousness has a normative meaning as well. If the persistence of a racially unjust status quo can be explained, in part, by the silent workings of racial assumptions or beliefs, then opposing such a status quo involves becoming conscious of those assumptions and beliefs. Baldwin conveys the meaning of race consciousness in this second sense in a letter he wrote to Angela Davis in 1971, as she awaited trial on charges of kidnapping, conspiracy, and murder: "Some of us, white and Black, know how great a price has already been paid to bring into existence a new consciousness, a new people, an unprecedented nation. If we know, and do nothing, we are worse than the murderers hired in our name."[5] Or, similarly, in the closing passage of *The Fire Next Time:* "If we—and now I mean the relatively conscious whites and the relatively conscious blacks, who must, like lovers, insist on, or create, the consciousness of others—do not falter in our duty now, we may be able, handful that we are, to end the racial nightmare, and achieve our country, and change the history of the world."[6] Consciousness, for Baldwin, is the active awareness and acceptance of the ways that circumstances shape an individual's life and the attempt to make those circumstances articulate to bring about change. Race consciousness in the normative sense thus entails the acknowledgment of race consciousness in the descriptive sense. Race consciousness is morally and politically imperative, according to Baldwin, as long as Americans' inability to talk honestly about race perpetuates racial injustice.[7]

Wary though Baldwin was of political theories and theorists, his conception of race consciousness enables him to inhabit the gap between democratic principles and American practices in ways that shed light on theoretical debates about identity and difference. One of these ways is Baldwin's elaboration of the idea of race consciousness as double consciousness, which offers a critical moral psychology of the color line. Although Baldwin never uses the term made famous by W. E. B. Du Bois, he exploits the concept of twoness, discrediting dreams of racial transcendence and, at the same time, undermining claims to racial authenticity.

Behind the Color Line

Writing in 1903, in the shadow cast by the dismantling of Reconstruction, Du Bois muses that understanding "the strange meaning of being black here in the dawning of the Twentieth Century" is of importance even for white readers, "for the problem of the Twentieth Century is the problem of the color-line."[8] Du Bois's comment is perhaps the most quoted statement of the significance of race in American life. And his description of the "double consciousness" to which the "problem of the color-line" gives rise is frequently cited, and criticized, as an expression of the dilemma confronting African Americans who aspire to be full members of American society.[9] The aim of revisiting Du Bois in conjunction with Baldwin is to shift this interpretive emphasis. Rather than reading double consciousness as a black problem, I mine *The Souls of Black Folk* for clues about how Du Bois uses double consciousness to convey the struggles of a whole society haunted by a history of racial oppression. I then turn to Baldwin for an expanded account of this American problem.

Du Bois understands double consciousness to be both a gift and a burden.[10] It is a second sight, a way of seeing that which escapes notice by the white majority. Endowed with an enlarged vision, Du Bois endeavors to take an uninformed white readership "behind the veil" that divides black from white so that they might see the beauty of the humanity that lives there. As second sight, double consciousness allows Du Bois to observe the distance between the American ideals he cherishes and the American practices of systematic racial degradation. Hence he contends that the experiences of slavery and exclusion allow African Americans to understand the promise of freedom in a way that white Americans cannot. "Actively we have woven ourselves with the very warp and woof of this nation," he reminds white Americans. "We fought their battles, shared their sorrow, mingled our blood with theirs, and generation after generation have pleaded with a headstrong, careless people to despise not Justice, Mercy, and Truth, lest the nation be smitten with a curse."[11] Double consciousness thus provides insight into the content of American promises as they are not understood by those who have the luxury of taking those promises for granted.

But double consciousness is a menacing insight. In "a world which yields [the Negro] no true self-consciousness," it compounds the misery inflicted on African Americans from without by providing an internal echo of white Americans' judgment of them.[12] For Du Bois, double consciousness involves participating in an "American" culture that sees his African heritage as degraded. From this dilemma arises "a painful self-consciousness, an almost morbid sense of personality and a moral hesitancy which is fatal to self-confidence."[13] Too often the result of this consciousness of dishonor, Du Bois remarks, is the resort to rebellion or hypocrisy.

Du Bois's efforts to reach out to a white audience reveal the price of inclusion. In decrying the economic barriers to African America freedom, he argues that the wretched are human, "even as you and I," thereby identifying himself with an "us" that is set apart from most African Americans.[14]

The gentle conviction with which Du Bois makes his appeal to the reasonable among his fellows belies the ambivalence engendered by double consciousness and mutes his outrage. Although Du Bois does hold fast to universal humanism, he also acknowledges that a strategy of dissemblance is a crucial component of making humanist claims; indeed, he indicates that it may be African Americans' only effective way of gaining access to a racist mainstream. Thus he seeks inclusion in a catholic culture, knowing that "the price of culture is a Lie."[15] The price of culture, furthermore, is the substitution of deception for the cultivation of the very virtues—"impulse, manliness and courage"—that he believes American society prizes most highly. From this requirement of deception for the purpose of inclusion arises "such a double life, with double thoughts, double duties, and double social classes, [which itself] must give rise to double words and double ideals, and tempt the mind to pretence or to revolt, to hypocrisy or to radicalism."[16]

Accompanying this account of double consciousness in African American lives there is another, less developed story of double consciousness in *The Souls of Black Folk*. This second story is that of the impact of "the swarthy spectre [that] sits in its accustomed seat at the Nation's feast."[17] For white Americans, whose place at the table is unquestioned, the ghostly presence serves as a constant reminder of hands that will never be clean. Implied in Du Bois's observation that white Americans always approach him haltingly, wondering, "How does it feel to be a problem?" is the suggestion that the omnipresence of the color line in American life effects a sort of double consciousness in white Americans as well.[18] Du Bois notices how the plight of African Americans lurks in the minds of their fellow citizens, despite white refusal to acknowledge or take responsibility for that plight. The ubiquity of the unasked question raises another question: "Whose problem?"

The place of the "problem" in white lives emerges clearly in Du Bois's depiction of the eerie order of life in the segregated South. By looking South, Du Bois does not absolve northern whites from censure. His elaboration of "the unasked question"—and its spoken counterparts, including: "Do not these Southern outrages make your blood boil?"—highlights northerners' insistent distancing of themselves from racial injustice.[19] Du Bois turns to the South of the late nineteenth and early twentieth century as the region in which there is the most extensive contact between black and white. He offers his analysis of relations there as a template for understanding the psychological ramifications of interracial contact more generally. What he finds is that southern women and men assiduously govern their lives by unspoken racialized rules. Like participants in some complicated dance, black and white come together and part on cue, never unaware of their relative positions, never needing to articulate the threat posed by transgression of the racial code.[20] Vividly, Du Bois describes the unhealthiness of this society that inhales "tainted air," that still breathes the "foul breath of slavery."[21] From this physically unhealthy situation comes emotional distress. The very existences of free blacks, Du Bois observes, incites "as deep a storm and stress of human souls, as intense a ferment of feeling, as intricate a writhing of sprit, as ever a people experienced."[22]

This "storm and stress" assaults white southerners' most deeply felt commitments. On the one hand, Du Bois writes, the belief in equality of all humanity and the Christian disavowal of caste division defeat attempts to justify the degrading effects of the color line. On the other hand, he relates that white southerners nonetheless respond to their uneasiness about the situation by pointing out that the African Americans they know live in ignorance and are prone to laziness and crime. "Can a self-respecting group hold anything but the least possible fellowship with such persons and survive?" they ask.[23] Du Bois rejects their protest on two grounds: It ignores the examples of African Americans who rise above the condition of the "masses," and it obscures the ways in which social, economic, and political structures serve to create the very masses it despises. Du Bois not only undermines white Americans' defenses against recognizing the humanity of black citizens, but he intimates how the presence of the color line forces the unacceptable choice between hypocrisy and rebellion on *all* Americans. When he writes about the double-trap laid for black Americans, Du Bois asks: "Is not this simply the writhing of the age translated into black—the triumph of the Lie?"[24]

Writing in the context of the segregation of midcentury, Baldwin similarly takes his mostly white readership behind the veil of color. Without using the term "double consciousness," he, too, considers the psychological impact of racial division on black and white Americans. Where Du Bois offers his portrait of life in the post-Reconstruction South as a key to understanding racial interaction in the United States, Baldwin plumbs his own experiences for insights into a broader racial order. When he writes that "to be a Negro meant, precisely, that one was never looked at but was simply at the mercy of the reflexes the color of one's skin caused in other people," Baldwin nearly echoes Du Bois's description of double consciousness.[25] He conveys the depth of the color line's imprint on American psyches by recalling how it feels to grow up circumscribed by mysterious boundaries: "The fear that I heard in my father's voice . . . when he realized that I really *believed* I could do anything a white boy could do, and had every intention of proving it, was not at all like the fear I heard when one of us was ill or had fallen down the stairs or strayed too far from the house. It was another fear, a fear that the child, in challenging the white world's assumptions, was putting himself in the path of destruction."[26] By learning to recognize his transgression of those boundaries in the reflexes of his parents, Baldwin begins to intuit what it means to measure his worth by the reactions of a hostile society.

In spite of the hurts inflicted by this coming to consciousness, Baldwin does not reduce black double consciousness to a reactionary moment. When he states that "in every aspect of his living [the Negro] betrays the memory of the auction block and the impact of the happy ending," Baldwin reiterates Du Bois's view that with the affliction comes the gift of insight.[27] He maintains that, by preventing black Americans from taking democratic values for granted, the memory of the auction block makes possible the genuine aspiration of freedom and equality.

Baldwin's assessment of the companionship of the ideals and the horrors of democracy in America represents a shift from Du Bois's account of double consciousness. The sting of Du Bois's double consciousness comes from an awareness that white Americans may never acknowledge the beauty of "the souls of black folk" and participate with their black neighbors in the merging of these two great streams of American culture. Baldwin echoes Du Bois in arguing for the essential role of African Americans in the creation of the United States. Yet, there is an important difference in Baldwin's account of the mutual implication of black and white Americans' fates and identities. When Baldwin writes that the land and institutions of the oppressor belong at least equally to those who blood was spilled involuntarily, he adds a new spin to the story:

The land of our forefather's exile had been made, by that travail, our home. It may have been the popular impulse to keep us at the bottom of the perpetually shifting and bewildered populace; but we were, on the other hand, almost personally indispensable to each of them, simply because, *without us, they could never have been certain, in such a confusion, where the bottom was;* and nothing, in any case, could take away our title to the land which we, too, had purchased with our blood. This results in a psychology very different—at its best and at its worst—from the psychology which is produced by a sense of having been invaded or overrun, the sense of having no recourse whatever against oppression other than overthrowing the machinery of the oppressor. We had been dealing with, had been made and mangled by, another machinery altogether. It had never been in our interest to overthrow it. It had been necessary to make the machinery work for our benefit and the possibility of its doing so had been, so to speak, built in.[28] (italics added)

The Souls of Black Folk offers a heroic portrait of African American participation in a history that is threatened, indeed from within, by racism. Baldwin's story, by contrast, pushes Americans to consider how the glory of that history is related to the maintenance of the color line. Baldwin would second Du Bois's claim that "actively we have woven ourselves with the very warp and woof of this nation," but he would expose as "the very warp and woof the heritage of the West, the idea of white supremacy."[29] Lacking evidence that Americans are prepared to grapple with the radical changes required to divorce democracy in America from the presumptions of white supremacy, Baldwin's response to his own twoness is even more ambivalent than Du Bois's endeavor to celebrate the cultural gifts of black and white Americans.[30]

One clue to that difference lies in Baldwin's account of the reach of double consciousness. Baldwin's version of double consciousness provides a critical metaphor for the experiences of white Americans as well as those of blacks, although it manifests itself differently in each case. Thus when Baldwin notes that the color of his skin functions "as a most disagreeable mirror," he demands that white readers look not only in the mirror but at it.[31] For in order to see the humanity of their black neighbors, Baldwin believes that whites must inquire how black degradation affirms their confidence in the value of being "American."

Crossing the Color Line: "Many Thousands Gone"

Perhaps Baldwin limns the interrelation of blackness and whiteness and the tensions that inhere in "American" identity most vividly in the essay "Many

Thousands Gone." There he deploys a rhetorical strategy that deliberately uncouples the narrator's "we" from any stable point of reference. By dividing "the Negro" from "Americans," the essay accepts the color line as fundamental to American society. But throughout the piece, Baldwin slips back and forth across the line—now aligning himself with African Americans, now looking at them from a distance, now obscuring the difference. With the economy of a simple juxtaposition he accomplishes in this essay what he strives for in a long career as a fiction writer whose first-person narrators might equally be bisexual and white or pregnant, nineteen, and black.

Baldwin's foray across the color line in "Many Thousands Gone" is different from the "we" employed by Du Bois to gain sympathy of an educated white audience. Whereas Du Bois defines double consciousness as a struggle with "two warring ideals" that are both worthy of celebration, Baldwin's maneuvering casts doubt on the reader's commitment to the ideals themselves. By the end of the essay, the number of possible "we's" has multiplied beyond accurate accounting (although the essay is most severe when the "we" in question refers to white northern liberals). The only sure thing left to say about white and black Americans' identity at the conclusion of "Many Thousands Gone" is that "we" know too little about who "we" are and how "we" are related to American democratic promises.[32]

It is worth pausing to try to follow Baldwin's trail as he moves back and forth across the color line, playing with the identity of his intended audience as deftly as he confounds readers' expectations about his own. Baldwin undermines the stable location of the color line from the very beginning of "Many Thousands Gone." He opens the essay as a distant commentator, noting that music is the only avenue through which "the Negro in America" can speak to "Americans." The narrator then observes that "Americans[']" selective interpretation of the tales told in this medium only confirms their assumptions about the order of the world, and black and white places within it. It is in the third sentence that he offers the warning with which I began: "We find ourselves until today oppressed with a dangerous and reverberating silence." Who is the "we" that is oppressed? Clearly, one of the themes of "Many Thousands Gone" is that African Americans have historically had no public language to make their suffering audible to white ears. But Baldwin also uses the "we" to indicate what whites lose by their inability to hear these voices and by their unwillingness to wrestle with what that deafness reveals about their own values. As he nears the end of the paragraph, the ambiguous "we" appears again: "The ways in which the Negro has affected the American psychology are betrayed in our popular culture and in our morality; in our estrangement from him is the depth of our estrangement from ourselves." And, finally, he observes that "we cannot ask: what do we *really* feel about him—such a question merely opens the gates on chaos. What we really feel about him is involved with all that we feel about everything, about everyone, about ourselves."[33]

The short paragraph that follows declares that "the story of the Negro in America . . . is the story of Americans." Read in this way, "the story of Americans" is not heroic. And "the Negro in America, gloomily referred to as that shadow which lies athwart our national life, is far more than that. He is a series of shadows, self-created, intertwining, which now we helplessly battle."[34] "The story of America" is thus, in important respects, a story of double consciousness. The shadows against which "we" battle are the memory of slavery and the knowledge that a coincidence of birth still condemns millions of Americans to life outside the promises of freedom and equality that "we" are all guaranteed. The fact that these shadows are "self-created" casts doubt on the possibility of a stable selfhood, an American identity untroubled by racial oppression.

Already, Baldwin is prodding a white readership, particularly readers who thoughtlessly trust in the possibility that racism and racial identity can be effortlessly transcended, to look upon their own beliefs about racial equality, and their beliefs about those beliefs, with mistrust. Above all, what Baldwin aims to undermine is the conviction that the present is divisible from the past. Until a real accounting of what was at stake in racial slavery and what that says about American democracy has been accomplished, Baldwin contends, white Americans will continue to be haunted by unasked questions. "In our image of the Negro breathes the past we deny, not dead but living yet and powerful, the beast in our jungle of statistics," he cautions. Like "the swarthy spectre" of Du Bois's imagination, Baldwin's beast never fully retreats from the consciousness of white Americans who aim to achieve racial equality by putting the past behind them without examining its traces in the present. According to Baldwin: "It is this [past] which continues to defeat us, which lends to interracial cocktail parties their rattling, genteel, nervously smiling air: in any drawing room at such a gathering the beast may spring, filling the air with flying things and unenlightened wailing. . . . Wherever the Negro face appears a tension is created, the tension of a silence filled with things unutterable."[35] To avoid dealing with the historical dehumanization of black Americans is thus to allow the beast to roam in white imaginations and the fear of the chaos brought on by true racial equality to rage unchecked.

If the "we" with whom Baldwin identifies as the essay opens is not white but black, then the question of what "we" feel about "the Negro" lends itself to another reading. Referring at once to all black Americans and to no one in particular, the term makes an abstraction of the lives subsumed by it. In many places in the essay, "the Negro" might just as easily be written as "the problem." The definite article and singular noun reinforce the sense that "we" understand to whom it refers. Moreover, the lumping together of all blacks into this objective-sounding category denies individual African Americans the capacity to voice feelings and opinions of their own. By leaving the racial identity of the "we" ambiguous, and by locating himself across the line from "the Negro," Baldwin asks whether his African American readers are the victims of Du Boisian double consciousness. He dares them to ask how much they have internalized the examples of successful assimilation or disastrous revolt, how much they measure their own lives "by the tape of a world that looks on in amused contempt and pity."[36] And he observes that the consequences of having one's identity and experiences compressed into "the Negro" are written indelibly on the consciousness of black Americans: "One must travel very far, among saints with nothing to gain or outcasts with nothing to lose, to find a place where [being a Negro] does not matter—and perhaps a word or gesture or simply a silence will testify that it matters even there."[37]

To expose what "we" might really think about "the Negro," Baldwin considers white and black Americans' relationship to Bigger Thomas. Baldwin's choice of the main character from Richard Wright's *Native Son* is complicated, but the most obvious reason is the novel's enormous influence in the postwar United States.[38] When Baldwin comments that Bigger "is the monster created by the American republic," he means that Wright's novel captures an American fantasy about the people it imported as slaves and eventually abandoned to a debased freedom.[39] The purpose of this essay, and of so much of Baldwin's writing, is to expose the myths perpetuated about African Americans and to explore what those myths reveal about the people who cling to them. By assuring "us" that the fear of the black other who was thereby created is justified, Bigger Thomas's violent passage from tenement to death row assuages "our" consciences. Baldwin's version of Bigger Thomas serves as a definitive marker of where the bottom is—in American society and in a broader moral order. But knowing where the bottom is, Baldwin admonishes, exacts a terrible price from both white and black Americans.

When he locates himself on the white side of the line between "us" and "the Negro," Baldwin argues that "our" image of Bigger serves as a barrier to real interracial communion. The remoteness of Chicago's black tenements insulates most of "us" from meeting Bigger himself. Nonetheless, his image is so ingrained in "our" consciousnesses that it prevents "us" (here he means, most pointedly, white liberals) from looking at African Americans simply as other human beings. "He stands at our shoulders when we give our maid her wages," Baldwin notes. "It is his hand which we fear we are taking when struggling to communicate with the current 'intelligent' Negro, his stench, as it were, which fills our mouths with salt as the monument is unveiled in honor of the latest Negro leader."[40] Baldwin's point is that the resonance of the image of Bigger Thomas (or O. J. Simpson?) in American culture exposes the virulence of white discomfort just below the surface of an avowedly interracial "we."

When Baldwin situates himself on the black side of the color line, the significance of Bigger Thomas is terrifying. For those whose lives are hidden in the formulation "the Negro," the force of the image may be especially destructive. "No American Negro exists," he avers, "who does not have his private Bigger Thomas living in the skull." Although Bigger's story flattens the variety of black lives into the monster represented by "the Negro," Baldwin contends that blacks are "compelled to accept the fact that this dark and dangerous and unloved stranger is part of [themselves] forever."[41] Baldwin dwells on the image of Bigger Thomas because prevailing racial images have a material bearing on the ways white and black Americans treat themselves and each other. But they do not exhaust the possibilities for African American identity. Part of Baldwin's challenge here is to make real the weight of racial oppression without reducing African Americans to that experience of oppression. This, then, is the "savage paradox" of Africans Americans' relationship to their own American culture. The culture that created Bigger Thomas and that denies the humanity of African Americans inhabits the very skulls of black citizens. It is a culture, unavoidably, to which African Americans belong.

"Many Thousands Gone" builds toward a conclusion that makes it clear that the point of Baldwin's incursions across the color line is to discredit the idea that it is possible to move beyond racial identity without working through its significance:

> Though there are whites and blacks among us who hate each other, we will not; there are those who are betrayed by greed, by guilt, by blood lust, but not we; we will set our faces against them and join hands and walk together into that dazzling future when there will be no white or black. This is the dream of all liberal men, a dream not at all dishonorable, but, nevertheless, a dream. For, let us join hands on this mountain as we may, the battle is elsewhere. It proceeds far from us in the heat and horror and pain of life itself where all men are betrayed by greed and guilt and blood lust and where no one's hands are clean. Our good will, from which we yet expect such a power to transform us, is thin, passionless, strident: its roots, examined, lead us back to our forebears, whose assumption it was that the black man, to become truly human and acceptable, must first become like us.[42]

However earnestly racial justice is desired, appeals to race-blindness disguise the degree to which the assumption still resonates that it is black Americans who need to prove themselves "truly human and acceptable." "This assumption once accepted," Baldwin warns, "the Negro in America can only acquiesce in the obliteration of his own personality, the distortion and debasement of his own experience."[43]

If the suppleness of language exhibited in "Many Thousands Gone" is among Baldwin's greatest rhetorical achievements, it is an achievement that could not be sustained in all political contexts. As the critiques of black nationalists, who saw in Baldwin's experimental embrace of a white persona "the obliteration of *his* own personality, the distortion and debasement of *his* own experience," mounted in the 1960s, and as white intransigence confirmed Baldwin's own suspicions that patient appeals to white consciences were merely abject, Baldwin abandons the racially ambiguous "we." Still, even as he locates himself definitively on the black side of the color line, Baldwin remains committed to an interracial "we." And even when he suppresses the ambivalence of his writing to demonstrate his allegiances, his essays provide moments of keen insight into the psychological burdens and the moral and political implications—for all citizens—of living with the color line.

Baldwin's Double Consciousnesses

To claim that Baldwin's account of double consciousness provides a moral psychology of the color line is to demand a place for his writing in contemporary debates about race and identity. But is this notion of doubleness sufficiently flexible to accommodate the range of experiences contained by racial categories? Or does Baldwin's emphasis on race consciousness require a certain degree of blindness to the differences *among* blacks or whites? Consideration of the multiple doublenesses of Baldwin's work indicates that, although Baldwin does sometimes fall prey to the temptation of making claims for a singular black experience, his public explorations of the tensions that inhere in his own identity make vivid the shortcoming of claims to racial authenticity.[44]

One sort of doubleness, the double existence Baldwin led as a "commuter" to the United States, provides him the necessary distance to write about Americans' racial predicament and simultaneously raises questions about Baldwin's qualifications as a commentator on black experience. Part of the value of Baldwin's contribution resides in the fact that he is at once conscious of how far he lives from the Harlem of his childhood and able to see how much Harlem lives in him. Hence when Swiss children shout, *"Neger! Neger!"* at a young Baldwin on his first day in their remote village, they unintentionally evoke in him a keen recollection of how it feels to be reduced to a name in the United States, where the epithet is not exotic but degraded.[45] The move to Europe teaches Baldwin that there is no running away from his identity, that the indelibility of experience precludes the attempt to drop out and find a new "us" to join or a new home in which to settle. If his flight reinforces Baldwin's sense of his American identity, however, his periodic moves back to the United States also remind him of the singularity of his own experience. This sort of double consciousness emerges poignantly in Baldwin's reports on trips he made to the South in the late 1950s and early 1960s. By discovering how ill-equipped he is to abide by the rules of Jim Crow, Baldwin comes to see how little he shares with the experiences of rural African Americans of the South, and how much.

In addition to this double identity as a commuter, Baldwin's notion of himself as an artist, an "incorrigible disturber of the peace," divides him from other Americans. Artistic consciousness, for Baldwin, involves the cultivation of a unique form of alienation. This alienation in turn enables him to hold a mirror to an unwitting society, for being an artist is as much about the courage to face what is ugly as the ability to create something beautiful.[46] Although Baldwin's views about the vocation of the artist or writer sometimes suffer from undue romanticization, his exploration of the double-edgedness of his talents still usefully complicates his understanding of racial identity.[47] The particular burdens that artistic estrangement places on black artists are a recurrent topic of Baldwin's essays. His critique of *Native Son* reveals Baldwin's own fears about what happens to the artist who is taken to be a "representative" of her or his race: "It is a false responsibility (since writers are not congressmen) and impossible, by its nature, of fulfillment. The unlucky shepherd soon finds that, so far from being able to feed the hungry sheep, he has lost the wherewithal for his own nourishment."[48] Not only do the pressures of acting as a spokesman threaten to alienate Baldwin from the very experiences that animate his art, but material success and acceptance by a largely white readership also divide him from the people whose lives inspire that art in the first place.

Of the many doublenesses in Baldwin's work, perhaps it is the sexual doublenesses that are most illuminating. The persistence of the color line is always related to issues of sexual division in Baldwin's estimation; the fears projected onto black Americans by whites are largely sexual. Moreover, Baldwin's handling of the divide between "normal" and "perverse" sexualities and between men and women proceeds from the same premise as his arguments against white supremacy. By showing how the exclusion of a degraded or subordinated group reassures members of the dominant group of their insulation from the fragility of human existence, Baldwin inquires what is at stake in asserting the fixity of identity.

That the author of "Many Thousands Gone" would refuse to adhere to sexual rules of order is not surprising. Making no secret of his own homosexuality, Baldwin crossed the color line artistically and bravely jeopardized a fragile reputation as a "Negro writer" when he published his second novel in 1956. Not only does the novel, *Giovanni's Room*, include no black characters, but it explicitly details a sexual relationship between two men. Despite his openness about his own attractions and his fictional exploration of homosexual love, however, Baldwin devotes little space in his essays to the question of what it means to be "gay."[49] Does this reticence indicate a submission on Baldwin's part to the requirements of racial authenticity? Although this question cannot be answered definitively, Baldwin's own response is instructive.[50]

Heterosexual, homosexual, and bisexual are "20th-century terms which, for me, really have very little meaning," Baldwin explains.[51] This comment may be attributed, in part, to his generation. (Baldwin came of age and left New York more than twenty years before the Stonewall uprising and the beginning of a national gay rights movement.) But there is, for Baldwin, a deeper reason for saying that the terms carry no meaning. Sexual labels and slogans, no less than racial labels and slogans, dehumanize insofar as they deny the complexity of human lives.[52] Baldwin implies that embracing a "gay" identity requires an unacceptable choice. It takes no account of the complications of his own experience as someone who nearly married three times early in life and whose intimate relationships with other men did not always conform to settled sexual categories. A believer in the redemptive possibility of genuine human communion, Baldwin views the quality of an individual's attachments as the measure of that individual's integrity.[53] Baldwin is thus most suspicious of any political stance that reduces human relationships to a formula. Hence when he complains that André Gide's homosexuality "was his own affair which he ought to have kept hidden from us," or when he declares to an interviewer that the question of sexuality is "absolutely personal," he is not suggesting that there is anything shameful in homosexuality.[54] Instead his aim is to protect that dimension of life which is most valuable to him. To make a political identity of sexuality, he fears, is to diminish the virtue of personal attachments and, thereby, to acquiesce to a society that would make those attachments shameful.[55]

Where Baldwin's essays do address "the homosexual problem," they shift attention away from finding solutions and turn instead to the investigation of what is invested in the idea that homosexuality is a problem. On the question of whether homosexuality is "natural," Baldwin remarks: "I really do not see what difference the answer makes. It seems clear, in any case, at least in the world we know, that no matter what encyclopedias of physiological and scientific knowledge are brought to bear the answer can never be Yes." The answer cannot be Yes, Baldwin reasons, because "it would rob the normal—who are simply the many—of their very necessary sense of security and order, of their sense, perhaps, that the [human] race is and should be devoted to outwitting oblivion—and will surely manage to do so."[56] Hence the persecution of gays and lesbians, like racial persecution, tells more about the fears that haunt the majority than about the minority they fear.

Baldwin develops his suspicions about the sources of homophobia by interrogating the naturalness of gender divisions and attacking swaggering ideals of masculinity. In "Preservation of Innocence," an essay published before his twenty-fifth birthday, Baldwin proposes an answer to the riddle of the natural relation between the sexes, an answer on which he elaborates throughout his career:

> Men and women seem to function as imperfect and sometimes unwilling mirrors for one another; a falsification or distortion of the nature of the one is immediately reflected in the nature of the other. . . . Matters are not helped if we thereupon decide that men must recapture their status as men and that women must embrace their function as women; not only does the resulting rigidity of attitude put to death any possible communion, but, having once listed the bald physical facts, no one is prepared to go further and decide, of our multiple human attributes, which are masculine and which are feminine.[57]

As soon as the decision of which attributes belong to which sex is made, he adds, one finds counterexamples everywhere, and the impulse behind the rigid division is even more keenly felt. The only way out of this paradox is to accept the fluidity of gender, or, as Baldwin argues at the very end of his career, androgyny: "We are, for the most part, visibly male or female, our social roles defined by our sexual equipment. But we are all androgynous, not only because we are all born of a woman impregnated by the seed of a man but because each of us, helplessly and forever, contains the other— male in female, female in male, white in black and black in white."[58] In dismissing stark divisions of male and female identity, Baldwin urges his readers to see how racial identity must be fluid as well.

Despite these gestures toward an account of the complicated interrelation of racial and sexual identity, Baldwin's essays do not go so far as to address how "blindness" to differences of sexual orientation and gender among African Americans compounds the injuries of race-blindness. Part of the explanation resides in Baldwin's desire to remain relevant to a changing struggle for black freedom. Of the nationalist attacks on Baldwin's authority, Eldridge Cleaver's "Notes on a Native Son" may be the most famous. Cleaver reviews Baldwin's fiction and nonfiction through *The Fire Next Time* and finds that "Baldwin's antipathy toward the Black race is shockingly clear."[59] What becomes shockingly clear in Cleaver's assessment, however, is that Cleaver's outrage is inseparable from his loathing of Baldwin's open homosexuality. By equating Baldwin's sexuality with "acquiescing in a racial death-wish," Cleaver emphasizes the policing that occurs when claims of racial authenticity are on the table.[60] Cleaver thus dismisses Baldwin's critique of the leaders of the Negritude movement as the *ressentiment* of an unmanly intruder: "Baldwin felt called upon to pop his cap pistol in a duel with Aimé Césaire, the big gun for Martinique."[61]

The effects of this policing on Baldwin's own writing become apparent not in any denial of the varieties of sexual attachment or of his own sexual orientation, but in the increasingly masculinist language of Baldwin's essays of the 1960s and 1970s. Baldwin's earliest essays do generalize about racial oppression from the emasculation of black men.[62] (He never considers what it might mean, for a woman, to have a "private Bigger Thomas living in the skull.") But his later writing goes further. Baldwin provides an example of how this masculinism reduces interracial struggles to the conflicts between white and black men in *No Name in the Street,* an autobiographical essay published as a book in 1972. There he asserts that "in the case of American slavery, the black man's right to his women, as well as to his children, was simply taken from him, and whatever bastards the white man begat on the bodies of black women took their condition from the condition of their mother: blacks were not the only stallions on the slave-breeding farms!"[63] Unsurprisingly, this rhetoric deafens Baldwin to claims about the gendered structure of power among African Americans. In a public dialogue with poet Audre Lorde, for example, the subtlety of Baldwin's understanding of how men and women mirror each other is lost in his reiteration that the great harm of American racism is that it takes from black men the capacity to support and protect their women and children. And it makes it difficult for him to hear Lorde's rejoinder that the inability to protect one's family is no less painful for a black woman than for her father, brothers, and sons.[64]

Insofar as Baldwin capitulates to this traditional understanding of manhood, he misses his own insights into the doublenesses of identity and, indirectly, repudiates his own experiences. Insofar as he investigates what it means to be, in this society, a commuter, an artist, a homosexual, and a man, however, he contributes substantially to his readers' understanding of what it means to be race conscious. "Princes and Powers" sums up as well as any essay Baldwin's attempt to mediate the conflicts that divide him both from white Americans and from other blacks. The critical power of Baldwin's ambivalence, his double consciousness, is suggested by this approving account of writer George Lamming's comments at the international conference of black writers and artists that convened in Paris in 1956:

> It seemed to me that Lamming was suggesting to the conference a subtle and difficult idea, the idea that *part of the great wealth of the Negro experience lay precisely in its double-edgedness.* He was suggesting that all Negroes were held in a state of supreme tension between the difficult, dangerous relationship in which they stood to the white world and the relationship, not a whit less painful or dangerous, in which they stood to each other. He was suggesting that in the acceptance of this duality lay their strength, that in this, precisely, lay their means of defining and controlling the world in which they lived.[65] (italics added)

Baldwin's Mirror and the Limits of Recognition

A writer who insists that the pretense of race-blindness allows racial injustice to persist, Baldwin might be identified as a proponent of what Charles Taylor calls "the politics of difference."[66] A writer, on the other hand, whose refusal to flatten the variety of individual experience for the sake of group identity leading to the conclusion that "a coalition has to be based on the grounds of human dignity," he seems a forceful advocate for what Taylor calls "the politics of equal respect."[67] Yet, Baldwin's double consciousness conforms to neither model. Taylor's rich story about the development of modern selfhood has contributed too much to contemporary thinking about identity and difference to be treated adequately here, but a brief consideration of "The Politics of Recognition" provides a fitting conclusion. For reading Baldwin against Taylor reveals two blind spots in Taylor's essay, blind spots that remind theorists why Americans' racial dilemmas have proved so intransigent. Hidden in the first blind spot are the effects of the historical misrecognition of black Americans on whites' sense of themselves as American citizens; lost in the second are the paradoxes of racial group membership. Without advancing an alternative "politics" of his own, Baldwin suggests the kind of grappling that still must be done for the promise of freedom and equality to be extended in fact to black Americans.

Taylor's sensitivity to the harms inflicted by misrecognition exposes connections between the psychological and political. Given that degrading images can deeply damage the psyches of blacks, or women, or other disfavored groups, Taylor observes that "due recognition is not just a courtesy we owe people. It is a vital human need."[68] Recognition in this sense is certainly part of what Baldwin's exposition of doubleness demands. One end of Baldwin's essays is to force an unwilling readership to acknowledge, truly, the humanity of African Americans. Yet, recognition of black Americans by whites cannot alone suffice.

Baldwin demands of his white readers not only that they accept the equal humanity of blacks but also that they admit the racial construction of their own identities and ask how that construction affects their commitments. Despite earnest claims to the contrary, the vulnerability of those commitments surfaces when white Americans perceive that the order of their lives is threatened or, tellingly, that their race-blindness is being called into question. According to Baldwin, white Americans refuse to see the degree to which the value of whiteness has historically derived from its distinction from a degraded sense of blackness. It is this will to innocence, rather than expressions of overt racism, that prevents his fellow citizens from acknowledging that democracy has not yet been truly tried, much less realized in this country. Without the interrogation of the effects of racial inequalities on "our" sense of what is normal, race-blind appeals to equal human dignity may thus appear hollow.

If it aims to speak to African Americans' American history, then "the politics of recognition" needs to be reconceived to take account of the pathos of both sides of the color line. To the extent that white Americans are haunted by racial guilt, and to the extent that unspoken assumptions about African Americans persist, Baldwin's double consciousness provides a basis for critical reflection. Although Baldwin welcomes the end of legal segregation and celebrates improvements in African Americans' status, he greets every change with a question: How far have "we" come from "our forebears, whose assumption it was that the Black man, to become truly human and acceptable, must first become like us"?[69]

The second blind spot relates to the first. Beyond pointing out that any "politics of recognition" needs to attend to the unacknowledged identity politics of the privileged, Baldwin warns against eliding tensions within the groups demanding recognition. Taylor's essay devotes much of its attention to Canadian struggles over cultural identity, yet it suggests more generally that minority groups seeking recognition are distinct from each other and unified internally. The end of the "politics of recognition," according to this view, is to sustain a group's distinctness in the face of the homogenizing forces of the majority of culture. But the challenge posed by race consciousness is not just to acknowledge that the "distinctness" of African American experience "has been ignored, glossed over, assimilated to a dominant or majority identity," although that certainly happens.[70] Nor is it captured by Taylor's account of the situation of "diasporic" peoples, for Taylor's assumption that every diaspora has a center—a center that lies elsewhere—misdescribes the experiences of that American portion of the African diaspora that is as old as the United States.[71] Rather, race consciousness requires that Americans confront their deep alienation from and attachment to each other. The root of "the Negro problem," Baldwin proposes, is that "it is not simply the relationship of oppressed to oppressor, of master to slave, nor is it motivated merely by hatred; it is also literally and morally, a *blood* relationship."[72]

Hence, when Baldwin alerts his readers to "the savage paradox of the American Negro's situation," he warns that race consciousness, in the normative sense, can be understood neither as a demand for the annihilation of difference nor as pure opposition. Blackness holds for Baldwin no intrinsic value, yet he insists that the particular contributions of African American men and women be acknowledged by the white majority. The difficultly consists in the impossibility of dividing, finally, the positive elements of black heritage from the negative and the black from the white. Commenting on "the relentless tension of the black condition," Baldwin writes: "Being black affected one's life span, insurance rates, blood pressure, lovers, children, every dangerous hour of every dangerous day. There was absolutely no way *not* to be black without ceasing to exist. But it frequently seemed that there was no way to be black either, without ceasing to exist."[73]

Attempts to overcome "the relentless tension of the black condition" may manifest themselves internally in battles for the mantle of authenticity. As Cleaver's assessment of Baldwin indicates, struggles over what Amélie Oksenberg Rorty calls "the right of authoritative description" serve to dehumanize members of the very group in whose name the struggle is undertaken.[74] Although Baldwin's essays articulate the distinctiveness of black citizens' experiences, no "politics of recognition" is acceptable to Baldwin that allows him to affirm his humanity as an African American by denying his worth as "an aging, lonely, sexually dubious, politically outrageous, unspeakably erratic freak."[75]

"Whatever may be their use in civilized societies, mirrors are essential to all violent and heroic action";[76] Virginia Woolf's observation intimates the power of Baldwin's double vision. Where would the British Empire be, she asks, without the reflective power of the stable of adoring women whose own weakness serves to puff up the confidence of the nation's leading men? What would the grandeur of the American experiment in democracy be, Baldwin demands, without slavery and the continued degradation of African Americans to confirm, by contrast, the value of the America "we"? By holding up his "most disagreeable mirror," Baldwin exhorts his readers, white and black, to ask this question and inquire how their own lives are reflected in the answer. Although he believes such scrutiny is necessary to make the promise of racial justice real, Baldwin knows that his attack on American democratic pretensions is not without its risks. For mirrors are double devices: they reflect and, as glass, they cut.

Notes

Originally published as Laurie Balfour, "'A Most Disagreeable Mirror': Race Consciousness as Double Consciousness," *Political Theory* 26, no. 3 (1998). Reprinted by permission of Sage Publications, Inc.

I want to thank George Kateb, Alan Ryan, Jeffrey Stout, and Cornel West for their contributions to many successive versions of this essay. I am also grateful for the thoughtful comments of Leora Batnitzky, Chad Dodson, Roxanne Euben, Robert Gooding-Williams, Kim Townsend, and Tracy Strong and the anonymous reviewers at *Political Theory*.

1. James Baldwin, "Many Thousands Gone," in *The Price of the Ticket: Collected Nonfiction, 1948–1985* (New York: St. Martin's/Marek, 1985), 64.

2. I will use the terms "African American" and "black" when referring to US citizens of African descent unless I am discussing a quotation in which another term is used. The matter of terminology is a difficult one both because the terms themselves are politically contested and charged with deeply personal significance and because they are ever-changing. In keeping with contemporary usage, I have sometimes opted for anachronism.

3. Baldwin is widely remembered as one of the greatest American essayists, but he was also a significant novelist and dreamed of being a great playwright. His corpus of published writing includes, in additions to dozens of essays, six novels, two plays, a screenplay, short stories, poetry, and a children's book. Although I will refer to Baldwin's fiction where it illustrates a point, I concentrate on the essays because it is there that Baldwin is most in command of his uncommon gifts as a writer and observer of American life.

4. Michael Omi and Howard Winant, *Racial Formation in the United States: From the 1960s to the 1980s* (New York: Routledge and Kegan Paul, 1986), 3.

5. James Baldwin, "An Open Letter to My Sister, Angela Y. Davis," in *If They Come in the Morning: Voices of Resistance,* ed. Angela Y. Davis (New York: Signet, 1971), 23.

6. James Baldwin, *The Fire Next Time,* in *The Price of the Ticket,* 379.

7. What it would mean to talk "honestly" about race is a knotty question. Although calls for color-blindness obscure the racial dimension of individual injustices and of systemic inequalities, they also prevent the expression of racial sentiments. One risk of "honesty," in a context in which those sentiments have been submerged but not eliminated, is that it could sanction the return of overt racism to public discourse. For an excellent discussion of this dilemma, see Kimberlé Williams Crenshaw, "Color-Blind Dreams and Racial Nightmares: Reconfiguring Racism in the Post–Civil Rights Era," in *Birth of a Nation'hood: Gaze, Script, and Spectacle in the O. J. Simpson Case,* ed. Toni Morrison and Claudia Brodsky Lacour (New York: Pantheon, 1997), 97–68.

8. W. E. B. Du Bois, *The Souls of Black Folk* (New York: Penguin, 1989), 1.

9. It is possible to dismiss the usefulness of double consciousness on the grounds that Du Bois's description only fits the experiences of an elite group of educated black men. But the more significant caution against bringing double consciousness into contemporary debates is that its misuses reinforce, rather than undermine, the idea that African Americans are a "problem" people. Adolph Reed argues that the term is resonant in contemporary American discourse because it confirms the assumption African Americans have a special incapacity for fitting into the America mainstream. Other critics, including Malcolm X, reject double consciousness altogether, identifying the problem of twoness with African Americans who bend to white supremacy but strive for both black and white approval without receiving satisfaction in either (Adolph Reed Jr., "Du Bois's 'Double Consciousness': Race and Gender in Progressive Era American Thought," *Studies in American Political Development* 6 [Spring 1992]: 95; Cornel West, *Race Matters* [Boston: Beacon, 1993], 96–97).

10. There is a good deal of scholarly disagreement about the intellectual origins of the term "double consciousness." I note only three helpful retreats of the issue

in passing. In *The Art and Imagination of W. E. B. Du Bois*, Arnold Rampersand argues that Du Bois's meaning reflects the influence of turn-of-the-century psychology, including the writings of "his favorite professor," William James. In contrast to Rampersand, David Levering Lewis contends that the influence of James's *Principles of Psychology*, and its allusions to "alternating selves" or "primary and secondary consciousness," is unclear. In addition to this murky psychological heritage, there is a philosophical one. Lewis notes that Du Bois's account of twoness suggests the impact of the fiction of Goethe and Charles Chesnutt and, possibly, of Emerson's late lecture "The Transcendentalist." (The term also appears in Emerson's "Fate.") A third argument, made by Shamoon Zamir, is that the idea of double consciousness, and indeed *Souls* as a whole, is best understood as a reworking of Hegel's *Phenomenology* (see Arnold Rampersand, *The Art and Imagination of W. E. B. Du Bois* [New York: Schocken, 1990], 74; David Levering Lewis, *Biography of a Race, 1868–1919* [New York: Henry Holt, 1993], 96, 280–83; and Shamoon Zamir, *Dark Voices: W. E. B. Du Bois and American Thought 1888–1903* [Chicago: University of Chicago Press, 1995], 113–68).

11. Du Bois, *The Souls of Black Folk*, 215.

12. Ibid., 5.

13. Ibid., 164.

14. Ibid., 118.

15. Ibid., 166–66.

16. Ibid., 165.

17. I am grateful to Robert Gooding-Williams for pointing out that the image of "the swarthy spectre" is that of Shakespeare's Banquo. The allusion to *Macbeth* suggests an alternative reading of the American founding narrative that casts doubt on the legitimacy of the United States and explains the hold of racial guilt on white American consciences. Also noted: Du Bois, *The Souls of Black Folk*, 7.

18. Du Bois, *The Souls of Black Folk*, 3.

19. Ibid., 4.

20. It is perhaps eerier still that such tacit rules continue to function as what Omi and Winant call "racial etiquette": a code based on racialized expectations of behavior that govern everyday interactions in the contemporary United States (see Omi and Winant, *Racial Formation in the United States*, 62).

21. Du Bois, *The Souls of Black Folk*, 35, 71.

22. Ibid., 147.

23. Ibid., 152.

24. Ibid., 165.

25. James Baldwin, "Notes of a Native Son," in *The Price of the Ticket*, 132.

26. Baldwin, *The Fire Next Time*, 342.

27. James Baldwin, "Encounter on the Seine: Black Meet Brown," in *The Price of the Ticket*, 39.

28. Ibid.

29. James Baldwin, "Stranger in the Village," in *The Price of the Ticket*, 87.

30. The complexity of this legacy is echoed in the writing of Patricia Williams, who reveals her ambivalence about claiming her connection to a long line of (white) lawyers, one of whom impregnated her great-great-grandmother Sophie: "Reclaiming that from which one has been disinherited is a good thing. . . . Yet claiming for myself a heritage the weft of whose genesis is my own disinheritance is a profoundly troubling paradox" (Patricia J. Williams, *The Alchemy of Race and Rights: Diary of a Law Professor* [Cambridge: Harvard University Press, 1992], 217).

31. James Baldwin, "White Man's Guilt," in *The Price of the Ticket*, 409.

32. This rhetorical strategy—which Baldwin deploys in several of his early essays—could be criticized as an attempt by Baldwin to situate himself "above the veil" as the sort of objective narrator who would appeal to the white liberal editors and readers or *Partisan Review*, where "Many Thousands Gone" first appeared. As Baldwin biographer David Leeming notes, the attempt to reach the consciences of white Americans by adopting what appears to be a white persona was in fact criticized at the time of publication and later exposed Baldwin to the scorn of cultural nationalists. Although the essays in which Baldwin uses this strategy were written for the readers of the *New Leader, Commentary,* and *Partisan Review*, their unsparing treatment of white liberal hypocrisies implies that Baldwin's end is to trouble rather than to curry favor (David Leeming, *James Baldwin: A Biography* [New York: Knopf, 1994], 101).

33. Baldwin, "Many Thousands Gone," 65.

34. Baldwin alludes to the passage that concludes Richard Wright's 1940 essay "How 'Bigger' Was Born." There Wright observes that, despite the general drabness of the United States as a young, industrial society, "We . . . have in the Negro the embodiment of a past tragic enough to appease the spiritual hunger of even a James; and we have in the oppression of the Negro a shadow athwart our national life dense and heavy enough to satisfy even the gloomy broodings of a Hawthorne. And if Poe were alive, he would not have to invent horror; horror would invent him" (Richard Wright, "How 'Bigger' Was Born," introduction to *Native Son* [New York: Harper and Row, 1966], xxxiv). Also noted: Baldwin, "Many Thousands Gone," 66.

35. Baldwin, "Many Thousands Gone," 68.

36. Du Bois, *The Souls of Black Folk*, 5.

37. Baldwin, "Many Thousands Gone," 67.

38. I will not attempt to sort through Baldwin's difficult relationship with his one-time mentor Richard Wright. Although an account of that relationship would

be necessary for a more comprehensive discussion of Baldwin's critique of *Native Son*, the choice of Bigger Thomas as an emblematic black figure is not unjustified. For example, in an essay critical of Baldwin and Ralph Ellison, Irving Howe states that "the day *Native Son* appeared, American culture was changed forever" (Irving Howe, "Black Boys and Natives Sons," *Dissent* [Autumn 1963]: 354).

39. Baldwin, "Many Thousands Gone," 76.

40. Ibid., 73.

41. Ibid., 77.

42. Ibid., 78.

43. Ibid., 78.

44. I refer to doublenesses rather than enumerating the number of dimensions of identity in question (threeness, fourness, and so on) because it allows me to hold two dimensions in tension and investigate the relationship between them. Yet the imprecision of the term—for there are never only two dimensions—serves as a reminder that an accurate accounting of all the relevant facets of an individual's identity and their relation to each other is not possible. For a forceful caution against the dangers of "additive analyses," see Elizabeth V. Spelman, *Inessential Woman: Problems of Exclusion in Feminist Thought* (Boston: Beacon, 1998).

45. Baldwin, "Stranger in the Village," 81.

46. James Baldwin, "The Creative Process," in *The Price of the Ticket*, 315–18.

47. At one point, Baldwin goes so far as to proclaim that "artists are the only people in a society who can tell that society the truth about itself" (James Baldwin, "Words of a Native Son," in *The Price of the Ticket*, 396).

48. Baldwin, "Many Thousands Gone," 71.

49. Baldwin's forthrightness about his sexuality was nonetheless groundbreaking, and his example continues to inspire black gay men (see *Brother to Brother: New Writings by Black Gay Men*, ed. Essex Hemphill [Boston: Alyson, 1991], esp. essays by Hemphill and Joseph Beam).

50. In an essay that provides a much more extended treatment of this topic, Kendall Thomas explores how a "heteronormative logic" undergirded attacks on Baldwin's racial authenticity when he was alive and informs attempts to "neuter" Baldwin in the making of his memory (see Kendall Thomas, "'Ain't Nothing Like the Real Thing': Black Masculinity, Gay Sexuality, and the Jargon of Authenticity," in *The House That Race Built: Black Americans, U.S. Terrain*, ed. Wahneema Lubiano [New York: Pantheon, 1997], 116–35).

51. James Baldwin qtd. in James Mossman, "Race, Hate, Sex, and Colour: A Conversation with James Baldwin and Colin MacInnes," in *Conversations with James Baldwin*, ed. Fred L. Standley and Louis H. Pratt (Jackson: University of Mississippi Press, 1989), 54.

52. Although always wary of the reductionism required by slogans, Baldwin

was considerably more comfortable with the use of racial slogans for the purpose of political mobilization than he was with sexual ones. Writing about "Black Power," for instance, he admits the importance of the phrase as "a political necessity," a means of providing a positive self-image to Americans to whom it has been denied. He nonetheless retains his critical posture, refusing to endorse any positive image that relies on the dehumanization of members of other groups (see James Baldwin, "Anti-Semitism and Black Power," letter to "Reader's Forum," *Freedomways* 7 [Winter 1967]: 75–77).

53. Baldwin's interest in the unifying power of sexual love—which he suggested by the image of the lovers in the closing passage of *The Fire Next Time* (quoted in the first section of this essay)—receives more explicit attention in his fiction than in his essays. *Another Century* (1960) provides the most extended exploration of the possibilities for and obstacles to connections across the divides of race and gender. By coupling and uncoupling the main characters in a variety of sexual relationships (none of them lesbian), Baldwin probes the fears that divide them and the needs that they share.

54. James Baldwin, "The Male Prison," in *The Price of the Ticket*, 102; James Baldwin qtd. in Richard Goldstein, "'Go the Way Your Blood Beats': An Interview with James Baldwin," in *James Baldwin: The Legacy*, ed. Quincy Troupe (New York: Simon and Schuster/Touchstone, 1984), 174.

55. In an interview with one of his biographers, Baldwin notes that his complaints about Gide were really directed at himself and his own defensiveness about his sexuality (Fern Marja Eckman, *The Furious Passage of James Baldwin* [New York: M. Evans, 1996], 135–36).

56. Baldwin, "The Male Prison," 102.

57. James Baldwin, "Preservation of Innocence," *Zero* 2 (Summer 1949): 17.

58. James Baldwin, "Here Be Dragons," in *The Price of the Ticket*, 690.

59. Eldridge Cleaver, "Notes on a Native Son," in *Soul on Ice* (New York: Dell, 1968), 97.

60. Ibid., 101.

61. Ibid., 98.

62. That the same criticism can be made of Du Bois indicates something about the masculinity of the qualities associated with American citizenship. Although the civic virtues mentioned in *Souls* are distinctly manly, Du Bois is in fact more attuned to the particular connections between the situation of black women and "the problem of the color-line" than is Baldwin. For a fuller expression of Du Bois's feminism, see "The Damnation of Women," in *W. E. B. Du Bois: A Reader*, ed. David Levering Lewis (New York: Henry Holt, 1995), 299–312.

63. For a general critique of the exclusion of black women's interests in anti-racist critiques of interracial rape, see Kimberlé Williams Crenshaw, "Mapping

the Margins: Intersectionality, Identity Politics, and Violence against Women of Color," in *Critical Race Theory: The Key Writings That Formed the Movement*, ed. Crenshaw, Neil Gotanda, Gary Peller, and Kendall Thomas (New York: New Press, 1995), 357–83. Also noted: James Baldwin, "No Name in the Street," in *The Price of the Ticket*, 482.

64. "Revolutionary Hope: A Conversation between James Baldwin and Audre Lorde," *Essence*, December 1984, 72–74, 129–33.

65. James Baldwin, "Princes and Powers," in *The Price of the Ticket*, 57.

66. Charles Taylor, "The Politics of Recognition," in *Multiculturalism: Examining the Politics of Recognition*, 2nd ed., ed. Amy Gutmann (Princeton, NJ: Princeton University Press, 1994).

67. Baldwin qtd. in Goldstein, "Go the Way Your Blood Beats," 181.

68. Taylor, "The Politics of Recognition," 26.

69. Baldwin, "Many Thousands Gone," 78.

70. Taylor, "The Politics of Recognition," 38.

71. Paul Gilroy uses the term "double consciousness" to capture the ambivalence that black peoples on both sides of the Atlantic feel in their relationship with societies of the modern West. For Gilroy, the black diaspora has no true center, because black cultures emerge as a response to perpetual homelessness (Taylor, "The Politics of Recognition," 63; Paul Gilroy, *The Black Atlantic Modernity and Double Consciousness* [Cambridge: Harvard University Press, 1993], 111).

72. Baldwin, "Many Thousands Gone," 76–77.

73. This comment illustrates something Taylor sometimes understates: the interrelation of fundamental issues of identity with issues of material deprivation and powerlessness. Using the example of women's and blacks' writings about the effects of degrading stereotypes, in an essay on Canadian struggles with the question of identity, Taylor observes that the absence of recognition "is portrayed as an act of aggression or domination so that the accent is displaced from the human need itself to the interhuman drama of power and exploitation." The displaced accent, Taylor writes, may be explained by the fact that making a claim for recognition entails an acknowledgment of vulnerability. But the writers Taylor chooses as his examples are already *publicly* vulnerable. Although I share Taylor's suspicions about the inadequacy of a politics of antidiscrimination to address or to overcome deep social division, his choice of examples shows that Taylor misses how opposing power and exploitation, even through a language of justice and rights, reflects a "human need." Further, he overlooks the possibility that it is the vulnerability of the privileged, the reliance on their sense of self on an unjust status quo, which requires public exposure (Charles Taylor, "Impediments to a Canadian Future," in *Reconciling the Solitudes: Essays on Canadian Federalism and Nationalism*, ed. Guy Laforest [Montreal: McGill-Queens University Press,

1993], 192). Also noted: James Baldwin, "Every Goodbye Ain't Gone," in *The Price of the Ticket*, 643.

74. Amélie Oksenberg Rorty, "The Hidden Politics of Cultural Identification," *Political Theory* 22 (February 1994): 158.

75. Baldwin, "No Name in the Street," 458.

76. Virginia Woolf, *A Room of One's Own* (New York: Harcourt Brace Jovanovich, 1981), 36.

2

The Race of a More Perfect Union

*James Baldwin, Segregated Memory,
and the Presidential Race*

P. J. Brendese

no whiteness (lost) is so white as the memory of whiteness
—Williams Carlos Williams, *The Collected Poems
of William Carlos Williams*, vol. 2

Memories of slavery disgrace the race, and race perpetuates memories
of slavery.
—Alexis de Tocqueville, *Democracy in America*, vol. 1

What really exercises my mind is not this hypothetical day on which
some other Negro "first" will become the first Negro President. What
I'm really curious about is just what kind of country he'll be President
of.
—James Baldwin, *The Cross of Redemption: Uncollected Writings*

When Barack Obama gave his revealing speech on race in America, he juxtaposed what he called "the white immigrant story" with the memories aired
in black barbershops and beauty salons. In what is now known as his "More

Perfect Union" address, Obama also made a distinction between his own generation's experiences of how race is lived in America and the memories of Reverend Jeremiah Wright's generation. In each case, Obama recognized a segregation of memory along the lines of color, class, and generation. The speech magnified the connection between America's segregated memories and its segregated polity.

Challenging the boundaries of what a viable presidential candidate was free to say about slavery, he contended that the racialized remainders endure as part of an unresolved history—and part of our union that "we have yet to perfect."[1] Obama's remarks indicated that the work of coming to terms with the tortured legacy of race in America involves different communities reckoning with the content of their respective stories, the distance dividing them, and how both are lived and performed in political spaces. Later on, the presidential hopeful offered a scene of grassroots democracy bending toward that perfected union. At an organizing meeting, a young, poor white woman found solidarity with an old black man on the basis of an intersecting memory.

The range of reactions to Obama's speech testified to the distance between the memories of which he spoke. While some praised his unprecedented candor, Newt Gingrich called it "intellectually, fundamentally dishonest," Rush Limbaugh compared Obama to Rodney King,[2] and another commentator argued that it was a flashback of "the same old con, the same old shakedown that black hustlers have been running since the Kerner commission."[3] If race functions as a third rail in American political discourse, then segregated memory is the current that electrifies its danger. Political thinkers with long memories have long contended that race is the shore upon which the American hope for a triumph over the past runs aground. Alexis de Tocqueville held that "it can happen that a man will rise above the prejudice of religion, country, race . . . but it is not possible for a whole people to rise, as it were, above itself."[4] Tocqueville expressed deep pessimism about the possibility that America could ever overcome the tragic bind where race and memories of a slave past are mutual triggers.[5] In the opening epigraph of this essay, the poetry of William Carlos Williams suggests why national self-overcoming would be so difficult. Whiteness is itself inflected with a "memory of whiteness," or innocence about the past.[6]

The peculiar correspondence between race and the American myth-history of a country born innocent absorbed one of the twentieth century's finest essayists, James Baldwin.[7] Responding to the relation between whiteness and a whitewashed memory, Baldwin deliberately played upon the double meaning of innocence as both a state of juvenile obliviousness and an absence of guilt, contending that it is "the innocence which constitutes the crime."[8] This innocence is a willful disavowal of the presence of the past that "sustains a mind-set that can accommodate both an earnest commitment to the principles of equal rights and freedom regardless of race and a tacit acceptance of racial division and inequality as normal."[9]

In this essay, I make the case that James Baldwin's insights illuminate and counter a willful innocence about the complex legacy of segregated memory in American politics in general, and the presidential race in particular. By bringing Baldwin's reflections on segregated memory to bear on the 2008 election of the first black president, I situate his theoretical contributions in a dialogue of mutual illumination with contemporary American racial politics. In so doing, I explore how present publics inherit the challenges of desegregating memory that Baldwin identified, and I assess the extent to which his contributions are generative for those who would take up such a task today.

Despite the distance between the circumstances of Baldwin's time and our own, there are several reasons why I take him to be a relevant resource for those seeking to understand the complexity of segregated memory at work in Obama's speech, as well as a broader need to speak to and name the remainders of the past that inhabit the racial contours of present-day political life. In an allegedly "postracial" era, Baldwin helps readers see the persistence of racial remainders as testament to the segregated memory we will confront in these pages. He writes with uncommon depth and clarity about both the conscious and unconscious aspects of that which we call memory. For Baldwin, the past is not merely an object of active recollection that memory can conjure or set aside at will. Rather, it lives and breathes beneath the surface of human interactions, rhythms, and aversions that shape our lived experiences of race. Put differently, his language subtly registers the racialized dimensions of what scholars such as Henri Bergson, Paul Ricoeur, and W. James Booth (among others) have theorized as habit-memory.[10] As we shall see, Baldwin's work also endeavors to reveal both what whites have invested in the faces of blacks and the assumptions they have yet to disclose about themselves.

Although race is a meaningful distinction for Baldwin, he disturbs it in provocative ways that generally (though not always) avoid the familiar trap of treating "Black Memory" or "The Black Community" as if the consciousness of African Americans moves with the singular, instinctive synchronicity of a school of fish.[11] He also provides leverage for those seeking to understand the generational divide that informs the variation in black memories thematized in Obama's reaction to Reverend Wright's damning indictment of American hypocrisy.[12] The particularity of Baldwin's historical prism provides access into the historical memories and the anger out which Wright's statement arose. In keeping with the Greek translation of the theorist as one who "travels in order to see," Baldwin's ability to penetrate and move between racial and generational lines is a key vehicle for broadcasting his many voices in a pitch audible to twenty-first-century political thinkers. Indeed, my contention is that his work offers readers a glimpse of how to use language as a shared medium of commonality through which different experiences of memory, time, and race can be articulated.[13] In the wake of a multiculturalism that was often more vocal about "celebrating diversity" than how inequalities of power attach to that diversity, Baldwin offers a window into an understanding of how power shapes memory and thereby perpetuates a collective inability to confront those inequalities.[14] As I read him here, Baldwin shows readers how the politics of marginalized people's memories is not innocent in the politics that relegates them to the periphery of contemporary political life.[15]

Lawrie Balfour and George Shulman have argued that Baldwin is also a valuable resource for theorists seeking to address the relative lack of attention in political theory to the role of race in American political life.[16] The field becomes narrower still when one seeks insight into the explicit correspondence between race and memory.[17] To the extent that legacies of racial violence *are* theorized, our points of reference remain largely in the orbit of European thinkers.[18] In Shulman's view, the consequence is that: "Our work seems cut off from the place where we Americans live and the prophetic voices haunting it."[19] Shulman's rich text draws attention to important ironies relevant to this essay. In particular, North American theorists often reach across the ocean to invoke Foucault in order to insist upon "local knowledge" and draw from Agamben on the virtues of bearing witness. Yet they often do so without turning to nonwhite American thinkers such as James Baldwin, whose intellectual and political vocation called him to witness and contest the endurance of segregated memory that continues to haunt US racial politics today.

This essay is divided into four sections. In the opening segment I provide a historical overview of the segregation of memory along racial lines as it extends from Reconstruction. I then offer an analysis of James Baldwin's relationship to memory and its impact on black and white consciousness in the face of dominant myth-histories. This is followed by an exposition of how Baldwin approaches desegregating memory by cultivating linguistic spaces better equipped to negotiate the legacy of time. Baldwin accomplishes this not merely by speaking on behalf of the dead but also by deliberately employing diction that requires the reader to imagine the impact of memory from black perspectives. In the third section, I probe the correspondences between his approaches to mnemonic divides and those of Barack Obama by exploring how segregated memory received contemporary expression in the 2008 presidential race. Finally, I close the essay by highlighting how Obama departs from the work of coming to terms with the past that Baldwin put forward, and the political significance of Obama's risky reliance on the exceptional American capacity to triumph over the past amid many unresolved problems where race figures prominently.

Segregated Memory, Race, and Reunion

Recent scholarship has witnessed a proliferation of histories casting a new light on the origins and trials of American democracy.[20] In order to elucidate the contemporary segregation of memory, a brief overview of the mnemonic divisions during the period of Reconstruction is instructive. In *Race and Reunion,* David Blight traces the segregation of Civil War memory by dividing the narratives into three categories: the reconciliationist, the white-supremacist, and the emancipationist memories.[21] Briefly stated, the reconciliationist narrative grew out of the gory process of dealing with the dead on the battlefields. Its emphasis centered on the reunion of North and South after a bitter fratricide. White-supremacist history featured a Lost Cause ideology where the South would rise again. This return of the repressed was embodied in the terrorism of the Ku Klux Klan, who professed to embody the ghosts of a vanquished Confederacy. Finally, the emancipationist narrative chronicled the passage of African Americans from bondage to freedom. Its foremost spokesman was none other than Frederick Douglass.[22] Blight contends that the reconciliationist theory colluded with the white-supremacist memory to exclude the emancipationist narrative. For purposes of exposition, we trace the outline of each below.

In the wake of the Civil War there were strong economic and political incentives to reunite northerners and southerners. As legions of wounded veterans returned home from bloody battlefields and a living death in prison camps, the nation was weary of war. The country's infrastructure was in tatters, and it seemed that hardly a household had been spared a loss. Horace Greeley, editor of the *New York Tribune,* posted bail for Confederate president Jefferson Davis in May 1867. Speaking to a mixed-race audience at the African Methodist Episcopal Church in Richmond, he gave voice to the spirit of reunion. As Greeley insisted on the reconstruction of the Union, it became clear what he thought the price of a reunion would be—a willful forgetting: "Men of Virginia! I entreat you to forget the years of slavery, and secession, and civil war now happily past. . . . [F]orget that some of you have been masters, others slaves,—some for disunion, others against it,—and remember only that you are Virginians, and all now and henceforth freemen."[23] Blight contends the speech was a kind of "founding text for sectional reconciliation" and that "variations of its themes would echo for decades with profound political consequences."[24]

In the years following Greeley's call to amnesia, the displacement of some memories in favor of others was policed by white power and took on a particular form. After the war, an infectious sentimentalism framed the recollection of the conflict in the memories of whites. This alchemy of selective memory and sentimentalism gained momentum until it reached its zenith at a ceremony commemorating the fiftieth anniversary of Gettysburg. There President Woodrow Wilson declared the war America's "quarrel forgotten."[25] As Blight puts it: "Like the politics of reconciliation, which was several decades old by 1913, this reunion was about forging unifying myths and making remembering safe."[26]

In his speech, President Wilson failed to recall the causes and results of the war. The forgetting he enjoined took on an embodied form—particularly when we consider Wilson's audience. The government had paid the transportation costs of far-flung white veterans from North and South to travel to the event but had neglected to include any of the surviving 180,000 black veterans who had served in the Union army and navy. The exclusion was more than symbolic: the reconciliation of the Blue and the Gray had been forged at the expense of healing the divide between black and white:

"Because the planters had allowed no space for surviving black veterans, they had left no space on the program for discussing the second great outcome of the war—the failures of reconciliation. . . . But the 1913 'Peace Jubilee' as the organizers called it, was a Jim Crow reunion, and white supremacy might be said to have been the silent master of ceremonies."[27]

The reconciliationist narrative had become parasitic upon white supremacy such that the two were fused together to exclude the emancipationist narrative. The *Louisville Courier-Journal* captured the spirit of amnesia by declaring: "God bless us every one, alike the Blue and the Gray, the Gray and the Blue! The world ne'er witnessed such a sight as this. Beholding, can we say happy is the nation with no history?"[28] Black newspapers took a much different view of the so-called Peace Jubilee, especially in light of the widespread lynching that by then had become frequent. The *Washington Bee* underscored the alarming contrast between how each community registered the presence of the past by recognizing that the premature celebration had made African Americans spectral. It bluntly asked: "A reunion of whom?"[29]

Wilson was an ardent segregationist, and his speech is remarkable in its performative displacement of both black presence and absence. Rather than acknowledging the complexity of the commemoration by invoking the multiple sacrifices that had made it possible, he disavowed those losses through the insinuation of a myth-historical reconciliation. It was a dangerous fiction that would continue a legacy lasting long into the twentieth century and, as we will see, stretched into the 2008 presidential race. The public staging of triumphal resolutions predicated on amnesia and African American exclusion would hardly end with Wilson's oration. As the work of Michael Rogin attests, this mythologized past extended itself in ways that were instrumental in perpetuating segregated memory and white supremacy amid a flood of European émigrés in the early twentieth century.[30] Rogin notes that the renowned (silent) film *Birth of a Nation* was based on Thomas Dixon's *The Klansman*.[31] The film's antagonist is a black rapist eager to predate on a white woman who is in desperate need of salvation by the resurrected ghosts of the Confederate dead.

By 1935, W. E. B. Du Bois declared that the African American experience had been effectively "seared" from public memory.[32] It was not until 1956 that John Hope Franklin became the first black historian appointed to a white institution. In different ways, both Du Bois and Franklin recognized the urgent need to deal with the stigma of color as an unresolved remainder of slavery that had been overwritten by a preemptive narrative of closure exemplified by Wilson's speech. In closing accounts with the past, Wilson's reconciliationist memory employed the most American of capstones: a happy ending.[33] Through a reunion built upon amnesiac white supremacy, the South—as the saying goes—"lost the war but won the peace." The tidy resolution of Wilson's narrative was mirrored in the triumph that sealed *The Birth of a Nation:* in both stories the distortion of history produced a "happy ending" brought about by whites lynching blacks. In a country arguably addled by its addiction to amnesiac redemption and its avoidance of tragedy—an aversion still so trenchant that even *Titanic* has a triumphal resolution—it is hardly surprising that in 1956 James Baldwin decried segregated memory by saying that in "every aspect of his living [the Negro] betrays the memory of an auction block and the impact of the happy ending."[34]

Baldwin and Desegregating Memory

One can view Baldwin's essays as a written record of his eloquent struggle to come terms with the past—both literally and figuratively. His was a lifelong labor to create linguistic and political spaces better equipped to deal with the legacy of time. In so doing, he posed a formidable challenge to white-supremacist memory by extending and deepening the emancipationist narrative initiated by Frederick Douglass.[35] Baldwin spoke of being called to do this work in much the same way one speaks of a religious vocation—one that obligated him to bear witness to a past that had been tragically disavowed.[36] To do so, he reaches for a language that can at once articulate the fact of this disavowal while also registering its legacy across racial lines.[37] To light our descent into the depths of his endeavor, let us consider a sequence of highly abbreviated remarks on three intimately related dimensions of Baldwin's essays: his relationship to memory, memory's conscious and unconscious impact on blacks and whites, and the collusion of myth-history in perpetuating white supremacy.[38]

Baldwin measures the distance segregating communities of memory by first diagnosing the United States as a land intoxicated by a peculiar kind of amnesia. The country's willful disavowal of any authentic connection to its past is the doorway opening onto the cloudless horizon of American political possibility: "The making of an American begins at the point where he himself rejects any other ties, any other history, and himself adopts the vesture of his adopted land."[39] What is the cost of this disavowal?[40] Although in different ways, the nation's inhabitants parted company with their forebears and, in the process, colored an American encounter with a core problem of modernity: they became unknown to themselves.[41]

Baldwin traces the path of the country's self-estrangement along racial lines. The European émigré story begins with a *voluntary* divorce from a land where children's futures were determined by their last name. Whereas "in the case of the Negro the past was taken from him whether he would or no; yet to foreswear it was meaningless and availed him of nothing, since his shameful history was carried, quite literally, on his brow."[42] Though whites do not "wear their history" in the same way as blacks, they live out the psychological impact of segregated memory as "the slightly mad victims of their own brainwashing."[43] Unlike blacks, who have "the great advantage of never having believed in that collection of myths to which white Americans cling," whites have been especially susceptible to the myth-historical trappings of a country born innocent.[44] They have assumed an innocence that their subterranean guilt will not let them sustain without considerable cost: "People who imagine history flatters them (as it does, indeed, since they wrote it) are impaled on their history like a butterfly on a pin and become incapable of seeing or changing themselves, or the world."[45]

The failure to confront these tortured legacies means that, in the tatter of an incomplete Reconstruction, "a bill is coming that I fear America is not prepared to pay."[46] In Baldwin's karmic economy of history, we "always pay for what we do, either willingly or unwillingly."[47] To insist that, one way or another, we must make good on outstanding personal and political debts, he invoked the image of Ezekiel's wheel, the wheel within a wheel, stating that "what goes around comes around."[48] That inherited obligations return to exact a cost is what Baldwin referred to as a "historical vengeance, a cosmic vengeance" or simply "the price of the ticket."[49]

Baldwin's subtle understanding of the demands of a haunting past penetrates beyond active recollection—though he clearly anticipated a palpable blowback from what he took to be the shortfalls of the civil rights movement and white-supremacist historiography.[50] To figure the price he speaks of is not merely to reckon with the divide between the conscious white immigrant/reconciliationist memory and the emancipationist narrative. It requires an assessment of how these histories are lodged in the subconscious registers, habituated practices, and presumptions that make up who we are. This is the case, in part, because history is "not merely something to be read. And it does not refer merely, or principally, to the past. On the contrary, the great force of history comes from the fact that we carry it within us, are unconsciously controlled by it in many ways, and history is literally present in all that we do."[51] Acknowledging the reality that we *are* history is key to beginning to decipher the "hieroglyph" of our circumstances.[52]

Baldwin consistently resists the language of memory as a simple facility of active recollection. The easy dichotomy of memory and forgetting is too reductive to adequately capture our experience of time. In "Many Thousands Gone," he offers one of his most famous expositions of the past's presence:

> In our image of the Negro breathes a past we deny, not dead but living yet and powerful, the beast in our jungle of statistics. . . . Wherever the Negro face appears a tension is created, the tension of a silence filled with things unutterable. It is a sentimental error, therefore to believe that the past is dead; it means nothing to say that it is all forgotten, that the Negro himself has forgotten it. *It is not a question of memory.* Oedipus did not remember the thongs that bound his feet; nevertheless, the marks they left testified to that doom toward which his feet were leading him. The man does not remember the hand that struck him, the darkness that frightened him as a child; nevertheless the hand and the darkness remain with him, indivisible from himself forever, part of the passion that drives him wherever he thinks to take flight.[53]

The sequence of the passage is illuminating. It posits "the Negro face" as carrying a silent tension where the strain of that which is unspeakable in mixed-race conversations functions to shape what *is* spoken. That this happens under the genteel veneer that envelops supposedly free speech means the complexion of those having a conversation speaks directly to its content. The poisoned, intractable wordlessness is a consequence of the disavowal of memory and guilt that whites have invested in the darkness of the black face. At worst, it confines blacks to the living death of Ralph Ellison's *Invisible Man*.[54] That whites remain unknown to themselves condemns them to be imprisoned by the psychic life of the fictions they inhabit—a delusion that ultimately dehumanizes all races. Without a reckoning, Baldwin warns in "The Fire Next Time," America is headed toward a self-immolation of biblical proportions.

With Oedipus as an analogue, Baldwin underscores the force of an intergenerational inheritance that makes up a historicity that even the most brilliant of intellects can neither map nor evade. By fleeing his parents, Oedipus tries to flee his history and thus his identity. He does this in spite of the fact that both are literally inscribed upon his skin.[55] To borrow a term from Frantz Fanon, Oedipus's past is *epidermalized*.[56] Unable to get away from his origins, he is compelled toward a homecoming of the worst order. In thinking he can escape the legacy that is his footprint, he runs into the very blindness his insight believed it could avoid. In referencing an indelible "hand that struck" the child, Baldwin accents the psychic power of parental authority from which even adults are never entirely emancipated. When the impact of white supremacy underlies and directs that authority (as it did for Baldwin), children's horizons of possibility are horribly disfigured.[57] The limits of freedom in the black political imagination have been so inscribed by white power, and the need to escape it, that the boundaries of that imagination are translated across generational lines. Parents impose these horizons on the psychic life of the future: their children. Baldwin accords this imposition significant personal and political influence in part because, for a black child, white supremacy "destroys his father's authority over him. His father can no longer tell him anything because his past has disappeared."[58] In short, Baldwin identifies an inherited poverty of positive freedom within the black political imagination.[59]

Regardless of whether we choose to remember the past, the past remembers us. Recalled or disavowed, the past inevitably returns to reconstitute its subjects.[60] Against this backdrop, any temptation to presume that active forgetting could be redemptive, emancipatory, or salvific is bound to be undone by the insurgent life of the present past. To portray the political relevance of the ongoing return of the past, Baldwin warns his readers to recognize that the history inherent in liberalism risks undermining freedom by tacitly conflating equality with sameness: "Our good will, from which we yet expect such power to transform us, is thin, passionless, strident; *its roots examined, lead us back to our forebears*, whose assumption it was that the black man, to become truly human and acceptable, must first become like us."[61]

Likewise, Baldwin reveals to readers of different colors the ways in which they have tacitly presumed liberal freedom to mean freedom from the past. For Baldwin, affirming the limits of freedom does not foreclose on its possibility. Rather, it is a precondition of any practice of freedom worthy of affirmation: "To accept one's past—one's history—is not the same as drowning in it; it is learning to use it. *An invented past can never be used. . . . It cracks and crumbles under the pressures of life like clay in a season of drought.*"[62]

Accepting the fact that "we are history" does not mean quiescence to the boundaries imposed by white power but is part of the work of "deciphering the hieroglyph" of one's circumstance. To translate an encrypted past allows one to acknowledge an inheritance that, while impossible to jettison, becomes available as a resource to those with the capacity to speak it in words: "A victim who can articulate the situation of the victim has ceased to be a victim: he, or she, has become a threat."[63] Just as understanding the limits imposed by the Anglo-Germanic linguistic heritage freed Baldwin to invent new possibilities of expression, using that language to avow an unchangeable past opens the possibility that memory might become enabling by changing one's relationship to it. In this, Baldwin agrees with Grillparzer that "he who knows his limits is free. He who imagines himself to be free is a slave to his own madness."

What tools does Baldwin offer to desegregate memory amid the complex legacies he identifies? Is he merely a poetic witness of segregated memory, or do his literary and dramatic innovations offer clues into how readers might democratize memory by desegregating mnemonic communities? It is to these questions that we now turn. By identifying the ways that history lives on not only in conscious memory but also in the unconscious minds and practices of whites and blacks, Baldwin is presented with the formidable challenge of speaking to multiple audiences with plural experiences of present pasts. Although there is no single panacea for the problems he identifies, Baldwin employs a series of illuminating lyrical maneuvers that force the reader to reposition herself in relation to the text. By alternating narrative voices between a first-person "I" and an ambiguous "we," the effect is a blurring of racial lines in a manner that requires both reader and author to imagine the reach of memory from different angles and expectations.

The phrase "in *our* image of the Negro breathes a past *we* deny" clearly implies a white perspective. The invocation of "*our* good will" allows him to disclose its unexamined roots in the assumption that blacks should become like the collective white "us" he employs as a starting point. Where he draws a racial divide, he often shifts perspective and then provocatively collapses distinctions: "The story of the Negro in America . . . is the story of Americans."[64] The moves allow Baldwin to begin to unlock what is hidden from white self-knowledge since "our estrangement from him is the depth of our estrangement from ourselves."[65] By moving between voices ranging from black and white individuals and collectives to a transracial "we," Baldwin seeks to convene another public that does not yet exist—a public that is both less alienated and less willfully blinded. The public he imagines is one that would extend the work his text initiates: the work of becoming co-creators of each other's awareness: "If we—and now I mean the relatively conscious whites and the relatively conscious blacks, who must, like lovers, insist on, or create, the consciousness of others . . . we may be able . . . to end the racial nightmare and achieve our country and change the history of the world."[66]

Toward this end Baldwin both prevails upon whites directly ("White men, Hear me!") and also lets them overhear his advice to the next genera-tion of African Americans through an open letter to his nephew.[67] Hence, the kind of insistence Baldwin performs in these textual spaces is transracial but also transgenerational. He interprets his calling to witness as requiring him to assume the burden of testifying on behalf of enslaved peoples de-nied a voice both in life and in death. During his own life, Baldwin repeat-edly denied being a spokesman for his black contemporaries. His diction, however, suggests something more ironic and complex, especially with re-spect to his ancestors. In an effort to desegregate memories that have been divided along race and generational time, Baldwin adopts the first-person perspective to make silence speak. He insists: "I am speaking very seriously, and this is not an overstatement: I picked cotton, I carried it to the market, I built railroads under someone else's whip for nothing. For nothing."[68]

At first it is not at all clear what Baldwin means when he says, "I picked cotton." Yet his remarks make more sense when heard in concert with those of the preceding section. Recall Baldwin argued that both the fearful trau-ma of black parents and the paternalistic "good will" of whites are conveyed through generational time. They are passed on. We literally embody history, in part because the body inherits the past's remainders: "This is, perhaps, the key to history since *we are history,* and since the tension of which I am speak-ing is so silent and so private, with effects so unforeseeable and so public."[69]

As a self-proclaimed "emotional historian" who speaks for the dead, Baldwin announces the continuity of black suffering breathing beneath the blues. Not only should the country know that whites and blacks need each other, but this need must not be translated into a request by blacks for a handout: "I am not an object of missionary charity, I am one of the people who built the country."[70] The mutuality of the necessity Baldwin expresses ought not to be used as a recipe for white paternalism. Paternalism would allow a power inequality to persist under the guise of white generosity and thereby further infantilize African Americans.[71] By taking on the voice of those whose dreams, labor, and blood went uncompensated and unstoried in the country's accumulation of wealth, he refuses as counterfeit the moral currency whites presume to accrue when they "give" to black people. Speaking on behalf of the unpaid dead, Baldwin resists the poisonous collusion of moral and political superiority that occurs when whites reduce blacks to objects of charity and "wards of America."[72]

In saying that he is not a spokesman, he makes an ironic distinction between himself and the ancestors who have seemingly taken possession of his tongue and pen.[73] His irony confronts the stigma of race that remains within "the image of the Negro" by allowing the specter of slavery to become articulate. In other words, by adopting the voice of a ghost he uses rhetorical and textual space to stage a relationship to a past where the dead have the power to channel themselves into spoken form in the present. The result compels his interlocutors to literally dialogue with history as embodied in the present, namely by engaging the form he assumes as its unappeased specter. Baldwin's ghostly personae aims to force readers to look on the country's railroads, infrastructure, and achievements with new eyes in order to see the landscape from above and below ground, to view the loss that inheres within the nation's every gain. For beneath America's fruited plain the soil is "full of the corpses of my ancestors."[74]

Does Baldwin speak on behalf of the dead in order to advance an *integrated* memory? Politically, he was notably opposed to both the black separatist movement as well as some forms that integration took on. Because integration is often a code word for assimilation into whiteness, the intersection of memories Baldwin speaks of cannot be understood as requiring a simple conflation of separate histories within the existing paradigm. His biting query "Do I want to be integrated into a burning house" also sounds a caution with respect to the politics of memory he endorses. With this in mind, we must interpret Baldwin with great care when he imagines "a fusion between what I remember and what you remember; then there will be no question about our separation. We are really one people—and this is part of our problem in fact—we spend all our time denying it."[75]

The "fusion" Baldwin speaks of might more accurately be described as transfiguration rather than integration. It would transform prior recollections and expose the fallacies at work in histories that arch over tragedy and bend toward the amnesiac redemption of a happy ending. The required reworking of both form and content would entail a comprehensive and thoroughgoing effort at the individual and collective levels because *"everything white Americans think they believe in must now be reexamined."*[76] Speaking again in the voice of the specter, he explains: "What happened to the Negro . . . is not simply a matter of *my* memory and *my* history, but of *American* history and memory. For the history the Negro endured . . . was endured by all the white people who oppressed him. . . . I was here, and that did something to *me*. But you were here on top of me, and that did something to *you*."[77]

Since Baldwin registers both the deep psychological and political impact of segregated memory, the examination he calls for is a core component of what he referred to as personal responsibility. In his use of the phrase, responsibility means literally *an ability to respond* to the conscious and unconscious limits and influences imposed by the past. It is a voluntary psychological excavation that occurs in "great pain and terror"[78] that "involves the honest appraisal of the historical roots, as well as the current conditions, of one's situation."[79]

The appraisal of one's condition is not simply an intellectual exercise involving the mere extraction and exchange of competing histories that will produce a geometric truth. Nor would a desegregated memory simply add another narrative to existing historical accounts. Given that "we are history," to simply expand the existing plurality of narratives would not be sufficient to bridge the wounded divide Baldwin identifies.[80] Rather, it requires an intensely personal dialogue with those whose presence and absence have been made spectral in our psychic and political lives. It is only by recognizing what has been excluded from our polity that we can hope to become less estranged from ourselves, our country, and our humanity.

Although Baldwin's insights are elegantly expressed, he is well aware that the spaces within which one writes and speaks the poetry of the possible are insufficiently equipped for the kind of transdermal mnemonic dialogue such a heavy history requires.[81] For the past to become useful, relationships to it must also be negotiated in *physical* proximity with others since body language transmits and authors visceral histories. The alternative is a politics of distance that achieves its crudest articulation in the contemporary prison industrial complex. This cannot continue "because there is a limit to the number of people any government can put in prison. . . . A bill is coming that I feel America is not prepared to pay."[82] I return to this point in the closing section.

To sum up, I have suggested that Baldwin poses a direct challenge to the form and content of the white-supremacist and reconciliationist memories. Where the Lost Cause ideology was embodied in the Klansmen who took the form of ghosts returning to avenge the Confederacy, Baldwin responds by speaking the specter of slaves in the first person. He speaks through multiple voices and a mobile, kaleidoscopic perspective in order to create spaces better equipped to deal with the legacy of segregated memory over time. By invoking and shifting between the vantage points and assumptions of whites and blacks, he begins to create a common medium through which the submerged racial and generational differences can become unearthed and articulate. Baldwin uses the terrain of the text to mediate between segregated memories and offer a relationship to the past that strives to create a less alienated, future public of the "relatively conscious." In the section that follows, we will see how the American democratic experiment inherits Baldwin's challenge to build a shared future from pasts that some would disavow.

The 2008 Presidential Race

Even before Barack Obama became a viable presidential candidate, the reconciliationist narrative outlined above once again became visible in the premature celebration of a new "postracial" era. Although the term is contestable on a number of levels, there is irony in a name that would invoke the very thing it professes to have moved beyond.[83] The lingering presumptions of the reconciliation narrative and unresolved legacy of segregated memory enumerated above returned to prevail upon the 2008 election. Remarkably, a certain spirit of James Baldwin also returned and was given voice by presidential hopeful Barack Obama. In this section, I explore how Obama adapts and extends Baldwin's approach to mediating segregated memory by moving between and within racial communities and temporalities to forge an agnostic space wherein the impact of those histories intersects.

In his first book, *Dreams from My Father: A Story of Race and Inheritance,* Obama acknowledges reading Baldwin.[84] Although he does not explore the parallels, the biographies of the two men bear some intriguing similarities.[85] As part of the work of coming to terms with their personal histories, both endured a struggle to forge their identities out of a vacancy left by their absent fathers.[86] This meant acknowledging and distinguishing between their respective father's blackness and their own.[87] The work of parsing a divide between generational struggles became relevant in a defining moment of the presidential race when the controversial comments of Reverend Jeremiah Wright compelled Obama to draw distinctions between his own generation and that of Wright and Baldwin. Indeed, there is a single word that Obama uses to describe his father, Wright, and Baldwin himself: "bitter."[88] Against this backdrop, Obama not only had to shift between the mnemonic subject positions of different racial communities, but he also had to occupy different temporal locations within black memories. Below we consider each in turn.

In a remarkable speech, Obama broke what Baldwin termed the "dangerous and reverberating silence" about race by airing an account that highlighted the contemporary political stakes of segregated memory. He did not rely on speechwriter Jon Favreau to script the remarks. He told campaign manager David Plouffe: "I already know what I want to say in this speech. I've been thinking about it for twenty years."[89] Quoting Faulkner to identify a slave past that is not past, he traced the story of emancipation through Jim Crow, segregated schools, the denial of loans for black housing and connected each to the prevalence of racialized economic inequalities. He made a deeper connection still by diagnosing America's inability to face those inequalities as perpetuated by divergent ways of relating to the past. The economic divides between and within racial communities accent complexities that we have never "really worked through" and threaten important possibilities for coalition politics. As such, they remain part of a "union that we have yet to perfect."[90]

Acutely aware of the political dangers of being typecast by whites as the face of angry black vengeance (a charge Baldwin did not escape), Obama attempted to disarm fears by portraying the grievances of different races as grounded in "legitimate concerns."[91] It was a high-wire oration that found the candidate reaching to cultivate a transracial receptivity strong enough to save the dialogue from being stranded on the shores of the recurring black anger and white guilt that Baldwin theorized as a self-proclaimed "emotional historian." To stake out a common experience of a present past, he pointed to a place where blacks and whites might identify with each other's anger despite the fact that its roots betray different genealogies. He told the story of working-class white Americans struggling to stave off financial ruin. As bearers of the "immigrant story," they feel neither implicated in the injustice of slavery nor wealthy as a result of its having occurred. Faced with economic hardship brought on by corporate greed and corruption, the perceived unfair advantage of African Americans in competition for jobs stokes anger and enmity. The perception is met with a conviction that, with resources so scarce, American opportunity "is a zero-sum game, in which your dreams come at my expense."[92]

In order to strategically disagree with Wright while not disowning him, Obama compared the preacher to his grandmother whose love for him is real, but who nevertheless had fears that were racialized.

> I can no more disown him than I can disown the black community. I can no more disown him than I can my white grandmother—a woman who helped raise me, a woman who sacrificed again and again for me, a woman who loves me as much as she loves anything in this world, but a woman who once confessed her fear of black men who passed by her on the street, and who on more than one occasion has uttered racial or ethnic stereotypes that made me cringe. These people are part of me. And they are part of America, this country that I love.[93]

By encouraging the listener to relate to Wright's remarks the way one would relate to those of an elderly relative, Obama was surely asking (white) listeners to view the incident more empathetically. Yet he was also drawing on his grandmother as an example of a particular kind of habit-memory that serves as a vehicle for her visceral reaction to black pedestrians. Recalling Baldwin's remark that "we are history" because it lives in our flesh, entrenched fears have legacies that can inform racial encounters in complicated ways that become articulate in habituated practices, aversions, and reactions. In this case, they became apparent in what Terrance MacMullan calls "habits of whiteness."[94] Such habits can often be unconscious and can exist in concert with conscious good intentions and, in the above case, a genuine love for one's grandson.

Beyond illuminating the differences between the white immigrant experience and the histories that erupt in the banter of black barbershops, Obama faced additional challenges. Reverend Wright's inflammatory remarks compelled him to address how memories diverge along generational lines within black communities. Here he simultaneously translates those memories for a wider audience while carefully establishing his own generation's distance from them:[95] "There were many who didn't make it—those who were ultimately defeated, in one way or another, by discrimination. That legacy of doubt was passed on to future generations. . . . *For the men and women of Reverend Wright's generation,* the memories of humiliation and doubt and fear have not gone away; nor has the anger and bitterness of those years. That anger may not get expressed in public, in front of white coworkers or white friends. But it does find voice in the barbershop or around the kitchen table."[96]

Strategically, Obama depicted Wright's anger as solidifying a relationship to time and memory so fixed that it disavows past progress and thereby forecloses upon the possibility of future change. In effect, he cast Wright's relationship to history as dangerous insofar as it had become what Nietzsche called a "disguised theology."[97] The controversial moves allowed Obama to contextualize Wright's angry memories as vacant of hope while making his grievances about race seem anachronistic—a point to which I shall return.

Obama cautions that, while the anger Wright expressed ought not to be dismissed by whites who fail to understand its roots, it is not necessarily an asset to blacks: "That anger is not always productive; indeed, all too often it distracts attention from solving real problems; it keeps us from squarely facing our own complicity in our condition, and prevents the African-American community from forging the alliances it needs to bring about real change."[98] By identifying anger as creating blindness to "our own complicity in our condition," Obama shifts between celebration, explanation, and risky critique in order to convene a public able to talk about race without the burden of imposed silences. Just as Baldwin employed his mobile perspective as an author to disclose how the power of racial tension constrains the "free" speech of whites, Obama confronted a similar constraint within black communities, a norm that rendered certain criticisms unutterable in mixed-race company.

Jesse Jackson's crude reproach of Obama arguably marked this enforced silence as part of a generational divide. Here is Zadie Smith's analysis:

> The Jackson gaffe, with its Oedipal violence ("I want to cut his nuts out") is especially poignant because it goes to the heart of a generational conflict in the black community, concerning what we will say in public and what we say in private. For it has long been a point of honor, among the civil rights generation, that any criticism or negative analysis of our community, expressed, as they are often by white politicians, without context, without real empathy or understanding, even if (*especially if*) the criticism happens to be true (more than half of all black American children live in single-parent households). Our business is our business. Keep it in the family; don't wash your dirty linen in public; stay unified. (Of course, with his overheard gaffe, Jackson unwittingly broke his own rule.)[99]

When Jackson criticized Obama for allegedly "talking down" to African American people, the implication was that the candidate had positioned himself *above* or *beyond* black people and therefore was no longer *of* them.[100] Looking through Jackson's generational prism, by offering a public criticism of African Americans, Obama wagered his blackness by assuming a role historically reminiscent of conservative white critics. Ironically, in his attempt to tend to future generations he found himself vulnerable to a critique by African Americans that bore a family resemblance to that which James Baldwin had endured a generation prior: he was vulgarly emasculated and accused of appeasing whites.[101]

It was hardly the case that all whites were appeased. MSNBC correspondent Patrick Buchanan's reaction to Obama's speech made strikingly visible the enduring legacy of segregated memory along racial lines. In an article entitled "A Brief for Whitey," Buchanan put forward a corrective to what he cited as the flaws in Obama's memory: "First, America has been the best country on earth for black folks. It was here that 600,000 black people, brought from Africa in slave ships, grew into a community of 40 million, were introduced to Christian salvation, and reached the greatest levels of freedom and prosperity blacks have ever known. . . . Second, no people anywhere has done more to lift up blacks than white Americans. . . . We hear the grievances. Where is the gratitude?"[102]

For the sake of brevity we will set aside the obvious omissions and historical inaccuracies of the statement. Nor is the point to suggest that Buchanan speaks for the memories of all whites, or that all whites have the same memories. Rather, consider how Buchanan's response highlights both the legacy of segregated memory as well as the ongoing momentum of the reconciliationist narrative.[103] The fusion of the reconciliationist memory with the white-supremacist historiography reaches its pinnacle in the view that blacks should look upon their slave past with gratitude to whites since it culminated in Christian redemption. Buchanan's redemption presumes a triumph over the past—a closure that renders some inequalities and memories unspeakable unless we are offering a thanksgiving for their resolution. In short, my contention is that the fusion of the white-supremacist and reconciliationist narratives received acute expression in Buchanan's willful disavowal of emancipationist memory, and that such a relationship to the past preempts a politics that remembers and addresses wounds across generations.

Taken together, Buchanan and Smith's remarks have provocative implications for which memories can be freely spoken, the extent to which habit-memories can become apparent, and what memories different American publics have ears to hear.[104] By situating Baldwin's essays in terms of the presidential race, I have argued on behalf of his relevance for contemporary political and theoretical encounters with the conscious and unconscious dimensions of segregated memory. Yet, if Baldwin is correct that what is spoken betrays the evidence of that which remains unsaid, Buchanan's false accusation that Obama is ungrateful draws our attention to important differences that separate Baldwin and Obama. The political relevance of this divide will be examined in the closing section.

Buchanan betrayed an absence of both long- and short-term memory when he registered Obama as a voice of ungrateful grievance. Throughout the campaign, the then-president and First Lady repeatedly attempted to disarm whites' latent fears of black resentment by expressing resentment's opposite: gratitude. With the crisp, euphonic alliteration that comes from having a mother from Kansas, and a father from Kenya, audiences repeatedly heard Obama give thanks for the gifts bestowed by the country, since "only in America" was his story possible. The effect was dimensional: he cultivated popular receptivity by casting his biography in the familiar vernacular of American exceptionalism. By expressing gratitude far more often than grievance, he assuaged the fears of black vengeance lodged in the emotional memories of whites. He positioned his candidacy on a broader arc of hopeful American triumphalism over adversity by deploying the reconciliation narrative, adopting the language of "change we can believe in," which effectively cast his coming in messianic terms as "The One."[105]

When Buchanan cited Christian salvation as part of his argument against the emancipationist narrative, he flagged another important distinction between Baldwin and Obama relevant to how memory is tied to political possibility in America. Unlike Obama, Baldwin rejected the black church on a number of grounds.[106] For his part, Baldwin was profoundly suspicious that the American "belief" in change is constituted by a liberal/Christian rebirth unaffected by the past and innocent of the memories we have been discussing in these pages. That is, Christian tropes of rebirth are too closely aligned with the self-making of liberalism insofar as both remain unconditioned by history.[107]

In his 1959 book *The American Adam*, R. W. B. Lewis chronicled the early American desire to begin the world anew, without reference to the past.[108] In a provocative article, John B. Judis draws parallels between the biblical figure of Adam, a patriarch unburdened by the weight of history, and Obama's future-oriented public appeal: "He is at once part of black America and also once removed from it and from its history—an Adam figure with respect to the country's oldest and most painful conflict."[109] If it is indeed the case that Obama's seductive powers grow out of the country's long-standing captivation with the ability to break with memory and begin the world anew, is the work of Baldwin that Obama took up in his speech on race fundamentally at odds with the very historical momentum that elected him? In other words, if Obama's appeal rests on resounding the biblically inflected idiom of a new birth, a hopeful future, and change we can believe in, then where does this leave the work of speaking and responding to the ghosts of the past that haunt the present moment in the form of enduring injustice?[110] Obama captured this tension in a single turn of phrase when asked by reporters whether he would investigate the past abuses of the previous administration. He replied: "I don't believe that anyone is above the law. . . . But we need to look forward as opposed to looking backwards."[111]

The Race of a More Perfect Union

I have argued that by adopting a Baldwinian lyrical dexterity to articulate and move between communities of memory, Obama began to shape a desegregated relationship to memory and time.[112] For a brief moment Obama occupied a contentious terrain that cultivates receptivity, translates memories, and situates them in an agonistic relationship to each other. Rather than endorse a singular, hegemonic, or integrated "black" relationship to the past, he identified the segregation of generational memory within black communities and beyond. When he did not suppose a disavowal of the past or a preemptive reconciliation, he directed his audience toward a future in common. Yet this account would be incomplete absent a consideration of how Obama strategically invoked what I have been calling a reconciliation narrative in order to portray himself as the vehicle through which America can, once again, leave the past behind in a dream-cloud of hope.

Complete with the visual imagery of sunrise renewal that recalled Ronald Reagan's "Morning in America," Obama distanced himself from Baldwin's emphasis on the price at which hope for future change is earned. He blurred key distinctions in narrative memories needed to make legible and confront the systemic nature of racial inequality, and sidestepped engagement with the stigma of blackness wherein memory conditions habituated practices of self-segregation. Of course, we do well to be mindful of the differences separating a president charged with embodying the union and a prophet seeking to re-member it. That said, I conclude this essay by offering critical reflections that emerge from several points where Obama has departed from the politics of working through the past in ways that disavow race. This is followed by a closing argument for the present-day political implications of the dimensional mnemonic approach that Baldwin's challenges make available—as well as the attendant limitation of addressing obstacles to desegregating memory through rhetoric alone.

While Obama's acknowledgment of a plurality of memories might make for clever campaign strategy, the obvious power differential between a presidential hopeful and a hopeful president recasts the consideration of memory as an issue of legitimacy. Moving too easily between mnemonic positions with presidential authority risks using executive power to author and legitimate a conflation of the memories of white immigrants and black emancipationists. Cornel West took notable exception to this maneuver, saying: "Do they [whites] have grounds for being upset? Absolutely. There have been excesses of affirmative action and so forth and so on, but Jim Crow de facto is still in place. . . . Who are the major victims of that? Poor, disproportionately, black and brown and red. You got to tell the truth, Barack. Don't trot this shit out with coded stuff."[113]

Such equivalence between histories imperils the case for responding to legacies of particularly racialized injustices still in need of redress today. As a candidate, Obama dangerously disregarded any notion that the roots of Reverend Wright's anger flare from memories much more recent than those of Jim Crow.[114] Namely, the complexion of the prison population, persistent residential and education segregation, and especially the devastation disproportionately wrought upon African Americans by Hurricane Katrina.[115] The government's inexcusable failure to provide an adequate response to black suffering was not without precedent and carries a legacy of neglecting African American people and their memories that is hardly vacant of contemporary relevance. To many, Hurricane Katrina exposed hidden horrors of historically entrenched, residential segregation. Yet Michael Dawson found that whereas 90 percent of blacks he surveyed believed the disaster showed that racial inequality remains a problem, only 38 percent of whites agreed.[116] The alarming disparity has prompted Dawson to argue, drawing on Jürgen Habermas, that blacks and whites occupy *separate lifeworlds*.[117]

Obama's incomplete account of the historical origins of Wright's anger risked perpetuating an image of black racial resentment that is unhinged from its causes and therefore less comprehensible to whites. The danger that this insufficient memory reinforces the caricature of the inexplicably "angry black man" in the white imaginary was precisely Baldwin's critique of Richard Wright's ahistorical portrayal of Bigger Thomas in *Native Son*. Beyond Obama's forced confrontation with the Wright controversy, the candidate was strategically silent about race. Accepting his party's nomination in Denver on the forty-fifth anniversary of Martin Luther King's "I Have a Dream" speech, Obama chose not to address the history of racial turmoil. Indeed, he did not even mention King by name, referring to him only obliquely as "a young preacher from Georgia."[118] Where King's ghost was largely an unspoken presence in Denver, the remainders of the unfinished work of Reconstruction that haunted King were less spectral—namely the mistrust in African American leadership, white paternalism, and the tendency to infantilize blacks as a strategy of maintaining power. Kentucky representative Geoff Davis gave voice to all of the above in a single quip about Obama's candidacy, saying: "That boy's finger doesn't need to be on the button."[119] As president, Obama has generally moved between silence and steadfast denial that race plays a role in the blowback his policies have ignited. The trend has prompted Michael Eric Dyson to remark: "This president runs from race like a black man runs from a cop."[120]

Remembering Baldwin in this context throws into relief how Obama has generally moved away from practices of openly invoking the legacy of the past whereby race is an issue that the country can "no longer" afford to ignore, and toward a much more frequent practice of dangerously performing the disavowal that he directly criticized in his speech—and Baldwin indicted in his writing. Intellectual historian James T. Kloppenberg contends that Obama's focus on commonalities and conciliation over differences and partisan division has a rich genealogy. Obama's influences not only span his time as a community organizer in Chicago but mark his deep debt to the pragmatism of James and Dewey, the tradition of civic republicanism, and an ethos of deliberative democracy.[121] Kloppenberg concedes that Obama's focus on compromise is a gamble he might well lose. Obama's "predilection to conciliate whenever possible is grounded in his understanding of the history of American thought, culture and politics" that views American history as "a dynamic process and project of widening opportunities and inclusion."[122] It is a difficult wager that left Obama vulnerable to critique from all sides. Obama's long-standing admiration of Lincoln leaves him haunted by the knowledge that—as the case of slavery attests—there are some issues where there can be no democratic compromise. As Obama writes, "I am robbed even of the certainty of uncertainty—for sometimes absolute truths may well be absolute."[123] By extension of this logic, Obama would be hard-pressed to deny the possibility that race-based grievances might be more trenchant and sustained than he has thus far allowed. Of course, whether he is prepared to confront these grievances—and whether conciliation and compromise are effective strategies for doing so in the context of the contemporary economic crisis—remains hotly contested.

In terms of divergent *conscious* memories, I have contended that the collective failure to apprehend the emancipationist narrative continues to play a significant role today. Clearly the intimate ties between race and memory in America are not limited to the fixation on the triumphal resolutions wrought by white supremacy—a false closure perpetuated by the abysmal state of history education in the United States.[124] The nature of this reality, however, means that too many Americans are unable to see the error in Pat Buchanan's facts when he argues that we need not recall legacies of black contributions to the country's wealth, or register an outstanding debt to black veterans (such as those that Woodrow Wilson neglected in his Gettysburg speech) because "whites were 100% of the people who died at Gettysburg."[125] The above points to an obvious disconnect between postracial rhetoric and postmnemonic political realities in which race and memory matter—and that too little has changed. At stake politically is the question of what terms, lexicons, and practices contemporary advocates of transracial democracy ought to use to make plural memories meaningful for a common future.

It is here where segregated memory is especially toxic for a forward-looking transracial coalition politics. It fails to acknowledge the progress of African Americans as the fruit of grassroots organizing long-standing black struggle and unlikely cross-racial alliances forged by groups like the Student Nonviolent Coordinating Committee (SNCC) and the Southern Christian Leadership Conference (SCLC).[126] It also disavows the ways that democratic initiatives have breathed new life into American politics, reimagined American freedom and political possibility, and transformed stories of tragedy into stories of human endurance. A more democratic relationship to the past would recall past struggles for democracy, not least of which those of the civil-rights generation. Absent a recollection of the Emancipationist memory, black advancements risks being cast as simply the product of the paternal generosity of beneficent white power. When tethered to a history that recalls how whites have already given *so* much, contemporary calls for a confrontation with racial inequality are cast as merely another request by blacks for a handout, "the same old shakedown that black hustlers have been running."[127]

In terms of making available possibilities for transracial coalition politics, Desmond King and Rogers Smith contend that Obama's emphasis on the *feelings* of blacks and whites did little to explain "how modern American politics has come to be shaped by rival coalitions of political actors and institutions (each including some members of all races), whose members take opposed policy positions on a wide range of issues that they perceive as having racial dimensions."[128] For instance, the tension between advocates of color-blind and color-conscious policies finds opposing groups contesting each other's respective standing as the true heirs to the civil rights movement.[129] Hence some whites hearing Obama's speech would be unlikely to comprehend why Wright would oppose color-blind policies as obstacles to racial equality. Nor would some African Americans glean why Wright's use of race-conscious rhetoric incurred charges of anti-Americanism and "reverse racism" from outraged whites. King and Smith emphasize that the failure to recognize how today's racial policy alliances are distinct from their historical precursors impairs the collective capacity to understand and move past the current climate of polarization that brokers so little compromise. Obama's tendency to lean rhetorically toward the color-blind position favored among whites leaves little room to argue on behalf of even a mix of race-neutral and race-conscious policies—even as it underscores the limits of what he could be expected to do in the speech.[130]

While it is widely accepted that it is the obligation of the citizenry to hold elected official accountable in a democracy, it is all too tempting to limit citizens' political obligations to an ongoing critique of the president. Such a posture relieves publics in general, and intellectuals in particular, of the burdens of memory and a great many political obligations entailed with legacies of injustice. It also represents a performative contradiction of democracy as the prerogative of the demos. Differently put, the danger here is not just "democracy without the citizen" à la Sheldon Wolin, or an undemocratic reliance on the exceptional messianic saviors so typical of Saturday-night cinemas and Sunday-morning sermons. It also risks entrapment by the long-standing tacit, racialized expectation that ours is a history preordained to be emplotted with a redemptive black figure whose primary purpose is to emancipate white protagonists from a condition they are otherwise helpless to rectify. In cinema, the trope is known as "the magic Negro," a term dating back to the 1950s, when Tony Curtis is saved by Sidney Poitier, who sacrifices himself in *The Defiant Ones*—a dynamic later satirized by Spike Lee in *Bamboozled*.[131] Playwright, poet, and raconteur Ariel Dorfman explains the curious phenomena this way: "The black character helps the white character, which demonstrates that [the former] feels this incredible interest in maintaining the existing society. Since there is no cultural interchange, the character is put there to give the illusion that there is cultural crossover to satisfy the need without addressing the issue. As a Chilean, however, I sense that maybe deep inside, mainstream Americans somehow expect those who come from the margins will save them emotionally and intellectually."[132]

With Obama cast as the leader of the "Joshua Generation," perhaps it is helpful to recall that the "Moses Generation" sought to intervene in history by contesting the views that segregation was either incapable of being changed or was bound to change on its own given enough time.[133] Martin Luther King Jr. repeatedly insisted that "even a superficial look at history" shows that social progress "does not roll in on the wheels of inevitability."[134] When political expediency continues to press Obama into maintaining an expressive silence about the historical role of race in struggles to oppose the inevitability of segregation, how are Americans to respond to their first black president's inaugural call for the country to take action and "choose" its "better history"? Smith and King offer a sobering response:

> One reason this promise is so challenging is Americans do not agree on what constitutes their "better history." Some see the spread of religious diversity and considerable secularity, for example, as advances for freedom. Others see those developments as a retreat from the United States' true calling to be a shining "Christian Nation." Some believe the country's "best history" centers on the realization of ideals arising in historically Anglo-American cultural traditions. Others see those cultural traditions as historically responsible for the repression of communities and identities that they regard as most valuable and most their own. Put more broadly, the difficulty is that it may well be impossible to give specific content to the putative shared, unifying values and purposes of Americans, without appearing to fail to recognize and accommodate adequately the diversity of values and purposes Americans in fact exhibit.[135]

As indicated by the passage above, race is hardly the only historical remainder worthy of political analysis. And there can be no doubt that criticism of the administration cannot, and ought not, be attributed to the president's race alone. Yet it is impossible to deny the entwined relevance of race and memory politics when conservative commentators defend their opposition to Obama's agenda by contending that his health-care and economic policies are actually a disguised bid by the president to secure reparations for slavery from whites.[136]

These expressions are symptomatic of the white resentment carried within the visceral memories Baldwin theorized. They further highlight the correspondence between white innocence and race-based emotions still available to be mobilized and leveraged as tools of entrepreneurial political strategists.[137] In the era of Obama, Baldwin's insistence that we require a persistent, public hermeneutics of how race encodes "the hieroglyph" of our circumstance draws our attention toward the habituated practices of a younger generation of voters key to Obama's election—a portion of the electorate with no living memory of slavery or Jim Crow, but who nevertheless inherit the political landscape shaped by that era's dreams, deficiencies, and achievements. From the vantage of habit-memory in general and habituated practices of self-segregation in particular, it means that we are still at a loss when confronted by Beverly Tatum's question: "Why are all the black kids sitting together in the cafeteria?"[138]

By probing deeper than the simple dichotomy between remembering and forgetting, Baldwin reminds readers that people find it very difficult to acknowledge even that which they consciously know to be true, particularly when it is not to their advantage to do so—and especially when it comes to race. At the same time, the implications of Baldwin's position suggest the limits of what might be accomplished through rhetoric, improved history lessons, and conscious practices of countermemory. In view of his dimensional approach to memory, a counternarration of history appears as a necessary, though not sufficient, condition of desegregating memory in a manner that anticipates a transracial democracy. A contemporary political example helps elucidate the relevance of Baldwin's caution.

The racial politics of what I have been calling the *habituated disavowal of segregated memory* made national headlines in April 2010. Elevated to power in an election hailed by Republicans as a direct repudiation of President Obama, Virginia governor Robert McDonnell disavowed the country's slave past when he reinstated Confederate History Month. Without any mention of slavery, the initial statement called for an understanding of the "sacrifices of the Confederate leaders, soldiers, and citizens during the Civil War."[139] The declaration publicly commemorated those who sacrificed for the "Lost Cause" while failing to mention that slavery was crucial to that cause—part of the southern "way of life" often euphemistically invoked to explain the war. Importantly, McDonnell was clear that he did not "forget" to mention slavery—neither in the sense that it slipped his mind nor in the sense that he was ignorant of slavery's historical role in the war. In a subsequent defense of his remarks to the *Washington Post,* McDonnell made the overt connections between race, power, and memory even more apparent. He explained that he was well aware that the Civil War "obviously involved slavery."[140] Yet he didn't mention it because he was simply "trying to focus on the aspects of the war that were most significant for Virginians."[141]

The casual nature of McDonnell's disavowal exemplified a reflexive practice of conditioned memory that remains within whites who continue to consider what "was significant for Virginians" by only considering whites *as significant* in the first place. McDonnell's disavowal of the emancipationist memory was a revealing, embodied performance of a particular "habit of whiteness" cast against black invisibility.[142] On the level of narrative memory, it is intimately tied to what, in the opening epigraph of this essay, William Carlos Williams called the "memory of whiteness." On the subterranean level Baldwin excavates, we witness how the white disavowal of the significance of African American history as *American history* is tethered to the perceived insignificance of African American presence in America today. Simply put, the incident dramatized the connection between marginalized people and marginalized memories.

The habituated, compulsive disavowal of the memories of emancipation is part of the historical legacy of segregated memory that accrues to a politics of black invisibility in the present. The self-segregation written into habit-memory means that, as Eduardo Bonilla-Silva argues, "Despite the civil rights revolution, whites, young and old, live a fundamentally segregated life":[143] "People cannot like or love people they don't see or interact with. This truism has been corroborated by social psychologists, who for years have maintained that friendship and love emerge when people share activities, proximity, familiarity, and status."[144]

From this vantage, the conditioned practices of disavowing the past and presence of racial others are hardly problems exclusive to the political right in general, or particular conservatives like McDonnell and Buchanan. Even those who openly express a "progressive" commitment to transracial relationships of various sorts are often betrayed by their own tendencies to self-segregate along racial lines. An inquiry into school segregation, residential segregation, and personal isolation found that, at least in principle, whites often expressed a *preference* for an interracial lifestyle. The empirical evidence, on the other hand, offered little proof to suggest that this commitment was embodied in practice. In a survey of Detroit residents, 57.7 percent were not consciously opposed to interracial marriage. However, of the 323 whites that responded to the survey, only 1 was actually married to a black person at the time of the interview, 89 percent had never had a romantic relationship with a black person, and 87 percent admitted that none of their closest friends were black.[145]

Contemporary schools and churches are *especially* glaring examples of segregation.[146] Regionally, "the South has become the first region in the country where more than half of public school students are poor and more than half are members of minorities."[147] Russell K. Robinson contends that this dynamic accrues to divergent psychological frameworks that amount to "perceptual segregation."[148] Too often, whites do not view their segregation as racial, and therefore not in need of explanation or action, because it is "just the way things are."[149]

Perhaps nowhere is segregation more dramatic than in the disproportionately African American prison population. A 2008 Human Rights Watch report indicated that black men are incarcerated at six times the rate of white men.[150] In the outsourcing of cheap inmate labor to corporations, the crack of the whip echoes in the sound of cell doors clanging shut.[151] In 2004, the Federal Bureau of Prisons reported that prisoners earn between eleven and thirty-six cents per hour.[152] In 2002 alone, prisoners produced goods and services worth an estimated $1.5 billion. Tom Daley, research economist for the Communications Workers of America, said: "Quite literally, they're taking advantage of a captive audience."[153]

The long-standing association of blackness with criminality that persists as grounds for enforced segregation, punishment, and disenfranchisement accents the lasting power of racial stigma.[154] While the divide between conscious memories makes calls for equality seem anachronistic to some, the perpetuation of racial stigma through spatial and role segregation serves to maintain entrenched exclusionary habits and norms whereby African Americans are treated as unequal—and therefore inferior. That is, the dimensional view of memory advanced in these pages points to the urgency of what Elizabeth Anderson aptly calls "the imperative of integration."[155] Where assimilation typically regards the disempowered group as the only subjects in need of change, capacious visions of integration aim at altering the habits, prejudices, and stigmas of dominant groups.[156] Importantly, integration does not suppose the emancipatory power of a "politically correct" view of history that can inoculate against unconscious racialized assumptions. Rather, Anderson's point is that "what most urgently needs to change are people's unconscious habits of interracial interaction and perception. Such *practical* learning can only take place in integrated settings."[157]

Although it would take at least another essay to unpack the relationship between integrated spaces, conditioned kinetic practices and racialized perceptions, the theoretical trajectory of Anderson's approach speaks directly to the need to collectively confront epidermalized histories that live on in the flesh as "habits of subordination and interaction rituals that reproduce stigmatization."[158] Partisans of democracy are called to theorize (in)equality not merely as legal standing but as a lived norm practiced by embodied beings over time, space, and stigma. In the wake of multicultural celebrations of diversity insufficiently attentive to how power inequalities frame difference in ways unworthy of celebration, a renewed focus on integration might make space for a contentious (re)construction of a "superordinate group identity . . . a 'we' is most importantly a shared identity as citizens."[159] That said, the mnemonic boundaries of such an emergent citizen-identity remain as open to question as the democracy toward which it would venture.[160] For my part, I have argued that the dimensions of segregated memory remain a persistent threat to transracial democratic equality in ways deeply implicated in the segregated polity termed "American apartheid."[161] Pace Obama, segregated memory does not, then, simply signal part of a "union we have yet to perfect." It is an imperfection that flags how race still pressures the limits of what, in political theory and political life today, we can only contestably call a union.

Looking forward, it is well worth contemplating how a rededication to novel practices of twenty-first-century integration might refigure spatio-temporal relationships in ways that address cognitive biases, compulsory invisibility, restricted access to opportunities, and racial "defaults"—not least of which is the presumption of black deviance that underwrites the contemporary incarnation of racialized social control achieved by mass incarceration and felon disenfranchisement. With an unprecedented number of people of color literally imprisoned by the past, there can be no illusions that desegregating memory exhausts the inventory of potential measures needed to grapple with the outrages of white supremacy discussed here. And memory counsels that progress toward racial equality is never inevitable—least of all in times of dire economic scarcity like our own.[162] But as Baldwin put it: "Not everything that is faced can be changed, but nothing can be changed until it is faced."[163]

When faced with a history that threatens to predetermine our possibilities for change, Baldwin counseled a change in how we remember our possibilities: "I know what I am asking is impossible. But in our time, as in every time, the impossible is the least that one can demand—and one is, after all, emboldened by the spectacle of human history in general, and American Negro history in particular, for it testifies to nothing less than the perpetual achievement of the impossible."[164] In times when a segregated polity is policed by segregated memory, reaching across race to remember the possibility of the impossible is one way for Americans to choose their better history.

Notes

Originally published as P. J. Brendese, "The Race of a More Perfect Union: James Baldwin, Segregated Memory and the 2008 Presidential Race," *Theory* 15, no. 1 (2012). Reprinted by permission of Johns Hopkins University Press Journals.

For generous and insightful feedback on earlier versions of this essay, I'd like to thank Lawrie Balfour, David W. Blight, Rom Coles, Greg Jackson, George Shulman, Jack Turner, and the editors and reviewers at *Theory & Event*.

First epigraph: William Carlos Williams, *The Collected Poems of William Carlos Williams*, vol. 2 (New York: New Directions, 1988), 245.

Second epigraph: Alexis de Tocqueville, *Democracy in America*, vol. 1, ed. J. P. Mayer, trans. George Lawrence (New York: Harper and Row, 1969), 356.

Third epigraph: James Baldwin, *The Cross of Redemption: Uncollected Writings*, ed. Randall Kenan (New York: Pantheon, 2010), 9.

1. Barack Obama, "Barack Obama's Speech on Race," *New York Times*, March 18, 2008, www.nytimes.com/2008/03/18/us/politics/18text-obama .html?pagewanted=6&_r=3.

2. David Remnick, *The Bridge: The Life and Rise of Barack Obama* (New York: Knopf, 2010), 525.

3. Patrick J. Buchanan, "A Brief for Whitey," March 21, 2008, http://buchanan .org/blog/pjb-a-brief-for-whitey-969. I am grateful to Jessie Casey Weatherwax for bringing this to my attention.

4. Tocqueville, *Democracy in America*, 1:356.

5. Writing roughly a century after Tocqueville, Patterson conveyed a related sentiment when he referred to the stigma of blackness as so freighted with slavery that it translated into a "social death" (see Orlando Patterson, *Slavery and Social Death: A Comparative Study* [Cambridge: Harvard University Press, 1985]).

6. Williams, *The Collected Poems of William Carlos Williams*, 2:245. Wil-

liams's contestable, yet provocative, implication is that racial borders shift with memory.

7. James Baldwin, "Stranger in the Village," in *Notes of a Native Son* (Boston: Beacon, 1984), 174–75. "People who shut their eyes to reality simply invite their own destruction, and anyone who remains in a state of innocence long after that innocence is dead turns into a monster."

8. James Baldwin, *The Price of the Ticket: Collected Nonfiction 1948–1955* (New York: St. Martin's, 1985), 336.

9. Lawrie Balfour, *The Evidence of Things Not Said: James Baldwin and the Promise of American Democracy* (Ithaca, NY: Cornell University Press, 2001), 27.

10. W. James Booth, *Communities of Memory* (Ithaca, NY: Cornell University Press, 2006), 27–29; Paul Ricoeur *Memory, History, Forgetting* (Chicago: University of Chicago Press, 2004), 40–42; Henri Bergson, *Matter & Memory*, trans. Nancy M. Paul and W. Scott Palmer (1912; Mineola, NY: Dover, 2004).

11. Balfour, *The Evidence of Things Not Said*, 16. "Baldwin sometimes . . . loses sight of the plight of other oppressed Americans, or despite his rejection of the violent reduction of African Americans male and female, old and young, into some category called 'the Negro,' his writing implies that what is most condemnable about such reductionism is what it takes from black men. Although such instances reinforce what Stuart Hall calls 'the innocent notion of the essential Black subject,' the sum of Baldwin's writings undermine the idea that such a subject exists."

12. Note how Obama strategically described the gap between his memory and that of Reverend Wright. Shortly thereafter, evidence of that divide irrupted from Jesse Jackson's sharp criticism.

13. Baldwin's investment in shared mediums of commonality that allow differences to be made meaningful offers a potentially helpful contrast to arguments focused on the infinity and inexpressibility of historically inscribed distinctions in subaltern communities.

14. Joel Olson, *The Abolition of White Democracy* (Minneapolis: University of Minnesota Press, 2004).

15. In this respect my reading of Baldwin keeps company with a sensibility at work in W. James Booth's treatment of Ellison as posing challenges and contributions for political theorists who are perhaps more accustomed to locating politics in the expressly political domain of broader legislative and juridical institutions (see W. James Booth, "The Color of Memory: Reading Race with Ralph Ellison," *Political Theory* 36, no. 5 [October 2008]: 684). Drawing on Ellison, Booth argues that an important dimension of politics can be "found outside the domain of high civics and in the vernacular, in how citizens live together, speak to one another, in what they remember and forget, in what they hope for, or in a future they ignore or reject."

16. See Lawrie Balfour, "Reparations after Identity Politics," *Political Theory* 33, no. 6, (December 2005): 787–88; Balfour, *The Evidence of Things Not Said;* George Shulman, *American Prophecy: Race and Redemption in American Political Culture* (Minneapolis: University of Minnesota Press, 2008).

17. Encouraging exceptions are cited throughout this essay. I draw readers' attention to the distinction between those that emerge from within political theory and beyond. See Thomas McCarthy, *Race, Empire and the Idea of Human Development* (Cambridge: Cambridge University Press, 2009); Thomas McCarthy, "Vergangenheitsbewältigung in the USA: On the Politics of Memory and Slavery," *Political Theory* 30, no. 5 (October 2002): 623–48; Thomas McCarthy, "Coming to Terms with Our Past, Part II: On the Morality and Politics of Reparations for Slavery," *Political Theory* 32, no. 6 (December 2005): 750–72; W. Fitzhugh Brundage, *The Southern Past: A Clash of Race and Memory* (Cambridge: Harvard University Press, 2009); Michael Rogin, *Blackface/White Noise* (Berkeley: University of California Press, 1998); Daniel Walkowitz and Lisa Mayer Knauer, eds., *Contested Histories in Public Space* (Durham: Duke University Press, 2009); Jessica Adams, *Wounds of Returning: Race, Memory, and Property on the Postslavery Plantation* (Chapel Hill: University of North Carolina Press, 2007); Josh Foa Dienstag, *Dancing in Chains: Narrative & Memory in Political Theory* (Palo Alto: Stanford University Press, 1997); and Melissa Williams, *Voice, Trust and Memory: Marginalized Groups and the Failings of Liberal Representation* (Princeton, NJ: Princeton University Press, 1998).

18. The historical reasons for this stem from the Nazi genocide and the significant influence of émigré political theorists who came to the United States seeking asylum. Confronting racial remainders on our own soil would seem an altogether fitting means of honoring our debts to European teachers, as well as our ethical and political obligation to "never forget" the lessons of the Holocaust (see John G. Gunnell, *The Descent of Political Theory* [Chicago: University of Chicago Press], esp. 175–98, where Gunnell chronicles the intellectual shift occasioned by the German émigré's fleeing the holocaust). Eric Voegelin published two books on the idea of race in the 1930s: Eric Voegelin, *Rasse und Staat* (Tubingen: J. C. B. Mohr, 1933); and *Die Rassenidee in der Geistesgeschichte von Ray bis Carus* (Berlin: Junker und Duennhaupt, 1933). On these texts, see Thomas W. Heilke, *Voegelin on the Idea of Race* (Baton Rouge: Louisiana State University Press, 1990).

19. Shulman, *American Prophecy*, 27. "Theorists read Agamben and Arendt on a genocide they did not cause or experience directly, but not Douglass, W. E. B. Du Bois, Baldwin or Morrison. . . . to address the racial holocaust that American caused and experienced directly, whose legacy still grips the lives of one and all."

20. See Jason Frank, *Constituent Moments: Enacting the People in Postrevolutionary America* (Durham: Duke University Press, 2010); Gary B. Nash, *The Un-*

known American Revolution: The Unruly Birth of Democracy and the Struggle to Create America (New York: Penguin, 2005); Alfred Blumrosen and Ruth Blumrosen, *Slave Nation: How Slavery United the Colonies and Sparked the American Revolution* (Naperville, IL: Sourcebooks, 2006); and Pauline Maier, *American Scripture: Making the Declaration of Independence* (New York: Vintage, 1998). For provocative historical fiction that shows the intersection of seemingly disparate stories on the basis of gender, see Toni Morrison, *A Mercy* (New York: Knopf, 2008).

21. David Blight, *Race and Reunion: The Civil War in American Memory* (Cambridge: Harvard University Press, 2001).

22. Frederick Douglass, *My Bondage and My Freedom,* ed. John Stauffer (1855; New York: Modern Library, 2003). The narrative is, of course, passed on by Douglass's luminous heirs; notably W. E. B. Du Bois and John Hope Franklin. See esp. W. E. B. Du Bois, *Black Reconstruction in America: 1860–1880* (New York: Free Press, 1998); and John Hope Franklin, *From Slavery to Freedom: A History of Negro Americans* (1947; New York: Knopf, 1967). See also Eric Foner, *Reconstruction: America's Unfinished Revolution 1863–1877* (New York: Harper Perennial Modern Classics, 2002).

23. Blight, *Race & Reunion*, 61.

24. Ibid., 60. Greeley invoked the prophetic idiom to make his plea: "Shall the sword devour forever? . . . So asked of an old Hebrew prophet, standing amid the ruins of his desolated country. So, I an American citizen, standing amid some of the ruins of our great civil war . . . shall speak in the spirit of the prophet, asking you whether time has not finally come when all the differences . . . should be abandoned forever?"

25. Ibid., 10–11.

26. Ibid., 9.

27. Ibid.

28. Ibid.

29. Ibid.

30. Michael Rogin, *Blackface/White Noise* (Berkeley: University of California Press, 1998).

31. Michael Rogin, "The Two Declarations of American Independence," *Representations* 55 (Summer 1996): 13–30.

32. McCarthy, "Vergangenheitsbewältigung in the USA: On the Politics of Memory and Slavery," 629.

33. See Howard Mumford Jones, *The Pursuit of Happiness* (Cambridge: Harvard University Press, 1953).

34. James Baldwin, "The Crusade of Indignation," in *The Price of the Ticket,* 157.

35. Baldwin understood his responsibility as a writer as symmetrical with what Sheldon Wolin speaks of when he refers to political theory as a vocation and invocation. It is a calling that calls us to recall (see Sheldon S. Wolin, "Political Theory from Vocation to Invocation," in *Vocations of Political Theory*, ed. Jason Frank and John Tamborino [Princeton, NJ: Princeton University Press, 2000], 3–22).

36. Fred L. Standley and Louis H. Pratt, eds., *Conversations with James Baldwin* (Jackson: University Press of Mississippi, 1989), 14.

37. The historical context in which Baldwin spoke and wrote meant that bearing witness took the form of an explicit portrayal of the brutal realities particular to his time—an era where the unredeemed promises of democracy bore the "strange fruit" eulogized by Billie Holiday.

38. One of Baldwin's achievements is his simultaneous use and critique of the prophetic tradition in American politics. As an ex-preacher, Baldwin had an acute sensitivity to the relationship between Christianity and white supremacy (see George Shulman, "James Baldwin and the Racial State of Exception: Secularizing Prophecy?," in *American Prophecy*, 131–74).

39. James Baldwin, "Many Thousands Gone," in *The Price of the Ticket*, 68–69.

40. One can ask the question by mixing Baldwin's metaphors with those of contemporary parlance: What is "the price of the ticket" to the "eternal sunshine of the spotless mind?" (see *The Eternal Sunshine of the Spotless Mind* [New York: Focus Features, 2004]).

41. Friedrich Nietzsche, *On the Genealogy of Morals & Ecce Homo*, ed. Walter Kaufmann (New York: Vintage, 1989). Nietzsche opens the first essay with a statement and a question: "We are unknown to ourselves we men of knowledge—we have never sought ourselves—how could it happen that we could ever *find* ourselves?"

42. Baldwin, "Many Thousands Gone," in *The Price of the Ticket*, 68–69.

43. James Baldwin, "The Fire Next Time," in *The Price of the Ticket*, 378.

44. Ibid., 377. The myths to which Baldwin refers include the notion that American "ancestors were all freedom-loving heroes, that they were born in the greatest country the world has ever seen, or that Americans are invincible in battle and wise in peace, that Americans have always dealt honorably with Mexican and Indians and all other neighbors or inferiors, that American men are the world's most direct and virile, that American women are pure. Negroes know far more about white Americans than that."

45. James Baldwin, "White Man's Guilt," in *The Price of the Ticket*, 410. See also George Shulman, "Hope and American Politics," *Raritan* (Winter 2002): 111–12.

46. Baldwin, "The Fire Next Time," in *The Price of the Ticket*, 378.

47. Standley and Pratt, *Conversations with James Baldwin*, 12.

48. James Baldwin, "Every Good-Bye Ain't Gone," in *The Price of the Ticket,* 644.

49. Baldwin, "The Fire Next Time," in *The Price of the Ticket,* 379; see also 354. "Time catches up with kingdoms and rends them; time reveals the foundations on which any kingdom rests, and eats at those foundations, and destroys doctrines by proving them to be untrue."

50. The worries he expressed publicly ran the gamut from segregation to extermination.

51. Baldwin, "White Man's Guilt," in *The Price of the Ticket,* 410.

52. Baldwin, "Every Good-Bye Ain't Gone," in *The Price of the Ticket,* 644.

53. James Baldwin, *Notes of a Native Son* (1955; New York: Bantam, 1964), 22; emphasis added. Baldwin thought that whites see blackness as a symbol of death itself. For whites, the underlying phenomenology of interracial encounters registers a terrifying mortality they have sought to purify. This mortality has been disowned and disappeared along with slavery to the point that it evacuates the humanity of black people altogether.

54. Ralph Ellison, *Invisible Man* (New York: Vintage, 1995). See also W. James Booth, "The Color of Memory: Reading Race with Ralph Ellison"; and Jack Turner, "Awakening to Race: Ralph Ellison and Democratic Individuality," *Political Theory* 36 (October 2008): 655–82.

55. For an analysis of the stigma of race as a remainder of the past, see Orlando Patterson, *Slavery and Social Death* (Cambridge: Harvard University Press, 1985); Glen Loury, *The Anatomy of Racial Inequality* (Cambridge: Harvard University Press, 2003); and Andrea Simpson, *The Tie That Binds* (New York: New York University Press, 1998).

56. Frantz Fanon, *Black Skin, White Masks* (1952; New York: Grove, 1967).

57. Baldwin, "The Fire Next Time," in *The Price of the Ticket,* 342. "Long before the Negro child perceives this [racial] difference, and even longer before he understands it, he has begun to react to it, he has begun to be controlled by it. . . . He must be 'good' not only in order to please his parents and not only to avoid punishment by them; behind their authority stands another, nameless and impersonal, infinitely harder to please and bottomlessly cruel. And this filters into the child's consciousness through his parents' tone of voice as he is being exhorted, punished or loved; in the sudden, uncontrollable note of fear heard in his mother's or father's voice when he has strayed beyond some particular boundary. . . . I heard it in my father's voice . . . when he realized I really *believed* I could do anything a white boy could do." For an illuminating gloss on the passage and the tensions Baldwin sees in the conflation of equality with conformity, see Lawrie Balfour, *The Evidence of Things Not Said,* 125.

58. James Baldwin, "The American Dream and the American Negro," in *The Price of the Ticket,* 404.

59. See James Baldwin's plays *Blues for Mr. Charlie* (New York: Vintage, 1995) and *The Amen Corner* (New York: Vintage, 1998). Baldwin was interested and provoked by a perception that the present is the stage upon which the legacy of these intersecting inheritances get played out in a manner analogous to a Greek tragedy. That is, memory often shapes human drama without the conscious knowledge of the players (see Standley and Pratt, *Conversations with James Baldwin*, 72–73).

60. Here one can draw generative parallels between Baldwin and Freud, who held that the past is latent within the subject and, like Oedipus, we often run into it unwittingly (see Sigmund Freud, *Civilization and Its Discontents*, ed. and trans. James Strachey [New York: Norton, 1961], 16–17). Freud writes: "Since we overcame the error of supposing that the forgetting we are familiar with signified a destruction of the memory trace—that is, its annihilation—we have been inclined to take the opposite view, that in mental life nothing which has once been formed can perish—that everything is somehow preserved and that in suitable circumstances (when, for instance, repression goes back far enough) it can once more be brought to light."

61. See Baldwin, "Many Thousands Gone," in *The Price of the Ticket*, 78; emphasis added. Like Goethe's insistence that when we cultivate our virtues we also cultivate our vices, Baldwin alerts whites to the irony in thinking that their liberal goodwill can transform and purify a latent deficiency within liberalism itself. When visions of the good come so freighted with the unexamined assumptions of one's ancestors, any practice of "goodwill" inevitably leads us in an Oedipal circle that reproduces those forebears—if not *with* them.

62. Baldwin, "The Fire Next Time," in *The Price of the Ticket*, 368; emphasis added.

63. James Baldwin, *The Devil Finds Work* (New York: Dial, 1976), 110.

64. Baldwin, "Many Thousands Gone," in *The Price of the Ticket*, 67.

65. Ibid., 65. Note that, in the context of the quote, the "our" is white, and "him" is black.

66. Baldwin, "The Fire Next Time," in *The Price of the Ticket*, 379.

67. Ibid., 333.

68. Baldwin, "The American Dream and the American Negro," in *The Price of the Ticket*, 404.

69. Baldwin, "Every Good-Bye Ain't Gone," in *The Price of the Ticket*, 644; emphasis added.

70. Baldwin, "The American Dream and the American Negro," in *The Price of the Ticket*, 407.

71. For an excellent critical race autobiography that engages paternalism from a white perspective, see Tim Tyson, *Blood Done Sign My Name* (New York: Three Rivers, 2005).

72. Baldwin, "The American Dream and the American Negro" in *The Price of the Ticket*, 407.

73. His is a present past that returns with the power to possess—a power that Toni Morrison fictionalizes in her novel *Beloved* (see Toni Morrison, *Beloved* [New York: Plume, 1988]).

74. Baldwin, "The American Dream and the American Negro," in *The Price of the Ticket*, 405.

75. James Baldwin, "Liberalism and the Negro: A Roundtable Discussion," *Commentary*, March 1964, 31.

76. Baldwin, "The Fire Next Time," in *The Price of the Ticket*, 364; my emphasis. On Baldwin's own account, the way many black Americans understand their past would be unsettled as well.

77. Baldwin, "Liberalism and the Negro: A Roundtable Discussion," 31.

78. Ibid.

79. Balfour, *The Existence of Things Not Said*, 131.

80. Baldwin, "The Fire Next Time," in *The Price of the Ticket*, 364. At bottom, Baldwin holds little hope for the power of sterile analytic persuasion alone. As he puts it, "One cannot not argue with anyone's experience or decision or belief."

81. Like the ancient Greeks, who used the space of tragic drama to negotiate the legacy of time, Baldwin's plays employed aesthetic space to speak to segregated political spaces and memories. In the set design of his play *Blues for Mr. Charlie*, Baldwin dramatizes spatio-temporal relationships through an open, yet split, stage design. The characters' thoughts are audible, and the lighting is cast to show the audience that, as one light designer put it, "Memories remain . . . but they're altered forever by what happens now."

82. Baldwin, "The Fire Next Time," in *The Price of the Ticket*, 378.

83. For his refutation of this misnomer, see Barack Obama, *The Audacity of Hope* (New York: Vintage, 2006), 275–80.

84. Barack Obama, *Dreams from My Father: A Story of Race and Inheritance* (New York: Three Rivers, 2004).

85. For an account that explores these intersections, see Colm Tóibín, "James Baldwin & Barack Obama," *New York Review of Books* 55, no. 16 (October 23, 2008). See also Herb Boyd, *Baldwin's Harlem: A Biography of James Baldwin* (New York: Simon and Schuster, 2008), 4–6.

86. Baldwin's father had been defeated by racism and became embittered, emotionally absent, and aggressively jealous of his young stepson James's prowess as a preacher. Upon his father's death in 1943, Baldwin realized that he "had hardly ever spoken to him." In Obama's case, he had met his father only once. His self-invention and personal discovery happened in the context of a mixed-race and cross-cultural heritage perennially haunted by the ghost of a parent he never really knew.

87. Tóibín, "James Baldwin & Barack Obama," 2. Quoting Baldwin, Tóibín writes: "He [Baldwin's father] along with thousands of other Negroes, came North after 1919 and I was part of that generation which had never seen the landscape of what Negroes sometimes called the Old Country." Tóibín notes: "Although Obama mentions in passing in *Dreams of My Father* that he had read Baldwin when he was a young community activist in Chicago, there is no hint in the book that he modeled his own story in any way on Baldwin's work. In both of their versions of who they became there are considerable similarities and shared key moments not because Obama was using Baldwin as a template or an example, but because the same hurdles and similar circumstances and the same moments of truth actually occurred almost naturally for both of them."

88. Obama, *Dreams of My Father,* 220; Obama, *The Audacity of Hope,* 86.

89. James T. Kloppenberg, *Reading Obama: Dreams, Hope and the American Political Tradition* (Princeton, NJ: Princeton University Press, 2010), 209.

90. Obama, "Barack Obama's Speech on Race."

91. Ibid.

92. Ibid.

93. Ibid.

94. Terrance MacMullan, *Habits of Whiteness* (Bloomington: Indiana University Press, 2009), 4. MacMullan argues that "the distance Obama sees between his grandmother's love for him on the one hand and her willingness to make racist comments on the other is the distance I see between the conscious good intentions and desire for justice that I think the overwhelming majority of white people hold in their hearts and the unconscious habits that are bred into the bones of these very same people, that lead many of them to do and say things that are at loggerheads with their commitment to principles of justice and fairness."

95. Obama also had to reach across an ever more cosmopolitan population of recent émigré voters who do not necessarily understand their experiences of economic hardship in black and white terms.

96. Obama, "Barack Obama's Speech on Race"; emphasis added.

97. Friedrich Nietzsche, "On the Uses and Disadvantages of History for Life," in *Untimely Mediations,* ed. Daniel Brazaele (Cambridge: Cambridge University Press, 2001), 58–123.

98. Obama, "Barack Obama's Speech on Race."

99. Zadie Smith, "Speaking in Tongues," *New York Review of Books* 56, no. 3, www.nybooks.com/articles/archives/2009/feb/26/speaking-in-tongues-2/?pagination=false.

100. Ibid.

101. Baldwin also placed strong emphasis on the need to take responsibility for future generations. The theme recurs repeatedly in his work.

102. Patrick J. Buchanan, "A Brief for Whitey," March 21, 2008, http://buchanan
.org/blog/pjb-a-brief-for-whitey-969.

103. Notice how Buchanan compares African Americans to blacks abroad rather
than to the relative standing of other racial and ethnic groups in the United States.

104. For an interesting discussion of "what we can hear" in the context of post-
9/11 American politics of memory, see Judith Butler, *Precarious Life* (London:
Verso, 2004), 1–19.

105. David Remnick, "The Joshua Generation," *New Yorker,* November 17,
2008, 4.

106. Among other things, Baldwin disagreed with the church's emphasis on
other-worldly salvation that served white supremacy by casting black suffering as
inherently redemptive rather than necessitating political resistance. In contrast,
Obama chronicles his conversion, and how his political memory became narrated
in theological terms. In his Philadelphia speech, Obama referenced how his own
memories became recast in biblical terms at Trinity Church: "I imagined the stories of ordinary black people merging with the stories of David and Goliath, Moses
and Pharaoh, the Christians in the lion's den, Ezekiel's field of dry bones. Those
stories—of survival, freedom, and hope—became our story, my story . . . until this
black church . . . seemed once more a vessel carrying the story of a people into
future generations and into a larger world. . . . [T]*he stories and songs gave us a
means to reclaim memories we didn't need to feel shame about . . . memories that
all people might study and cherish—-and with which we could start to rebuild.*"
For a discussion on how the Exodus story figured historically into African American conceptions of time and liberation, see Eddie Glaude Jr., *Exodus!: Religion,
Race and Nation in Early Nineteenth-Century Black America* (Chicago: University of Chicago Press, 2000).

107. The amalgam of Christianity and liberalism in the United States concerned
Baldwin in part because an anemic posture toward the past contributed to the nation's impaired orientation to the future. Baldwin found the moral denunciation of
the flesh inherently homophobic. This raises another set of distinctions between
Obama and Baldwin that cannot be treated within the space of this essay but are
nevertheless relevant.

108. R. W. B. Lewis, *The American Adam* (Chicago: University of Chicago
Press, 1959).

109. John B. Judis, "American Adam," *New Republic,* March 12, 2008, 4.

110. Jeff Spinner-Halev, "From Historical to Enduring Injustice," *Political Theory* 35, no. 5 (October 2007): 574–97.

111. Jim Lobe, "U.S. Calls Mount for Obama to Appoint Truth Commission," *Inter
Press Service,* February 19, 2009, www.globalissues.org/news/2009/02/19/670.

112. Obama, *The Audacity of Hope,* 303. Obama adopts Baldwin's strategy of

an ambiguous "our" when talking about media portrayals of blacks: "Rather than evoke our sympathy, our familiarity with the lives of black poor has bred spasms of fear and outright contempt. But mostly it's bred indifference."

113. See David Remnick, *The Bridge: The Life and Rise of Barack Obama* (New York: Knopf, 2010), 526.

114. In speaking of righteous anger and its roots, once cannot help but think of Baldwin's critique of Richard Wright's *Native Son* in "Many Thousands Gone." There Baldwin deftly acknowledged the scream that lives within black people (or as he put it, a "private Bigger Thomas") while resisting any caricature of blacks that portrays them as simply vengeful while failing to examine the historical conditions out of which their psychology arises.

115. See Lawrie Balfour, "Remembering Obama," *The Imminent Frame*, April 2009, http://blogs.ssrc.org/tif/2009/05/21/remembering-obama/.

116. Michael C. Dawson, "After the Deluge," *Du Bois Review* 3, no. 1 (2006): 240.

117. Ibid., 240–41.

118. See Gwen Ifill, *Breakthrough: Politics and Race in the Age of Obama* (New York: Anchor, 2009), 53.

119. Kate Phillips, "GOP Rep. Refers to Obama as 'That Boy,'" *New York Times*, April 14, 2008, http://thecaucusblog.nytimes.com/2008/04/14/gop-refers-to-obama-as-that-boy/.

120. Michael Eric Dyson, MSNBC interview, qtd. in Dinesh D'Sousa, *The Roots of Obama's Rage* (Washington, DC: Regnery, 2010), 8.

121. Kloppenberg, *Reading Obama*.

122. Ibid., 82–83.

123. Obama qtd. ibid., 244.

124. James Oliver Horton, "Presenting Slavery: The Perils of Telling America's Racial Story," *Public Historian* 21 (1999): 23.

125. Patrick Buchanan qtd. from MSNBC's *The Rachel Maddow Show*, July 16, 2009, http://mediamatters.org/research/200907170007. One can rightly contend (drawing from Baldwin himself) that Buchanan does not (and cannot) represent *the* single (official) voice of white memory—-as if there were such a thing. And many conservative whites would not argue that blacks should be grateful for slavery.

126. Charles Payne, *I've Got the Light of Freedom: The Organizing Tradition and the Mississippi Freedom Struggle* (Berkeley: University of California Press, 2007).

127. Buchanan, "A Brief for Whitey."

128. Desmond S. King and Rogers M. Smith, *Still a House Divided: Race and Politics in Obama's America* (Princeton, NJ: Princeton University Press, 2011), 7.

129. The divide is especially pronounced with respect to the specific policies entailed by Martin Luther King's desire for judgment based on content of character over skin color.

130. King and Smith, *Still a House Divided*, 287–88.

131. Likewise, the character Morpheus, played by Laurence Fishburne in *The Matrix*, helps an intellectually bankrupt Neo (Keanu Reeves) become a Messiah (see Rita Kempley, "Movies' 'Magic Negro' Saves the Day—but at the Cost of His Soul," *Black Commentator* 49 [July 2003], www.blackcommentator.com/49/49_magic.html).

132. Ibid.

133. Remnick, *The Bridge*, 493. Remnick writes: "The opening of the Iowa speech ['they said this day would never come'] deliberately echoed King, but it was not explicitly racial; it was a way of intensifying a universalist purpose with a specific historical ring. 'I knew that it would have multiple meanings to multiple people,' [speechwriter Jon] Favreau said."

134. Martin Luther King Jr., *A Testament of Hope* (San Francisco: HarperCollins, 1986), 296.

135. Rogers Smith and Desmond King, "Barack Obama and the Future of American Racial Politics," *Du Bois Review* 6, no. 1 (2009): 33.

136. *The Rush Limbaugh Show*, June 22, 2009. Limbaugh has previously argued that Obama deliberately seeks higher unemployment in order to enact a policy of an expanded welfare state and reparations (see Melissa Harris-Lacewell, "Rush and Reparations," *Nation*, May 12, 2009, www.thenation.com/blogs/notion/435392/rush_and_reparations).

137. Recent history gives ample reason to suspect that Obama's forward-looking emphasis on reconciliation and consensus makes him especially vulnerable to such tactics. For an illuminating, historically sensitive account of race as a tool of political entrepreneurs, see Thomas Edsall, *Chain Reaction: The Impact of Race, Rights and Taxes on American Politics*, with Mary Edsall (New York: Norton, 1992).

138. Beverly Daniel Tatum, *Why Are All the Black Kids Sitting Together in the Cafeteria and Other Conversations about Race* (New York: Basic, 2003).

139. See Maria Newman, "April in Virginia," *New York Times*, April 7, 2010, http://thecaucus.blogs.nytimes.com/2010/04/07/april-in-virginia/?emc=etal.

140. Anita Kumar and Rosalind S. Helderman, "McDonnell's Confederate History Month Proclamation Irks Civil Rights Leaders," *Washington Post*, April 7, 2010, www.washingtonpost.com/wp-dyn/content/article/2010/04/06/AR2010040604416.html?hpid=topnews.

141. Ibid.

142. See MacMullan, *Habits of Whiteness*.

143. Eduardo Bonilla-Silva, *Racism without Racists* (Lanham, MD: Rowman and Littlefield, 2010), 125.

144. Ibid., 124.

145. Ibid., 105. Similarly, in a survey of students, the vast majority of whites (92 percent) had "no objection" to inviting a black person for dinner. When those same respondents were asked whether they had actually "invited a black person for lunch or dinner recently," 68.5 percent said "no."

146. See Mary McClintock Fulkerson, *Places of Redemption* (Oxford: Oxford University Press, 2007), 15–16.

147. See Sheila Dewan, "Southern Schools Mark Two Majorities," *New York Times*, January 6, 2010, www.nytimes.com/2010/01/07/us/07south.html?emc=etal.

148. Russell K. Robinson, "Perceptual Segregation," *Columbia Law Review* 108 (2009): 1093–180.

149. To those who would respond by arguing that school integration is the answer, Bonilla-Silva's study revealed that tracking insulates whites in schools that are nominally integrated. Even in schools where the minority population was 40 percent or more, white respondents indicated that their classes were "mostly white." Unsurprisingly, students who attended these integrated schools were found to have social lives that were overwhelmingly self-segregated.

150. Human Rights Watch, "World Report 2009," www.hrw.org/en/node/79365.

151. See Tara Herival and Paul Wright, eds., *Prison Profiteers: Who Makes Money from Mass Incarceration* (New York: New Press, 2007).

152. See Jon Swartz, "Inmates vs. Outsourcing," *USA Today*, July 6, 2004, www .usatoday.com/money/economy/employment/2004–07–06-call-center_x.htm.

153. Ibid. Although there is not space to survey the growing literature on the complexion of the contemporary U.S. prison population here, the revelations of this research are appalling (see Michelle Alexander, *The New Jim Crow: Mass Incarceration in the Age of Colorblindness* [New York: New Press, 2010]; Loïc Wacquant, "Deadly Symbiosis," *Punishment & Society* 3, no. 1 (2001): 95–134; Glen Loury, *Race, Incarceration, and American Values* [Cambridge: MIT Press, 2008]; and Bruce Western, *Punishment and Inequality in America* [New York: Russell Sage Foundation, 2007]).

154. See Michael Tonry, *Punishing Race* (New York: Oxford University Press, 2011).

155. Elizabeth Anderson, *The Imperative of Integration* (Princeton, NJ: Princeton University Press, 2010).

156. Ibid., 116–17.

157. Ibid., 186. See also Orlando Patterson, *The Ordeal of Integration* (Washington, DC: Civitas Counterpoint, 1997).

158. Anderson, *The Imperative of Integration*, 123.

159. Ibid., 184.

160. Although a topic of this breadth cannot be adequately addressed here, I

treat the subject at length in my book *The Power of Memory in Democratic Politics* (New York: Rochester University Press, 2012).

161. Douglas S. Massey and Nancy Denton, *American Apartheid: Segregation and the Making of the Underclass* (Cambridge: Harvard University Press, 1991).

162. See Philip A. Klinker with Rogers M. Smith, *The Unsteady March: The Rise and Decline of Racial Equality in America* (Chicago: University of Chicago Press, 1999).

163. Baldwin qtd. in Tatum, *Why Are All the Black Kids Sitting Together in the Cafeteria*, xix.

164. Baldwin, "The Fire Next Time," in *The Price of the Ticket*, 379.

3

James Baldwin and the Politics of Disconnection

Susan J. McWilliams

Out in the wide world, Kitty—wide
Night—*far across the sea* . . . Some guardian accent
   grows
Below the soft voice, brusque:
"You are: not what you wished but what you were."
          —John Berryman, "The Long Home"

How hath hard fate undone me!
Oe'r the wide earth unto what goal
Blind am I borne, in fate's control?
          —Sophocles, *Oedipus Rex*

Giovanni's Room begins with its protagonist, a young, white American named David, staring out the window of a house in the south of France. There, brooding on the events that he is about to recount, David emphasizes that they "were acted out under a foreign sky." He suggests that this fact undergirds all others in the narrative, that if you didn't know he was an American abroad, you wouldn't be able to understand the nature of what has transpired. To understand David, and David's story, you must understand that he is an American who has traveled outside of America. "There is," he says, "something fantastic in the spectacle I now present to myself of having run so far, so hard, across the ocean."[1]

In James Baldwin's corpus, this "fantastic spectacle" of an American who has traveled long distances—an American who has sought tangible disconnection from history and home—is also a frequent one. Few of Baldwin's characters are, to quote Yeats, "rooted in one dear perpetual place."[2] In *Another Country,* we meet Eric, an American who "prolongs his sojourn" in Paris.[3] The second book of *Tell Me How Long the Train's Been Gone*—its title is "Is There Anybody There? Said the Traveler"—details the first time that Leo Proudhammer and his friends roar away from home to pursue their acting careers.[4] And Baldwin himself spent a good amount of time abroad; much of his nonfiction centers on the experiences he had while traveling and on the phenomena of American travel and movement more generally. In Baldwin's hands, the American ideal of mobility becomes a matter of physical practice; Americanness becomes defined largely by the fantastic spectacle of so many, running so far. It is a spectacle that involves Americans of all races, genders, sexualities, and classes.

This pervasive American mobility, in Baldwin's writings, suggests something important about his understanding of the American understanding of freedom. How could it not? After all, travel invokes freedom, as Hannah Arendt has explained. "Of all the specific liberties which may come into our minds when we hear the word 'freedom,' freedom of movement is historically the oldest and also the most elementary," she writes. "Being able to depart for where we will is the prototypal gesture of being free, as limitation of freedom of movement has from time immemorial been the precondition for enslavement." In addition, we associate the ability to travel with the ability to act in the world, the ability to assert one's own will and make basic changes to the circumstances of one's life; "freedom of movement is also the indispensable condition for action, and it is in action that men primarily experience freedom in the world."[5]

But the story of American freedom that Baldwin is telling through the depiction of all that movement is not a simple one, not straightforward and not merely productive of liberation. It's a depiction of American movement, and a picture of American freedom, that complicates Arendt's account. In fact, central to Baldwin's thinking is the idea that Americans misunderstand freedom—both what it is and how to achieve it—and as a result perpetuate a political world of delusions and dominations. That misunderstanding is revealed in the ways Americans move through the world.

Consider what David, the protagonist of *Giovanni's Room*, has to say about his own American forebears: "My ancestors conquered a continent, pushing across death-laden plains, until they came to an ocean which faced away from Europe into a darker past."[6] David's account is that his (white) ancestors traveled both to conquer and to escape—to assert themselves forcefully and even violently in the world, chasing some dream of domination over the terms of life, while at the same time hoping to avoid a determined fate. Their ambitions, that is, are more suggestive of dreams of mastery rather than dreams of freedom (though it's not hard to imagine that they confused the ambition to be masters with the ambition to be free). Moreover, David suggests that his ancestors' ambitions of mastery were eventually thwarted; having moved so fast and so far to create a new future on their own terms, they end up stopped by the natural limit of the ocean, with no choice but to turn back or to stand still and look across the sea, imagining on the other side the "darker" continent there on which they had tried to turn their backs, the continent that they had constructed as a site of enslavement.[7]

As David allows us to see it, the further in thrall to the dream of mastery his ancestors became, the closer they moved to the truth of the enslavement they had wrought. The further they moved in their quest to dominate the continent, the closer they came to being chastened by the fact of natural limits. The further they thought they were moving toward the future, the more they moved into the past. Such is the intersection of American illusion with geographical and temporal fact: although to Americans, the West has always represented future possibility, the geographical and temporal fact is that the farther west you go, the farther you move back in time. (When the sun has set on the East Coast, daylight still reigns in the West.) Another American illusion crashes into geographical and temporal fact here, too: although to Americans, Africa has largely been imagined as a "backward" (or "underdeveloped") continent, the temporal fact is that Africa is always ahead of the United States, watching the sun rise on a new day when Americans are getting ready to go to bed the night before.

From the beginning of *Giovanni's Room*, then, Baldwin has David suggest that what Americans—and white Americans in particular—take to be pursuit of freedom is both misguided and illusive. It is misguided in that what they have taken to be the pursuit of freedom is in fact the pursuit of mastery. It is illusive in that it imagines possible what is in fact impossible, and it imagines limitless what is subject to natural limits.

In their travels, Baldwin's Americans typically are seeking to escape what is inescapable, whether it be the color of their skin, their sexual desires, their romantic and familial attachments, their history, or their mortality. They so often are trying to free themselves from that from which they cannot be freed; they are trying to assert mastery in realms where mastery is denied to human beings. The "freedom" that Americans so often seek is really a kind of control that human beings cannot have, and thus the American idea of freedom is fatally flawed. The way in which Baldwin's Americans travel through the world exposes their misunderstanding of freedom itself and the tragic consequences of that misunderstanding. That is why David, having acted with an unthinking faith in this flawed notion of freedom, comes to think of freedom itself as a problem. That "these nights were being acted out under a foreign sky, with no one to watch, no penalties attached— it was this last fact which was our undoing," he muses, "for nothing is more unbearable, once one has it, than freedom."[8]

Moreover, there are hints in David's early musings—hints here that Baldwin makes as explicit arguments elsewhere—that the racial politics of American life are somehow explained, or at least implied, in American forms of mobility. White supremacy and racial domination are incompatible with a true understanding of and aspiration to freedom; to bastardize a saying of Martin Luther King Jr.'s, unfreedom anywhere is a threat to freedom everywhere. But white supremacy and racial domination are wholly compatible with an aspiration to mastery; the historical meaning of "master" testifies to that well enough. The incoherence of American creed and American conditions—the oft-noticed fact that Americans are a people who say they celebrate freedom and yet systematically deny freedom to large numbers of (largely dark-skinned, homosexual, and foreign) people—can best be explained by the flawed American understanding of what freedom is, the mistaking of the pursuit of mastery for the pursuit of freedom.

Part of Baldwin's project can be understood, then, as the attempt to walk his readers through journeys that, in exposing the incoherence and innocence of the way that Americans tend to move through the world, redirect his largely American audience toward a truer definition of freedom.

The Discovery of Disconnection

Baldwin's account of some of his own journeying is telling. He says he traveled outside the United States—that he disconnected physically from the United States—in order to achieve some measure of freedom from its gruesome racial politics. "I left America," Baldwin writes, "because I doubted my ability to survive the fury of the color problem here": "I wanted to prevent myself from becoming *merely* a Negro; or, even, merely a Negro writer. I wanted to find out in what way the *specialness* of my experience could be made to connect me with other people instead of dividing me from them. (I was as isolated from Negroes as I was from whites, which is what happens when a Negro begins, at bottom, to believe what white people say about him.)"[9] Baldwin's point of departure, both literal and figurative, was the problem of race in America, the problem bound up in the legacy of slavery in America. He left America not only because other Americans were inclined to see him only as a "Negro" but also because he was starting to have trouble seeing *himself* in another way. He felt alien to himself, and Baldwin left for Europe to reground himself in order to find connection with others—the kind of connections that he assumed could only be realized via a disconnection from the United States.

The underlying dynamics here are ones that, with only minor variations, appear time and again in Baldwin's writing. We get the story of an American individual who feels trapped at home. That sense of being trapped has to do both with feelings of helplessness and feelings of disconnection. The American individual feels helpless in the face of some difficult truth and imagines there might be some way to become unshackled from that difficult truth. At the same time, the American individual feels disconnected—from country, from countrymen, from self—and longs to find a surer and more secure grounding in the world. The American individual thus leaves home, trying to assert control over the conditions of his or her life, seeking both freedom and connection.

So we get David in *Giovanni's Room,* who like Baldwin leaves the United States for Paris, though in his case he feels trapped because of his homosexuality, because of familial assumptions that it is time for David settle down with a girl. And we get Hella, in the same novel, who comes to Europe because she feels trapped by her gender and by the American social expectations about how women are supposed to behave. Or we get Arthur, in *Just Above My Head,* who "wanted, really, to leave home" because "it was as though, at home, he found himself trapped in a play, acting a role he had played too long."[10]

Baldwin makes it hard not to sympathize with these characters—not to mention with himself—and to understand the reasons that, in each of their cases and others, one might see travel as a way out or a way forward. It makes sense that someone who feels out of control would seek to exert more control over the conditions of his or her existence. It makes sense that if you feel trapped in a place, you would want to leave it. But at the same time he makes us sympathetic to these motivations, Baldwin shows that there are obvious problems with the American inclination to use physical movement as a way to gain control and in doing so find freedom and friendship, or find liberation and love.

The first obvious problem is what Ralph Waldo Emerson had in mind when he called travel a "fool's paradise," saying that "my Giant goes with me wherever I go."[11] All of Baldwin's travelers are people whose sense of being trapped owes not just to external conditions but to internal confusions. They go somewhere else only to realize that they have taken the problem—their own anxieties, struggles, and ambivalences—with them. They learn that the prison in which they have felt trapped is not the prison of home; it is the prison of the self. To that extent, their travels have been at best an escape or distraction from the core problems they face. (Says David in *Giovanni's Room:* "I had decided to allow no room in the universe for something which shamed and frightened me. I succeeded very well—by not looking at the universe, by not looking at myself, by remaining, in effect, in constant motion.")[12] Again and again in Baldwin's writings, it is as Rufus realizes in *Another Country:* "He had merely been taking refuge in the outward adventure in order to avoid the clash and tension of the adventure proceeding inexorably within."[13] Baldwin consistently posits Americans as a people who make the mistake of believing that their psychic turmoil can be resolved (or at least evaded) through physical motion.

To some degree, that mistake is an understandable one. If you feel trapped because of the political conditions or social systems in the place where you are—trapped by the institutionalized white supremacy in the United States, for instance, or trapped by its restrictive gender roles—it makes sense to try to move somewhere outside the grip of those political conditions or social systems, to leave the place where you are. But as

Baldwin teaches, things are not that simple. Because we are creatures who internalize our early experiences and environments, it is impossible to fully separate ourselves from those experiences and environments just by walking away. (Think of the many variations of this old saying: "You can take the boy out of the country, but you can't take the country out of the boy.") Years before it was common to talk about "social construction," in other words, Baldwin became one of social construction's greatest theorists. So Baldwin, along with his characters, run again and again into the fact that is possible to leave the American landscape but not the American mindscape. It is not so simple as to try to control the atmosphere around you, when—largely out of your control—you've spent years breathing in the atmosphere of home. In leaving home in its physical instantiation, you think you are freeing yourself (and you may be, to some extent), but in large measure you are trying to control what is beyond your control. You think you seek freedom, but in fact you seek mastery.

Baldwin captures his understanding of things forcefully in recounting his journey, in 1953, to a tiny Swiss village that, as far as anyone could ascertain, no black person had visited before. The villagers, Baldwin wrote, regarded him as a "living wonder": "and the children shout *Neger! Neger!* as I walk along the streets." Baldwin said he "knew that they did not mean to be unkind," that "the children who shout *Neger!* have no way of knowing the echoes this sound raises in me." But "it is necessary, nevertheless, for me to repeat this to myself each time that I walk out of the chalet." The Swiss children, he knew, were unaware of the overtones of the word within the broader historical context that had defined Baldwin's life. But *he* could not be unaware of the overtones of the word, and that made all the difference. "Joyce is right about history being a nightmare—but it may be the nightmare from which no one *can* awaken," he wrote. "People are trapped in history and history is trapped in them."[14] Outside the physical confines of the United States, Baldwin realized that the United States existed within his own confines. By traveling, he had sought to escape or control a feeling that turned out to be both within him and resistant to his intellectualizations.

That realization points to the naiveté of thinking that travel is likely to produce liberation. But it also points to the naiveté of thinking that travel is likely to produce more profound or more effortless human connection. Baldwin faulted his younger self for that kind of naiveté: he tells the story of finding in France that it was much harder to find recognition and common ground with others than he had imagined. He'd had "rather exaggerated hopes of the French," he writes, and thought he would find easy intellectual communion on the other side of the Atlantic.[15] When he did converse with French people in France, though, he found what was only obvious in retrospect: that the French have their own cultural predispositions, know America only through the distortions of distance, and were unfamiliar with Baldwin's formative experiences. As a result, in France Baldwin said he found himself "involved, in another language, in the same old battle: the battle for his own identity."[16] In fact, Baldwin discovered, the battle might be a more difficult one on these terms: not only would he have to fight through a caricature of himself *and* of his country, but also he would have to fight through a language barrier.

Baldwin tells an important variation of this story when he talks about the lack of connection he felt when meeting African immigrants in Europe—people with whom he had imagined he would share some kind of racial recognition. But that, as he writes, was not the case; Baldwin found instead a vast experiential gulf: "The African before him has endured privation, injustice, medieval cruelty; but the African has not yet endured the utter alienation of himself from his people and his past. His mother did not sing 'Sometimes I Feel Like a Motherless Child,' and he has not, all his life long, ached for acceptance in a culture which pronounced straight hair and white skin the only acceptable beauty." These and other differences mattered, and mattered deeply: "They face each other, the Negro and the African, over a gulf of three hundred years—an alienation too vast to be conquered in an evening's good-will, too heavy and too double-edged ever to be trapped in speech."[17] The gulf between Africans and African Americans was one Baldwin articulated time and again, usually in essays about his own travels. The gulf he saw came down to a "banal and abruptly quite overwhelming fact" that they had been born in different societies: "We had been dealing with, had been made and mangled by, another machinery altogether."[18]

As Baldwin tells the story of his own travels in Europe, those failures to connect were even more discomfiting because they stood in sharp contrast to the connections he made with white Americans in Paris. Though the interactions of black and white Americans in Paris had the "high potential" to be "awkward" or "ugly," Baldwin was shocked to sense something beneath the superficial guardedness of those conversations.[19] "It became terribly clear in Europe, as it never had been here," he writes, "that we knew more about each other than any European ever could": "In my necessity to find the terms on which my experience could be related to that of others, Negroes and whites, writers and non-writers, I proved, to my astonishment, to be as American as any Texas GI. And I found my experience was shared by every American writer I knew in Paris. Like me, they had been divorced from their origins, and it turned out to make very little difference that the origins of white Americans were European and mine were African—they were no more at home in Europe than I was." It was a conclusion that caused Baldwin to suffer "a species of breakdown." But the breakdown comprised his "breakthrough." He had to do what he realized no American really wants to do, which is to face himself and the place from whence he came. He had to come to terms with his Americanness—a fact about himself from which he could not be freed, no matter how far he moved. To free himself, Baldwin realized that he had to give up on the dream of limitless liberation and instead turn within, and turn toward home. Prefiguring his character David, Baldwin "unhappily" realized that freedom would come only from giving up on the American fantasy of freedom, the fantasy that people can "invent their mooring posts, their lovers and their friends, any more than they can invent their parents."[20] And so there, in Europe, he reported, "Armed with two Bessie Smith records and a typewriter, I began to try to recreate the life that I had first known as a child and from which I had spent so many years in flight."[21]

The Dynamics of Disconnection

That language of "flight" is important because Baldwin makes recourse to it often, in both his autobiographical writings and fictions, when describing the behavior and mind-set of Americans. "To flee or not," Baldwin writes, seems to Americans to be their primary choice, not realizing that "it is all the same" whether they stay or go.[22] "The Americans always fly," says Guillaume, a French character in *Giovanni's Room*. "They are not serious."[23] In Baldwin's writings, both white and black Americans seem possessed of the conviction that fleeing will lead to freedom—that fleeing will lead to both liberation and self-realization—when in fact flight is "a reckless, desperate state."[24] In fleeing, Baldwin's Americans are trying to escape what cannot be escaped and control what they cannot control. They are not freeing, but rather evading, themselves—and often doing great damage to themselves (and others) in the process. The "freedom" that Americans so often seek is really a desperate move of evasion and a reckless grab for control—a desperate move to evade what cannot be evaded, and a reckless grab to control what cannot be controlled, and thus the American idea of freedom is fatally flawed.

Before considering the costs of all that fleeing, though, Baldwin considers why Americans are inclined toward their reckless, desperate acts of flight. To answer that question, he draws attention to the American idiom that one travels or leaves home to "find oneself." ("My flight," Baldwin says of his own journeying, "had been dictated by my hope that I could find myself.")[25] As David puts it in *Giovanni's Room*, "finding oneself" is "an interesting phrase, not current as far as I know in the language of any other people." He muses that the phrase "does not mean what it says but betrays a nagging suspicion that something has been misplaced."[26]

Throughout his corpus, Baldwin argues that what Americans suspect they have lost is something at their very core: their identity. He writes that he discovered that during his own travels, when he interrogated his feelings of connection to white Americans and realized that they, like he, like all the other Americans in Paris, were "searching for our separate identities," and that the search itself connected them. That discovery—the "discovery of what it means to be an American"—pointed Baldwin to one of his most fundamental claims about Americanness.[27] Americans are caught up in a "crisis of identity," Baldwin writes, which goes to the depths of the national soul.[28] "The necessity of Americans to achieve an identity is a historical and a present personal fact," Baldwin muses, "and this is the connection between you and me."[29] In the United States, identity requires "achievement" or work, a kind of work that is difficult and fraught. American society is one "in which the individual must fight for his identity."[30]

That's where things get difficult for Americans—because of course, having to work to "achieve" your identity makes that identity feel perilous or forced. Having to seek to "achieve" your identity may make you feel disconnected from your identity, since if something needs to be sought, that something is distant or obscured. So to the extent that Americans must seek their identity, Americans feel distant from their identity. And to be distant from one's identity is to be distant from one's self. A pervasive theme in Baldwin's writing, accordingly, is that Americans are constantly, on some level, "confronted with the extent of their own alienation, and the un-imaginable dimensions of their own poverty."[31] As Baldwin understands it, "depthless alienation from oneself and one's people is, in sum, the American experience."[32]

That alienation comes in part from the historical fact that in an ancestral sense, all Americans find themselves, as Meridian Henry intones in *Blues for Mister Charlie,* "in a strange land. In a strange land!"[33] For the descendants of former slaves, Baldwin writes, the United States is still their Egypt, the house of bondage that has violently separated them from their ancestors and cut them off from the freedom of self-determination and communal self-governance. Similarly, Native Americans, whose forbears were dispersed to the point of being "almost destroyed," live under conditions of violent separation from their forbears.[34] To some degree, white Americans—themselves all the children of immigrants—share those conditions; few of them know from whence they or their families came, and "the missing identity aches." For them, too, "one can neither assess nor overcome the storm of the middle passage. One is mysteriously shipwrecked forever, in the Great New World."[35] (The language seems meant to evoke a parallel to the transportation of slaves, enhancing the sense of common history.) Says Baldwin, alienation from self that comes with alienation from one's past "has been faced by all Americans throughout our history—in a way it *is* our history— and it baffles the immigrant and sets on edge the second generation until today."[36] The struggle to articulate one's birthright, Baldwin concludes, is a distinctively American struggle, and for each American, it is "in this need to establish himself in relation to his past he is most American."[37]

Note that here, if we accept Baldwin's formulation that "people are trapped in history and history is trapped in them," a curious—and particularly American—problem reveals itself.[38] Americans, across races, are trapped in a history of being without a history, of being disconnected from history. American history "is the history of the total, and willing, alienation of entire peoples from their forebears." This disconnection from origins manifests itself throughout American life. Under everything else, as described above, it expresses itself in an "entirely unprecedented people, with a unique and individual past," which encourages "the alienation of the American from himself."[39] It is that disconnection and alienation that Baldwin sees Americans trying to overcome, futilely, through travel. Effectively estranging themselves from America in order to overcome their essential feelings of estrangement, all they do is exacerbate their original condition; after all, trying to relieve your homesickness by leaving home is a rather insensible remedy.[40] Rather than becoming freer and more self-realized, as they'd hoped, Americans are enmeshed in patterns of behavior that trap them ever more thoroughly in an alienated, disconnected state.

Of course, even if Americans of all races share this underlying condition of alienation, the nation's racial history allows people of different skin tones to manage the shared condition of alienation differently. Indeed, this makes all the difference. By changing their names, European immigrants—for whom "*Giorgio* becomes *Joe, Pappavasiliu* becomes *Palmer, Evangelos* becomes *Evans, Goldsmith* becomes *Smith* or *Gold,* and *Avakian* becomes *King*"—it happens that "in the twinkling of an eye, one becomes a white American."[41] Though they and their descendants are left with an underlying, nagging fear that they lack a "true" identity and have sold out their past, they paper over that fear by clinging to their new racial identity; "the price the white American paid for his ticket was to become white." Baldwin elaborates: "The Irish middle passage, for but one example, was as foul as my own, and as dishonorable on the part of those responsible for it. But the Irish became white when they got here and began rising in the world, whereas I became black and began sinking. The Irish, therefore and thereafter—again, for but one example—had absolutely no choice but to make certain that I could not menace their safety or status or identity: and, if I came too close, they could, with the consent of the governed, kill me."[42] It is thus that the American condition of disconnection, the alienation of self that pervades American experience, manifests itself in practice in systematic racial oppression and violence. The people who are the children of those who aspired to masterlessness become not a free people but a new breed of master. The dream of freedom, which may always have been a dream of mastery, resolves itself—upon reflection, rather unsurprisingly—in white supremacy.

The Anxiety of Disconnection

Again: Baldwin described the American republic as a kind of "bottomless confusion," where no one is sure where they belong. All the Americans he met abroad, Baldwin said, shared the fact that they "didn't know who they were."[43] He captures this sense in *Giovanni's Room,* when David walks into an American Express office and contemplates the countrymen he finds there. What he sees are people of all ages, races, and conditions—a superficially diverse group—who, below it all, share this quality of confusion: "Beneath these faces, these clothes, accents, rudenesses, was power and sorrow, both unadmitted, unrealized, the power of inventors, the sorrow of the disconnected."[44] In other words, the American condition is one of disconnection tied to the dream of power. How could it not make sense that these people who, riding on an underlying current of loss and disconnection, seek to overcome their sorrow by seeking control and power (that they imagine to be freedom)?

So Americans, Baldwin thought, as befits part of their reputation, invent. Specifically, they invent status markers and in so doing "use status to make up for identity."[45] In a place where "identity is almost impossible to achieve," people reorient their desire to achieve toward the more manageable matter of status.[46] In America, "status became a kind of substitute for identity," especially material status.[47]

That substitution is understandable. Americans have become obsessed with material status because it is easier to access and measure than the inaccessible matter of identity; "nearly everyone prefers to be defined by his status, which, unlike his virtue, is ready to wear."[48] Moreover, a materialist culture sorts and ascribes power to people, and it makes that power both visible and tangible.

But from the perspective of the control-seeking American, there is a problem with a reliance on material status, at least as far as that status is used to sort and measure individuals. That problem is that one's material status is not permanently fixed; it does not provide the solid grounding that anxious Americans might seek. Material status can change, and this causes Americans no small amount of discomfort. So, says Baldwin, "People are perpetually attempting to find their feet on the shifting sands of status" in America.[49] Of course, one cannot be obsessed with status, with its achievement and maintenance and improvement, without being beset by the terrible fear of losing status. So Americans are plagued by a "social panic, with our fear of losing status," says Baldwin: "This really amounts sometimes to a kind of social paranoia. One cannot afford to lose status on this peculiar ladder, for the prevailing notion of American life seems to involve a kind of rung-by-rung ascension to some hideously desirable state. If this is one's concept of life, obviously one cannot afford to slip back one rung. When one slips, one slips back not a rung but back into chaos and no longer knows who he is."[50] Americans are creatures of "confusion, dishonesty, [and] panic, trapped and immobilized in the sunlit prison of the American dream."[51] The American dream, of increasing one's tangible social status, is a rickety (at best) spiritual apparatus. One climbs in part because one does not know what else to do. One climbs because one fears falling. One climbs because one feels connected only to the ladder—not to others, not to one's self, not to any deeper or intangible purpose.

In this kind of shaky spiritual contraption, even phenomenal levels of material well-being do not assuage the underlying terror. The "illusion" that being materially rich and powerful makes us happy or better actually creates more fear than comfort: "The principal effect of our material well-being has been to set the children's teeth on edge." And so "this illusion certainly prevents us from making America what we say we want it to be," writes Baldwin.[52] Even when we strip the illusion away, we are left staring at the difficult disconnection that motivated the turn to status in the first place. Baldwin saw this in the character of the mother in *The Exorcist*, for instance, a woman who was guilt-ridden and anxious about her elite status, her high anxiety belying "her essentially empty and hypocritical and totally unanchored life."[53]

Everything in America returns to the fact of disconnection. The social anxiety that makes itself seen and felt throughout American life—which, among other things, causes Americans to be preoccupied with material concerns—emerges because of the American obsession with social status. That obsession, in turn, has emerged because Americans would rather struggle with status than with identity—the struggle with identity being a monumental task in a nation premised on disconnection of all kinds. The spiritual disconnection of the American people results in social and material dysfunction. "The problem of status in American life became," intones Baldwin, "and it remains today acute."[54]

Disconnection and Racial Oppression

This observation, that the American sense of disconnection creates and contributes to widespread status anxiety, leads to an even more indicting reality. Baldwin argues that the American sense of disconnection—especially when combined with the status anxiety that it helps to create—is ground zero for white supremacy. The sense of disconnection lurking in the American soul expresses itself, largely through the status anxiety it feeds, in racism.

Throughout his writing, Baldwin argues that it is the social anxiety of white Americans that leads them to promote and embrace white supremacy. "One of the real reasons for the status of the Negro in this country," he writes, is that "in a way, the Negro tells us where the bottom is: *because he is there*, and *where* he is, beneath us, we know where the limits are and how far we must not fall. We must not fall beneath him. We must never allow ourselves to fall that low, and I am not trying to be cynical or sardonic. I think if one examines the myths which have proliferated in this country concerning the Negro, one discovers beneath these myths a kind of sleeping terror of some condition which we refuse to imagine."[55] In other words, white Americans—fearful of losing status for all the reasons limned above—placate themselves by imagining a class of citizens, black Americans, who are *in every case* lower than them on the ladder. So the white American can be somewhat relieved of his most pervasive fear of falling; no matter how low he falls relative to other white Americans, he knows that he will not fall to the level of the black American. White Americans, then, are spiritually invested in the oppression and exclusion of black Americans.

Much if not most of the racial hierarchy in the United States, Baldwin argues, emanates from the anxieties produced by a culture of disconnection, and the self-preserving attempt on the part of white Americans to conceal their past from themselves. White Americans have dealt with their historical alienation and loss of identity in the United States by asserting a position of superiority-in-status over black Americans: in the absence of a sense of birthright identity, they constructed a racial identity—a thin, false, sense of status that only holds so long as a racial hierarchy can be supported and enforced. "It was impossible for Americans to accept the black man as one of themselves, for to do so was to jeopardize their status as white men," writes Baldwin.[56] White supremacy, that is, is inextricably connected to status anxiety, which is itself inextricably connected to the spiritual disconnection of Americans: "In this country, chaos connects with color."[57]

And the American obsession with status, and the white supremacy it engenders, exerts itself powerfully on every new generation of citizens. Baldwin notes that for those first reaching the United States, there can be at first a kind of camaraderie among black and nonblack immigrants. They sense that they share, as indeed they do, a sense of disconnection from the past and a sense of confused identity—those enduring bedrocks of American experience. But within a generation, the white immigrant pushes the black immigrant beneath him. "Within a generation, at most two, he is at home in the new country and climbing that ladder," says Baldwin. "If there is trouble in the Irish, Italian, or Polish ward, say, the trouble can be contained and eliminated because the demands of these white people do not threaten the fabric of American society."[58] White immigrants become quickly socialized into the culture of white supremacy because of the evident benefits such a system offers them: "To be white was to be forced to digest a delusion called white supremacy."[59]

Ultimately, the American sense of disconnection results in a desperate grab for status that leads to the perpetuation of racial oppression and politically and legally sanctioned inegalitarianism. "The Americans' ladder is not Jacob's ladder," says Baldwin, "their pillow is not Jacob's pillow."[60] Americans do not climb with the promise of salvation awaiting them, or with much comfort along the way. Americans climb because of the fear of falling, and the only promise that white Americans in particular can find is that someone—the black American—is always going to be beneath him. It is an awful comfort in a frightening climb.

As Baldwin makes clear, white Americans deal with their internal status anxiety not by addressing it directly—for what terrible things that might reveal!—but by externalizing their sense of the problem: "It has always been much easier (because it has always seemed much safer) to give a name to the evil without than to locate the terror within."[61] Tellingly, to externalize an evil is to feel like you have greater control over it than you do. To externalize an evil is to feel like you have freed yourself from it, even though in fact you've really turned yourself into a master.

The same dynamics that send Baldwin's American characters into their flights from home, in other words, are the dynamics that underlie American white supremacy. Mobility in America is, in many dimensions, tied to white supremacy in America. The American love of travel exposes that what Americans imagine to be their desire for freedom is really their desire for control.

Baldwin had traveled abroad only to come home to himself—and to his native country. He said had come to the "discovery of what it means to be an American" while in Europe. It was in wrestling with this apparent paradox, he wrote, that he made his "first breakthrough" as an American writer trying to understand American identity.[62] Thus Baldwin's art imitated Baldwin's life, or at least drew heavily upon it: Baldwin narrated the experiences of American travelers as a means of laying bare certain fundamental dynamics of American political life.

And central to those dynamics is the idea of disconnection. When writing about American travel and mobility, the idea of disconnection is always at the fore. Baldwin drew from his experiences and observations of American travelers the conclusion that Americans—regardless of race—are animated by pervasive feelings of disconnection: disconnection from origins and the past, and disconnection from human fellowship and community. As a result of this sense of disconnection, the American yearns—to use two familiar idioms—"to find a place where he fits in" or "to find himself." This yearning is closer to the surface and more apparent in Americans who travel abroad simply because such Americans have traveled—whether they realize it or not—in order to relieve that yearning. Having mistaken a spiritual disconnection for a geographic one (or an internal sense of disconnection for an external one), they have tried to escape that sense of disconnection through travel. But in Baldwin's depiction of their travels it becomes clear the extent to which their dislocation is internal. Abroad, their interior, spiritual disconnection is set in stark relief.

That the American's interior world is so dominated by feelings of disconnection has two problematic impacts on his exterior world—on the dynamics of American politics. First, Baldwin argued that this sense of disconnection feeds a more generalized status anxiety in American life. The "social paranoia" of status anxiety, for Baldwin, gets to the heart of things in America.[63] He described the American republic as a kind of "bottomless confusion," where no one is sure where he or she belongs. All the Americans he met, Baldwin said, "didn't know who they were."[64] And critically, that lack of self-knowledge stems from a lack of connectedness—a theme Baldwin returns to again and again. Second, Baldwin believes that the American sense of disconnection—especially when combined with the status anxiety that it helps to create—helps to maintain and might even aggravate the racist system of white supremacy. The sense of disconnection lurking in the American soul expresses itself, often through the status anxiety it feeds, in recourse to aggressive racial typing and hierarchizing. This sense of disconnection, then, is a crucial part of what Lawrie Balfour has so well articulated (in her essay in this volume) as American's "subterranean reality," the truths on the "level of assumptions and unacknowledged beliefs" in a system of race consciousness and racial injustice.[65]

More theoretically, Baldwin's depiction of American mobility reveals the tragic flaw in the American conception of freedom. Americans often imagine they are seeking freedom when what they are really seeking is control—the ability to invent the conditions of their own lives, to escape the past, to engage in acts of fundamental self-creation. They fail to understand both that there are limits to the degree one can liberate oneself and that freedom in fact comes from a hard reckoning with those things that cannot be escaped. Freedom comes from fight, not flight. Baldwin's Americans reliably choose flight over fight—fleeing from the truth of their lives rather than fighting with, and for, it. That fact underscores that, especially in the moments when Americans think they are pursuing freedom, they are pursuing mastery—and a mastery of that which cannot, in the end, be mastered. Just as Baldwin's American travelers come to realize the futility of their travels—"I think now if I had any intimation that the self I was going to find would turn out to be only the same self from which I had spent so much time in flight, I would have stayed at home," says David, in *Giovanni's Room*—Baldwin hopes that his readers will come to realize the futility (not to mention the recklessness) of the way Americans misunderstand freedom.[66]

For the way that Americans misunderstand freedom is tied, through a number of knots, to white supremacy and systematic racial domination. Tragically, it is precisely when Americans think they are on the path to liberation that they are in fact courting oppression. As long as Americans misunderstand what it means to be free, America will itself not be freed from the white supremacy that has endured and thrived throughout its history.

One of the other great tragedies here is that the American misunderstanding of freedom— the misunderstanding that leads to racial domination—comes from the sense of disconnection and anxiety about identity that, at its core, is *shared* by Americans of all races. Baldwin at several points seems to suggest that the sense of disconnection that all Americans share could be a source of connection and hope. On some level, all Americans are disconnected from their past, alienated in their present, homeless in their home, and beset by "the question of identity: *Who am I? And what am I doing here?*"[67] There is an underlying uncertainty that connects the children of master and slave, the inheritors of a shared legacy that leaves them both feeling like strangers in a strange land.

But rather than face that shared condition, and the shared legacy to which it owes, Americans take flight. They take literal flight, crossing state lines and borders and winging themselves far from home. They take intellectual flight, covering their eyes and diverting themselves in distraction and veiling themselves in claims of innocence, habits that are made visible in the phenomena of American mobility. Americans embark on these flights from reality by convincing themselves that flight is the means to freedom, and that freedom is what they seek. But the truth is that what they seek is control after a lifetime of feeling its lack. And so what Americans think of as quests for freedom are in fact projects of mastery. What Americans think of as journeys to knowledge are in fact reckless attempts to maintain innocence. These American misunderstandings become resolved, among other ways, in racial domination. So the American idea of freedom, flawed as it is, results tragically in unfreedom—the violent unfreedom of white status and supremacy.

Against that damning pattern, Baldwin retained at least some hope that Americans could redirect themselves toward real freedom. If travelers, for Baldwin, embodied the broader problems of Americanness, they also embodied potential. So many of Baldwin's American travelers—not least of whom is himself—find, when the reality of self runs up against the fantasies of travel, that they are only going to be freed when they stand still and look within rather than run around and try to get out. One who has always chosen flight still retains the possibility of fight. And the fight of confrontation—confrontation with the past, with home, with the self—is where the possibilities of freedom lie. For Baldwin, "not everything that is faced can be changed; but nothing can be changed until it is faced."[68] There, at least, is some hope for the birth of a real freedom in the United States.

Notes

First epigraph: John Berryman, "The Long Home," *Short Poems* (New York: Farrar, Straus and Giroux, 1948), 85.

Second epigraph: Sophocles, *Oedipus the King,* trans. E. D. A. Morshead (London: Macmillan, 1885), 107.

1. James Baldwin, *Giovanni's Room* (New York: Modern Library, 1956), 5–6.

2. William Butler Yeats, "A Prayer for My Daughter," in *The Poems,* ed. Richard J. Finneran (New York: Scribner, 1997), 191.

3. James Baldwin, *Another Country* (New York: Vintage International, 1993), 215.

4. James Baldwin, *Tell Me How Long the Train's Been Gone* (New York: Vintage International, 1968), 127.

5. Hannah Arendt, *Men in Dark Times* (New York: Harcourt, Brace, and World, 1955), 9.

6. Baldwin, *Giovanni's Room,* 5.

7. Baldwin here adds a possibility to Hegel's dictum that America will never come to terms with itself until "the inhabitants," reaching the Pacific shore, "instead of pressing outwards to occupy the fields, press inwards upon each other" (see G. W. F. Hegel, *Lectures on the Philosophy of History,* trans. J. Sibree [London: Henry G. Bohn, 1861], 90). Baldwin suggests that part of that coming to terms will be realizing that, even when Americans think they have most distanced themselves from and turned their backs on Africa, they end up staring that continent in the face.

8. Baldwin, *Giovanni's Room,* 5.

9. Ibid., 171.

10. James Baldwin, *Just Above My Head* (New York: Delta, 2000), 268.

11. Ralph Waldo Emerson, "Culture," in *The Conduct of Life* (Boston: Ticknor and Fields, 1867), 127; "Self-Reliance," in *Self-Reliance and Other Essays* (New York: Dover, 1993), 34–35.

12. Baldwin, *Giovanni's Room,* 22.

13. Baldwin, *Another Country,* 133.

14. James Baldwin, "Stranger in the Village," in *The Price of the Ticket: Collected Nonfiction 1948–1985* (New York: St. Martin's, 1985), 81, 85.

15. James Baldwin, "Encounter on the Seine: Black Meets Brown," in *The Price of the Ticket,* 36.

16. Ibid., 35–39.

17. Ibid., 38–39.

18. James Baldwin, "Princes and Powers," in *The Price of the Ticket,* 45.

19. Baldwin, "Encounter on the Seine," 36–37.

20. Baldwin, *Giovanni's Room,* 5.

21. James Baldwin, "The Discovery of What It Means to Be an American," in *The Price of the Ticket,* 172.

22. James Baldwin, "Everybody's Protest Novel," in *The Price of the Ticket,* 33.

23. Baldwin, *Giovanni's Room,* 169.

24. James Baldwin, *Going to Meet the Man: Stories* (New York: Vintage, 1995), 221.

25. James Baldwin, *No Name in the Street* (New York: Vintage, 1972), 40.

26. Baldwin, *Giovanni's Room*, 22.

27. Baldwin, "The Discovery of What It Means to Be an American," 172.

28. James Baldwin, "Nothing Personal," in *The Price of the Ticket*, 386.

29. James Baldwin, "In Search of a Majority," in *The Price of the Ticket*, 234.

30. Baldwin, "The Discovery of What It Means to Be an American," 175.

31. Baldwin, "No Name in the Street," in *The Price of the Ticket*, 546.

32. Baldwin, "Encounter on the Seine," 39.

33. James Baldwin, *Blues for Mister Charlie* (New York: Dell, 1964), 104.

34. James Baldwin, *Conversations with James Baldwin*, ed. Fred L. Standley and Louis H. Pratt (Jackson: University Press of Mississippi, 1989), 148.

35. James Baldwin, "The Price of the Ticket," in *The Price of the Ticket*, xix.

36. James Baldwin, "Many Thousands Gone," in *The Price of the Ticket*, 69.

37. Baldwin, "Encounter on the Seine," 39.

38. Baldwin, "Stranger in the Village," in *The Price of the Ticket*, 81.

39. James Baldwin, "A Question of Identity," in *The Price of the Ticket*, 99.

40. Though Baldwin spent much of his adult life outside of the United States, he resisted the idea that he was an expatriate. "For better or worse, my ties with my country are too deep, and my concern is too great," he told an interviewer. "I am an American artist, and I know what Nathaniel Hawthorne meant when he wrote, from England, around 1861, that 'the United States may be fit for many purposes, but they are not fit to live in.' Nearly all American artists have felt this, and for very good reasons; but we have all—usually, anyway—gone home. The danger of being an expatriate is that you are very likely to find yourself living, in effect, nowhere" (see *Conversations with James Baldwin*, ed. Standley and Pratt, 60).

41. Baldwin, "The Price of the Ticket," xix.

42. Ibid., xix–xx.

43. James Baldwin, "Notes for a Hypothetical Novel," in *The Price of the Ticket*, 241.

44. Baldwin, *Giovanni's Room*, 97.

45. *Conversations with James Baldwin*, ed. Standley and Pratt, 74.

46. Baldwin, "The Fire Next Time," in *The Price of the Ticket*, 371.

47. Baldwin, "In Search of a Majority," 231.

48. James Baldwin, "The Devil Finds Work," in *The Price of the Ticket*, 562.

49. Baldwin, "The Fire Next Time," 371.

50. Baldwin, "In Search of a Majority," 232.

51. Baldwin, "Everybody's Protest Novel," 31.

52. James Baldwin, "Nobody Knows My Name," in *The Price of the Ticket*, 184.

53. Baldwin, "The Devil Finds Work," 634–35.

54. Baldwin, "In Search of a Majority," 231.

55. Ibid., 232–33.

56. Baldwin, "Stranger in the Village," 88.

57. James Baldwin, "Here Be Dragons," in *The Price of the Ticket*, 689.

58. Ibid.

59. James Baldwin, "Dark Days," in *The Price of the Ticket*, 657.

60. James Baldwin, "Every Good-Bye Ain't Gone," in *The Price of the Ticket*, 644.

61. Baldwin, "Nothing Personal," 383.

62. James Baldwin, "The Discovery of What It Means to Be an American," 173.

63. Ibid., 173–74.

64. Baldwin, "Notes for a Hypothetical Novel," 241.

65. Lawrie Balfour, *The Evidence of Things Not Said: James Baldwin and the Promise of American Democracy* (Ithaca, NY: Cornell University Press, 2001), 7.

66. Baldwin, *Giovanni's Room*, 22–23.

67. James Baldwin, "Of the Sorrow Songs," in *The Cross of Redemption: Uncollected Writings*, ed. Randall Kenan (New York: Vintage, 2010), 149.

68. James Baldwin, "As Much Truth as One Can Bear," in *The Cross of Redemption*, 42.

4

What William F. Buckley Jr. Did Not Understand about James Baldwin

On Baldwin's Politics of Freedom

Nicholas Buccola

"The American Dream is at the expense of the American Negro." This was the motion up for debate when the Cambridge Union Society hosted James Baldwin and William F. Buckley Jr. in February 1965. Baldwin, who was by then an internationally acclaimed novelist, playwright, essayist, and activist, was invited to argue on behalf of the motion, and Buckley, who, as editor of the *National Review* magazine and author of the books *God and Man at Yale* and *Up from Liberalism,* was fast emerging as a leading voice of American conservatism, was invited to argue against the motion. The scene of the debate was a remarkable one. According to the *New York Times,* this prestigious debating society, which was "modeled after England's House of Commons," was marking its 150th anniversary that year and the Baldwin-Buckley debate was one of the biggest events of the term. At the time of the debate, the civil rights movement and southern backlash were urgent topics of concern both in the United States and abroad. Indeed, the level of interest in the topic—and these two debaters—was evident by the massive turnout. According to the *Times,* "More than 700 students crowded the high-ceiling debating chamber and 500 others packed the bar, the library and other rooms to watch over closed-circuit TV."[1]

After two undergraduates weighed in on the motion—one in support and one in opposition—Baldwin rose to the podium. He began by saying that he found himself, "not for the first time, in the position of a kind of Jeremiah." One's "response" to the question before the house, he explained, "depends on where you find yourself in the world, what your sense of reality is. That is, it depends on assumptions we hold so deeply as to be scarcely aware of them."[2] Baldwin then proceeded to offer a series of thoughtful and nuanced reflections on the history, economics, politics, and morality of race relations in the United States. At the conclusion of his "masterful per-formance," legal scholar Carl Bogus has written, both sides of the chamber "rose and gave Baldwin long and lusty applause—something that was rare, if not unprecedented, in the history of the Union."[3] The standing ovation must have seemed to last an eternity to Buckley, who was finally invited to rise to offer his speech in opposition to the motion. Buckley demonstrated some of the skills that would eventually lead him to be recognized as one of the premier debaters and wordsmiths of the conservative movement, but upon the conclusion of his speech, the votes were cast, and Baldwin was the overwhelming victor. The motion carried by a vote of 544 to 164.[4]

In the foregoing description of this remarkable debate, I have been rather coy about the specific arguments presented by Baldwin and Buck-ley on that day in 1965. I will return to some of these specifics below, but what follows will *not* be an exhaustive study of the arguments offered at Cambridge. Instead, what I propose to do in this essay is to use Buckley's arguments in the debate (and in some of his other writings) as the basis of an analysis of Baldwin's political thought. I focus in particular on a se-ries of things Buckley did not understand about Baldwin. Buckley believed Baldwin was a wild-eyed extremist who was bent on overturning "American civilization." Buckley saw Baldwin as a threat, to borrow the language of the *National Review* "Mission Statement," to the "tradition of fixed postulates having to do with the meaning of existence, with the relationship of the state to the individual, of the individual to his neighbor, so clearly enunci-ated in the enabling documents of our Republic."[5] In what follows, I argue that Buckley was right to perceive Baldwin as a threat to his worldview, but that he fundamentally misunderstood the nature of Baldwin's critique. In order to make this case, I challenge Buckley's portrayal of Baldwin as an ideological extremist, and I compare what Buckley and Baldwin had in mind when they talked about freedom. My focus in this essay is on Baldwin, so my explication of Buckley's ideas is necessarily cursory and, admittedly, rather superficial. My aim, in other words, is not to offer a comprehensive comparative analysis of Buckley and Baldwin but rather to use Buckley's misunderstanding of Baldwin as the basis for an exploration of how Baldwin challenged—and attempted to transform—how Americans tend to think about freedom.

My argument will proceed as follows. After I reconstruct Buckley's portrayal of Baldwin in the debate, I challenge Buckley's claim that Baldwin was a radical ideologue. I show that Baldwin was deeply suspicious of ideologies of the Right *and* the Left and that Buckley was wrong to view him as a wild-eyed extremist animated by a simple mantra of "Hate the System." I then compare what Buckley and Baldwin had in mind when they talked about freedom in order to show that Baldwin was up to something far more complex than simply calling for the overthrow of "American civilization." Instead, he was attempting to go *beyond* conventional views of liberty by arguing that one cannot be free unless one is liberated from domination and delusion—precisely the forces to which Buckley showed himself, in the debate, subject. I conclude the essay by revealing how I think Baldwin would explain Buckley's failures to understand not only his project but also the goals of the civil rights movement: Buckley did not, in a meaningful way, accept the equal dignity of African Americans.[6]

"Mr. Baldwin's Aspirations": On Buckley's Understanding of James Baldwin

In the debate, Buckley's case consisted of two major components: a critique of Baldwin as a dangerous ideologue and a two-pronged suggestion of how the "race problem" ought to be addressed. In this section, I take up the first component of Buckley's case: his claim that Baldwin was a dangerous ideologue. Throughout his speech, Buckley sought to establish himself as the defender of American (and Western) civilization and to portray Baldwin as a revolutionary who was seeking its overthrow. Baldwin's "indictments of our civilization," Buckley announced in his introductory comments, "are unjustified," and "if his counsels were listened to," he "would be cursed by all his grandchildren's grandchildren." Buckley contended that in Baldwin's debate speech and "his copious literature of protest," his argument was "that we ought to recognize that American Civilization, and indeed Western Civilization, has failed him and his people, [and] that we ought to throw it over."[7] A few weeks after the debate, Buckley repeated these charges in his column "On the Right": "Mr. Baldwin's indictment of our society," he declared, "is total."[8] Baldwin's views, Buckley wrote later, are marked by "swollen irrationalities," and he "and his coterie of America-haters" ought to "be ghettoized in the corners of fanaticism."[9]

What, precisely, did Buckley think Baldwin was seeking to overthrow? Baldwin, he argued, calls for the overthrow of "Christianity," "the teachings of Plato and Aristotle," "the constitutional system, the idea of the rule of law, [and] the idea of individual rights of the American citizen."[10] In other words, Baldwin sought to overturn many of the things Buckley set out to defend in his *National Review* magazine. The magazine, Buckley had announced in 1955, would stand "athwart history, yelling Stop" as the United States drifted from the "tradition of fixed postulates . . . so clearly enunciated in the enabling documents of our Republic" to the latest plans of liberals, socialists, intellectuals, "Social Engineers," communists, "Fabian operators," internationalists, the United Nations, the League of Women Voters, Henry Steele Commager, the *New York Times*, and all others with a "cynical contempt for human freedom."[11] And, he might well have added in 1965, the *National Review* would be yelling stop to "Negroes" tempted "to adopt the kind of cynicism, the kind of despair, the kind of iconoclasm that is urged by Mr. Baldwin."[12]

What, according to Buckley, did Baldwin seek to erect in the place of these "fixed postulates . . . enunciated by the enabling documents of the Republic"? This is not entirely clear from Buckley's remarks, but given the historical context of the debate, it is evident what he had in mind. In the conclusion to his speech, Buckley expressed concern that "Negroes . . . will seek to reach out for some sort of radical solutions" to the "race problem."[13] As the two engaged in debate, the Cold War was, of course, urgent in the minds of citizens and statesmen around the world. Baldwin, Buckley was warning his audience, may well be tempting his readers to replace the "faith of our fathers" with the "satanic utopianism" of the communists. Buckley would make this accusation more explicitly in his writings after the debate in which he would argue that Baldwin's criticisms of "the capitalist system" and his "common cause" with the editors of *Dissent* magazine should lead all to wonder about his true sympathies.[14] In the face of this radicalism, Buckley pledged to fight not only with rhetoric but with arms if necessary: "If it finally does come to a confrontation between giving up the best features of the American way of life and fighting for them, then we will fight the issue. We will fight the issue not only in the Cambridge Union, but we will fight as you were once asked to fight—on the beaches, in the hills, in the mountains."[15] If Baldwin and others like him "reach out" to the Communists to solve the "race problem," Buckley said, he and other American patriots would be willing to fight them to the death.

"I Think All Theories Are Suspect": Baldwin's Skepticism of Ideology

In "Down at the Cross," Baldwin describes a gripping moment in his meeting with Nation of Islam leader Elijah Muhammad. Baldwin had told Muhammad and others present at the dinner: "I left the church twenty years ago and I haven't joined anything since." In response, Muhammad asked, "And what are you now?" Baldwin admits to hesitating a bit—unwilling to be "stampeded" into saying he was still a Christian—before offering: "I'm a writer. I like doing things alone. . . . I don't, anyway, think about it a great deal." To this, Muhammad said to his followers at the table, "I think he ought to think about it *all* the deal."[16] Although Baldwin describes the scene as a relatively awkward exchange, I think it provides a revealing contrast between Baldwin's self-understanding as a "writer" and Muhammad's status as a kind of ideologue (a contrast that is similar to one that might be drawn between Baldwin and Buckley).[17] Baldwin's self-identity as a writer was deeply at odds with ideological thinking. In the "Autobiographical Notes" for his first essay collection, *Notes of a Native Son*, Baldwin set two goals for himself: "I want to be an honest man and a good writer."[18] Baldwin's pursuit of these interrelated goals led him to be deeply suspicious of ideology. Good writing, he argued throughout his life, was rooted in honesty about human experience. As a writer, he hoped to be a witness who told the truth about his own experiences and the experiences of those around him. "One writes," he declared in the "Autobiographical Notes," "out of one thing only—one's own experience."[19] Experience was the proper source of good writing, he argued, because it is the best source of truth. As he said in his opening remarks at the debate, "one's response" to questions often "depends upon where you find yourself in the world, what your system of reality is."[20] It is from this experience-based "system of reality" that Baldwin sought to engage in what he considered to be an important part of the "business of a writer"—"to examine attitudes, to go beneath the surface, to tap the source."[21] In order to accomplish these tasks, one cannot be guided by abstraction; instead, one must "trust life."[22] This idea is not just what Baldwin believed ought to guide the writer; he believed this ought to guide all human beings in their quest to discover truth.

When one trusts life, Baldwin teaches, one begins to distrust theories and ideologies. Human beings, he writes, are "raised to believe in formulas," but experience reveals to us the complexity of the world, our selves, and others. In the words of Wilson Carey McWilliams, Baldwin "regarded all ideologies as overly abstract efforts to simplify human complexity."[23] Theories and ideologies are, by design, tools to help us simplify the world. They provide us with markers, signposts, and categories that are supposed to orient us and offer us means to evaluate and, if necessary, change the world. This "passion for categorization," this desire to "have life neatly fitted into pegs," Baldwin argues in "Everybody's Protest Novel," often moves us further from the truth.[24] In a critique of the leftist writer Daniel Guérin in 1956, for example, Baldwin declared: "A man whose vision of the world remains as elementary as Mr. Guérin's can scarcely be trusted to help us understand it."[25] What one needs to tell the truth about the world is *not* ideology but rather a willingness to respond to one's experiences with intellectual honesty and dynamism. In the "Autobiographical Notes," Baldwin writes: "I think all theories are suspect, that the finest principles may have to be modified, or may even be pulverized by the demands of life, and that one must find, therefore, one's own moral center and move through the world hoping that this center will guide one aright."[26] Almost thirty years after these "Autobiographical Notes" were published, Baldwin returned to this theme during a question-and-answer session at the University of California at Berkeley: "The reason it is difficult for me sometimes to discuss my political views," he told the audience, "is because [politics demand] a vast amount of improvisation from day to day."[27] When one's assumptions and principles are "pulverized" by the ever-changing world of politics, one must be ready to adapt.

One of the remarkable things about Baldwin's suspicion of ideology is how consistently he applied it across the political spectrum. Baldwin's critical eye landed on thinkers of the Left such as Jean-Paul Sartre, Simone de Beauvoir, and Daniel Guérin as well as figures on the Right such as Barry Goldwater and Ronald Reagan, and also individuals more difficult to place on the traditional Left-Right spectrum such as Elijah Muhammad. One might wonder why Baldwin expressed such uniform concern about ideological thinking. It is important to note that his concern was not just epistemological—that ideologies can cause people to misunderstand the world—but, more importantly, that his concern was moral. Ideological thinking, Baldwin worried, provides theoretical justification for people to behave unjustly. Baldwin expressed reservations about "Sartre, de Beauvoir, and company" because it seemed to him "that ideas were somewhat more real to them than people."[28] In his discussion of Guérin, he said that while the author is surely right to identify the shortcomings of capitalism, he worried about the attitude toward other people invited by Guérin's "elementary vision of the world": "[Capitalism] may indeed be doomed, and we may all be the slothful and pussy-footing creatures [he] says we are. But his own tone is so extremely ungenerous that I cannot avoid a certain chill when I think of the probable fate of dissenters in his vari-colored brave new world."[29]

Baldwin linked his epistemological and moral concerns about ideology by saying that one of the common casualties of ideological thinking (and the righteous indignation it tends to breed) is "personal humility." Once personal humility has died, one enters "into a dialogue with that terrifying deity, sometimes called History, previously, and perhaps again to be referred to as God, to which no sacrifice in human suffering is too great."[30] Armed with ideological certainty, human beings are capable of truly terrifying things indeed.

Baldwin's encounter with Nation of Islam leader Elijah Muhammad was a complicated affair, but in his reflections on the meeting in "Down at the Cross" we can see further into the nature of his skepticism of ideology. Muhammad's "merciless formulation" of racial hierarchy was not entirely novel, Baldwin writes, but it was remarkable due to "the explicitness of its symbols and the candor of its hatred."[31] Unlike white supremacists (who will be discussed below), Muhammad and his followers in the Nation of Islam operated from a genuine sense of grievance. Nation of Islam speakers, Baldwin noted, spend "very little time" on the elaborate "theology" Muhammad developed, for one did not need to prove to a "Harlem audience that all white men were devils."[32] Baldwin himself acknowledged that he knew "through ugly experience, what [white policemen] were like when *they* held the power." He had, he said, "been carried into precinct basements often enough" to know that "when a white man faces a black man, especially if the black man is helpless, terrible things are revealed."[33] What the Nation of Islam spokesmen understood was that the "brutality with which the Negroes have been treated in this country simply cannot be overstated" and that the experiences of this brutality could leave the victim with the sense that he has nothing to lose.[34] The problem with the leaders of the Nation of Islam, Baldwin argued, lies not in their identification of grave injustice but rather in their explanation of this injustice and the path to rectification. In short, Baldwin could not accept the ideology of racial hatred and separation at the core of the Nation of Islam's philosophy because its rigid categorization and absolutism were not consistent with his experience: "Yes, I knew two or three people, white, whom I would trust with my life, and I knew a few others, white, who were struggling as hard as they knew how, and with great effort and sweat and risk, to make the world human."[35] The "glorification of one race and the consequent debasement of another" had, furthermore, been revealed by experience to be a "recipe for murder": "If one is permitted to treat any group of people with special disfavor because of their race or the color of their skin, there is no limit to what one will force them to endure, and, since the entire race has been mysteriously indicted, no reason not to attempt to destroy it root and branch."[36] As Baldwin describes his departure from Muhammad's mansion, he concludes that Elijah's perception of "reality" and his own have led them to very different conceptions of "responsibility" and that, as a result, they "would always be strangers, and possibly, one day, enemies."[37]

It is not hard to imagine that Baldwin regarded Buckley in similar fashion.[38] It is worth noting, though, that Buckley thought of himself as a skeptic of ideology. There are many examples of this in his speeches and essays, but I will limit myself to a comment he made during the Cambridge debate. Toward the end of his speech, he said: "There is no instant cure for the race problem in America. Anyone who tells you that there is a quick solution is a charlatan and ultimately a boring man—a boring man precisely because *he is then speaking in the kind of abstractions that do not relate to the human experience.* The trouble is a . . . very complicated one. I urge those of you who have an actual rather than a purely *ideologized* interest in the problem to read the book *Beyond the Melting Pot* by Professor Nathan Glazer."[39]

Based on what I have already argued and cited, it is clear that Baldwin would agree we ought to avoid "speaking in the kind of abstractions that do not relate to the human experience" and that we ought to strive to achieve something beyond an "ideologized" understanding of the "race problem" or any other problem. Despite Buckley's professions of ideological skepticism, it was he—not Baldwin—who was guilty of "ideologized" thinking on the "race problem in America." It was, furthermore, precisely by thinking in "abstractions" about the freedom and dignity of African Americans that Buckley was able to go so grievously wrong in his response to the civil rights movement.

To state it clearly: Baldwin was not a radical ideologue who wanted to bring about a complete overthrow of "American civilization." He was up to something far more interesting. Rather than rejecting Buckley's "tradition of fixed postulates" in their entirety, Baldwin asks us to go beyond blind reverence for this tradition (if it can indeed be regarded as a unitary tradition) by considering the ways in which we have failed to realize these postulates in practice and the ways in which we may need reimagine and go beyond these postulates to achieve true justice. Such a reimagining, Baldwin argued, "might bring new life to Western achievements and transform them" in valuable ways.[40] In order to illustrate and illuminate all of these claims, I now turn to how Buckley and Baldwin understood freedom.

"Freedom Is Hard to Bear": Buckley and Baldwin on the Meaning of Freedom

There is little doubt that Buckley believed Baldwin had a "cynical contempt for human freedom."[41] In what follows, I argue that Buckley was wrong. Although it is certainly true that Buckley and Baldwin understood freedom in very different ways, it would be more accurate to say that Baldwin *went beyond* Buckley's conception of freedom (as opposed to simply rejecting it). Buckley, as you will soon see, understood freedom in classical liberal or libertarian terms: to be free is to be free from interference (or coercion). The most serious threat to one's freedom, on this view, is the state. There is no evidence that Baldwin rejected freedom from interference as an important dimension of liberty. In fact, Baldwin longed for a world in which African Americans were free from unjust interference by agents of the state *and* private citizens.

And yet, while Baldwin acknowledged that freedom from interference was a necessary part of justice, he recognized that it was not sufficient for justice to be achieved. He went beyond this conception of freedom in two important ways. First, he realized that one's freedom is threatened by conditions of inequality. In other words, an individual's freedom is threatened not just by coercion but also by domination. Under conditions of significant inequality, Baldwin says, some individuals and groups are able to dominate others; under these conditions, the dominated groups cannot be said to be free. Second, Baldwin believed an individual could not truly be free unless he was free from delusion about himself, others, and history. This idea of freedom as nondelusion was at the core of Baldwin's political thought, and, I believe, it constitutes one of his most significant contributions to political theory. Baldwin's understanding of freedom is far more consistent with human dignity than the "ideologized" conception defended by Buckley.

Let us begin by considering Buckley's understanding of freedom. A "negative" conception of liberty was at the core of Buckley's conservative philosophy. In *Up from Liberalism,* he explains:

> Still, for all the confusion and contradiction, I venture to say it is possible to talk about "the conservative position" and mean something by it. At the political level, conservatives are bound together for the most part by negative response to liberalism; but altogether too much is made of that fact. Negative action is not necessarily of negative value. Political freedom's principal value is negative in character. The people are politically stirred principally by the necessity for negative affirmations. Cincinnatus was a farmer before he took up his sword, and went back to farming after wielding some highly negative strokes upon the pates of those who sought to make positive changes to his way of life.[42]

Buckley's language in this passage is very telling, and it is worth keeping in mind below when I discuss his views of the right of southerners to maintain their "way of life." Perhaps most importantly, note that Buckley identifies those who seek "to make positive changes to [one's] way of life" as significant threats to one's freedom. It was on the basis of this negative conception of liberty that Buckley rooted his view of the proper role of government: "It is the job of the centralized government (in peacetime) to protect its citizens' lives, liberty, and property. All other activities of government tend to diminish freedom and hamper progress. The growth of government (the dominant social feature of this century) must be fought relentlessly. In this great social conflict of the era, [the *National Review* is], without reservations, on the libertarian side."[43] Just as Cincinnatus was prepared to wield his sword to defend his "way of life" against those who sought to make "positive changes" to it, this negative conception of freedom must have been in Buckley's mind when he promised, in the debate with Baldwin, to take to the hillsides and the beaches to defend "the best features of the American way of life."[44]

Although Buckley imagined he might have to take up arms against those who followed Baldwin down the path of radical despair (and hence, in Buckley's mind, rejected liberty), there is little evidence to suggest that Baldwin objected to the idea of liberty as noninterference. To the contrary, Baldwin wanted to achieve a world in which African Americans were free from the interference of both state and nonstate actors. In "Down at the Cross," Baldwin makes this point clear: "they, the blacks, simply don't wish to be beaten over the head by the whites every instant of our brief passage on this planet."[45] Baldwin's writings are rife with examples of both state actors and private citizens interfering with African American liberty. American society would be making a long stride toward justice, Baldwin counseled, if all people were free from unjust interference. As Baldwin told a congressional committee in 1969: "That is all the Negro wants: his autonomy. Nobody hates you. The time is far gone for that. I simply want to live my life."[46]

But Baldwin's understanding of freedom went *beyond* negative liberty in significant and compelling ways.[47] In a 1964 essay called "The White Problem," Baldwin argues that "liberty" and "freedom" ought to be distinguished from each other. "Liberty," he writes, "is a genuine political possibility, in spite of the fact that the word is so often used as a slogan," and "freedom" is "beyond politics, though affecting politics and affected by" politics.[48] The liberty that is a "genuine political possibility" is the freedom from interference described above as well as the equal right to participate in self-government. Freedom, on the other hand, is something very different in Baldwin's political thought. For Baldwin, true freedom is the liberation from delusion about oneself, others, and history. By "delusion," I mean nothing more than the dictionary definition: "an erroneous belief that is held in the face of evidence to the contrary."[49] Without this kind of freedom—what I am calling "freedom as nondelusion"—"liberty and justice for all" will remain but a dream.

Before proceeding to an extensive discussion of Baldwin's understanding of freedom as nondelusion, though, a brief word must be said about his appreciation for ways in which domination threatens freedom. Although freedom from interference was important to Baldwin, an individual free from interference is not yet free. One of the remaining threats to this individual's freedom is domination. According to the theory of freedom as nondomination, "liberty might best be understood as a sort of structural relationship that exists between persons or groups, rather than as a contingent event."[50] A structural relationship can threaten a person's freedom if he is subject to the "arbitrary or uncontrolled power" of another person or group.[51] The dominant person or group need not actually interfere with an individual to deprive him of his freedom; the power of the dominant person or group might be so great that intentional or explicit interference is not a necessary ingredient of their ability to control others.

There are many examples of Baldwin discussing freedom in language that evokes the idea of nondomination. Perhaps the most powerful passage comes from an essay about his journeys through the South called "Take Me to the Water": "I remember the Reverend S., for example, a small, pale man, with hair resembling charred popcorn, and his tiny church, in a tiny town, where every black man was owned by a white man. In democratic parlance, of course, one says that every black man *worked* for a white man, and the democratic myth wishes us to believe that they worked together as men, and respected and honored and loved each other as men."[52] It is worth pausing for a moment here to take note of the "democratic myth." I will discuss the ways in which myths and illusions threaten freedom below, but for the time being, note what the democratic myth conceals. The recognition of the nature of such myths is central to Baldwin's idea of freedom as nondelusion (and its connection to the idea of freedom as nondomination). Here is how Baldwin proceeded in the passage: "But the democratic circumlocution pretends a level of liberty which does not exist and cannot exist until slavery in America comes to an end: in those towns, in those days, to speak only of the towns, and only of those days, a black man who displeased his employers was not going to eat for very long, which meant that neither he, nor his wife, nor children, were intended to live for very long."[53] If we accept only the idea of liberty as noninterference, then the black man described in the passage must be considered free. There is no indication that his employer is coercing him and he is "free" to leave the job (and the town for that matter) at will. Baldwin captures the idea of nondomination when he says we must "pretend" a "level of liberty which does not exist" to accept that this black man is truly free. When Baldwin looks at the situation of this man, he does not see freedom; he sees slavery.[54] What would Buckley see?

Baldwin's attentiveness to the impact that systemic inequality and domination can have on individual freedom is the first way in which he goes beyond Buckley's understanding of freedom as noninterference. In addition, the example cited above directs us to the idea Baldwin usually had in mind when he spoke of freedom: freedom as nondelusion. In "Take Me to the Water," Baldwin says the "democratic *myth*" asks to imagine these two human beings worked together as equals, but this myth "*pretends* a level of liberty which does not exist." This language of "myth" and "pretending" invites us to think about freedom in a different way. When Baldwin discusses freedom (or liberation), more often than not he has in mind the idea of a human being who has come to grips with a truth—an individual, in other words, who has come to *recognize* the erroneousness of a belief by accepting compelling evidence that undermines that belief. This is an extraordinarily demanding conception of freedom, which is rarely pursued or achieved. If it is achieved, it can only be achieved in a limited way, for a limited amount of time. One does not, on this conception, *become* free and stay that way; one must constantly *strive* to be free. It is precisely because freedom, as Baldwin understands it, is so difficult and uncomfortable that *most* people have no interest in pursuing it. In the passage from "The White Problem" quoted above, recall that Baldwin distinguishes between "liberty," which he calls a "genuine political possibility," and "freedom," which he says is "beyond politics, though affecting politics and affected by it." In that passage, he goes on to say that freedom "may be the very last thing that people want. The very last thing."[55] This echoes a line from "Down at the Cross" in which he offers a more detailed explanation of both the symbiotic relationship between freedom and politics *and* the idea that freedom is not something most people want: "I have met only a very few people—and most of these were not Americans—who had any real desire to be free. Freedom is hard to bear. It can be objected that I am speaking of political freedom in spiritual terms, but the political institutions of any nation are always menaced and ultimately controlled by the spiritual state of that nation."[56] As you will see in great detail below, freedom is hard to bear because it requires us to rise from a soothing state of delusion into the world of truth.[57] This is upsetting precisely because it forces us to confront truths about ourselves, and our society, that we would rather not acknowledge. These truths, Baldwin argues, will in all likelihood force us to rethink the core of our identity. Freedom, thus understood, affects politics and is affected by politics in myriad ways. Consider, for example, the discussion of noninterference and nondomination above. Freedom as nondelusion is related to these other concepts of freedom in a very important way. If we are not striving to be free from delusion, Baldwin teaches, we are more likely to accept a society in which individuals are subject to unjust interference and arbitrary domination. The failure to pursue freedom from delusion was (and is) largely to blame for the acquiescence of many Americans while their black fellow countrymen were (and are) subject to great injustice.

Freedom as nondelusion is a capacious and complex idea in Baldwin's thought, and here I would like to consider it in a systematic way. In order to do so, I seek to answer three questions. First, what delusions are preventing Americans from being free? Second, why do Americans cling to these delusions? Third, what does Baldwin prescribe to liberate Americans from delusion? Although Baldwin's idea of freedom as nondelusion has implications beyond the American "racial nightmare," I will limit my discussion to this problem since it was at the center of his disagreement with Buckley.

The Great American Illusion: Baldwin on the Nature of Our Delusions

In the penultimate line of "My Dungeon Shook," Baldwin tells his nephew: "We cannot be free until they are free."[58] This sentence directs us to the primary and most urgent task of liberation from delusion: to inspire those with power to free themselves from their "striking addiction to irreality."[59] In the American context, this addiction to irreality is fed and reinforced by "that collection of myths to which white Americans cling": "that their ancestors were all freedom-loving heroes, that they were born in the greatest country the world has ever seen, or that Americans are invincible in battle and wise in peace, that Americans have always dealt honorably with Mexicans and Indians and all other neighbors or inferiors, that American men are the world's most direct and virile, that American women are pure."[60] Baldwin argued that the power of this collection of myths was immense.

Underlying Baldwin's argument here is his conviction in the power of myths, more generally speaking. Myths, Baldwin taught, not only serve to delude those who believe in them but also contain the seeds of their own perpetuation. In the 1964 essay "Nothing Personal," Baldwin says it is "in the very nature of myth" to lead its "victims" and "perpetrators" to be "rendered unable to examine the myth, or even to suspect, much less recognize, that is a myth which controls and blasts their lives."[61] To be in the grip of myth is, in Baldwin's words, to be "locked in the past": "To be locked in the past means, in effect, that one has no past, since one can never assess it, or use it: and if one cannot use the past, one cannot function in the present, and so one can never be free. I take this to be, as I say, the American situation in relief, the root of our unadmitted sorrow, and the very key to our crisis."[62] Baldwin's critique here differs significantly from one that holds that the "dead hand of the past" prevents us from being free. To the contrary, Baldwin is making clear that "the past" has an important role to play in our quest for freedom. But the past can only be useful if we demythologize it. I will return to the role of history in the process of liberation below, but for the time being it is important to note that danger is presented by "the past" only if we pretend that it is something other than what it really is.

Baldwin's sense of the power of myth should now be evident, but more must be said on the function that myth plays in deluding us. Myth, Baldwin argues, allows us to engage in "moral evasion."[63] The "collection of myths" to which we "cling" function as ideological weapons we use to ward off taking responsibility for ourselves—as individuals and as communities. In the American case in particular, these myths serve not only as defensive weapons but also as the source of irrational exuberance about our virtue as individuals and our "exceptionalism" as a nation.

The relevance of this idea to the "race problem" is obvious enough. The American myth prevents us from authentic appreciation of the history of African Americans. The mythologized narrative emphasizes the ways in which slaveholders like Thomas Jefferson agonized over slavery while he wrote so eloquently of universal natural rights, the unfortunate "compromises" that allowed slavery into the Constitution, the triumphant "Second American Revolution" brought about by the Civil War that allowed us to "complete the Constitution" by allowing African Americans a place at the political table, etc. What this mythologized narrative ignores or downplays is not only the "bloody catalogue of [racial] oppression" but also the heroic struggle of African Americans in the face of this oppression.[64] In "Down at the Cross," Baldwin explains:

> This past, the Negro's past, of rope, fire, torture, castration, infanticide, rape; death and humiliation; fear by day and night, fear as deep as the marrow of the bone; doubt that he was worthy of life, since everyone around him denied it; sorrow for his women, for his kinfolk, for his children, who needed his protection, and whom he could not protect; rage, hatred, and murder, hatred of white men so deep that it often turned against him and his own, and made all love, all trust, all joy impossible—this past, this endless struggle to achieve and reveal and confirm a human identity, human authority, yet contains, for all its horror, something very beautiful.[65]

I return to the beauty Baldwin finds in this past later, but for the time being I wish to reiterate the precise nature of his argument about the delusion that haunts Americans in the context of the race problem: Americans cannot be free, he contends, until they come to grips with the history and present reality of race in this country. If we are honest with ourselves about this history, we can begin the process of freeing ourselves from delusion. In an essay called "The White Man's Guilt" that was published just a few months after his debate with Buckley, Baldwin describes the intimate connection between history and freedom as nondelusion. It is mere speculation to say so, but perhaps Buckley was the "white man" (or one of the white men) Baldwin had in mind when he wrote these words: "White man, hear me! History, as nearly no one seems to know, is not merely something to be read. And it does not refer merely, or even principally, to the past. On the contrary, the great force of history comes from the fact that we carry it within us, are unconsciously controlled by it in many ways, and history is literally *present* in all that we do. It could scarcely be otherwise, since it is to history that we owe our frames of reference, our identities, and our aspirations."[66] In this passage, Baldwin reconstructs and expands upon his opening statement in the Cambridge debate in which he said that "one's system of reality" was, in large part, determined by one's point of view. He then proceeded to make plain just how seriously he took the idea that history is *"present"* in all that we do by saying: "I am speaking now very seriously, and this is not an overstatement: *I* picked the cotton, *I* carried it

                                                        Nicholas Buccola

to the market, *I* built the railroads under someone else's whip for nothing. For nothing."[67] The political, social, moral, and economic implications of this connection between history and identity are profound. We cannot even begin to approach freedom until we reflect on how history has shaped our understanding of, to borrow Buckley's language, "the meaning of existence," "the relationship of the individual to the state," and "of the individual to his neighbor."[68]

In *The Fire Next Time* (which contains "My Dungeon Shook" and "Down at the Cross"), Baldwin masterfully weaves autobiography, social criticism, moral philosophy, and political theory. One of the most powerful strategies Baldwin employs in the book is to utilize his discussion of the mythology and ideology of the Nation of Islam as a way to nudge white readers to reflect on the relationship between their own mythologies and ideologies. Baldwin knew that most white readers would find "the truth" that was promoted by Elijah Muhammad to be absurd. Here is Baldwin's description of that "truth":

> The truth is that at the very beginning of time there was not one white face to be found in all the universe. Black men ruled the earth and the black man was perfect. This is the truth concerning the era that white men now refer to as prehistoric. They want black men to believe that they, like white men, once lived in caves and swung from trees and ate their meat raw and did not have the power of speech. But this is not true. Black men were never in such a condition. Allah allowed the Devil, through his scientists, to carry on infernal experiments, which resulted, finally, in the creation of the devil known as the white man.[69]

This mythology served as the basis for Elijah Muhammad's claim that there is "by definition, no virtue in white people." In other words, this mythology served as foundation of Muhammad's ideology of black supremacy. Baldwin knew that his white readers would regard this mythology (and the resulting ideology) to be delusional. But he hoped they would go a step further by recognizing that it is not any more delusional than the mythologies to which they cling that allow them—in direct and indirect ways—to embrace white supremacy. "An invented past," Baldwin concludes, "can never be used; it cracks and crumbles under the pressures of life like clay in a season of drought."[70]

Why Do Americans Cling to Delusion? Or, Why Don't Americans Want to Be Free?

Baldwin's idea of freedom as nondelusion presents each of us with a most unwelcome invitation. What he is asking us to do is to confront what he promises will be some very uncomfortable truths. If we are honest with ourselves about history, we are likely to discover things that, if taken seriously, will force us to rethink our identities and our relationships with other people. In "White Man's Guilt," Baldwin describes the existential confrontation that one invites when one strives to be free:

> It is with great pain and terror that one begins to realize [that history is literally *present* in all that we do]. In great pain and terror one begins to assess the history which has placed one where one is, and formed one's point of view. In great pain and terror because, thereafter, one enters into battle with that historical creation, Oneself, and attempts to re-create oneself according to a principle more human and more liberating: one begins that attempt to achieve a level of personal maturity and freedom which robs history of its tyrannical power, and also changes history.[71]

The historical creation "Oneself" is "locked in the past" by a mythologized understanding of the past and, hence, an inability to achieve the critical distance necessary to assess it.[72] We are reluctant to seek this critical distance because we are terrified by what we might see.

The "race problem" in the United States was, of course, at the center of Baldwin's mind as he formulated these ideas. Rather than viewing white supremacists and indifferent whites as fundamentally evil, he viewed them as terrified.[73] These individuals are terrified—and have no desire to be free—because their identity is rooted in their sense of relative status, where status is invariably racialized. In a 1956 essay called "Faulkner and Desegregation," Baldwin opens the piece with an explanation of this idea: "Any real change implies the breakup of the world as one has always known it, the loss of all that gave one an identity, the end of safety. And at such a moment, unable to see and not daring to imagine what the future will now bring forth, one clings to what one knew, or thought one knew; to what one possessed or dreamed one possessed."[74] Baldwin returned to this idea in his opening remarks at the Cambridge debate when he said that the "white

South African or Mississippi sharecropper or Alabama sheriff has at bottom a system of reality" that leads him to view an African American demanding an end to racial oppression as "insane." After all, one would have to be insane "to attack the system to which he owes his entire identity."[75] If someone comes along and challenges the legitimacy of this order, our first reaction might be to treat them as out of touch with reality. The whites Baldwin is describing have fallen into "the stunning and intricate trap of believing that they *deserve* their fate, and their comparative safety," and they cannot imagine how any sane person would question what is rightfully theirs.[76]

Race has a special place in the annals of American status anxiety.[77] In a 1960 lecture at Kalamazoo College entitled "In Search of a Majority," Baldwin explains:

> Some of the [reasons for racial oppression] are social, and these reasons are more important [than political or economic reasons] because they have to do with our social panic, with our fear of losing status. This really amounts sometimes to a kind of social paranoia. One cannot afford to lose status on this peculiar ladder, for the prevailing notion of American life seems to involve a kind of rung-by-rung ascension to some hideously desirable state. If this is one's concept of life, obviously one cannot afford to slip back one rung. When one slips, one slips back not a rung but back into chaos and no longer knows what he is. And this reason, this fear, suggests to me one of the real reasons for the status of the Negro in this country. In a way, the Negro tells us where the bottom is: *because he is there,* and *where* he is, beneath us, we know where the limits are and how far we must not fall.[78]

Baldwin's "bottom rung" explanation of the status of African Americans has something to do with power and something to do with psychology. There is obviously much that white people have gained (and continue to gain)—politically, economically, and socially—through the subordination of African Americans. But Baldwin argues that this is only part of the story and perhaps not the most important part. Racial subordination plays a crucial psychological role: the delusion of racial supremacy allows us to escape from freedom.

As Baldwin explained in the "In Search of a Majority" lecture, "if the Negro were not here, we might be forced to deal within ourselves and our own personalities, with all those vices, all those conundrums, and all those mysteries with which we have invested the Negro race."[79] As Baldwin says in "Down at the Cross," "identity is *almost* impossible to achieve" where "people are perpetually attempting to find their feet on the shifting sands of status."[80] This is why "the Negro" plays such a crucial function as "the bottom rung." Although the sands of status are constantly shifting, the black man "has functioned in the white man's world . . . as an immovable pillar: and as he moves out of his place, heaven and earth are shaken to their foundations."[81] When "the Negro" moves from "his place," Baldwin argues, all who have relied on his subjection for so long would be forced to engage in a process of introspection that would put them on the path to that terrifying thing called freedom. In a country where "the delusion of white supremacy" is sewn into the social fabric, Baldwin said late in his life, "any real concept of education" is as "remote" and "feared" as "freedom itself."[82] Remote and feared though it may be, education is our only hope.

Liberation by Education: Baldwin on the Educative Function of History and Creativity

The roots at the foundation of American delusion are very strong indeed. Our identities rest comfortably in the hammock of delusion, and the last thing we want is to leave this comfort and ascend into the terrifying realm of true freedom. But this, Baldwin hopes, is precisely what we will do.

Near the end of the Cambridge debate, Buckley claimed that Baldwin was a prophet of despair, but this is yet another thing the young conservative got wrong about the young writer. Baldwin was asked throughout his life if he was in despair over the racial situation in the United States. Despair, Baldwin consistently said, is not an option. In order to live, he believed, one must have hope. "It is necessary, while in darkness," he wrote in 1964, "to know that there is light somewhere, to know that in oneself, waiting to be found, there is light."[83] Baldwin's hope rested on the idea that no matter how "dismal and shocking" human nature appears to be, "people can be better than they are."[84] As he told an audience of high school students in 1963, although people do many wicked things, we cannot allow ourselves to conclude that they are, at their core, wicked.[85] People can be made better, he believed, through education. The "purpose of education," Baldwin wrote in 1963, "is to create in a person the ability to look at the world for himself, to make his own decisions" because "to ask questions of the universe, and then learn to live with those questions, is the way he achieves his own identity."[86] Through the process of introspection and critical examination of the world, Baldwin hoped, individuals might achieve identities of their own.

The language of *achievement* is significant here. To achieve an authentic identity, one cannot simply accept one's identity and status as given; one must be willing to ask hard questions about oneself and society. The process of education (and liberation) by introspection is an intensely "complex, difficult—and private—thing," but Baldwin did believe there are two things essential to this process of achieving freedom from delusion: coming to grips with history and exercising creativity.

One of the most fascinating commonalities between Buckley and Baldwin was their shared belief in the importance of history. When Buckley spoke of "the faith of our fathers," our "tradition of fixed postulates," the "organic moral order," and "our civilization," he was drawing on a core tenet of the conservative worldview. In the words of his *National Review* colleague Russell Kirk, conservatives believe in "the principle of prescription," which he described as "things established by immemorial usage." In politics, Kirk taught, "we would do well to abide by precedent and precept and even prejudice" because the accumulated wisdom of history provides us with a "prescriptive wisdom far greater than any man's petty rationality."[87]

Buckley applied the conservative principle of prescription to the race question in two primary ways. First, he argued that we ought to feel constrained by the "enabling documents of our Republic" in our responses to the question. Whatever the virtues of desegregation, for example, Buckley argued that federal promotion of desegregation should be opposed because it is inconsistent with the American Constitution.[88] The Constitution, he believed, was a wise document that has proved its worth in part by withstanding the test of time. But perhaps more interestingly, Buckley relied on the language of "civilization" to articulate how the past ought to inform the present. Most infamously, Buckley and his colleagues at *National Review* penned an editorial in 1957 entitled "Why the South Must Prevail."[89] In this essay, Buckley argued that the "central question" raised by the civil rights struggle is not "answered by merely consulting a catalogue of the rights of American citizens, born Equal." Instead, the central question "is whether the White community in the South is entitled to take such measures as are necessary to prevail, politically and culturally, in areas in which it does not dominate numerically?" The "sobering answer," he declared, "is *Yes*—the White community is so entitled because, for the time being, it is the advanced race."[90] It "is more important," he continued, "for any community . . . to affirm to live by civilized standards, than to bow to the demands of the numerical majority." White southerners, he concluded, have the right to maintain their political and cultural superiority rather than to allow "Negro backwardness" to take power.[91] There are so many startling things about this editorial that one hardly knows where to begin. Since my primary focus is on Baldwin, I will say only two things about the ideas expressed by Buckley et al. that can be most usefully contrasted with Baldwin's view of the educative potential of history.

First, note the invisibility of African Americans implied by the title and arguments of the editorial. "The South" that must prevail does not seem to include black southerners. They are, quite literally, not a part (or at least not a significant part) of the southern "civilization" as Buckley understands it. Second, note the fact that according to Buckley's view of the prescriptive value of history, "civilization" trumps the principles expressed in the "enabling documents of our Republic." Recall that in the Cambridge debate, Buckley accused Baldwin of aspiring to convince Americans to "desert the constitutional system" and "the idea of the individual rights of the American citizen."[92] Although there is no evidence that this was indeed Baldwin's aspiration, Buckley's argument in "Why the South Must Prevail" reveals how quickly Buckley himself was willing to desert the "catalogue of the rights of American citizens" and the idea that we are "born Equal" in the name of some mythic and amorphous "civilization."

It is not hard to imagine how Baldwin might respond to these two ideas, but that imagining sheds light on the nature of Baldwin's understanding of the educative potential of history. First, consider the invisibility of African Americans in Buckley's view of "the South." This is a clear manifestation of the American myth discussed above. "The South," in Buckley's mind, consisted of the white South. The "Negro" exists, from this perspective, not as a human being but as "a problem." I will return to the perils of this way of thinking later in this essay, but for the time being I would like to say something about how problematic it is *as an understanding of history.* History can only educate and liberate us *if* we read it with open eyes. In "The White Man's Guilt," Baldwin puts it this way: "The record is there for all to read. . . . It might as well be written on the sky. One wishes that Americans . . . would read, for their own sakes, this record, and stop defending themselves against it. Only then will they be enabled to change their lives."[93] How can an honest reading of history enable us to change our lives? For one thing, Baldwin believes we must come to grips with the role oppression has played in our political, economic, moral, religious, and psychological development. When one comes to grips with history, one begins to see that the hierarchies that exist have not been ordained by God, established by nature, or produced by merit. Through the examination of history, Baldwin hopes, we will get a sense of our "inescapable responsibility" for the world in which we live.[94] Baldwin was not interested in making people feel guilty but rather in making people feel responsible. In a 1964 essay entitled "Words of a Native Son," Baldwin explained: "Please take note. I'm not interested in anybody's guilt. Guilt is a luxury that we can no longer afford. I know you didn't do it, and I didn't do it either, but I am responsible for it because I am a man and a citizen of this country and you are responsible for it, too, for the very same reason: As long as my children face the future they face, and come to the ruin that they come to, your children are very greatly in danger, too."[95] When we begin to appreciate the inescapability of responsibility we have for our history, we move closer to Baldwin's understanding of freedom as nondelusion.

The invisibility of African Americans in Buckley's vision of "the South" is offensive to Baldwin's view of history in another way. The turn to history is not just liberating because it forces us to take responsibility for things we would rather ignore. The turn to history can also be liberating because it reminds us that human beings are capable of great things. By ignoring the existence (in a meaningful way) of African Americans in the South, Buckley missed the very best that southern "civilization" had to offer. In "Down at the Cross," Baldwin argues that the "Negro boys and girls who are facing mobs today come out of a long line of improbable aristocrats—the only genuine aristocrats this country has ever produced." These civil rights activists are the inheritors of a tradition that includes the "unsung army of black men and women" who have managed to live and struggle and love and create in the face of unspeakable horrors are, in a real way, the very best thing this country has created. As we look to the past for positive guidance for how we ought to live, Baldwin argues that these "improbable aristocrats" would be a good place to start.[96]

The second point from "Why the South Must Prevail" that Baldwin would find deeply objectionable is Buckley's jettisoning of the guidance provided by "the enabling documents of our Republic." In his references to the "catalogue" of American rights and the idea that all men were "born Equal," Buckley quickly dismisses the Constitution and the Declaration of Independence as relevant historical guides to how we should behave in the present. Given the stark contrast Buckley seeks to draw in the debate between himself as the defender of American civilization and Baldwin as its would-be overthrower, it is telling that we should find Baldwin, not Buckley, appealing to the enabling documents of the American republic in response to the race problem. In "Nobody Knows My Name," Baldwin reveals just how seriously he takes the relevance of the *principles* enunciated in the Declaration.

> Human freedom is a complex, difficult—and private—thing. If we can liken life, for a moment, to a furnace, then freedom is the fire which burns away illusion. Any honest examination of the national life proves how far we are from the standard of human freedom with which we began. The recovery of this standard demands of everyone who loves this country a hard look at himself, for the greatest achievements must begin somewhere, and they always begin with the person. If we are not capable of this examination, we may yet become one of the most distinguished and monumental failures in the history of nations.[97]

Baldwin was under no illusion about the Declaration of Independence or those who signed it. He made very clear that he did not believe the document was meant to include him, and he also believed the document was "more commercial than moral."[98] In the passage quoted above, though, it is difficult to imagine what he could have had in mind when he appealed to "the standard of human freedom with which we [as a nation] began" other than the *principles* enunciated in the famous second paragraph of the Declaration of Independence: "We hold these truths to be self-evident, that all men are created equal, that they are endowed by their creator with certain inalienable Rights; that among these are the rights to Life, Liberty, and the pursuit of Happiness."[99] Rather than simply celebrating the enunciation of these principles and pretending that they have been the animating principles of our history, Baldwin urges the "recovery of this standard" so that we might use it as a lens through which to take "a hard look" at ourselves. This is what is demanded of "everyone who loves this country"; this is true patriotism.

In order to make this "standard of human freedom" meaningful in our own time, Baldwin says we must be creative. As we attempt to free ourselves from delusions we hold about our selves and our society, we cannot simply regurgitate the ideas expressed in the Declaration. In order to "bring new life" to principles like those expressed in the Declaration and "transform" them to make them meaningful in the present, we must engage our creative faculties.[100] Although coming to grips with history can provide human beings with a sense of their "inescapable responsibility" for themselves and society and can provide human beings with "standards" and "models" of how one ought to live, creativity is needed to "conquer the great wilderness" of the self and "to illuminate that darkness, blaze roads through that vast forest" in order "to make the world a more human dwelling place."[101] In order to conquer the wilderness within and discover the beauty of our lives, Baldwin argues, we must liberate ourselves from the delusions—the "totems, taboos, crosses, blood sacrifices, steeples, mosques, races, armies, flags, [and] nations"—that "imprison" us.[102] It is only if we are able to accomplish this individually that we will be able to achieve the social transformation necessary to "achieve our country" and "make the world a more human dwelling place."[103] Creativity is essential to this process of liberation because in order to transcend these things, we must be able to imagine a world in which we no longer need them to sustain our identities.

In order to bring out more fully what Baldwin means by creativity, I want to consider the ideal of "the artist" he sketches in "The Creative Process." Although Baldwin does not expect all of us to *become* artists, he did believe that there is much all of us can learn from the artist about seeking freedom and living well. The "artist is present," Baldwin writes, "to correct" our "delusions" about reality. This is his "purpose," and he "cannot allow any consideration to supersede his responsibility to reveal all that he can possibly discover concerning the mystery of the human being."[104] The nature of the artist's responsibility puts him at odds with society in a fundamental way. In his quest to reveal all that he can about the "mystery of the human being," he must subject many social ideals and institutions to vigorous scrutiny. The artist must "never cease warring with [society], for its sake and for his own"; his obligation is to "drive to the heart of every answer and expose the question the answer hides."[105] The artist, Baldwin says, is engaged in a project that is beyond and against ideologies. Indeed, he must seek to "defeat all labels and complicate all battles."[106] As noted above, Baldwin believes all of these things to be essential to the vocation of the artist, but they are not solely the artist's province. As he explained in a 1963 essay called "A Talk to Teachers," the duty to "ask questions of the universe, and then to learn to live with those questions" is the responsibility of all human beings, and the "obligation of anyone who thinks of himself as responsible is to examine society and try to change it and to fight it—at no matter what risk."[107]

What might Buckley make of Baldwin's praise of the artist as a freedom fighter in the battle against delusion? A few months after the Cambridge debate, Buckley penned a second "On the Right" column in order to critique Baldwin. In this column, Buckley conceded that Baldwin was a "fine writer" but added that his "reputation" had also been earned due to "implacability of his theme (Hate the System)."[108] In the same column, Buckley accused Baldwin of leading a "coterie of America-haters" whose principal strategy is to threaten "us" whenever "we disagree with whatever poetical locution he comes up with concerning the delinquencies of the white people in this country."[109] This echoed Buckley's theme in the debate: Baldwin loathes our society and would like to see it altered beyond recognition. Buckley's likely response to Baldwin's conception of "the artist" would be to condemn it as more rabble-rousing and system-hating nonsense.

In "The Creative Process," Baldwin anticipates and responds to criticisms like those raised by Buckley in the debate and in his "On the Right" columns. As noted above, Baldwin pits the artist against "society" in a perpetual war. To be at war with "society" is, in an important sense, to be at war with conservatives, who take as their purpose the conservation of "the best features" of the society. What Buckley did not understand about Baldwin was that his embrace of the artist was not rooted in hatred, but in love.[110] "Societies never know it," he concludes in "The Creative Process," but "the war of an artist with his society is a lover's war, and he does, at his best, what lovers do, which is to reveal the beloved to himself, and with that revelation, make freedom real."[111] It is precisely because "I love America more than any other country in the world," Baldwin once declared, "and, exactly for this reason, I insist on the right to criticize her perpetually."[112]

Conclusion: "A Man Is a Man, a Woman Is a Woman, a Child Is a Child"

In 1956, Baldwin published a remarkable essay entitled "Faulkner and Desegregation." In the essay, Baldwin describes the novelist William

Faulkner's explanation of what he believes to be his "middle of the road" position on desegregation. Faulkner thought his position was moderate because it was situated between what he perceived to be the extreme views espoused by the White Citizens' Council on one side and the National Association for the Advancement of Colored People on the other. From this "middle of the road" position, Faulkner encouraged his fellow countrymen to "go slow" on the segregation question because, although the segregationist position is "wrong and untenable," it is "not wise to keep an emotional people off balance." Faulkner said all of this while at the same time speaking of the indestructibility of man, which is rooted in his "simple will to freedom."[113] In response to this, Baldwin argued that it would be easy to dismiss Faulkner as a mere hypocrite. But this would be a mistake. Faulkner "is not being hypocritical. . . . [He] means everything he says, means them all at once, and with very nearly the same intensity."[114] Faulkner, Buckley, and other defenders of the racial status quo, cling "to two entirely antithetical doctrines, two legends, two histories": the "beliefs and principles expressed in the Constitution" and a system of "naked and brutal oppression."[115]

How are we to explain this apparent paradox? Baldwin says the explanation is simple: for Faulkner, Buckley, and others like them, "Man is one thing, . . . and the Negroes . . . are quite another."[116] This is the delusion from which Americans most urgently need to be liberated. We must come to realize the simple but profound truth that a "man is a man, a woman is a woman, a child is a child."[117] This recognition of equal human dignity is an essential step toward meaningful liberation.

Notes

This project would not have been possible without the research and editorial assistance of Maggie Hawkins. I would also like to thank Emily Buccola, Rich Schmidt, and Ellie Forness for their assistance with this project.

1. "The American Dream," *New York Times Magazine*, March 7, 1965, 32. This is a "slightly condensed" transcript of the Cambridge Union debate between Baldwin and Buckley. Hereafter this transcript will be cited as "American Dream," *NYT Sunday Magazine*, followed by the page number.

2. James Baldwin, "The American Dream and the American Negro," in *Collected Essays*, ed. Toni Morrison (New York: Literary Classics of the United States, 1998), 714.

3. Carl Bogus, *William F. Buckley and the Rise of American Conservatism* (New York: Bloomsbury, 2011), 171.

4. "The American Dream," *NYT Sunday Magazine*, 88.

5. *National Review*, "Our Mission Statement," November 19, 1955.

6. It should be noted that later in his life Buckley did recant some of his views on race and civil rights. When asked by *Time* magazine if the passage of time had caused him to rethink any of his previously stated views, Buckley answered: "Yes. I once believed we could evolve our way up from Jim Crow. I was wrong: federal intervention was necessary." As qtd. in Bogus, *William F. Buckley and the Rise of American Conservatism*, 173.

7. "The American Dream," *NYT Sunday Magazine*, 87.

8. William F. Buckley, "On the Right: The Negro & the American Dream," April 6, 1965, syndicated column.

9. William F. Buckley, "Negroes' Cause Harmed by Extreme Militancy," June 18, 1965, syndicated column.

10. "The American Dream," *NYT Sunday Magazine*, 87–88.

11. "Our Mission Statement," *National Review*, November 19, 1955.

12. "The American Dream," *NYT Sunday Magazine*, 88.

13. Ibid.

14. Buckley, "Negroes' Cause Harmed by Extreme Militancy," June 18, 1965. For more on this column and the joint television appearance that inspired it, see W. J. Weatherby, *James Baldwin: Artist on Fire* (New York: Dell, 1989), 312–13; and David Leeming, *James Baldwin: A Biography* (New York: Penguin, 1994), 249.

15. "The American Dream," *NYT Sunday Magazine*, 88.

16. Ibid., 327.

17. By ideology, I have in mind the definition provided by political theorists Terence Ball and Richard Dagger: a "set of ideas" that helps its adherent "explain" the political world, that helps its adherents "evaluate" the political world, that "orients" adherents as to where they fit within the political world, and that provides its adherents with a program to change the political world (see, generally, Terence Ball and Richard Dagger, *Ideologies and the Democratic Ideal* [New York: Pearson, 2010], chap. 1).

18. James Baldwin, "Autobiographical Notes," in *Collected Essays*, ed. Morrison, 9.

19. Ibid., 8.

20. Baldwin, "The American Dream and the American Negro," in *Collected Essays*, ed. Morrison, 714.

21. Baldwin, "Autobiographical Notes," in *Collected Essays*, ed. Morrison, 7.

22. James Baldwin, "The White Man's Guilt," in *Collected Essays*, ed. Morrison, 727.

23. Wilson Carey McWilliams, "*Go Tell It on the Mountain:* James Baldwin and the Politics of Faith," in this volume, 195; originally published in *Democracy's Literature*, ed. Patrick Deneen and Joseph Romance (Lanham, MD: Rowman and Littlefield, 2005), 153. Baldwin biographer David Leeming reached a similar conclusion: "Baldwin was never a believer in ideology" (Leeming, *James Baldwin: A Biography* [New York: Penguin, 1994], 294).

24. James Baldwin, "The New Lost Generation," in *Collected Essays*, ed. Morrison, 662.

25. James Baldwin, "The Crusade of Indignation," in *Collected Essays*, ed. Morrison, 608.

26. Baldwin, "Autobiographical Notes," in *Collected Essays*, ed. Morrison, 9.

27. James Baldwin, Questions and Answers, Wheeler Auditorium, UC–Berkeley, April 26, 1974.

28. James Baldwin, "Alas, Poor Richard," in *Collected Essays*, ed. Morrison, 249.

29. Baldwin, "The Crusade of Indignation," in *Collected Essays*, ed. Morrison, 607. It is worth noting that later in life, Baldwin did become sufficiently convinced of the shortcomings of capitalism that he accepted "the necessity of establishing a form of socialism in this country." Baldwin's discussions of such an alternative, though, are always tentative and nondoctrinaire: such a system would have to be "an indigenous socialism, formed by, and responding to, the real needs of the American people" (see James Baldwin, "To Be Baptized," in *Collected Essays*, ed. Morrison, 461).

30. Baldwin, "The Crusade of Indignation," in *Collected Essays*, ed. Morrison, 609.

31. Baldwin, "Down at the Cross," in *Collected Essays*, ed. Morrison, 325.

32. Ibid., 315.

33. Ibid., 315, 317.

34. Ibid., 326.

35. Ibid., 328.

36. Ibid., 334.

37. Ibid., 332.

38. I will not address Baldwin's critiques of white supremacy or conservatism here since these will be discussed below.

39. "The American Dream," *NYT Sunday Magazine*, March 6, 1965, 88; emphasis mine.

40. Baldwin, "Down at the Cross," in *Collected Essays*, ed. Morrison, 340.

41. "Our Mission Statement," *National Review*, November 19, 1955.

42. William F. Buckley, "The Conservative Position" (an excerpt from *Up from Liberalism*), in *Athwart History*, ed. Roger Kimball (New York: Encounter, 2010), 14.

43. "Our Mission Statement," *National Review*, November 19, 1955.

44. "The American Dream," *NYT Sunday Magazine*, March 6, 1965, 88.

45. Baldwin, "Down at the Cross," in *Collected Essays*, ed. Morrison, 299.

46. James Baldwin, "The Nigger We Invent," in *The Cross of Redemption: Uncollected Writings* (New York: Vintage, 2010), 116. In the "Autobiographical Notes," Baldwin spoke the language of noninterference: "Most [Negroes] care nothing whatever about race. They want only their proper place in the sun and the right to be left alone, like any other citizen of the republic" ("Autobiographical Notes," in *Collected Essays*, ed. Morrison, 7).

47. It should be noted that Buckley might find even this more modest goal—to go *beyond* freedom as noninterference—as an offensive manifestation of "relativism." To take the question of freedom's meaning seriously, one reveals oneself to be flirting with "elasticity of standards" (see William F. Buckley Jr., "The Intellectuals and Socialism," in *Essays on Hayek*, ed. Fritz Machlup [New York: New York University Press, 1976], 105).

48. James Baldwin, "The White Problem," in *The Cross of Redemption: Uncollected Writings* (New York: Vintage, 2010), 91.

49. Wordnetweb.princeton.edu entry for "delusion."

50. Frank Lovett, "Republicanism," *The Stanford Encyclopedia of Philosophy*, Summer 2014 ed., ed. Edward N. Zalta, http://plato.stanford.edu/archives/sum2014/entries/republicanism/.

51. Ibid.

52. James Baldwin, "Take Me to the Water," in *Collected Essays*, ed. Morrison, 402.

53. Ibid.

54. Another telling example of Baldwin's view that domination threatened freedom can be found in his televised debate on British television with the journalist Peregrine Worsthorne. During the debate, Worsthorne says to Baldwin: "You've never been a slave and your father wasn't a slave. . . . [He was] a free man." In response, Baldwin appeals to the idea of freedom as nondomination: "I beg your pardon, I beg your pardon. A man, who is trapped in, I repeat, a ghetto, who makes 27 dollars a week and can't make anymore, not because he's stupid, who worked life away in a factory all of his life to support 9 children and cannot get out of the ghetto and cannot get out of the factory . . . that man is a slave" (see "A Television Conversation: James Baldwin, Peregrine Worsthorne, and Bryan Magee," in *Conversations with James Baldwin*, ed. Fred L. Standley and Louis H. Pratt [Oxford: University of Mississippi Press, 1989], 122).

55. James Baldwin, "The White Problem," in *Collected Essays*, ed. Morrison, 91.

56. Baldwin, "Down at the Cross," in *Collected Essays*, ed. Morrison, 337. For

more on Baldwin's "accent on the moral" in his discussions of freedom, see Lawrie Balfour, *Evidence of Things Not Said* (Ithaca, NY: Cornell University Press, 1998), 23–24.

57. Balfour captures the essence of this idea beautifully when she writes, "Baldwin maintains that freedom requires the exercise of moral agency in the face of disagreeable truths" (see Balfour, *Evidence of Things Not Said*, 130).

58. James Baldwin, "My Dungeon Shook," in *Collected Essays*, ed. Morrison, 295.

59. James Baldwin, "Nothing Personal," in *Collected Essays*, ed. Morrison, 702.

60. Baldwin, "Down at the Cross," in *Collected Essays*, ed. Morrison, 344.

61. Baldwin, "Nothing Personal," in *Collected Essays*, ed. Morrison, 694.

62. Ibid.

63. James Baldwin, "East River, Downtown," in *Collected Essays*, ed. Morrison, 183.

64. "The American Dream," *NYT Sunday Magazine*, 32.

65. Baldwin, "Down at the Cross," in *Collected Essays*, ed. Morrison, 342–43.

66. Baldwin, "The White Man's Guilt," in *Collected Essays*, ed. Morrison, 723.

67. Baldwin, "American Dream and the American Negro," in *Collected Essays*, ed. Morrison, 715.

68. "Our Mission Statement," *National Review*, November 19, 1955.

69. Baldwin, "Down at the Cross," in *Collected Essays*, ed. Morrison, 325.

70. Ibid., 333.

71. Baldwin, "The White Man's Guilt," in *Collected Essays*, ed. Morrison, 723.

72. By "one's history," I suppose it is obvious by now, Baldwin and I have in mind something far more vast than an individual's natural life.

73. Baldwin argued that only about 5 percent of white southerners were true believers in segregation; everyone else was merely a "passive adherent" to the system (see James Baldwin, "The Dangerous Road before Martin Luther King," in *Collected Essays*, ed. Morrison, 652).

74. James Baldwin, "Faulkner and Desegregation," in *Collected Essays*, ed. Morrison, 209. For an excellent discussion of the relationship between this idea and democracy, see Jack Turner, *Awakening to Race: Individualism and Social Consciousness* (Chicago: University of Chicago Press, 2012), 101.

75. Baldwin, "The American Dream and the American Negro," in *Collected Essays*, ed. Morrison, 714.

76. Baldwin, "The White Man's Guilt," in *Collected Essays*, ed. Morrison, 724.

77. I borrow the term "status anxiety" from the philosopher Alain Botton (see his *Status Anxiety* [New York: Vintage, 2005]).

78. James Baldwin, "In Search of a Majority," in *Collected Essays*, ed. Morrison, 218–19.

79. Ibid., 219. In his discussion of Baldwin in *The Idea of Fraternity in America*, Wilson Carey McWilliams says that Baldwin believed that man "delights in the suffering of others because it helps him to forget his own" (see Wilson Carey McWilliams, *The Idea of Fraternity in America* [Berkeley: University of California Press, 1973], 610). I am not sure the word "delight" captures Baldwin's view since he sees this sort of behavior as the product of great suffering. As Baldwin said in an interview with Studs Terkel in 1961, "the key" thing to understand about the "terrifying mobs" of whites in the South is this: "It isn't hatred that drives those people in the streets. It is pure terror" (Fred L. Standley and Louis H. Pratt, eds., *Conversations with James Baldwin* [Oxford: University of Mississippi, 1989], 8).

80. Baldwin, "Down at the Cross," in *Collected Essays*, ed. Morrison, 337.

81. Baldwin, "My Dungeon Shook," in *Collected Essays*, ed. Morrison, 294.

82. James Baldwin, "Dark Days," in *Collected Essays*, ed. Morrison, 798.

83. Baldwin, "Nothing Personal," in *Collected Essays*, ed. Morrison, 704.

84. Baldwin, "Down at the Cross," in *Collected Essays*, ed. Morrison, 300, 338.

85. James Baldwin, "Living and Growing in a White World," talk with students at Castlemont High School in Oakland, California. This talk was broadcast on June 23, 1963. It is available on the Black Media Archive at www.thebma.org.

86. James Baldwin, "A Talk to Teachers," in *Collected Essays*, ed. Morrison, 678.

87. Russell Kirk, "Ten Conservative Principles," in *The Politics of Prudence* (Wilmington: ISI, 1993).

88. Bogus, *William F. Buckley and the Rise of American Conservatism*, 155–57.

89. Although the editorial is unsigned, scholars have concluded Buckley was the author of this essay (see ibid., 158). Furthermore, when National Public Radio talk show host Terri Gross brought up the essay in an interview with Buckley in 1989, Buckley accepted the essay as his own (see "William F. Buckley Remembered," February 28, 2008, episode of *Fresh Air*).

90. "Why the South Must Prevail," *National Review*, August 24, 1957.

91. Ibid.

92. "The American Dream," *NYT Sunday Magazine*, 88.

93. Baldwin, "The White Man's Guilt," in *Collected Essays*, ed. Morrison, 722.

94. Ibid. For a compelling discussion of the relationship between Baldwin's conception of freedom and the idea of responsibility, see Balfour, *The Evidence of Things Not Said*, 129–32.

95. James Baldwin, "Words of a Native Son," in *Collected Essays*, ed. Morrison, 713.

96. Baldwin, "Down at the Cross," in *Collected Essays*, ed. Morrison, 343.

97. Baldwin, "Nobody Knows My Name," in *Collected Essays*, ed. Morrison, 208.

98. See Baldwin's interview with R. H. Darden on KPFK Radio in Los Angeles (April 1, 1968). This interview is available at: https://archive.org/details/Baldwin

AndDarden1968. See also James Baldwin, "Freaks and the American Ideal of Manhood" in *Collected Essays*, ed. Morrison, 816.

99. Declaration of Independence, paragraph 2.

100. For a wonderful discussion of the significance of "creativity" in Baldwin's political thought, see Turner, *Awakening to Race*, 99–105.

101. Baldwin, "The Creative Process" in *Collected Essays*, ed. Morrison, 669.

102. Baldwin, "Down at the Cross," in *Collected Essays*, ed. Morrison, 339. For a fantastic discussion of Baldwin's ideas on the transformation of rage into "creative energy," see Nicholas Bromell, *The Time Is Always Now: Black Thought and the Transformation of U.S. Democracy* (New York: Oxford University Press, 2013), 30–33.

103. Baldwin, "Down at the Cross," in *Collected Essays*, ed. Morrison, 347.

104. Baldwin, "The Creative Process," in *Collected Essays*, ed. Morrison, 669–70.

105. Ibid., 670.

106. James Baldwin, "Why I Stopped Hating Shakespeare," in *The Cross of Redemption: Uncollected Writings* (New York: Vintage, 2010), 69.

107. Baldwin, "A Talk to Teachers," in *Collected Essays*, ed. Morrison, 678–79.

108. As qtd. in Weatherby, *James Baldwin: Artist on Fire*, 312.

109. Ibid.

110. In the words of Wilson Carey McWilliams, Baldwin "was a fervent critic of the American regime precisely because he was an anguished lover" (see McWilliams, "*Go Tell It on the Mountain:* James Baldwin and the Politics of Faith," in this volume, 195; originally published in *Democracy's Literature*, ed. Deneen and Romance).

111. Baldwin, "The Creative Process" in *Collected Essays*, ed. Morrison, 672. For more on Baldwin's understanding of love as "a battle," see his "In Search of a Majority," in *Collected Essays*, ed. Morrison, 220.

112. Baldwin, "Autobiographical Notes," in *Collected Essays*, ed. Morrison, 9.

113. Baldwin, "Faulkner and Desegregation," in *Collected Essays*, ed. Morrison, 209–11.

114. Ibid., 211.

115. Ibid., 212.

116. Ibid., 211. It is worth noting that Baldwin did not believe this was a rare problem. "Most people," he wrote in 1962, are not able to look on each other as human beings, and, in spite of everything, to treat each other that way. Until that happens, freedom is only an empty word" (James Baldwin, "Color," in *Collected Essays*, ed. Morrison, 677).

117. Baldwin, "The White Man's Guilt," in *Collected Essays*, ed. Morrison, 726.

II

Prophecy, Religion, and Truth

5

Baldwin, Prophecy, and Politics

George Shulman

Although James Baldwin's essays depict the relationship of white supremacy to the formation of American society and the shaping of national identity, prevailing forms of liberal and Marxist political thought, as well as most versions of so-called democratic theory, do not recognize him as a political thinker or even contributing to the understanding of politics. Their resounding silence about race, and his exclusion from their canons, bespeak the very conditions he analyzes as a political and moral catastrophe. These conditions are, in short, ongoing racial domination as the foundation of American life, and its disavowal by those it enfranchises. On the one hand, Baldwin analyzes the price of this silence in American life, and by extension our theoretical practice: what is occluded and obscured, about life and politics, when thinkers ignore race? On the other hand, what kind of theorizing, or critical practice, is required or called forth by the issue of race, in what thinkers must say and how they must say it? In both regards, Baldwin shows how attention to the issue of race transforms prevailing views of (how to theorize) politics.

Surely, Baldwin would have white readers "see" race, which is invisible to them. But what does this mean? Partly, seeing race means grasping the related meanings of whiteness and blackness—the impossible purity and unmarked authority of one and the unspeakable horror of embodiment and vulnerability invested in the other—as a symbolic code, discursive system, and collective imaginary shaping every aspect of life in the United States. Partly, seeing race means grasping how this discursive system is woven into practices of inequality and exclusion, not only in slavery and then the legal apartheid called Jim Crow but in their legacy, contemporary residential patterns, labor markets, criminal justice institutions, cultural practices, and state policies.

But just as high theory has narrated modernity in terms of capitalism or disenchantment, but not slavery and the color line, so for Baldwin American culture and politics are also engendered by *disavowal* of their traumatic origin and continuing ground in racialized domination. It is not possible to understand the shaping and character of American life, he argues, unless we credit the generative centrality of racial domination—and its disavowal. In Baldwin's version of what some theorists now call constitutive exclusion, American nationhood is constituted by disavowed domination; what he calls "innocence" of domination is a willful, and so culpable, form of bad faith, to use the existentialist idiom of his formative years, a willful not-seeing and disclaiming of responsibility, which fundamentally corrupts American life: every aspect of public and private life; every cultural practice; and every literary or theoretical production. Innocence names a condition not only moral and political but "spiritual," he claims, for it bespeaks a failure to acknowledge human finitude and the "tragedy" of life, a denial of the very nature of reality as well as the reality of others. In turn, he argues, those disenfranchised as "black" (and their allies) must name and confront the disavowals that both privilege and imprison those enfranchised as white. To move from innocence to the kind of acknowledgment he calls "acceptance" would reconstitute the America regime.

This project of provoking acknowledgment—which Baldwin witnesses in the civil rights movement and enacts in his texts and worldly speech-acts—is a political practice meant to reconstitute a regime, by confronting the bad faith that sustains it and thus by recasting at visceral levels what and who are counted as real by the enfranchised. So the question becomes: By what language does he take exception to the racial state of exception constituting American liberal nationalism? Working not within a democratic frame, but to engage the domination and disavowal that both found and violate it, he echoes neither the idealization of reason and deliberation in liberal political thought nor the idealization of plurality and difference in its poststructural critics. He depicts himself as addressing not a problem of ignorance to remedy by knowledge but a failure to acknowledge, as Stanley Cavell puts it, what people do know but disavow; he depicts himself as facing not so much a dogmatism of identity hostile to plurality as an identity inseparable from domination.[1] Correspondingly, Baldwin does not speak like Habermas, as if to prove the validity of truth claims about the structure of society, nor does he speak quite like poststructuralists, who expose the contingency of identity to foster irony and openness to difference. Rather he makes a claim about willful blindness, a claim that is not a contestable interpretation but a truth those who call themselves white must accept, or they live in denial of the true meaning of their conduct and history. Given this claim, he must undertake a form of persuasion that expects resistance, values rhetoric, and relies on literary art.

For these reasons among others, I argue, he draws on the genre of biblical prophecy even as he inflects it in nontheist ways. This secularized prophecy enacts registers of voice—urgent, intense, uncompromising, probing, accusatory, demanding, provoking—that are devalued or even demonized both by liberal discourse and by prevailing genres of political theory. But as he uses prophecy to confront the issue of racial domination, we see how such speech, and the kinds of political claims it bears, are needful and not only dangerous in democratic politics.[2]

Disavowal, Acknowledgment, and Prophecy

One passage from *The Fire Next Time* especially exemplifies his critical practice and its characteristic idiom. In the first part of the book, "My Dungeon Shook" (a "Letter to My Nephew on the 100th Anniversary of Emancipation"), he says: "The crime of which I accuse my countrymen, and for which neither I nor time nor history will ever forgive them, is that they have destroyed and are destroying hundreds of thousands of lives and do not know it and do not want to know it. One can be and indeed must strive to become, tough and philosophical concerning destruction and death . . . but it is not permissible that the authors of this destruction should also be innocent. It is the innocence which constitutes the crime."[3] He then says: "This innocent country set you down in a ghetto in which, in fact, it intended that you should perish. You were born where you were born and faced the future you faced because you were black and for no other reason." Having positioned white readers to overhear him, he urges his nephew: "Try to remember that what they do and cause you to endure does not testify to your inferiority but to their inhumanity and fear. Indeed, there is no basis for their impertinent assumption that they must accept you. The really terrible thing . . . is that you must accept them . . . with love. For these innocent people have no other hope. They are still trapped in a history they do not understand and until they understand it they cannot be released form it."[4] Accordingly, "we, with love, will force our brothers to see themselves as they are, to cease fleeing from reality and begin to change it."[5] The alternative is not only the continuing subjugation of African Americans; switching to a we that joins blacks and whites as Americans, he adds: "If we, who can scarcely be considered a white nation, persist in thinking of ourselves as one, we condemn ourselves . . . to sterility and decay, whereas, if we could accept ourselves as we are, we might bring new life to Western achievements and transform them."[6]

A language of innocence as disavowal, and of acknowledgment as "accepting ourselves as we are," is Baldwin's way to address race and secularize prophecy as a language of politics. He thus imagines the critic not as God's messenger but as an artist whose struggle with society he depicts in terms of love: "The war of an artist with his society is a lover's war, and he does, at his best, what lovers do, which is to reveal the beloved to himself and, with that revelation, to make freedom real."[7] Meaning love not "in the infantile American sense of being made happy, but in the tough and universal sense of quest and daring and growth," he links critics with artists and lovers to imagine not only himself but blacks as a collective subject, acting as a "disagreeable mirror" to "block the door to the spiritual and social ease" of whites.[8] "Love" thus names an engagement to move whites not from ignorance to knowledge but from innocence to acknowledgment, and so from sterile repetition into the freedom of the unknown.

That engagement is a calling likely to fail: "A person does not lightly elect to oppose his society. One would much rather be at home among compatriots than mocked and detested by them. But the mockery of the people, even their hatred is moving because it is so blind: it is terrible to watch people cling to their captivity and insist on their destruction."[9] From his self-authorizing election to their blindness, captivity, and self-destruction, and so to the pathos of witnessing choices he has failed to change and suffering he cannot forestall, Baldwin forges a nontheist prophecy to confront white supremacy. To assess its political bearing, we must unpack his idea of innocence and then how he organizes critical and political practices around the idea of impelling whites to acknowledge what and whom they disavow.

The Concept of Innocence

Baldwin uses the moral category of innocence ironically: it denotes not excusable ignorance but a blindness that is culpable because it is willful. Destruction and domination are commonplace in history; rendering others invisible is an injustice built into human life by hierarchy and power. But innocence is a refusal not only to recognize these others but to acknowledge that we enact this denial. Innocence is disowning social facts we in some sense know. It is disavowing the exercise of power, the practice of inequality, and their benefits.

In one dimension, this innocence signals a society invested in both egalitarian ideals and in slavery. "Confronted with the impossibility of remaining faithful to one's beliefs [because one is invested in slavery] and the impossibility of becoming free of them [because one remains committed to equality]," Euro-Americans are "driven to the most inhuman excess."[10] Excess is the idea of blackness, which they invent to justify inequality by racializing subalterns in demonic and debased terms. But masters are haunted and crazed: "It was impossible for Americans to accept the black man as one of themselves, for to do so was to jeopardize their status as white men. But not to accept him was to deny his human reality, his human weight and complexity, and the strain of denying the overwhelmingly undeniable forced Americans into rationalizations so fantastic that they approached the pathological."[11] In Baldwin's view, then, Euro-Americans invent fictions of race and melodramas of black pathology to justify domination and protect an innocence they voice in claims to whiteness, moral virtue, exceptional liberalism, and an exemplary nationalism.

But the symbolic meaning invested in blackness also signals another form of innocence: "The racial tensions that menace Americans today have little to do with real antipathy—on the contrary indeed—and are involved only symbolically with color. These tensions are rooted in the very same depths from which love springs, or murder. The white's unadmitted—and apparently, to him, unspeakable—fears and longings are projected onto the Negro."[12] Whiteness is formed by projecting blackness, which becomes a site not just of aversion but of longing for what is split off.

Partly, the meaning of blackness is linked to death: "White Americans do not believe in death, and this is why the darkness of my skin so intimidates them." But "death" does symbolic work for Baldwin; it bears the meaning of a finitude he links to time, change, and mortality, thus to embodiment and incompletion, hence to desire and thereby to vulnerability, suffering, and violence. Accordingly, "My black flesh is the flesh that Saint Paul wanted to have mortified," for in the name of pure disembodied spirit, Christianity "splits itself into dark and light."[13] But secular liberalism also denies the meaning of carnal mortality by its idolatry of self-determination as sovereignty, a wish sustained by lodging license, irrationality, passion, dependence, and violence in racialized others, who signify what normative citizens must master to achieve "self-determination."[14]

"White" thus denotes not skin color, says Baldwin, but a "moral choice" to "opt for safety instead of life."[15] That choice is a symptom of *ressentiment* and a form of violence. Indeed, disassociating from their own destructiveness, those who call themselves white invoke morality to exorcize the specter of darkness in others, as if to master their own impulsive life, and life itself, by controlling the symbolically charged bodies of others. Blackness is then the Dionysian, and innocence is the bad faith that moralizes and racializes it. As racial categorization yields moral dichotomy, both make the "American" vision of life abstract and rigid: "The American vision of the world—which allows so little reality, generally speaking, for any of the darker forces in human life, which tends to pain moral issues in glaring black and white—owes a great deal to the battle waged by Americans to maintain between themselves and black men a human separation which could not be bridged."[16] Lastly, therefore, innocence connotes disavowal of the past: "It is a sentimental error . . . to believe that the past is dead. . . . It is not a question of memory. Oedipus did not remember the things that bound his feet; nevertheless the marks they left testified to that doom toward which his feet were leading him."[17] To address people invested in Christian ideas of rebirth, or in the liberal romance of self-making, Baldwin invokes the image of Oedipus—whose wish to make his own destiny seals his doom, whose insistence on escaping the past tightens its grip, and whose claim to know himself assures misrecognition of his identity. As a tragic truth-teller Baldwin might be a Tiresias, but in a biblical culture he calls himself "a kind of Jeremiah"[18] who must address citizens willfully blind to what is self-defeating in their self-making: "White man, hear me! History . . . does not refer merely or even principally to the past. On the contrary, the great force of history comes from the fact that we carry it within us, are unconsciously controlled by it in many ways, so history is literally *present* in all that we do. It could scarcely be otherwise since it is to history that we owe our frames of reference, our identities, and our aspirations."[19]

To summarize, by casting whiteness as "innocence," Baldwin denotes: partly a denial of the Dionysian that he links to carnal mortality and what he calls the "tragic" nature of life; partly a denial of the reality of others and a disclaiming of this refusal; and partly a denial of history, the past constituting the inescapably situated particularity of every human life. In each regard, innocence is a dream of safety, sovereignty, or purity, of not being subject to sentience and dependence on others, to time, loss, and death. But finitude in these senses is socially mediated: people undergo "life" through subjection to—and privileging by—social categories, domination, and violence. Innocence also means denying this social landscape of power and our differential positioning in it. Whiteness thus signals a regime that disavows its investment in inequality and a culture animated by bad faith.

From Disavowal to Acknowledgment

As the weak invent true worlds or fixed racial categories to seek an impossible kind of protection from life, and as "those who cannot suffer never grow up," so "freedom and innocence" are antithetical.[20] The alternative to innocence, it is therefore crucial to emphasize, is not so much guilt as a capacity for responsibility Baldwin associates both with adulthood and with agency. To depict this alternative he uses the idiom of acceptance: white supremacy is an idolatry that produces sterility, "whereas, if we could accept ourselves as we are, we might bring new life to western achievements and transform them." Always naming "the price of the ticket," the cost not only of domination and its disavowal but also of their overcoming, he adds that "the price" of renewal is "the unconditional freedom of the Negro: it is not too much to say that he . . . must now be embraced and at no matter what psychic and social risk." Freedom means resisting innocence as bad faith, by "accepting" what (and who) has been disavowed.[21]

Partly, the freedom of those who call themselves white depends on "accepting" national origins in violence and slavery, not in consent, and "accepting" an abiding national investment in inequality, not equality. Partly, whites remain trapped by this history unless they accept how racial domination and black agency have shaped American culture in every regard: "What happened to the Negro . . . is not simply a matter of *my* memory and *my* history, but of *American* history and memory." For "the history the Negro endured . . . was endured on another level by all the white people who oppressed him. . . . I was here, and that did something to *me*. But you were here on top of me, and that did something to *you*." Right now, what "this republic does to the Negro, it does to itself."[22] Indeed, the relation of white and black is not only oppressor to oppressed, he insists, but a blood bond of family and an erotically charged marriage:

> Love does not begin and end in the way we think it does. Love is a battle, love is a war; love is a growing up. No one in the world . . . knows Americans (i.e. whites) better or, odd as it may sound, loves them more than the American Negro. This is because he has had to watch you, outwit you, deal with you, bear you, and sometimes even bleed and die with you, ever since both of us, black and white, got here—and this is a wedding.[23]

Baldwin moves between metaphors of family in which one brother confronts another and metaphors of wedding in which a lover confronts a beloved, to register and engender investment in a bond readily disavowed but impossible to escape. What he calls "achieving our country" means accepting the gothic reality of this wedding and the people we have become by it: only if "we" "accept" that American history is shaped by domination and miscegenation can we initiate a democratic nation-building never yet attempted. Baldwin here "accepts" a national frame for politics, not because he loves an ideal America but because freedom means wrestling with the fatality of the actual one. Whereas Richard Wright answers white disavowal with refusal, Baldwin forges a collective black subject by blocking ideas of divorce and of racial purity. Instead he encourages blacks to "accept," and in all ambivalence engage, a miscegenated attachment he depicts as grievously flawed. It may be irredeemably flawed, but until 1968 he believes a history of domination and miscegenation can be made into a condition of action.[24]

Baldwin himself models the acknowledgments he seeks from blacks and from whites as constituent members of a national subject. In "great pain and terror," he says, he grasped the depth of his own historical constitution, but "only then can one enter into battle with that historical creation, oneself," and attempt to re-create oneself according to a principle more humane and liberating: "One begins the attempt to achieve a personal maturity and freedom which robs history of its tyrannical power and also changes history. . . . Obviously I speak as a historical creation which has had to bitterly contest its history, to wrestle with it, and finally accept it in order to bring myself out of it."[25] He cannot escape his past or fix what went wrong in it, as if to change it. Only by accepting his historical constitution can he, paradoxically, make a future different from the one the past seems to dictate. In a Nietzschean sense, accepting the past diminishes the power it accrues from denial; those ruled less by resentment of it or by fantasies of escaping it can wrestle with it to act otherwise.

Baldwin does not ask African Americans to simply "accept" hegemonic images of blackness; to accept that "categorization alone is real" and "surrender to the image" is to give life "no other possible reality" than self-hatred and hatred. Yet "bitter railing" at a category is "the only motion needed to spring the trap on us," for we reinstate it in our protest.[26] To elude the trap, paradoxically, means "accepting" that "the American image of the Negro lives in the Negro's heart," that "this dark and dangerous and unloved stranger is part of himself forever." For "only this recognition sets him in any wise free," and it is "this necessary ability to contain and even, in the most honorable sense of the word, to *exploit* the 'nigger' which lends Negro life its high element of the ironic."[27] To "accept" this stranger within is to credit, at once, carnal humanity and internalization of its estranged white image; such doubleness yields the tragic insight and freedom that enable creativity.

Whites, too, must "wrestle" with the constitutive power of the past as the inherited categories they internalize and live by and as the segregated, unequal world they sustain. But one trapped within the safe sterility of whiteness must also seek "fruitful communion with the depths of his own being." To contact such "depths" is in effect "to become black himself, to become part of that suffering and dancing country that he now watches wistfully from the heights of his lonely power."[28] If whites can "accept and love themselves" by learning to accept the "dark stranger" within each person "—which will not be tomorrow and may very well be never—the Negro problem will no longer exist for it will no longer be needed."[29] They must risk the idol of racial identity, not by minstrel inversions, but by contacting the Dionysian:

> It is the responsibility of free men to trust and celebrate what is constant—birth, struggle, and death are constant, and so is love, though we may not always think so—and to apprehend the nature of change, to be able and willing to change. I speak of change not on the surface but in the depths—change in the sense of renewal. But renewal becomes impossible if one supposes things to be constant which are not, safety for example, money or power. One clings then to chimeras, by which one can only be betrayed, and the entire hope—the entire possibility—of freedom disappears.[30]

Assessing Baldwin's Politics as a Practice of Prophecy

How shall we assess the political bearing of a critical practice cast in terms of disavowal and acknowledgment? Begin with the criticisms of white and black audiences at the point of Baldwin's greatest visibility and since. Many whites express rage at his view of their willful innocence, which makes any resistance to his view evidence of its truth. He imposes an interpretation of history as a truth whites must accept or, he insists, they live in self-denial. Resenting the judgment and aggression in such claims, they say that critics, to be effective, must use other registers of voice, to persuade by argument, not self-righteous testimony. Inversely, black critics object that Baldwin acquiesces to white power: by investing in dialogue and casting blacks in the role of redeeming whites, his idiom of love sacrifices black political autonomy in a vain effort to free people who cannot listen and to change a regime invested in racial rule.

We can translate these historic and recurring reactions into questions. First, what is the status of Baldwin's claims about innocence and disavowal: what kind of truth is this? Does it moralize white supremacy or politicize it? Does this idiom clarify how people know something, say, about inequality and the humanity of excluded others, and yet do not acknowledge or count as salient, and so cannot act on, what they know? But what fosters such acknowledgment? Second, therefore, is his way of addressing the nation as a subject: does his analogy of the personal and the collective collapse the plural space of politics or conjure a subject of attribution to undertake what

Hannah Arendt calls "collective responsibility"? Third, does his language of love romanticize nationhood and escape from politics or, rather, depict miscegenation and gothic ambivalence, to name the only terms on which a democratic politics in the United States could begin? Last, is he binding blacks not only to whites and a national frame but also to the past and what Wendy Brown calls "wounded attachment"? Or on the model of Nietzschean redemption, does he use his art to "compose fragments, riddle, and dreadful accident" into *amor fati?*[31] I can't answer these questions in any detail here, but they suggest the many ways in which Baldwin enriches the conversation of political theory.

Most broadly, Baldwin's texts reveal a modernity whose legacy is divided because it is founded in slavery, not only enlightenment, and because secularism remains entangled in religious faith, as the subjection and resistance of African Americans attests. Through him we confront a modernity neither white nor secular, and we can thereby reimagine the meaning and making of a "countermodernity." More specifically, his account of white supremacy transforms how we view American liberalism.

His basic political claim is that democratically authorized racial domination has formed the regime of liberal nationalism: the liberal freedoms of the enfranchised depend on the material subordination and cultural exploitation of racially marked others. How does this change our view of liberalism? Carl Schmitt depicts liberalism as antipolitical because an inclusive and pluralist, consensual and procedural creed avoids the "decision," and refuses the "friend-enemy" distinction, by which he defines the properly political. What Schmitt laments as a loss is praised by defenders of liberalism, but Baldwin sees how race is what Schmitt calls "political theology," the organizing discourse defining the constitutive outside and internal other of American liberalism.[32] What Michael Rogin calls "counter-subversive" politics is thus Schmittian decision in American drag: a liberal regime forges sovereignty and normative citizenship by imposing a racial and sexual frontier.[33] A black man of "dubious sexuality," Baldwin stands with the enemy or subversive against which a nation forms itself as a political community. Naming the state of racial exception enabling liberal nationalism, he takes exception to American exceptionalism.[34] But what, then, could suspend the state of exception that sustains the liberal rule of the American ordinary?

The dominant story of equal rights, individual mobility, and ethnic pluralism is not so much invalidated by Baldwin's story of white supremacy as recast as a form of innocence; as he makes ghettos signify not black inferiority but white domination, and as he makes riots signify not irrationality but insurrection, he shifts the gaze from black to white pathology, and he links black agency to justice not anarchy. Both stories seem validated by experience, but neither can be proven; each is a background narrative preceding what we even count as facts, let alone how we endow them with meaning. Baldwin's rhetorical and political task is thus to confront a prevailing narrative perspective and shift the deep judgments it sustains.

He provokes that shift in part by visiting the standpoint of whites to voice what is unspeakable by them, both their fearful fantasies of blackness and the meaning of unmarked whiteness. But he also testifies to what blacks do not directly say to whites. In effect he asks: how would your view of your conduct and history change, and how would our life together change, if you took my perspective seriously and counted as real my experience of domination and resistance to it? In this way he creates a textual space for dialogue that parallels the political space being taken and created in the 1950s and early 1960s by African American collective action. To craft these voices and mediate them, I believe, he draws on the biblical genre of prophecy, which depicts the public office of messengers who announce, witnesses who testify, watchmen who warn, and singers who lament.[35]

As messengers announce what is, so Blake argues that prophets are poets. For their seminal fictions—Wallace Stevens says supreme fictions—become truths by which subsequent generations live.[36] In this sense Baldwin voices a perspective that remakes the passionate frame of reference by which people orient self-reflection and agency. But messengers announce *unspeakable* truths, which people deny at great cost to themselves and others: Amos thus declares that God does not unconditionally support the Hebrews but holds them accountable for injustice and declares war against them, whereas Nietzsche assumes the office of prophecy to announce the death of God. To announce the conditions we *must* acknowledge *if* we are to flourish—whether a just god or a universe beyond good and evil—is a prophet's office.

In this sense Baldwin speaks imperatively not because of dogmatism but because of the kind of claim he makes; he seeks not obedient submission to dogma but acknowledgment—of conditions of finitude we must accept, and of idolatrous fictions we must relinquish, if we are to escape imprisonment. Imperative assertions—about how we must see our situation and our history to bring ourselves out of it—take conditional form: you *must* stop doing *x* and start doing *y* *if* you would flourish. We feel we cannot argue back, but he is stating the price of the ticket, not commanding us to obey, and we are free to ignore him, albeit at our peril.

Baldwin also repeatedly insists that he speaks as a witness rather than as a spokesman. He says what he sees, like a legal witness, but like a prophet he also stands against it: making present voices long made absent or un-counted, he bears witness against the exclusion and disavowal by which a democratic regime constitutes and betrays itself, but he also bears witness to capacities for resistance and self-overcoming. His judgment is militant be-cause he believes he addresses not a lack of knowledge to fix by information or a cognitive error to remedy by reasoned argument, as liberal reformers have argued since Gunnar Myrdal's *American Dilemma*, nor an inescapable partiality of vision due to our imbrication in discourse, as Foucault argues, but a motivated blindness about the reality of others that is culpable because it can be overcome. He testifies to no mere gap between people's professed ideals and their actual conduct but to a denial of reality so profound that every value seems hollow, and people seem deranged, not just hypocritical.

As prophets therefore warn that self-destruction is the penalty paid by those who deny reality, so arguments about disavowal entail a prudential and futural dimension, and prophets call themselves watchmen who would forestall the danger they foresee. When he warns of "the fire next time," therefore, Baldwin does not decree or predict a fate; rather, he names the consequence of conduct as a contingent future we can avoid if we "amend our ways," as Jeremiah puts it. But like the biblical prophets, he also warns of the point when it may be too late to avert the relentlessly unfolding con-sequences of prior conduct.

What, then, is Baldwin's answer to disavowal and its penalties? Bibli-cal prophets claim that what God requires is not esoteric but accessible, not a transcendent Archimedean point to reach by abstraction but a "turn" toward what is nearby, to become present to it. As the Hebrew for "turn" is translated as "repentance," so Baldwin uses narrative and personal testi-mony to turn us toward what we disavow. That turn reconstitutes political community by recasting at visceral levels whom we count as real, how we judge social practices, and the way we practice first principles.

He knows his perspective is contestable, but for him, we who contest it are denying the meaning of our history and conduct. Here he stands, and he cannot speak otherwise, for he would betray his vocation by moving if we are offended. Depicting amnesia, disavowal, and self-destruction, he expects our resistance, for he offers not opinions or stories whose comparable validity we must grant to achieve civility, but urgent judgments on which our lives depend. He does not attack dogmatism to pluralize valuable optics, then, but names a willful blindness about domination to reconstitute a regime. As Martin Buber argues that biblical prophets do not predict the future but demand a "decision" in the present, so Baldwin seeks a fateful decision about constitutive practices.[37]

What is dangerous and needful in prophetic speech, and in Baldwin's revision of it, is the claim that people are willfully blind to the truth of their conduct and history, and this demand for decisive choices between commitments, practices, and narratives depicted as antithetical. The danger shadows the Schmittian provenance of "decision," which seems to deny plurality as an axial principle of democratic politics, and yet for Baldwin, this register of speech is needful if the issue is domination and its disavowal. Jacques Rancière's *Dis-Agreement* suggests why.[38]

Rancière argues that any regime enfranchises some by excluding others; every "whole" is partial, presuming a "part that has no part." The subordinated exist demographically, so to speak, but become properly political subjects only as they translate their "injury" into claims about "wrong" that dispute who a regime counts, and how. By their speech and action those who Rancière calls "the part with no part" create a "scene" of argument to engage the enfranchised and reconstitute the regime as a whole. What Baldwin calls love is thus the engagement Rancière calls dis-agreement, not a movement beyond it. For Baldwin knows that speech relating a part to a whole may fail to persuade the enfranchised, and his goal is not to produce an agreement that ends politics but to suspend a state of exception that makes democratic politics stillborn.

I have used Cavell's idea of acknowledgment, therefore, to suggest that the political problem for Baldwin is not ignorance but disavowal and that his political remedy is not so much new information or public deliberation as a different relationship toward what we (individually and collectively) already know, say, and do. But contra Cavell, Baldwin must turn people not toward criteria of ordinary language they have refused but toward practices of domination they have disavowed. In turn, taking seriously Baldwin's focus on disavowed domination would reorient how we theorize politics.

We would shift focus from epistemology (as if to guarantee the truth of claims or establish the shared truth that identities are partial and contingent) to rhetorical arts (which use vernacular idioms to "turn" people toward what they know but disavow). Rather than validate truth claims by deliberative procedures, pluralize avowedly contestable faiths and contingent identities, or foster an ethical ethos of openness to difference, our critical practice would seek conflict about constitutive (racial) practices we must end, not learn to forbear or work to pluralize. Politics does entail dialogue about plural identities and perspectives, as well as deliberation about action, but it also must be adversaries struggling to reconstitute regimes that privilege some by subordinating others. Baldwin thus seeks not only openness to excluded voices but judgments about which practices (and stories) to mandate or oppose. His voice intensifies our awareness of domination, and his intensity—of anger, grief, and judgment—signals dimensions of political speech that are not only scary and indeed dangerous but also needful and transforming.

I have invoked Schmitt to emphasize the register of decision in Baldwin's story of disavowal overcome by acknowledgment, but it is also important to see how Baldwin reworks the distinction between friend and enemy. As his famous encounter with Elijah Muhammad suggests, he neither reifies nor defuses the friend-enemy polarity. He does see a worldly adversary in whites invested in domination, but the "enemy" he faces is also internal to every person, a capacity for bad faith he impels each to name and overcome. He thus stands with some and against others but also in an agonal stance toward each and every citizen. Still, he never chastens his judgment of white supremacy, which remains an evil fundamentally at odds with democratic life.

Since forbearance toward the other means complicity in racial domination rather than receptivity toward difference, the appearance (even the reality) of moralism is not the greatest danger that Baldwin sees. Indeed, it is no surprise that whites cast him as an invasive moral fanatic opposed to democratic process: a racial state of exception requires him to question the authority of law, majority rule, local self-rule, and the idioms of pluralism, for each is wholly contaminated by racialized exclusion and domination. Yet overcoming white supremacy remains *the* condition of democratic possibility, period; the alternative is a fraudulent pluralism among whites. For Baldwin, then, politics is not a process of deliberation or mediation of plural identities, but a structure of rule, and a *democratic* politics must struggle against it. Still, he insists that every accusation contains a plea for community, and he argues that overcoming white supremacy will truly benefit those who call themselves white, though they cannot yet see how. Instead of polarization or pluralization, therefore, he mediates parts and whole to reconstitute political community.[39]

If Rancière theorizes the constitutive exclusion that Baldwin interprets as a state of exception, it is but a step to say that amnesia is its symptom; to reconstitute community, political actors must mediate parts and wholes, as Rancière argues, but also, like prophets, remember what people forget. In a way Rancière does not emphasize, Baldwin (like other critics of white supremacy) turns to prophecy to emphasize the historical and thus narrative dimension in politics. We therefore should note the stories that he rejects. He refuses the story of a providentially chosen people but also the nationalist jeremiad that redeems this people from corruption by making good their liberal creed. Unlike Abraham Lincoln, he does not invoke an ideal America to make real by acts of dedication and sacrifice. Unlike Martin Luther King, he does not redeem founding principles to authorize protest by African American sons and daughters, and unlike Hannah Arendt, he does not return to 1776 to recover a "revolutionary treasure."[40] Depicting a nation founded in slavery, whose ideals have been practiced only in viciously exclusionary ways, he denies that progress is the telos of American history.

He instead narrates a tragic story in which a disavowed past generates barren repetition. He insists on this story not to produce despair, but as a condition of opening a possibility for new possibilities. To quote Jonathan Lear, he seeks not "an ordinary possibility, like all the others only new," but "an alteration in the world of possibilities."[41] Is there some other way forward, except by coming to terms with the past? Baldwin denies it. Possibility is not produced by deliberative rationality, nor is it inherently emergent in the ontological process of becoming; it is entirely dependent on coming to terms with the past. Again, his claim-making is both imperative and conditional, as he offers the kind of story that might, in turn, make other stories possible.

Baldwin quickly grasped the failure of the civil rights era as a second Reconstruction, and he lived long enough to grasp, too, that the strange complexities of a post–civil rights era did not signal fundamental change. He had hoped to take strategic advantage of the opening for racial change created by Cold War public relations, though he also privileged nationhood as the scene of political redemption, but by the late 1960s he came to think otherwise. Some critics depict his decline into ideology and bitterness rather than credit his view of the intractability of white supremacy.[42] But he never relinquished faith in the possibility of reconstituting the field of possibility: "I know that what I am asking is impossible. But in our time, as in every time, the impossible is the least one can demand—and one is, after all, emboldened by the spectacle of human history in general and American Negro history in particular, for it testifies to nothing less than the perpetual achievement of the impossible."[43]

In registering the "achievement of the impossible" Baldwin is attesting not only to the ontological fact of contingency, an apparently miraculous exception recurrently rupturing the rule, but also to the ongoing countersovereignty and communal rites of black agency, situated between nation and empire. Continuing to write despite political defeat, he leaves as a legacy a political ethos that holds in tension two necessary but incompatible ideas: "The first idea is . . . acceptance totally without rancor, of life as it is and men as they are: in the light of this idea it goes without saying that injustice is a commonplace. But this does not mean that one can be complacent, for the second idea is . . . that one must never in one's life accept these injustices as commonplace, but must fight them with all one's strength."[44] For as he declares at the end of "The Fire Next Time," "everything now, we must assume, is in our hands; we have no right to assume otherwise."[45]

Notes

Originally published as George Shulman, "Baldwin, Prophecy, and Politics," in *American Prophecy: Race and Redemption in American Political* Culture (Minneapolis: University of Minnesota Press, 2008). Reprinted by permission.

1. See Stanley Cavell, *The Claim of Reason* (New York: Oxford University Press, 1979).

2. For my broader argument about prophecy, and for the full chapter on Baldwin from which this essay is drawn, see George Shulman, *American Prophecy: Race and Redemption in American Politics* (Minneapolis: University of Minnesota Press, 2008).

3. James Baldwin, *The Fire Next Time,* in *The Price of the Ticket: Collected Nonfiction, 1949–1985* (New York: St. Martin's, 1985), 334.

4. Ibid., 334–35.

5. Ibid., 335.

6. Ibid., 374.

7. James Baldwin, "The Creative Process," in *The Price of the Ticket*, 317–18.

8. Baldwin, *The Fire Next Time*, in *The Price of the Ticket*, 370; "disagreeable mirror" is from James Baldwin, "White Man's Guilt," in *The Price of the Ticket*, 409.

9. James Baldwin, *No Name in the Street* (New York: Dial, 1972), 172–73.

10. James Baldwin, "Stranger in the Village," in *The Price of the Ticket*, 89.

11. Ibid., 88.

12. Baldwin, *The Fire Next Time*, in *The Price of the Ticket*, 375.

13. James Baldwin, "White Racism and World Community," in *The Price of the Ticket*, 440.

14. In *The Fire Next Time*, he says that "we sacrifice the beauty of our lives" and "imprison ourselves in totems, taboos, crosses, blood sacrifices, steeples, mosques, races, armies, flags, nations in order to deny the fact of death," whereas we should "rejoice" in and "earn" it "by confronting with passion the conundrum of life" (373–74).

15. James Baldwin, "On Being White and Other Lies," *Essence*, April 1984.

16. Baldwin, "Stranger in the Village," in *The Price of the Ticket*, 89.

17. James Baldwin, "Many Thousands Gone," in *The Price of the Ticket*, 68.

18. James Baldwin, "The American Dream and the American Negro," in *The Price of the Ticket*, 403.

19. Baldwin, "White Man's Guilt," in *The Price of the Ticket*, 410.

20. Baldwin, *The Fire Next Time*, in *The Price of the Ticket*, 376–77.

21. Ibid., 374. My claim, which I cannot justify in this chapter, is that Baldwin criticizes innocence to move beyond guilt, not to generate it; indeed, he is trying to free whites from the unconscious guilt they already feel. He is trying to evoke responsibility without reinstating the moral apparatus and guilty subject of Christianity. See also, in this context, Hannah Arendt, "Collective Responsibility," in *Responsibility and Judgment*, ed. Jerome Kohn (New York: Schocken, 2003).

22. James Baldwin, Nathan Glazer, Sidney Hook, Gunnar Myrdal, and Norman Podhoretz, "Liberalism and the Negro: A Roundtable Discussion," *Commentary*, March 1964, 31.

23. James Baldwin, "In Search of a Majority," in *The Price of the Ticket*, 234. The relations of people of African descent and Anglo-Europeans is "more terrible, more subtle, and more meaningful than the relationship of bitter possessed to uncertain possessor" or of "master to slave." It is "literally and morally a blood relationship, perhaps the most profound reality of the American experience, and we cannot begin to unlock it until we accept how very much it contains of the force and anguish and terror of love" ("Many Thousands Gone," in *The Price of the*

Ticket, 76). The "interracial drama," by a literal and figurative miscegenation, has created "a new black man, and a new white man too" ("Stranger in the Village," in *The Price of the Ticket,* 89).

24. Refusing the path of separation is one lesson Baldwin teaches in his famous story about meeting Elijah Muhammad in *The Fire Next Time,* though it often goes unnoted that Baldwin also agrees with Elijah's critique of white supremacy. But after 1968, Baldwin increasingly doubts the possibility of an interracial movement to reconstitute the republic; even as he continues to deny ideas of racial purity and to insist that black and white are in fact mixed, he rarely says "we" of "Americans," by which he now means whites, and he argues that blacks must redeem *themselves,* not whites.

25. Baldwin, "White Man's Guilt," in *The Price of the Ticket,* 410.

26. James Baldwin, "Everybody's Protest Novel," in *The Price of the Ticket,* 32–33.

27. Baldwin, "Many Thousands Gone," in *The Price of the Ticket,* 77.

28. Baldwin, *The Fire Next Time,* in *The Price of the Ticket,* 375.

29. Ibid., 340.

30. Ibid., 373.

31. Wendy Brown, "Wounded Attachments," *Political Theory* 21, no. 2 (1993); Arendt, "Collective Responsibility" in *Responsibility and Judgment,* ed. Jerome Kohn; Friedrich Nietzsche, "On Redemption," in *Thus Spoke Zarathustra* (New York: Vintage, 1980).

32. Carl Schmitt, *The Concept of the Political* (Chicago: University of Chicago Press, 1996); Carl Schmitt, *Political Theology* (Chicago: University of Chicago Press, 1985).

33. Michael Rogin, *Ronald Reagan, the Movie* (Berkeley: University of California Press, 1987).

34. Baldwin, *No Name on the Street,* 18. Baldwin left America because of race, but he left Harlem because of homophobia: homosexuality still signifies as an internal frontier demarcating racially authentic community, that is, the internal dimension of the friend-enemy distinction.

35. I draw the idea of "visiting" from Hannah Arendt, and I draw the idea of saying the unspeakable from Toni Morrison.

36. William Blake, "There Is No Natural Religion," in *Blake: Collected Writings,* ed. Geoffrey Keene (New York: Oxford University Press, 1972), 97–98; William Blake, "The Marriage of Heaven and Hell," ibid., 148–58; Wallace Stevens, *The Necessary Angel: Essays on Reality and Imagination* (New York: Vintage, 1951).

37. "The Israelite prophet . . . hardly ever . . . foretells a plainly certain future. God does not deliver into his hand a completed book of fate with all future events

written on it. . . . It was something of this kind that 'false prophets' pretended. . . . Their main 'falsity' lay not in the fact that they prophesy salvation but that what they prophesy is not dependent on question and alternative. . . . The true prophet does not announce an inevitable decree. He speaks into the power of decision lying in the moment" (Martin Buber, *Prophetic Faith* [New York: Harper and Row, 1949], 103–4).

38. Jacques Rancière, *Dis-Agreement* (Minneapolis: University of Minnesota Press, 1999).

39. Rather than endlessly unmask the falsity of every claim to universality, Baldwin believes a greater good can be engendered by particular voices seeking freedom, if they see themselves as reconstituting a whole. For an analogous argument, see Nikhil Pal Singh, *Black Is a Country: Race and the Unfinished Struggle for Democracy* (Cambridge: Harvard University Press, 2004).

40. Hannah Arendt, *On Revolution* (New York: Viking, 1971).

41. Jonathan Lear, *Therapeutic Action: An Earnest Plea for Irony* (New York: Other Press, 2003), 204.

42. See esp. Henry Louis Gates, "The Fire Last Time: What James Baldwin Can and Can't Teach America," *New Republic*, June 1992. See also Hilton Als, "The Enemy Within: The Making and Unmaking of James Baldwin," *New Yorker*, February 16, 1998; Julius Lester "Some Tickets Are Better than Others: The Mixed Achievement of James Baldwin," *Dissent* 33 (1986).

43. Baldwin, *The Fire Next Time*, in *The Price of the Ticket*, 379.

44. James Baldwin, "Notes of a Native Son," in *The Price of the Ticket*, 145.

45. Baldwin, *The Fire Next Time*, in *The Price of the Ticket*, 379.

6

The Negative Political Theology of James Baldwin

Vincent Lloyd

Religious language, ideas, and images pervade the essays, plays, stories, and novels of James Baldwin. A product of Black Pentecostalism and a teenage preaching prodigy, Baldwin describes his writing style as influenced by the King James Bible and the storefront church.[1] Verses from the Bible and snippets of gospel music pervade Baldwin's texts. Yet religion also appears in Baldwin's work as something he has overcome, a distasteful encounter with authoritarianism that he passed through to reach his present secular, democratic enlightenment. If this is the case, the religious language that appears in Baldwin's texts could be read as rhetorical flourish, leveraging the persuasive power of a Christian idiom without any commitment to Christian beliefs.

Some have suggested that Baldwin occupies a religious office, that of the prophet. Standing at the margins of a community, the prophet makes explicit that community's values, and the prophet condemns the community for its present deviations from those values.[2] Now that the world has secularized, the prophet no longer must invoke God's name in her condemnations. Furthermore, instead of holding out the promise of otherworldly rewards, the secularized prophet would hold out the promise of this-worldly happiness once we accept human finitude. On this reading, Baldwin is the quintessential democratic prophet, explicating democratic values and enumerating the ways nations ostensibly committed to democracy fall short—where an acceptance of human finitude is a core commitment of democratic politics.[3]

A focus on either Baldwin's religious language or his prophetic posturing, though, fails to consider the possibility that a specifically Christian set of ideas might frame Baldwin's political vision. Scholarship on political theology has shown the fruitfulness of examining subtle connections between theological and political ideas, of examining how they can mirror each other and how they can shift together. Recovering these connections can help us understand a writer's political vision more clearly. It can reveal weaknesses in that political vision by illuminating incoherence or by showing how the theological premises on which a political argument once implicitly relied no longer have traction.

I will argue that James Baldwin transformed, rather than rejected, his father's Christianity. The components of that Christianity—ideas about innocence, salvation, sin, truth, and much else—are reworked by Baldwin, and in their new form they are inextricably linked with Baldwin's political vision. Race is essential to this theological transformation, for Baldwin charges most Christians with misunderstanding race and so misunderstanding their religion; the condition of blackness produces a natural (although often suppressed) attunement to truth. As he writes, "Black is a tremendous spiritual condition."[4] In Baldwin's transformed theology, whiteness represents idolatry, represents worldly interests elevating themselves to the place of the transcendent, defining the true, the good, and the beautiful. The theology that Baldwin offers in its place is negative, part of the long tradition of Christian negative theology for which the only true thing that can be said about God is what God is not: the work of theology is the critique of idolatry. Baldwin does not offer a black theology to oppose white theology; he offers a thoroughgoing critique of the religion of whiteness, and he posits a name for what remains when that critique is successful: love.

Fathers and Gods

Baldwin's negative political theology begins with his father, who serves as the paradigmatic symbol of authority, and of idolatry. Fathers play central roles in Baldwin's fiction and essays, from his first books (a working title for his first novel was "In My Father's House"; his first essay collection is *Notes of a Native Son*) to his last. Throughout, fathers are identified with gods—false gods. They seem to have absolute power, but in fact that power is compromised and precarious. Fatherhood itself is unsettled, with apparent fathers revealed to not be fathers at all, creating a world of bastards. Baldwin describes himself as a "bastard of the West."[5] He names black Americans "nameless and unnamable bastards" living in "the great Western house."[6] Yet the need for a father persists; Baldwin is haunted by the question—posed by his first minister and by Elijah Muhammad, as well as by the even more idolatrous gods of the street—"whose little boy are you?" To which he responds, in retrospect, "I unquestionably wanted to be somebody's little boy."[7] We long for a father, or for a god; for an authority in absolute control. Acknowledging this longing and rejecting any object that would sate it is at the center of Baldwin's political theological vision.

The eponymous essay of *Notes of a Native Son* is the story of two days in which Baldwin's father, a preacher, dies; Baldwin's sister is born; Baldwin himself comes of age (it is his nineteenth birthday); and the world descends into chaos, into race riots. It is the story of the collapse of absolute authority and its aftermath, personally and politically. Chaos and violence could result, or new life could result. With proper reflection—and, ultimately, with the activity of writing itself—we are able to opt for the latter. We are able to critically appropriate the legacy of the father, of the god, accepting how that legacy shapes us but also acknowledging its pathologies.

Baldwin introduces his father, the preacher, as almost mythical, as god-like. No one knew his age. He was handsome and proud and "very black." He looked "like pictures I had seen of African tribal chieftains: he really should have been naked, with war-paint on and barbaric mementos, standing among spears."[8] His power, it would seem, came from time immemorial, and it was sanctioned by the heavens; indeed, its provenance was the heavens. He "lived, like a prophet, in such unimaginably close communion with the Lord that his long silences which were punctuated by moans and hallelujahs and snatches of old songs . . . never seemed odd to us."[9]

The seemingly absolute power of this god-father, of this father-sovereign, was, Baldwin recalls, undermined as soon as he encountered the white world. In the essay, Baldwin recalls how one of his white teachers took an interest in him and went to his home to ask permission from the young Baldwin's parents to take him to a play: "It was clear, during the brief interview in our living room, that my father was agreeing very much against his will and that he would have refused permission if he had dared. The fact that he did not dare caused me to despise him."[10] The will of the father was not absolute, and the young Baldwin now knew it. It was always already undermined by another will, the will of the white world that surrounded them, putting fatherhood under erasure for black Americans. If the father's role is traditionally to teach the child social norms, to impose rules so that the child can learn the rules of a society, the black father necessarily fails at this task. As Baldwin puts it in a later essay, the black child "must be 'good' not only in order to please his parents and not only to avoid being punished by them; behind their authority stands another, nameless and impersonal, infinitely harder to please, and bottomlessly cruel."[11] Here we start seeing how blackness is a "tremendous spiritual condition," for Baldwin wants to claim that this precariousness of authority—divine, paternal, or political— is a part of the human condition writ large; black Americans just have the opportunity, as it were, to encounter it much earlier, and more frequently, than whites.

The result of trying to be a father in a land that makes fatherhood impossible is madness; Baldwin's father went mad, and it eventually killed him. At the same time, the world also went mad. Race riots left New York in disarray: "As we drove him to the graveyard, the spoils of injustice, anarchy, discontent, and hatred were all around us."[12] And so, too, did the young James Baldwin, but only for a moment. When confronted, at the "American Diner," with a waitress who refused him service because of his race, Baldwin felt hatred become madness in him, hatred that he imagines his father also felt, hatred that animated his father's life. But then, Baldwin grew up. Unlike his father, he was able to acknowledge his own hatred and to see how it could detrimentally affect his life. He saw how his father's Christianity was motivated by this hatred, how its apocalypticism and denial of the world were a product of American race relations—and how they would not remedy racial injustice.

At the end of "Notes of a Native Son," as Baldwin recalls his father's funeral, recalls the officiant speaking Christian words that so falsely described the man he knew, he reflects on a biblical passage his father would preach: "But as for me and my house, we will serve the Lord." Baldwin decides to embrace this sentiment, and in doing so he affirmed his faithfulness to both a divine and a human father. Instead of rejecting any figure of fatherhood, Baldwin would—impossibly—affirm it, affirm a figure of authority that could never come into existence in the world as it is. In doing so, Baldwin professed a faith that entailed not blind belief but the difficult work of identifying and disavowing idolatry. For Baldwin, faith in a god-father ought to mean "acceptance, totally without rancor, of life as it is, and men as they are," which leads, Baldwin continues, to rejecting every distortion of life, indeed, fighting every such injustice.[13] The god-father is not rejected, but he comes to motivate criticism rather than adherence, to motivate the struggle against purported god-fathers, encapsulated by the regime of white supremacy—the "Great White Father."[14]

Baldwin's semi-autobiographical first novel, *Go Tell It on the Mountain*, is also a story of impossible fatherhood. It begins with an alienated son, destined to follow his father into the pulpit, turning fourteen and seeing himself as a sinner. His mother affirms the omniscience of his father: "Your father knows best. You listen to your father, I guarantee you you won't end up in no jail." Then, in the next words out of her mouth, it is God who provides assurances: "there ain't no safety except you walk humble before the Lord."[15] One of the sons ponders, "I know the Lord ain't as hard as Daddy." The novel culminates in the protagonist's conversion, a conversion that effectively replaces the human father with a less stringent divine father. At the very end of the novel, the protagonist and his father have a quiet confrontation: "He turned to face his father—he found himself smiling, but his father did not smile."[16] The father recognized his authority undercut by another; indeed, it was undercut twice. After the conversion, on the way home, the father is reminded by his sister that he is not actually a biological father at all but rather a stepfather. Just as in *Notes of a Native Son*, seemingly absolute authority is exposed as less than absolute. In this case, the relationship between authority and biology is also destabilized (to be a father is not necessarily to be genetically related to a son; Baldwin's own "father" was a stepfather, though this is not mentioned in *Notes*). Yet at the same time that the narrator of *Go Tell It on the Mountain* is refusing his father's authority, he necessarily remains within its orbit: his father, after all, is a preacher, and the protagonist, because of his apparent patrimony, was destined to follow his father into the church.

Baldwin's 1974 novel *If Beale Street Could Talk*, published some twenty years after his first novel, continues to press the question of the impossibility of black fatherhood in America—that is to say, the question of the impossibility of black authority. The novel opens with a woman on her way to tell her unjustly imprisoned lover, Fonny, that she is pregnant. It ends with the birth of this baby coinciding with the suicide of Fonny's father. The book's epigraph, "Mary, Mary, / What you going to name / That pretty little baby?," from a hymn, presses the religious significance of fatherhood. The female protagonist, whose lover was her childhood friend and who persists in a childish innocence about the world, is in a sense mysteriously inseminated (her lover, after all, is in prison, though he was not when she conceived). Where Jesus's paternity was otherworldly, the father of this new, unnamed baby is also taken away by the world—to "the Tombs," the Manhattan Detention Center. The protagonist remarks to the reader that "when I first had to go and see him in the Tombs, and walked up those steps and into those halls, it was just like walking into church."[17] Fonny, imprisoned, can only be an absent father to his Mary-like lover; Fonny's father, in the ghetto, a prison without bars, can never do enough for his son. Despite working long hours and stealing from his employer, there are always more lawyer's fees and a high bail: "I don't know if I was ever any kind of father to him—any kind of *real* father—and now he's in jail and it ain't his fault and I don't even know how I'm going to get him out. I'm sure one hell of a man."[18] Enraged by the impossibility of his position, the father ultimately kills himself. Baldwin dramatizes this crisis of authority by depicting Fonny's father's divine aspirations. Fonny's mother is an assertively pious woman; Fonny overhears his parents making love: "And she'd say, Oh, Frank, let me bring you to the Lord. And he'd say, Shit, woman, I'm going to bring the Lord to *you. I'm the Lord.*"[19]

The fathers depicted in Baldwin's works are authoritarian and aspire to omnipotence, omniscience, and omnipresence. Those aspirations are rejected, but the fathers are not. Fatherhood is inescapable, and the attempt to escape brings doom. Rather, Baldwin calls on us to acknowledge the impossibility of their position, and we must take that paradox of authority-under-erasure as an invitation to purge ourselves of the false authorities that grip us. The same is true—and not merely by analogy—for Baldwin's God. Discussions of political theology, following Carl Schmitt, often focus on the relationship between political sovereign and God's sovereignty, accepting the need for some concept of sovereignty as a given. Perhaps we can read Baldwin as questioning the sovereignty of God and father—and so, the purported sovereignty of political entities, of states or rulers. Then, Baldwin would be posing the question: How can we think sovereignty without authoritarianism?

Idolatry and Theology

When Baldwin discusses religious ideas—that is, when he does more than employ religious language for rhetorical force—he contrasts two types of theology, or, more properly, idolatry and theology. Idolatry is the religion of his father, of Richard Wright, and of Elijah Muhammad, to name a few. Theology is Baldwin's own constructive proposal for how religion ought to fit together. Commitment to idolatry leads to (and is fed by) confusion, anger, hatred, and fallacy; correct theology results in communion and salvation. Baldwin has much more to say about idolatry than theology. This is because the primary content of theology, for him, is the critique of idolatry, and Baldwin is always critiquing idolatry.

On Baldwin's account, idolatry, first and foremost, is motivated by the desire for safety, which in turn is motivated by fear of death: "Perhaps the whole root of our trouble, the human trouble is that we will sacrifice all the beauty of our lives, will imprison ourselves in totems, taboos, crosses, blood sacrifices, steeples, mosques, races, armies, flags, nations, in order to deny the fact of death, which is the only fact we have."[20] Because we fear death, we turn to symbols, rituals, and institutions that promise us safety—but at a high cost. The "principles governing the rites and customs" of churches, black and white, are "Blindness, Loneliness, and Terror, the first principle necessarily and actively cultivated in order to deny the two others."[21] Christianity most often functions as idolatry, offering ways to worship but ultimately concealing truth, ultimately enforcing blindness about ourselves and our worlds. The result is that we feel alone, that we fear, and so we seek safety—back in church.

The desire for safety may be the desire to know that one is saved in the afterlife, or it may be the desire to live in a neighborhood free of crime, or it may be the refusal to acknowledge one's own complicity in sin. Closely related to the desire for safety, but often concealed, is the desire for innocence. Baldwin worries that the desire for innocence necessarily simplifies the world, overlooks the way that we are not in control of ourselves, overlooks the way that sinful histories continue to shape us, and overlooks the culpability we have for the actions of those with whom we relate, even when their actions are not clearly caused by our own. We make distinctions and create categories that insulate us, keeping us safe, protecting our innocence, and we cling to them with religious fervor. We make out of our history a myth, refusing critical engagement in favor of stories about the past that comfort us in the present. Idolatry is supremely dangerous: "The dream of safety can reach culmination or climax only in the nightmare of orgasm or genocide."[22] Safety ultimately means complete elimination of that on which one's fears are projected, or pseudo-communion in rape. It motivates hate crimes that, even when committed by an individual alone, represent idolatrous "communion." Such hate crimes are acts of pseudoreligious sacrifice of the innocent: "the orgasm of the mob is drenched in the blood of the lamb."[23]

The quintessential form of idolatry, for Baldwin, is the belief in a white god. Sometimes this white god has a religious name, but not always. Belief in a white god entails belief in a black devil, in blackness as evil. As Baldwin puts it, "The black man has functioned in the white man's world as a fixed star, as an immovable pillar."[24] Whites are safe when sin is projected onto blacks, allowing whites to ignore their own misdeeds and the complications of their own lives—and to ignore the fact that the fantasy of blackness was created by whites. Baldwin sympathetically cites Bobby Seale's notion that "one of the things that most afflict white people is their disastrous concept of God; they have never accepted the dark gods, and their fear of the dark gods, who live in them at least as surely as the white God does, causes them to distrust life."[25] Life, for Baldwin, is what idolatry conceals. It is complex, impossible to systematize, and always morally ambiguous.

The idolatry of the white god also affects blacks. Some blacks believe it: they believe that whites are inherently superior. This is the problem, Baldwin asserts, with Wright's Bigger Thomas: "Bigger's tragedy is . . . that he has accepted a theology that denies him life, that he admits the possibility of his being sub-human and feels constrained, therefore, to battle for his humanity according to those brutal criteria bequeathed him at his birth."[26] This is also the problem with Baldwin's own father. (Baldwin, it should be noted, describes Wright as "alas! My father.")[27] Despite angrily rejecting whites' belief in God (he describes them as heathen), he accepts their theology. As Baldwin writes in the letter to his nephew that begins *The Fire Next Time,* his father "was defeated long before he died because, at the bottom of his heart, he really believed what white people said about him. This is one of the reasons that he became so holy."[28] Baldwin's father believed, in effect, that by becoming a better idolater he could be saved; this is why he was defeated.

Other blacks, such as Elijah Muhammad, construct their own gods in opposition to the white god, but in so doing reproduce the structure of idolatry—the desire for safety, innocence—that comes with the white god. Baldwin feels as if Muhammad is asking him, "whose little boy are you?," the essential appeal for safety and innocence: for a father-protector, for a god-sovereign. And he feels as if Muhammad is volunteering his services as substitute father. Baldwin appreciates the anger that motivates Muhammad, the urgency with which he speaks, and the need to affirm the worth of black life. But Baldwin cannot accept that race is fundamental to theology, only to idolatry. Further, he cannot accept the mystification of the past that he felt the Nation of Islam promoted. Baldwin cannot accept a substitute father. He must honor his own father—his Christian father—by developing a more compelling theological vision, a political theological vision. Essential to this vision is the notion that idolatry, ultimately, is cowardice: it is faithlessness.

"Complexity is our only safety," Baldwin writes.[29] Baldwin's own statement of the theology he has developed, found in a late essay, begins by repudiating fear and the desire for its elimination as a religious motivation. "Salvation is not precipitated by the terror of being consumed in hell: this terror itself places one in hell. Salvation is preceded by the recognition of sin, by conviction, by repentance."[30] Idolatry, religion motivated by fear, results in damnation; souls are saved when they have faith and turn away from sin—coolly, as it were; motivated not by immediate emotion but by clear perception. Baldwin does not offer a crisp statement of what he means by sin, but he specifies that it is "not limited to carnal activity" and that such activity is not "the most crucial or reverberating of our sins."[31] Once salvation is approached in this way, we near supreme communion, "union with all that is or has been or will ever be."[32] This vision of union is also specific and personal. It involves making whole our broken selves, and making whole our broken relationships with others. Salvation is approached but never achieved. It is a process that happens in time rather than a one-off event. As a process, Baldwin maintains that the need for faithfulness and disavowal of sin (both themselves processes, and interconnected ones) is immediate: as he famously writes, "The time is always now."[33] This temporality of redemption helps to decipher the apocalyptic conclusion of *The*

Fire Next Time. If the faithfulness and disavowal of sin are not happening now, salvation is impossible: we are condemned to damnation.

This is not simply an expansive use of religious rhetoric, adding oomph to a moral or political argument. Baldwin describes salvation as a relationship with God ("accepting and reciprocating the love of God"), although of course the theological and the political are inextricable here.[34] I am arguing that we should understand God in Baldwin's theology negatively, as the name for what remains when idolatry is rejected, rather than metaphorically. Some would see Baldwin as affirming, in the tradition of American Transcendentalists, transcendence without the transcendent, a sense of the divine without God. Such a reading misses the specifically Christian commitments that Baldwin maintains. Unlike the Christian caricature of Judaism, as a religion in which salvation is achieved by strictly following rules, in Baldwin's theology salvation has already been achieved for us. We just need to accept it—by rejecting false belief. Baldwin develops a specifically Christian name for this acceptance: love. In a sense, the idolatries that Baldwin rejects are precisely those that Christ rejects: the beliefs of those who claim to condemn in the name of God, who cultivate fear for their own benefit, and who refuse to critically examine themselves and their worlds. Specific worldly practices are not needed, on Baldwin's account; all that is needed is faith, lived in daily life, manifesting as love.

Secrets of the Heart

Baldwin writes, "The value of the human being is all that I hold sacred."[35] But, given the deeply Christian outlook that informs his theological (and political) writings, Baldwin is not best understood as a humanist. He is not simply rejecting the projection of human desires onto a god-father and instead affirming the divinity of the human, her inherent worth and dignity. Baldwin does, indeed, value the human being greatly, but he values the human being insofar as the human being contains the image of God—remembering that, for Baldwin, the image of God is the rejection of idolatry, is that which exceeds and eludes human concepts. The "human riddle," writes Baldwin, is that a "mighty, unnameable, transfiguring force . . . lives in the soul of man."[36] This soul, in which Baldwin clearly and emphatically believes, is a mystery, and that mystery humbles us and reminds us that the world is saturated with mysteries that no ideology can ever explain. The attempt to explain them, to the soul or to the world, inevitably does violence, both metaphorically and literally. Yet the attempt to understand the soul, and the world, is crucial: this is Baldwin's main article of faith. It is a task of understanding that will always fall short. Our job is to try again, and to fail better. This is just the opposite of the humanist claim to respect the human being for certain reasons, because of certain attributes. Baldwin calls for reverence, not respect, and this reverence is due precisely because the human has a soul that is indescribable, that is incomprehensible by reason. Accepting such ineffability is difficult work; it is the work of faith. But the indescribable nature of the soul is the only proposition which, for Baldwin, deserves the label of truth.

Particularly in Baldwin's early writings, what might be called, somewhat misleadingly, the question of identity is the driving force. It is not quite right to call this the question of identity because the answer to the question of who Baldwin is, of who the protagonist is, is an essential opacity accompanied by an affirmation of the continuing urgency of the question. The question of identity has overwhelming importance and requires rigorous attention but will never yield clarity, except that one must clearly reject those who peddle in clarity. Of his adolescent experience as a pious Christian, Baldwin writes: "I rushed home from school, to the church, to the altar, to be alone there, to commune with Jesus, my dearest Friend, who would never fail me, who knew all the secrets of my heart. Perhaps He did, but I didn't, and the bargain we struck, actually, down there at the foot of the cross, was that He would never let me find out."[37] The young Baldwin, puzzled by his changing body and desires, sought clarity in God, who knew what the boy could not discern about himself. In this religious phase, this idolatrous phase, Baldwin delegated the task of self-examination to God (it had once been delegated to his father). This is the structure of idolatry that Baldwin would later disclaim, the thought, *deep down I have a secret that God knows,* rather than, *knowing that deep down I am opaque is how I can know God.* The former thought is what leads to pathologies, sexual and political; it supports blindness, the desire for safety. The latter thought motivates self-examination, and it gives meaning to life—Baldwin affirms the Socratic maxim that the unexamined life is not worth living.[38]

The opacity of the human being makes the human being sacred, that is, marks the image of God in the human. Recognizing that essential characteristic (or rather noncharacteristic) of humans is what allows for communion: we recognize that "all men are brothers."[39] Baldwin writes that Americans are "in desperate search for something which will help them re-establish their connection with themselves, and with one another."[40] In a world of heterogeneity, community can be achieved only by recognizing and probing the sacred opacity of each human, and so reverencing each human (this is, for Baldwin, salvation). The result is neither heterogeneity nor homogeneity, but complex connection. The world conspires to conceal essential humanity, to categorize people by race, and in other ways, asserting that color marks humanity all the way down. In accepting this, we are refusing our own humanity. As Baldwin remarks, "It is a terrible, an inexorable, law that one cannot deny the humanity of another without diminishing one's own: in the face of one's victim, one sees oneself."[41] A victim is not attacked because of who they are but because of what they are, because of the way their humanity is categorized. An attacker deceives himself into believing that questions of who can be reduced to questions of what, a belief applied to the victim and so becoming definitive of the attacker.

All humans, even the most stubborn and prideful, contain a sacred remainder, and they sense it. Such a remainder manifests as charisma. As Baldwin writes of his father: "There was something else in him, buried in him, which lent him his tremendous power and, even, a rather crushing charm. It had something to do with his blackness, I think—he was very black—with his blackness and his beauty, and with the fact that he knew that he was black but did not know that he was beautiful."[42] Baldwin's father was black, that is what he was, but he was also more, he also had a sacred remainder—a remainder that was good, and true, and beautiful—but it was a remainder of which Baldwin's father was unaware. It was the source of his charisma, of his power. Baldwin sees in the white world only the faintest hints of a sacred remainder, of a who beyond a what. The secrets of the heart can continually be contained, the categories structuring the world seeming to fit well. But this is a refusal. When the terms "you think describe and define you inevitably collide with the facts of life," we are posed with "a very narrow choice." We can do as Baldwin's father did, and have a mighty but tragic power, or we can say "*Yes, Lord.* Which is to say yes to life."[43] We can welcome God by welcoming his image in our hearts. Blacks are confronted with this choice more pressingly than whites, and this is a grand opportunity. Baldwin concludes that blacks "grow up under the necessity of questioning everything—everything, from the question of one's identity to the literal, brutal question of how to save one's life in order to begin to live it."[44] In this way, blacks have privileged access to the sacred, live with that "tremendous spiritual condition."

Most people do not have an opportunity to reflect on the ways that the world misrepresents them. Most people depend on the wisdom of the world, on the concepts and categories of the world, to go about their lives. (Most blacks realize there is misrepresentation at work but do not have time to reflect; most whites do not realize there is misrepresentation.) Writers are the exception. Such reflection is the writer's vocation, according to Baldwin. It is, in a not particularly metaphorical sense, a religious vocation, in pursuit of the good, the true, and the beautiful. The only "real" conversation Baldwin ever had with his father, he recalls, is when his father asked him, "You'd rather write than preach, wouldn't you?," to which Baldwin responded, "Yes." The religion of the father is preaching, law; the religion of the son is writing, grace. Preaching is the practice of idolatry; writing is practical theology. Writers, he writes, are "the only people who know the truth about us." He adds: "Art is here to prove, and to help one bear, the fact that all safety is an illusion. In this sense, all artists are divorced from and even necessarily opposed to any system whatever." Baldwin is not here proclaiming allegiance to art for art's sake. He is making a theological assertion, a negative theological assertion: the pursuit of the beautiful (aligned with the true and the good) means the rejection of all worldly attempts to describe the beautiful, the true, or the good—the rejection of "any system whatever." The alienation of the artist—"for reasons he cannot explain to himself or to others, he does not belong anywhere"—is not alienation at all but faithful commitment to the ineffability of the human soul, to probing the secrets of the heart. In so doing, the writer reminds those who are swept up in the inertia of ordinary life about that "mighty, unnamable, transfiguring force" that resides within them, and within every human being—and so, the writer serves to the reader words as communion wafers, making of humanity a sacred unity, and bringing redemption. At least this ought to be the writer's aspiration, argues Baldwin.[45]

The writer, as a member of the spiritual elite, embodies freedom, and the writer is an evangelist for this freedom. For Baldwin, freedom, genuine freedom, is not freedom from constraint, nor is it freedom as constraint, freedom achieved by following a set of religious rules. Rather, Baldwin understands freedom in a highly Christian sense: "Ye shall know the truth, and the truth shall set you free."[46] Freedom comes when we are not con-strained by worldly concepts and categories, when idolatries are discard-ed and we are left in what remains, which is truth. Americans, Baldwin charges, make freedom synonymous with comfort, that supreme idol. On his view, in contrast, "to be free . . . you have to look into yourself and know *who you are*."[47] Baldwin describes realizing that he, like his father, was not free, that he was in bondage to his hatred, of whites. Whiteness, after all, is a worldly category and the ultimate idol. The result of Baldwin's bondage: "I thus gave the world an altogether murderous power over me . . . in such a self-destroying limbo I could never hope to write."[48] Acknowledging and accepting that feeling of hatred, rather than repressing it, made him free: free of the world's power over him, not to "be himself" in some anodyne sense but to participate in the beautiful, the true, and the good: to write.

No Salvation without Love

Baldwin's early work poses a question and makes questioning the answer. Later, Baldwin offers a new answer, an even more Christian answer: *Who am I? I am a lover.* When idolatry is refused, when we realize our essential identity, the proper response to that opacity is not simply reverence; it is love. Like writing, love is difficult: "Love is a battle, love is a war; love is a growing up."[49] Love is "quest and daring and growth."[50] This work, though, offers a rich reward. Baldwin writes, "Only that work which is love and that love which is work will allow one to come anywhere near obeying the dictum laid down by the great Ray Charles, and—tell the truth."[51] Baldwin's early work focused on the opacity of the self, whereas his later work fo-cuses on the opacity of others, of those we love (including ourselves). When we experience love, we realize that we cannot control our lover, not with our bodies or our desires or our concepts. For the same reason, we can-not merge with our lover, despite our desires. Love happens as we explore the opacity of the other, as we desire to know her (as we desire to know ourselves), knowing that we will never know her, knowing that we can at best fail better. In that process of failing better, fueled by desire, comes pleasure—not from attaining or capturing an object but from accepting distance, accepting it as sacred: "When two people love each other, when they really love each other, everything that happens between them has something of a sacramental air."[52]

Put another way, if writing is a practice for the spiritual elite, Baldwin turns later to love as a practice for the masses. Baldwin recalls that his first love affair, in France, taught him the significance of love as a practice accessible to all. Love, he found, "was breathing and belching beside me, and it was the key to life. Not merely the key to *my* life, but to life itself."[53] In other words, love offers access to that world beneath ideology, beneath concepts that always misrepresent. Love does not offer this access through fantasy or through the imagination, but through the direct contact it entails with the unsentimentalized realities of life: "breathing and belching." Through love, according to Baldwin, "the masks that we fear we cannot live without and know we cannot live within" are removed.[54] In other words, love functions to expose and critique idolatry. But love also names Baldwin's eschaton, the state in which all idolatry has been removed, the state of perfect communion. This is not, in fact, a state, but a process in which we participate when we love. In other words, we do not love (or write) so that we can eventually achieve a state of perfect harmony, of communion. The work of loving (or writing) is itself participation in that communion. In political terms, we do not struggle so that one day we can live in peace. We struggle because the process of struggling itself is desirable—indeed, is salvific: "There is absolutely no salvation without love."[55]

Love, for Baldwin, means seeing rightly (a formulation that strikingly resonates with the reflections of Simone Weil and Iris Murdoch). When we love an object, we see it in truth, its imperfections as well as its virtues. We are compelled to be honest about both. Baldwin describes himself as a lover of America, and so a critic of America. If his affection for America resulted only in praise, it would not be love at all but fantasy. Love allows its object freedom to be what it is, and so assures that the lover maintains her own freedom, to live truthfully. Baldwin asserts that blacks are privileged lovers of America because the stakes are so high in their ability to see America rightly: their life depends on it. Is it then the case that seeing rightly requires love in the same way that love requires seeing rightly? Baldwin would seem to respond in the affirmative, for the process of seeing rightly, of carefully observing, and reacting, recalibrating, observing some more, the process of what Simone Weil would call attention, *just is love*. It brings with it affective investment. It is not a process directed at most objects in our worlds, just those we care about—whether because of our desire or by necessity. (Similarly, the writer only writes well about things she cares about.) For most objects in our worlds, we accept the wisdom of the world; we regurgitate the things most people say about them. This is why Baldwin's theology remains pre-eschatological. This side of the eschaton, it is only in small corners of our lives that we can aspire to see rightly, truthfully—to love.

Idolatrous love is motivated by fear; it distorts and it controls. It is, in fact, not love at all. Baldwin describes his youthful preaching in this way: "I hoped to love them more than I would ever love any lover and, so, escape the terrors of this life." Eventually, he realized the destitution of such love, how it made him "a liar": "I did not want my love to become manipulation. I did not want my fear of my own desires to transform itself into power—into power, precisely, over those who feared and were therefore at the mercy of their own desires."[56] Such love produces sexual pathologies: consider Baldwin's story "Going to Meet the Man," in which a white policeman is only able to make love to his wife when remembering the arrest and lynching of black men. Whites, on Baldwin's view, systematically deceive themselves in all areas of their lives. Because of their privileged position and their desire for safety, their fantasies are not tested against the realities of life, so their love is systematically deformed. It often requires the presence of blacks, on whom unacknowledged fear and desire is projected. But this is a service that blacks can, and should, according to Baldwin, refuse. The only hope whites have of salvation lies in blacks who might genuinely love them: "we, with love, shall force our brothers to see themselves as they are, to cease fleeing from reality."[57] Blacks have privileged access to truth, and to the truth about white Americans; it is truth, practiced in love, that brings salvation.

Genuine love, because it is love of who rather than what a beloved is, disregards race: "one must accept one's nakedness."[58] The nakedness involved in love, whether of baby or lover or aging parent, or nation, brings with it vulnerability, exposure, risk: the opposite of safety. This points toward the political implications of Baldwin's account of love. It is an ethical practice, a practice that teaches us to live well, and to live well together. Love prepares us for democratic politics: when our souls are accustomed to uncertainty and risk, and to the distortions of worldly wisdom, we are well equipped for the precariousness of democratic political processes, processes that demand commitment and imply contingency at once. Moreover, it is the least of these—in the case of Baldwin's America, blacks—who are best equipped for democratic politics. Whites, because of the unexamined fears and desires accompanying their loves, including their love for America, enter democratic deliberation with antidemocratic tendencies.

In Baldwin's political theology, must authorities love? Baldwin concludes that his father, despite much harsh treatment and apparent cruelty, did, in fact, love his children, albeit "in his outrageously demanding and protective way."[59] His father's love was misshaped by hatred and fear, distended but not destroyed. Fatherhood brings love because it brings attentiveness, close observation from birth through life. Love, Baldwin asserts, is "constant" even if "we may not always think so."[60] This seems quite different from the love Baldwin described in France, the love that first awakened him to love. But for Baldwin there is only one type of love, for truth is unequivocal. Love may be more or less intense, may be more or less revelatory, but it is still love, whether it is of a sexual partner or a father or a son. Indeed, love blends into sensuality, which Baldwin describes, in rather religious terms, as presence, "from the effort of loving to the breaking of bread."[61] Indeed, the closeness of the protagonist and his brother in *Tell Me How Long the Train's Been Gone*—they hold each other in bed, and masturbate together—points to the way Baldwin blurs the lines between intimacy, love, and sensuality. Ratcheting up the intensity of love is desirable because it thrusts the lover toward truth. Hence Baldwin promises his nephew, Big James, to love him "hard, at once, and forever, to strengthen you against the loveless world."[62] Given the pervasive distortions of the world, given the prevalence of idolatry, it is necessary for fatherly figures to love as much as possible. Love, says Baldwin, provides a home, but home does not mean safety and security. It means being comfortable with risk, with the precariousness of life.

Love or Lust?

Political theology has traditionally focused on political and theological concepts of sovereignty; Baldwin's negative political theology, naming as idolatry each attempt to establish a sovereign authority—sovereign God, sovereign father, sovereign self, and political sovereign— offers a refreshing alternative approach. Politically troubling, however, is Baldwin's second move: christening as love what remains after (or, better, through) the critique of idolatry. This is politically troubling because love stands astride the division between ethics and politics. Martin Luther King Jr., for example, famously suggested a deep connection between love and social justice, yet love is also a virtue, one of the three theological virtues, together with faith and hope. If all Baldwin were claiming for love was its ethical relevance, that it shaped the soul in a way that made citizens ready for democratic deliberation, say, this seems reasonably defensible. But Baldwin claims something more. For him, love happens between individuals, sexually, between family members, between friends, between enemies, between citizens and nations, and between authorities and their subjects. He suggests that there is genuine love and a false kind of love, animated by fear and unacknowledged desire. But beyond this distinction, Baldwin offers no help in picking out what we might call, following Augustine, rightly ordered love. There can be no right ordering, on Baldwin's account of love, because love precisely names that which is without norms, that which remains when worldly concepts recede.

Baldwin's novels, most of all *Another Country,* explore the varieties of love and desire, and the way that race in America shapes desire. But Baldwin has a tendency to remain descriptive, rather than normative, when giving accounts of desire: they are all part of the work of love, all examples of failing, and then failing better. Even in *Go Tell It on the Mountain,* where Baldwin has a very clear position with respect to authority, accounting for its transfer from father to God catalyzed by the self's opacity, he remains curiously equivocal on his protagonist's sensuality, particularly his attraction to the older Elisha. Sensuality is present in the narrative, but it only functions as evidence of our opacity to ourselves, evidence of the self's sacred remainder. Read in light of Baldwin's later work, where this opacity is named love, *Go Tell It on the Mountain* becomes a struggle between idolatrous loves, of father and God, and genuine love, the sensual/sexual love of John and Elisha, a love emanating directly from the boys' opaque selves, a love performing the end of idolatry.

I worry that the political potency of love, which comes about when love is connected with justice, is lost when love is placed in a realm free of norms. Recalling his relationship with his father, paradigmatic for his relationship with authority, Baldwin decides that "serving the Lord," the god-father, means putting new content in old form: "All of my father's texts and songs, which I had decided were meaningless, were arranged before me at his death like empty bottles, waiting to hold the meaning which life would give them for me."[63] Such images point to the distance at which Baldwin holds norms. His father provides empty bottles that can be filled with anything; it is only the bottles that are given. Paternal love might involve struggle, but it is the struggle to make sense of what is given; whatever results from that struggle (essentially with oneself) will be free of judgment. Every art project receives an A+ so long as it is not captive to the father's rules. But what can it mean to work with the father's texts and songs but not the father's rules, not his judgment?

It was with the rise to national prominence of Martin Luther King Jr. that Baldwin began extoling love, but for King, love and power were always deeply entwined. As he famously put it: "Power without love is reckless and abusive, and love without power is sentimental and anemic. Power at its best is love implementing the demands of justice, and justice at its best is power correcting everything that stands against love." In contrast, it seems that for Baldwin power is necessarily disjunct from love. The imperative to love may demand the use of power, to oppose idolatry, but this use of power is instrumental. Certainly, for Baldwin love is not an end state but a process, a struggle. But this struggle, which happens through worldly things—words and bodies—is directed toward a communion of souls free of worldly things. Put theologically, the worry is about the desire to bring about the eschaton in a world of sin, and the degrading of creation that results. For Baldwin, we can approach redemption when worldly distinctions are eliminated, between familial and sexual love, between love and sensuality, between love of nation and love of self. Bodies and pleasures mingle without form as souls commune. But in the Christian tradition the image of God in humans is not an indiscernible secret of the heart soliciting love. It is manifested in words and bodies; it is these that are to be loved. These are to be loved for the way in which they image God, for their beauty, goodness, and truth. All words and bodies participate in beauty, goodness, and truth to some extent, but that extent varies. It is in this way that love, power, and justice combine. Loving rightly does not require accepting and so bracketing all worldly distinctions to commune with the soul; it requires judging worldly distinctions, the good and the bad, the beautiful and the ugly, and embracing the good and the beautiful while using power to correct the bad and the ugly. Baldwin has much to say about lust: about its motivations in fear and false consciousness, specifically, in fantasies of racial difference. But instead of seeing lust as disordered love in need of correction, he places it in a different category than love, which is blind to race. This is the position of Baldwin's essays; in novels such as *Giovanni's Room* and *Another Country*, Baldwin seems to be doing quite the opposite: teaching the reader lessons in how love can be disordered, lessons in the continuity between love and lust.

Baldwin generally avoids discussing political institutions (are we to love the president? the presidency?). This could lead us to read Baldwin as, strictly, a political theorist of social movements, movements that can, more plausibly than political institutions, be animated by love. But Baldwin does consider, in both his fiction and nonfiction, one political institution: the criminal justice system. The legal system brings to the fore the issue with which Baldwin's political theology is least well equipped to deal: judgment and condemnation. Judgment, of course, is the essence of courts; ideally, judgment animated by justice. Baldwin's negative political theology reserves judgment and condemnation only for idolatry, not for individuals. To condemn an individual, for Baldwin, implies a commitment to idolatry. Baldwin describes condemnation as "fueled by terror and self-hatred": "Salvation repudiates condemnation, since we all have the right, for many reasons, to condemn one another. Condemnation is easier than wonder."[64] Law enforcement is, expectedly, viewed by Baldwin as theology gone wrong: as idolatry: "Both the white fundamentalist minister and the deputy are Christians—*hard-core* Christians, one might say. Both believe that they are responsible, the one for divine law and the other for natural order. Both believe that they are able to define and privileged to impose law and order; and both, historically and actually, know that law and order are meant to keep me in my place."[65] The legal system, like Christianity of the worst sort, condemns, and the burden of condemnation most often falls on the backs of blacks. Yet what Baldwin's alternative would be, in the political rather than religious realm, remains unclear. His reconfiguration of theology does not so easily transform into a reconfiguration of politics. What is a court system that would reverence the souls of the accused?

Baldwin writes, "I do not claim that everyone in prison here is innocent, but I do claim that the law, as it operates, is guilty, and that the prisoners, therefore, are all unjustly imprisoned."[66] It is unclear what implications Baldwin intends from statements such as these. It is clear, from his reflections elsewhere, that he is not simply concerned with particularly high incarceration rates in the United States, or particularly harsh prison conditions (though he is concerned with them). Baldwin is concerned with the institution of the prison itself, and the prisoner. But it is unclear whether he is saying that prisons should be abolished (together with courts?), or if he is reminding us that any human institution that purports to judge guilt and innocence will fail in that task. This latter claim seems to be, in effect, a reminder that there is sin in the world, that we live on the near side of the eschaton, rather than a statement about politics. If politics means figuring out how to live together in a fallen world, it does not seem to be a topic that interests Baldwin much at all. On his account, making judgments, for individuals, is inescapable, but when judgment is institutionalized, it becomes farcical: "Each of us knows, though we do not like this knowledge, that a courtroom is a visceral Roman circus. No one involved in this contest is, or can be, impartial . . . the ability to suspend judgment is, in each of us, suspect."[67]

The injustice of the criminal justice system is a theme that pervades Baldwin's writings, from his early autobiographical essay about his arrest in Paris through his reflections on the persecution of the Black Panthers juxtaposed with the persecution of his much more anonymous black friend Tony in *No Name in the Street* to his late account of the Atlanta child murders, and the trial that resulted, in *The Evidence of Things Not Seen. If Beale Street Could Talk* is a novel that entirely revolves around unjust policing and imprisonment. Police harassment follows Fonny and lands him in jail for rape, navigating a byzantine legal system with the "help" of a morally ambiguous lawyer. Fonny's friend, significantly named Daniel, is released from prison and tells of the horrors he experienced. Fonny reflects on his own captivity, realizing that he is not in jail because of his acts, and the other prisoners are not, either: "These captive men are the hidden price for a hidden lie: the righteous must be able to locate the damned."[68] In contrast to the world of unjust and irrational condemnation in *Beale Street*, Baldwin presents a world of love: Tish's love for Fonny. It is love that reveals truth: she is our trusted narrator, giving us an honest account of her experiences, an honest picture of the misunderstood Fonny (who only wants to create, to sculpt). The world is dishonest, its norms and concepts misleading, to the extent that Tish and Fonny can live honestly only when they use names that have no relation to their own (Clementine and Alonzo). *Beale Street* is such a hopeless novel because the two worlds, of love and of justice, have nothing to do with each other.

This worry about Baldwin's account of love may be addressed by recalling his account of writing, for love and writing do the same work of revealing truth. They are both, for Baldwin, spiritual practices. Writing has the effect of conveying truth, but the writer does not simply write truth. "I do not like people who are *earnest* about anything," he writes.[69] To write truth—to write *earnestly*—would be to suppose that words had the ability to represent reality perfectly, but they do not. Words do quite the opposite, on Baldwin's view, functioning as idols, keeping us safe from the complexity of ourselves and our worlds. The writing that Baldwin commends manipulates, persuades, in the service of truth. The "protest novel," in contrast, manipulates and persuades in the service of politics. Baldwin does not position his own writing as apolitical, but as doing politics better, more thoroughly, more rigorously. To do the work of persuasion that is necessary for writing, the writer must be "thoroughly disciplined," must be fully versed in social norms (and the norms of literary traditions).[70] The writer looks out onto a mix of the good and the bad, the true and the false, the beautiful and the ugly, and the writer produces work that draws an audience toward the good, the true, and the beautiful. The writer does not simply condemn the false and wallow in truth. The writer does not condemn—that would be too earnest—but her writing has the effect of condemnation, the effect of judgment.

Yet Baldwin's account of love seems to be missing this sense of judgment, this acknowledgment of the power of lovers, their partiality, the condemnation that can be implicit in their love. All of that Baldwin casts as accompanying lust. The result is that Baldwin's political theology, his constructive account of love, is apolitical. It is his negative political theology, his dogged critique of idolatry—of ideology—that is of lasting import.

Notes

1. See Clarence E. Hardy, *James Baldwin's God: Sex, Hope, and the Crisis in Black Holiness Culture* (Knoxville: University of Tennessee Press, 2003).

2. Michael Walzer, *Interpretation and Social Criticism* (Cambridge: Harvard University Press, 1987).

3. George Shulman, *American Prophecy: Race and Redemption in American Political Culture* (Minneapolis: University of Minnesota Press, 2008).

4. James Baldwin, *Collected Essays* (New York: Library of America, 1998), 471.

5. Ibid., 7.

6. Ibid., 468.

7. Ibid., 303.

8. Ibid., 64.

9. Ibid., 66.

10. Ibid., 68.

11. Ibid., 302.

12. Ibid., 63.

13. Ibid., 84.

14. Ibid., 410.

15. Baldwin, *Early Novels and Stories* (New York: Library of America, 1998), 23.

16. Ibid., 215.

17. Baldwin, *If Beale Street Could Talk* (New York: Dial, 1974), 26.

18. Ibid., 126.

19. Ibid., 16.

20. Baldwin, *Collected Essays*, 339.

21. Ibid., 305.

22. Baldwin, *The Evidence of Things Not Seen* (New York: Holt, Rinehart and Winston, 1985), 102.

23. Baldwin, *Collected Essays*, 840; cf. René Girard, *Violence and the Sacred* (Baltimore: Johns Hopkins University Press, 1977).

24. Baldwin, *Collected Essays*, 294.

25. Ibid., 437.

26. Ibid., 18.

27. Ibid., 253.

28. Ibid., 291.

29. Baldwin, *The Cross of Redemption: Uncollected Writings* (New York: Pantheon, 2010), 165.

30. Ibid., 164.

31. Ibid.

32. Ibid.

33. Baldwin, *Collected Essays*, 214.

34. Baldwin, *The Cross of Redemption*, 164.

35. Ibid., 205.

36. Ibid., 56.

37. Baldwin, *Collected Essays*, 307.

38. Ibid., 391.

39. Baldwin, *The Cross of Redemption*, 205.

40. Ibid., 6.

41. Baldwin, *Collected Essays*, 179.

42. Ibid., 64.

43. Baldwin, *The Cross of Redemption*, 73; Baldwin's emphasis.

44. Baldwin, *Collected Essays*, 431.
45. Baldwin, *The Cross of Redemption*, 42.
46. Baldwin, *Collected Essays*, 432.
47. Baldwin, *The Cross of Redemption*, 70; Baldwin's emphasis.
48. Baldwin, *Collected Essays*, 8.
49. Ibid., 220.
50. Ibid., 341.
51. Ibid., 426.
52. Baldwin, *If Beale Street Could Talk*, 143.
53. Baldwin, *Collected Essays*, 365.
54. Ibid., 341.
55. Baldwin, *The Cross of Redemption*, 164–65.
56. Ibid., 160.
57. Baldwin, *Collected Essays*, 294.
58. Ibid., 366.
59. Ibid., 64.
60. Ibid., 339.
61. Ibid., 311.
62. Ibid., 292.
63. Ibid., 83.
64. Baldwin, *The Cross of Redemption*, 165.
65. Ibid., 161–62; Baldwin's emphasis.
66. Baldwin, *Collected Essays*, 444.
67. Baldwin, *The Evidence of Things Not Seen*, 1.
68. Baldwin, *If Beale Street Could Talk*, 192.
69. Baldwin, *Collected Essays*, 9; Baldwin's emphasis.
70. Baldwin, *The Cross of Redemption*, 8.

7

Go Tell It on the Mountain

James Baldwin and the Politics of Faith

Wilson Carey McWilliams

James Baldwin was a constant American despite all his years of expatriation, a native son whose subjects and audiences were primarily American, even when (as in *Giovanni's Room*) he set his story overseas. He was a fervent critic of the American regime precisely because he was an anguished lover, and nothing is clearer in Baldwin's work than the depth of his concern for American political life and culture.

Baldwin's direct involvement in political affairs, however, was relatively slight, skeptical, and infrequent, confined almost entirely to the edge of movements, parties, and events.[1] He practiced a version of what Neal Riemer has called "prophetic politics"; he spoke of "political freedom in spiritual terms," Baldwin said, out of a conviction that the "spiritual state" of a nation ultimately controls its institutions and laws.[2] Politics, so understood, is starkly at odds with the prevailing doctrine of contemporary liberalism: Baldwin's politics had "foundations"; except in the narrowest legal sense, religious neutrality is impossible; and most of what passes for politics is only so many shadows on the wall of the Cave.[3]

In Baldwin's view, social categories and institutions—all the distinctions that do and must mean so much in practice—are ultimately incomplete definitions of our identities, at best useful and at worst distortions that obscure or diminish our humanity.[4] Race, obviously, was Baldwin's primary example, but almost as frequently he pointed to gender; similarly, he regarded all ideologies as overly abstract efforts to simplify human complexity.[5] At the same time, conventions are inevitable: the Cave is real, its partial truths and illusions have power, and it is extremely difficult, even "virtually impossible," to step beyond the terms and assumptions of one's society and time. Still, nature tests convention, and society itself is not free from ambivalence: "The paradox of education is precisely this: that as one begins to become conscious, one begins to examine the society in which [one] is being educated. The purpose of education, finally, is to create in a person the ability . . . to ask questions of the universe and then learn to live with those questions. . . . But no society is really anxious to have that kind of person around. What societies . . . want is a citizenry that will simply obey rules."[6] In American practice, one cannot exist without being "black" or "white," but one cannot inwardly be either without ceasing to exist: a self-definition in terms of race (or in terms of sexual orientation) abridges or rejects one's humanity.[7] Practical politics matters, but—engrossed with the issues as they appear in the half-light of convention—neither the "protest novel" nor protest politics is "profound and tough" enough to get to the human heart of things.[8] The effectual truth is not the *whole* truth, and it is the whole truth that justice demands.[9]

Politics depends on people who excel at the cave art of getting results, but it also needs voices to articulate the human universals, not only our dependence and mortality but also the recognition of the self in the other (and the other in the self), the fact of commonality, the self as a part of a whole.[10] In one sense Baldwin argued for the proposition—the too-often garbled cornerstone of multiculturalism—that the human is naturally sovereign over the cultural, the theoretical over the experiential.[11] Love, Baldwin's Grail, he saw as the dynamic of a journey that points to the love of all, that "opens the door to that which is greater than oneself" and, ultimately, even greater than humanity itself.[12]

At the same time, Baldwin recognized—in part from firsthand experience—that the impulse to love is dangerous, that it is all too easy to be deceived by one's hopes and illusions, and that human love at its best involves the certainty of loss.[13] Moreover, Baldwin knew that it is only in rare moments of the soul that human beings catch a glimpse of his vision and that our yearning for the extraordinary can endanger the commonplace.

Nevertheless, he was persuaded that human fraternity, ultimately beyond human realization, always draws us. Even in his most pessimistic moments, Baldwin emphasized the need to keep the faith, seeking to find words for the too-often voiceless promptings of the spirit.[14] Early on, Baldwin wrote that he left the pulpit to preach the gospel: he became, in other words, an evangelist of the pen.[15]

Yet, while his work had echoes of evangelical politics—Lawrie Balfour calls him "preoccupied with personal transformation"—writing imposes its own discipline on the evangelical mantra, "one soul at a time."[16] Potentially accessible to all literate persons, writing addresses an audience far less specific, less known, and more varied in the states and qualities of soul of which it is composed than that reached by an evangelist's voice or person. And the writer who would speak of high things, consequently, is even more strongly impelled to speak in parables, embedding extraordinary teaching in conventional stories for those "who have ears to hear."[17]

Balfour shrewdly titled her study of Baldwin *The Evidence of Things Not Said*, a paraphrase of the definition of faith in Hebrews 11:1—"the evidence of things not seen"—which itself leaves unsaid the first part of that text, "the assurance [or substance] of things hoped for." The African American heritage, as Baldwin understood it, is premised on an assurance offered by the unseen and unsaid, the word beyond words.[18] *Go Tell It on the Mountain* includes any number of autobiographical elements; it describes a dimension of African American experience with unique power.[19] But it is much more than a record of a time or culture. In one sense a parable about racial identity, the book is also a teaching about human identity, and Baldwin devotes his eloquence and craft to leading his reader beyond the categories of practice, and the evidence of eyes and words, toward the unseen city.[20]

Go Tell It on the Mountain describes a day in the life of a Harlem family in 1935, John Grimes's fourteenth birthday, a traditional marker of entry into manhood. And from the beginning, Baldwin signals his own artistry.

The novel is divided into three parts, "The Seventh Day," "The Prayer of the Saints," and "The Threshing Floor," each broadly sermonic and furnished with a scriptural text.[21]

The first, "The Seventh Day," is prefaced by a reference to the last chapter of the last book of the Christian scriptures, as if to mirror that testament's promise that the "last shall be first," a reversal of conventional order and perception. The citation itself, to Revelation 22:17, invites "him that heareth" to join the "Spirit and bride" in yearning for Christ's coming, also promising the "water of life" to "him that is athirst." The following verse in the text, however, warns against adding to or subtracting from the words of the book, "For I testify unto every man that heareth the words of the prophecy of this book."[22] Baldwin's citation indicates that the effectiveness of a teaching depends on hearers who are able and disposed to discern and receive it; emphasizing that a written doctrine depends on care in writing and attention in reading, Baldwin's subtext is a guide and caution when approaching his own book.

"The Seventh Day" introduces the principal characters in *Go Tell It on the Mountain,* the Grimes family and their church, the storefront Temple of the Fire Baptized. Like "The Threshing Floor," "The Seventh Day" is distinctively John's story, and the major characters in John's version of the family drama—himself; his mother, Elizabeth; and his stepfather, Gabriel—evoke the account of the birth of John the Baptist in the first chapter of Luke.[23] There, the Angel Gabriel silences Zacharias, Elizabeth's husband, for his failure to believe in her miraculous conception of John. Baldwin's Gabriel, however, in part plays the role of Zacharias, unable to see that his stepson, John, is the child of his spirit because he is fixated on Royal, the child of his body. But unlike Zacharias, Gabriel Grimes is decidedly not silent.

For that matter, John, when he meets him, is no prophet in the wilderness. He knows that his power lies in words, but he intends to use his talent as a writer to *resist* God, to escape the life of "his father and his father's fathers," the poverty and humiliation he associates with the "way of the cross."[24] At the very least, he yearns for some way around "God's injustice," the choice between righteousness and the things of the world.[25] Of course, John has reason to be angry at the oppressiveness of his circumstances, but his rebellion—rejecting the African American heritage as little more than a record of shame—mirrors and validates the prevailing doctrine of white society.

Liberalism, for all its varieties, is united by the conviction that liberty is humanity's defining characteristic and excellence, a good to be preserved and enhanced to the greatest possible extent, even—as F. W. J. Schelling called it—"the one and all of philosophy."[26] Liberty is linked to dominion:

political society, which sets limits to the will of individuals, is justified when it adds to our safety and our mastery over nature, pushing back the boundaries of that great constraint, making us, in one way or another, freer than we were before. While the liberal tradition regards self-preservation as an instinctive goal, its strong voice also advises us that without our fundamental liberties, nothing is secure, so that we must defend our rights even at the risk of life, because it is unendurable to be less than free. Generations of young Americans learned the lesson from Patrick Henry: "Is life so dear or peace so sweet as to be purchased at the price of chains and slavery? Forbid it Almighty God, I know not what course others may take, but as for me, give me liberty or give me death."[27] The great majority of African Americans trace their descent to ancestors who made the other choice, and in these terms, the verdict of liberalism is that the African American past is founded on a preference for life that is at best understandable but low, and at worst, a mark of dishonor.[28]

In *Go Tell It on the Mountain,* a large part of Baldwin's concern is the effort to help African Americans reclaim their past rather than feel obliged to reinvent it, to set a truer value on the teachings and human qualities that liberalism deprecates.[29] At the same time, in speaking *of* African Americans, Baldwin is talking, through John, *to* all Americans: African Americans found support and inspiration in the texts and teachings of biblical religion, and Baldwin's broader aim is to rearticulate that second voice of American culture and, in the process, to rededicate all of us to the proposition that all human beings are created equal.[30]

As Baldwin introduces it in "The Seventh Day," the Grimes family's church teaches a gospel that is unyielding and harsh: two teenagers, Ella Mae and Elisha, the friend of John's heart, humiliatingly are called to the front of the church and warned against sin, even though—Elisha says—"we didn't have nothing on our minds at all," because the pastor caught the scent of temptation to come.[31] "Ain't no such thing as a big fault or a little fault," Sister McCandless explains. "Satan got his foot in the door, he ain't going to rest until he's in the room. You is in the world or you ain't—ain't no halfway with God."[32] Yet, Baldwin lets his readers see that this stern teaching has its reasons. Initially, he was furious at his pastor uncle, Elisha says, but "the Lord made me see that he was right."[33] In practice, African American churches were necessarily the champions of the community in its efforts to resist the demoralizations of racism. Facing a world in which the "temptations of the street" were the more alluring when set against the certainty of secular indignity and frustration, churches insisted on moral discipline in the name of immortal destiny.[34] "People say it's hard," Elisha tells John, "but . . . it ain't as hard as living in this wicked world and all the sadness of the world where there ain't no pleasure nohow, and then dying and going to Hell."[35]

The church's doctrinal militancy, moreover, is amplified by the ways in which the practice of racism is entangled with theoretical tenets of American secularity. In general, liberalism and modernity have been inclined to define human nature and identity in terms of the body, discounting if not rejecting the soul.[36] This view, in turn, encourages us to see social or political reality in terms of appearances, the motion and collision of bodies; thus, it adds *intellectual* authority to the human disposition to group or categorize by eye and, hence, by race. More subtly, these doctrines urge us to be guided by the evidence of our senses and, hence, by experience, a persuasion that still might lead us to regard blacks—disproportionately poor, ill educated, and apt to fall afoul of the law—as somehow inferior. In Shakespeare's Venice, when Brabantio argues that it is against "all rules of nature" for Desdemona to love Othello, "in spite . . . of years, of country, credit, everything," the Doge dismisses the evidence of "these thin habits and poor likelihoods of modern seeming."[37] In modern America, by contrast, it is modernity that occupies the position of authority, and African American churches have reason to "Put on the whole armor of God" for their combat against the "rulers of this present darkness."[38]

Battle and war, however, are simplifiers that call for slogans rather than subtleties. The logic of combat includes a tendency to make oneself a mirror image of one's enemy, a negation rather than an affirmation. Virtually all American churches, for example, know the danger that African American churches encounter with special force: in resisting the doctrine that their members are nothing but bodies with desires, the church becomes preoccupied with the sins of the flesh, neglecting those of the spirit. For African Americans, this includes a temptation to reverse racism—especially potent because, as a general rule of practice, whites *are* the enemy.[39] Gabriel taught John "that all white people were wicked," with no shortage of historical evidence to support that view, and John—envying whites their advantages and reflecting on the inevitable exclusions of racism—"knew that one day he could hate them if God did not change his heart."[40] And more subtly, the same inclination is evident in Gabriel's preoccupation with his "royal line," the child of his blood as opposed to the child of his spirit.[41]

Baldwin had good reason to expect that the great majority of his readers would agree with—and even anticipate—the foregoing critique of the church. For Baldwin himself, however, the more fundamental criticism was one that most of his readers would not share: in its battle with American society, the church's principal weapon is words, but words used as instruments distort the Word, the "power which outlasts kingdoms," reducing Christ to culture and the quest for truth to ideology.[42]

Religion's higher wisdom, as Baldwin understood it, runs counter to the modern doctrine that the art and science of politics consists of mastering nature and her seasons (as in Bill Clinton's inaugural promise to "force the spring"). It teaches, by contrast, that political action depends on discerning, or even ransoming, the times.[43]

"The Prayers of the Saints" is introduced by a quotation from Revelation, in which those "that were slain for the word of God" ask for belated justice: "And they cried with a loud voice, saying, How long, O Lord, holy and true, dost thou not judge and avenge our blood on them that dwell on the earth?" In the succeeding verse, they are told to "rest yet for a little season," warned that their "fellow servants and brethren" must also endure martyrdom but robed in glory and assured of ultimate vindication.[44]

That promise, Baldwin will remind his readers, has found supporting testimony in African American experience. In *Go Tell It on the Mountain*, Florence recalls her mother's memories of slavery:[45]

For it had been the will of God that they should hear, and pass thereafter, one to another, the story of the Hebrew children who had been held in bondage in the land of Egypt, and how the Lord had heard of their groaning, and how His heart was moved; and how he bid them wait but a little season till he should send deliverance. . . . She had only to endure and trust in God. She knew that the big house, the house of pride where the white folks lived, would come down: it was written in the Word of God. They, who walked so proudly now, had not fashioned for themselves or their children so sure a foundation as was hers. They walked on the edge of a steep place and their eyes were sightless . . . and one day the time to forsake evil and do good would be finished, and then only the whirlwind . . . awaited those people who had forgotten

God. . . . The word was fulfilled one morning, before she was awake. . . . There was a great running and shouting . . . everywhere outside, and as she opened her eyes to the light of that day, so bright, she said, and cold, she was certain that the judgment trumpet had sounded. . . . In rushed Bathsheba and . . . shouted, "Rise up, rise up, Sister Rachel and see the Lord's deliverance. He's brought us out of Egypt just like He promised, and we's free at last!"[46]

That oppression had reasserted itself in new forms only emphasized the lesson. Slave-owning society, false to nature and to humanity, rested on illusion and was doomed to fall by its own error and lie, and as with slavery, so with its successors: one need only remain in readiness, alert but waiting for the time.

In fact, "The Prayers of the Saints" is prefaced by a sign, the presence in church of John's Aunt Florence for "John knew that it was the hand of the Lord that had led her to this place, and his heart grew cold. The Lord was riding on the wind tonight."[47]

Baldwin knew, of course, that most of his readers would confront the temple as outsiders, and he is being characteristically artful: Florence, whose reflections open "The Prayers of the Saints," is the bridge between us and the inner experiences of the faithful.[48]

Her name—one of the few nonbiblical names in John's family—evidently evokes Renaissance humanism and the rejection of "cities that have never been seen," and Florence herself has qualities that secular and modern readers can be expected to like and admire.[49] She is tough, savvy, irreverent about Gabriel's pieties and pretentions, and fiercely independent—self-sufficiency is *her* pretension—and it probably helps white readers identify with her that she is a bit of a racist, despising "common niggers" out of her own ambition and pride.[50] But Florence has cancer, and doctors and folk cures have failed her: she is brought to the altar by her recognition that "death's got a warrant out for you."[51] Just as the fear of death is liberalism's civilizing passion, the fact of death—that inevitable limit to human mastery and freedom—makes even very secular liberals more open to faith.[52]

Gabriel, John's stepfather, has had a more orthodox experience of dependence and rebirth. While his mother lay dying, holding on to life in hope of seeing his birth in Christ, Gabriel—something of a roisterer—had fled into the arms of harlot. Returning home the next morning, Gabriel encountered a moment of dreadful silence—the "very birds had ceased to sing, and no dogs barked, and no rooster crowed for day"—a stillness that emphasized his isolation, his vulnerability, and his exposure to the judgment of God.[53]

But Gabriel's surrender to God, which he dates from that day, defines itself as an alliance with God's power: "Yes, he wanted power—he wanted to know himself to be the Lord's anointed. . . . He wanted to be master, to speak with that authority which could only come from God."[54] Gabriel's motto or text, we are told, is "set thine house in order," God's command to Hezekiah, given in view of that king's impending death.[55] But Hezekiah's righteous obedience to God wins him an *extended* span, beyond the limits of nature: for Gabriel, the ordered house is shorthand for expanded dominion.

And Gabriel does see himself as a king: he is caught up by the vision of establishing a "royal life" composed of the children of his body, a dream that raises many questions about his faith.[56] Angered, Gabriel speaks of John as the "son of the bondwoman" and not the "rightful heir," adopting Sarah's tone of complaint against Hagar.[57] However, in Galatians, Paul argues that the *true* "child of the bondwoman" is one born "after the flesh"; the child of the free woman is the one born "by the promise."[58] Identifying the "rightful heir" with his bloodline, Gabriel reverses Paul's teaching: he sees the body but is blind to the spirit.[59]

In a similar reversal, confronted by God in and through *silence,* Gabriel seeks to fill the world with *words:* "I opened my mouth to the Lord that day and Hell won't make me change my mind."[60] By the time of the story in *Go Tell It on the Mountain,* Gabriel only rarely occupies the pulpit: he is "a kind of fill-in speaker, a holy handyman." But in his younger days, in the South, he had a "mighty reputation," and in Gabriel's own mind, preaching is his calling, virtually equivalent to "his life as a man."[61]

It is appropriate, then, that Gabriel's prayer includes two sermons, complete with texts. In the first, he brings a sinner to the mercy seat; in the second, his failure to draw the sensual Esther to the altar anticipates his own surrender to his adulterous passion for her, his words proving less powerful than the flesh. Closely examined, however, both of these sermons prove to miss the scriptural point of their respective texts, a lesson Gabriel himself needs: God's cause, like God's love, transcends ours, and the effort to speak for God, as opposed to yearning for God, is inevitably tainted by pride and folly.

The text of the first sermon is Isaiah 6:5: "Woe is me, for I am undone, because I am a man of unclean lips and I dwell in the midst of a people of unclean lips, for mine eyes have seen the King, the Lord of hosts." Gabriel uses it as a basis for a denunciation of sin, especially the sins of the flesh, a praise of God that emphasizes the woe of unrighteous humanity.[62] Yet, the text itself goes on to tell us that an angel seared the prophet's mouth with a live coal, purging his sin, suggesting that he must be silenced in order to be redeemed. God then calls the prophet and sends him to speak to the people, foreknowing that he will not be understood. God, in other words, gives the prophet a second, humbled mouth. The lips of the people are not "unclean" in any conventional sense; Israel speaks of God, but in a way that debases His glory, as any human speech inevitably must do. The real defect is in the ear: the people's ears are stopped because, hearing words, they reject or ignore their meaning, the Word beyond words.

Moreover, Isaiah tells us that his vision occurred "in the year King Uzziah died."[63] At the beginning of his reign, Uzziah "set himself to seek God," but a string of military successes made him feel invulnerable, secure because of his army and his technology of war, so that he was "lifted up to his presumption."[64] He claimed the right to enter the sanctuary, contrary to the law, and leprosy "broke out upon his forehead." Uzziah's piety, the text suggests, was only a matter of appearance; his corruption, like leprosy in the scriptural view, was internal, only waiting for its moment to become manifest.[65] The king valued God as an ally of his will to power, but strength and success tempted him to believe that he could command God: inwardly, it was not God he sought, but mastery, and only relative weakness kept that desire under wraps. This, however, is not a teaching Gabriel could be expected to discern.

Gabriel's second sermon is preached on 2 Samuel 18:29, where Ahimaaz answers David's demand for "tidings" by saying, "I saw a great tumult, but I knew now what it was." Gabriel uses this remark as an example of the confusion of the unredeemed, and he urges his hearers to know the meaning of "tumult" so they will be able to give proper tidings to the Lord.[66] This is a genuinely startling misreading. Ahimaaz is not at all hesitant. He is eager to bring tidings to the king—after all, David's army has won a great victory—and he persists in asking to be sent even after Joab's warning that there will be no reward for these tidings, because the king's son, Absalom, is dead. It is only when he is in David's presence that Ahimaaz recognizes the truth that the king is more loving and forgiving than Ahimaaz recognized and that the victory Ahimaaz saw as grounds for celebration is reason for mourning for the king. And what is true of David is even more true of the Lord: a king knows that in practice there are battles that must be fought and that the relatively just side is to be preferred, but he laments the necessity; the goal of royalty is the good of the whole, not the triumph of a part.[67] That higher dimension of politics, however, is one that Gabriel (and to a lesser degree, the church), devoted to the God of power and judgment, is all too prone to ignore.

By contrast, John's mother, Elizabeth, who offers the concluding prayer, is the voice of human love. As a child, she was love starved: her mother, for whom she felt little affection, died when Elizabeth was eight. Her father, whom she adored, left her to the care of a sternly respectable aunt, whose pious version of love—very much like Gabriel's—Elizabeth recognized as in reality only "a bribe, a threat, an indecent will to power."[68] By contrast, Elizabeth knew that "the kind of imprisonment love might impose was also, mysteriously, a freedom for the soul and spirit, was water in the dry place, and had nothing to do with the prisons, churches, laws, rewards, and punishments that so positively cluttered the landscape of her aunt's mind."[69] But Elizabeth, echoing the young Augustine, was "in love with love," cherishing love as her own version of pride and power, building her life around her devotion to Richard, John's biological father.[70]

Like Florence, Richard has a nonbiblical name, emblematic of his secularism (and one that, given Baldwin's preoccupations, inevitably suggests Richard Wright). Elizabeth's attraction to him is at least largely explained by the ways in which he is like her father, an individualist of "deadly pride" who taught her "to weep, when she wept, alone; never to ask for mercy; if one had to die, go ahead and die, but never let oneself be beaten."[71] Richard is at least as prideful and as devoted to independence, defiantly irreverent, cultivating an air of "indifferent aloofness," and pursuing knowledge as a means to mastery:[72] "I just decided me one day that I was going to get to know everything the white bastards knew, and I was going to know it better than them, so could no white son-of-a-bitch *nowhere* talk *me* down and never make me feel that *I* was dirt, when I could read him the alphabet, front, back and sideways. Shit—he weren't going to beat my ass, then. And if he tried to kill me, I'd take him with me, I swear to my mother that I would."[73] Events shatter that confidence. Richard is arrested for a crime he did not commit. He is in the wrong place at the wrong time, and the police sweep him up along with the guilty: "They were all colored, they were all about the same age, and . . . they stood together on the subway platform."[74] The police are predictably brutal, but the system works, more or less, and Richard is released. Richard, however, is devastated by his inability to control his fate: being freed is as humiliating as his arrest, an exclamation point added to the experience of dependence and vulnerability. His love for Elizabeth is not strong enough to override the blow to his individualist's pride: he commits suicide, a final and futile gesture of independence that overpowers the claims of her love and the obligations of his own.

Elizabeth is left with the lesson that human love at its best is unable to command the world and is sure to be defeated by it. Recognizing the brittleness and desperation of Richard's prose, she sought to make her love his fortress, "the indisputable reality to which he could always repair," but her love's reality proved inadequate to the test of the world's strength and Richard's illusions.[75] Humanity's strength, and love's, rests on a deeper yearning: "For the world called to the heart, which stammered to reply; life, and love, and revelry, and, most falsely, hope, called the forgetful, the human heart. Only the soul, obsessed with the journey it had made, and had still to make, pursued its mysterious and dreadful end; and carried, heavy with weeping and bitterness, the heart along."[76] Elizabeth's soul carried her until John's birth, "the beginning of her life and death," and from there, through Florence, to Gabriel. And after a time, Gabriel, in a moment of "grace and humility," pledged to love and provide for Elizabeth and her son.[77] There is no indication that Elizabeth loved him; she was touched by his kindness, and she saw in him a means of returning to respectability and providing for her son. And Gabriel "kept the letter of his promise" to care for John, even though, predictably, "the spirit was not there."[78] John's coming into the world, however, was Elizabeth's second birth, a travail followed by joy that pointed beyond itself, "toward that moment when she would make her peace with God."[79]

In sum: Baldwin presents his readers with three reflective prayers, each with its thematic motive—the fear of death (Florence), the desire for power (Gabriel), and the love of love (Elizabeth). These are primary dynamics of social and political practice, inevitable concerns of custom and law. Taken together, in fact, they constitute a kind of psychological Augustinian subtext to the unalienable rights mentioned in the Declaration of Independence. All of them have touched and helped to nurture John, but by the end of "The Prayers of the Saints," their inadequacies have been exposed: human life cries for something more. It is no surprise, then, that the section ends with John on the threshing floor or that his cry is "not the cry of the child, newborn, before the common light of earth; but the cry of the man-child, bestial, before the light that comes down from Heaven."[80]

The scriptural preface to "The Threshing Floor" repeats Isaiah 6:5, the text of Gabriel's first sermon, underlining the difference between that preaching and Baldwin's own evangel. On the threshing floor, John experiences the full force of his rage and agony and fear, his fury at his father and his love for Elisha, and above all, the desolating sense of being utterly abandoned— particularly by his father's rejection—in darkness and alone. All of this is bound up with his dread of the past and the fate of his race; the "ironic voice" of temptation tells him to go his own way, to "rise from that filthy floor if he did not want to become like all the other niggers."[81]

> And he struggled to flee—out of this darkness, out of this company— into the land of this living, so high, so far away. Fear was upon him, a more deadly fear than he had ever known, as he turned and turned in the darkness, as he moaned, and stumbled, and crawled through the darkness, finding no hand, no voice, finding no door. *Who are these? Who are they?* They were the despised and rejected, the wretched and the spat upon, the earth's offscouring; and he was in their company, and they would swallow up his soul. The stripes they had endured would scar his back, their punishment would be his, their portion his, their humiliation, anguish, chains, their dungeon his, their death his.[82]

Even at this bleak moment, however, there is a hint of a turn in the road. John is reminded of Paul's account of his travails, which he associates with the "dread testimony" and "desolation" of his people.[83] But Paul gloried in these things, assured of the ultimate sufficiency of God's grace and power and of its paradoxical corollary, the proposition that "when I am weak, then I am strong."[84] So, it proves for John, at any rate. Despairing of human help and his own power, reduced to his flawed and vulnerable humanity, John has an instant of dazzling insight—"the darkness, for a moment only, was filled with a light he could not bear"—that leaves him with an abiding truth.[85] Creation, the fundamental nature of things, has power against its condemners. Even what is most shameful in human life and conduct—and "no one's hands are clean"—testifies to something beyond itself.[86]

> Then John saw the river, and the multitude was there. And now they had undergone a change; their robes were ragged, and stained with the road they had traveled, and stained with unholy blood; the robes of some barely covered their nakedness; and some indeed were naked. And some stumbled on the smooth stones at the river's edge, for they were blind; and some crawled with a terrible wailing, for they were lame; some did not cease to pluck at their flesh, which was rotten with running sores. All struggled to get to the river, in a dreadful hardness of heart: the strong struck down the weak, the ragged spat on the naked, the naked cursed the blind, the blind crawled over the lame. And someone cried, *"Sinner, do you love my Love?"*[87]

Human beings, spiritually blind and crippled, savagely competitive and self-seeking, are universally drawn by a higher end, seeking the river. This unity of human striving testifies to the obedient soldier's courage that underlies the "way of the cross," keeping one's human station up to the sacrifice of life, confident that God and nature will prevail against the illusions of mastery.[88]

> They moved on the bloody road forever, with no continuing city, but seeking one to come: a city out of time, not made with hands, but eternal in the heavens. No power could hold this army back, no water disperse them, no fire consume them. One day, they would compel the earth to heave upward, and surrender the waiting dead. They sang, where the darkness gathered, where the lion waited, where the fire cried, and where blood ran down: *My soul, don't you be uneasy.*[89]

Almost immediately, John recognizes that his life has been bought with a price, his ancestors' pilgrimage of faith and suffering, and that his own life—like all human lives—is lived under obligation.[90]

If it needs saying, that John is "saved" means that his life has undergone a turning, that its agony has become a conscious struggle, permanently affected by the memory of his moment in light.[91] In his conversation with Elizabeth, and even more in his exchanges with Elisha and Gabriel, lower motives are quite evidently mingled with spiritual affirmations, but John's new insight remains an insistent whisper.

Talking with Gabriel, John tries and fails to find "the authoritative word" that will "conquer the great division" between him and his stepfather, and "in the silence something died in John, and something came alive." Recognizing that he must speak and that "his tongue only could bear witness to the wonders he had seen," John finds "common testimony" in the text of one of Gabriel's sermons, Job 16:19: "My witness is in heaven and my record is on high."[92]

Yet, the interpretations of that common text differ: the gap between prophecy and practice can be bridged—the effort to do so is a major office of politics—but it cannot be eliminated. For Gabriel, the text apparently implies a confident appeal to God against men. Job, however, is denouncing those who offer him the comfort of pious words. God's design, Job argues, is beyond human speech, and certainly beyond human ideas of justice, since God knows ("my record is on high") that Job has not merited his afflictions. Consequently, Job observes, one cannot plead with God as one *can* plead for one's neighbor.[93] By implication, human words, so inadequate for capturing the divine, should primarily be devoted to seeking justice between human beings, just as the recognition of human vulnerability before God should lead us to support and sustain each other. John's politic appeal to Job indicates that he has come full circle, that his words will now proclaim his unity with the humble rather than afford a means to escape them.

The Grimes family's mantelpiece is adorned with two mottoes: the first is an invitation to guests—and especially, to the Guest—to come without warning, assured of a welcome; the second is the familiar words of John 3:16, "For God so loved the world." These sentiments, Baldwin remarks, are "somewhat unrelated," a comment that begs us to ask in what ways they *are* related.[94] That inquiry would lead us to John, the cited text, and to the observation that established its context: no man has ascended to heaven, but God descended to man.[95] Heaven cannot be scaled, that passage suggests; God must be awaited, made inwardly welcome (as in the Grimes family's first motto), and recognized as the light of and in this world.[96] Baldwin appears to be arguing that the church, even in hands more unambiguously benign than Gabriel's, is, first of all, too eager to speak with authority and too unwilling to seek and listen, and second, too indifferent to this world, where human speech and action can make a difference in alleviating pain.[97]

This is, however, no merely secular teaching. The Spirit can be heard, if not bidden, if one listens with the right ears. The cognition of God's love for all His children and for all His creation, the lesson of Jonah, is necessary for any people, but perhaps especially for those, like African Americans, who are justly furious at oppression. The demand for justice—the victorious retribution Ahimaaz is so ready to trumpet—needs to be softened by a desire for reconciliation, and especially by the need to avoid "victories" that make one into the image of one's oppressors and enemies.

If in one sense Baldwin points people of faith—and human beings in general—toward greater politicality, his message is also that they must be guided by the city founded not on victory or utility but the truth. John hears the music on the threshing floor:

> *I, John, saw a city, way up in the middle of the air,*
> *Waiting, waiting, waiting up there.*[98]

We are all, Baldwin declares, "meant to be witnesses to a truth we will never see," most evidently the high, half-terrifying fact of human equality.[99]

Notes

Originally published as Wilson Carey McWilliams, *"Go Tell It on the Mountain: James Baldwin and the Politics of Faith,"* in *Democracy's Literature: Politics and Fiction in America,* ed. Wilson Patrick J. Deneen and Joseph Romance (Lanham, MD: Rowman & Littlefield, 2005). Reprinted by permission of Rowman & Littlefield Publishing Group.

1. Baldwin, writes Lawrie Balfour, *The Evidence of Things Not Said: James Baldwin and the Promise of American Democracy* (Ithaca, NY: Cornell University Press, 2001), 138, had "virtually nothing to say about political institutions and policies." See also David Leeming, *James Baldwin: A Biography* (New York: Knopf, 1994), 18, 216–30. For that matter, Baldwin's judgments about people and events in political practice were not always fortunate, especially when he strove to avoid seeming irrelevant to younger black militants, although even then he retained a certain ironic detachment: in 1968, he listed Henry James's *The Princess Casamassima* as a book he would recommend to Black Power militants (Leeming, *James Baldwin,* 284–302).

2. Neal Riemer, ed., *Let Justice Roll: Prophetic Challenges in Religion, Politics and Society* (Lanham, MD: Rowman and Littlefield, 1996); James Baldwin, *The Fire Next Time* (New York: Dell, 1963), 88, 89. David Leeming's verdict is the more telling because of its balance: Baldwin, he writes, was "not a saint . . . not always psychologically or emotionally stable. But he was a prophet" (Leeming, *James Baldwin*, xii; for Kenneth Clark's similar judgment, see ibid., 138).

3. On the philosophic impossibility of religious neutrality, see Roy Clouser, *The Myth of Religious Neutrality* (Notre Dame, IN: University of Notre Dame Press, 1991).

4. James Baldwin, *Nobody Knows My Name* (New York: Dial, 1961), 42–43; Balfour, *Evidence of Things Not Said*, 58; Leeming, *James Baldwin*, 352–52, 358. "We are all under the same mental calamity," G. K. Chesterton wrote, "we have all forgotten our names. We have all forgotten what we really are" (see G. K. Chesterton, *Orthodoxy* [New York: Dodd Mead, 1908], 97).

5. James Baldwin, *Notes of a Native Son* (Boston: Beacon, 1955), 9; Balfour, *Evidence of Things Not Said*, 95–96; Leeming, *James Baldwin*, 294–369. Baldwin's arguments, Henry Louis Gates Jr. wrote, were "richly nuanced and self-consciously ambivalent . . . far too complex to serve straight forwardly political ends" ("The Fire Last Time," *New Republic*, July 1, 1992, 38).

6. James Baldwin, "A Talk to Teachers," *Saturday Review* 46 (December 21, 1963): 46.

7. James Baldwin, *The Price of the Ticket* (New York: St. Martin's, 1985), 643. "The world tends to trap and immobilize you in the role you play," Baldwin wrote, "and it is not always easy—in fact, it is always extremely hard—to maintain a kind of watchful, mocking distance between oneself as one appears to be and oneself as one actually is" (Baldwin, *Nobody Knows My Name*, 173). See also Balfour, *Evidence of Things Not Said*, 7; Leeming, *James Baldwin*, 268–69, 335, 338, 358, 362.

8. Baldwin, *Notes of a Native Son*, 20, 23, 35–36, 113. Baldwin's examples of protest novelists were Harriet Beecher Stowe and, inevitably, Richard Wright.

9. "Though we do not fully believe it yet, the interior life is a real life, and the intangible dreams of people have a tangible effect on the world" (Baldwin, *Nobody Knows My Name*, 23). The importance of the inner life is underlined in America by the fact that "society is much given to smashing taboos without thereby managing to be liberated from them" (Baldwin, *Nobody Knows My Name*, 23).

10. David Leeming, "An Interview with James Baldwin on Henry James," *Henry James Review* 8 (1986): 47–56; Balfour, *Evidence of Things Not Said*, 56–58; James Baldwin, *The Evidence of Things Not Seen* (New York: Holt, Rinehart and Winston, 1985), 101–2; Baldwin, *Nobody Knows My Name*, 13, 66.

11. As Henry Louis Gates writes, "our histories, individual and collective, do

affect what we wish to write and what we are able to write. But that relation is never one of fixed determinism. No human culture is inaccessible to someone who makes the effort to understand, to learn, to inhabit another world" ("'Authenticity,' or the Lesson of Little Tree," *New York Times Book Review*, November 24, 1991, 30).

12. James Baldwin, "To Crush the Serpent," *Playboy.* June 1987, 66ff.; Baldwin, *Nobody Knows My Name*, 113; Leeming, *James Baldwin*, 30, 125, 321, 369, 375.

13. Josh Kun, "Life According to the Beat: James Baldwin, Bessie Smith and the Perilous Sounds of Love," in *James Baldwin Now*, ed. Dwight McBride (New York: New York University Press, 1999), 307–28.

14. Baldwin, *The Fire Next Time*, 105, 119. See also James Baldwin, *Just above My Head* (New York: Dial, 1979); and Leeming, *James Baldwin*, 351.

15. Baldwin, *Notes of a Native Son*, 9; Leeming, *James Baldwin*, 146. Balfour points to Baldwin's effort to develop a "moral vocabulary" adequate for citizenship and "democratic ideals" (*The Evidence of Things Not Said*, xi). Of course, Baldwin was often sharply critical of Christianity—although that goes with the prophetic vocation—and notoriously departed from conventional sexual morality. (He was troubled, Baldwin said, by "demons," as well as "the Lord"; see Leeming, *James Baldwin*, 309.) Yet Baldwin was a believer, convinced of sin and human shortcoming and devoted to a morality that was often surprisingly traditional (Balfour, *Evidence of Things Not Said*, 33); for example, when asked by an unmarried graduate student for advice about her unwanted pregnancy, Baldwin told her—Leeming says that he "ordered" her—to "carry and keep" the child (*James Baldwin*, 340–41). He spoke of himself as bearing witness to a truth learned "in the church where I was raised," as devoted to the Bible as a text (along with gospel songs), and as being definitively "in the hands of the Living God" (Baldwin, *Notes of a Native Son*, 113; Leeming, *James Baldwin*, 309, 367, 370).

16. Balfour, *Evidence of Things Not Said*, 23.

17. Mark 4:1–32.

18. On the general point, see Toni Morrison, "Unspeakable Things Unspoken," *Michigan Quarterly Review* 28 (1989): 1–31.

19. Citations to *Go Tell It on the Mountain* (orig. 1953) refer to the Modern Library edition (New York, 1995); hereafter cited as *GTM*.

20. Leeming, *James Baldwin*, 84–85.

21. "The Prayers of the Saints" is further divided into three chapters, each identified as the prayer of a member of the Grimes family, of which the second (and longest) is Gabriel's prayer, making it central among the book's subdivisions.

22. Revelation 22:18.

23. John's stepbrother Royal and his stepsisters Sarah and Ruth are essentially secondary characters in John's imagination and in Baldwin's story.

24. Baldwin, *GTM*, 14–15, 35. See also Balfour, *Evidence of Things Not Said*, 146–47n52; and Baldwin, *Nobody Knows My Name*, 168–69. John's literary talent evidently links him to Baldwin, as do many details in the story. It is also notable that Baldwin frequently gave his central characters the name "John," for example, in his story "Peace on Earth" (Leeming, *James Baldwin*, 29) and in the more autobiographical "Death of the Prophet" (*Commentary* 9 [March 1950]: 257–61), to say nothing of Giovanni in *Giovanni's Room* (New York: Dial, 1951). The choice of a name, especially in broadly autobiographical fiction, is suggestive, since Baldwin repeatedly wrote about and in terms of a search for a name beyond conventional names, as in *Nobody Knows My Name* or Baldwin's *No Name in the Street* (New York: Dial, 1972). James is the apostle who speaks of the importance of deeds; John—whether we think of John the Baptist (prophecy), John the Apostle (the word beyond words), or John of Revelation—is associated with a vision beyond appearances: I suspect that just as James or Jimmy was Baldwin the person we see, identity in practice, Baldwin thought of John as a kind of inward identity, the person who sees.

25. Baldwin, *GTM*, 44.

26. F. W. J. Schelling, "Philosophische Untersuchungen über das Wesen der menschlichen Freiheit und die damit zusammenhängenden Gegenstände," in *Sammtliche Werke* (Augsburg: Cotta, 1860), 6:351.

27. Speech to the Virginia Convention, March 23, 1775, in William Wirt, *Sketches of the Life and Character of Patrick Henry* (Philadelphia: Thomas, Cowperthwait & Co., 1838), 141–42. Mark Twain has Tom Sawyer forget Henry's peroration during his school's exercises—implausibly, since a glory seeker like Tom would have cherished that line if he forgot everything else, but significantly, if Twain wanted to raise questions about America's devotion to freedom (see *The Adventures of Tom Sawyer* [Berkeley: University of California Press, 1982], 155).

28. A judgment evidently reflected in Eldridge Cleaver's late-1960s demeaning of his own patronage in *Soul on Ice* (New York: Dial, 1968), 210: "A Slave who dies of natural causes cannot balance two flies in the Scales of Eternity."

29. Horace Porter, *Stealing the Fire: The Art and Protest of James Baldwin* (Middletown, CT: Wesleyan University Press, 1989), 99; Leeming, *James Baldwin*, 86–87, 89. Baldwin never obscured the lamentable aspects of African American experience or culture; he only insisted that there was a vital "something more" (*Notes of a Native Son*, 121).

30. Cornel West, *Keeping Faith* (New York: Routledge, 1993), 72–73, 85, 290–91.

31. Baldwin, *GTM*, 65.

32. Ibid., 70.

33. Ibid., 65.

34. Balfour, *Evidence of Things Not Said,* 68, 123–24. This effort is evident in religion's worst manifestations: Gabriel calls on the Lord as he beats his son, Royal, precisely because he resists the lesson of secularity offered by his sister, Florence: "You can't change nothing, Gabriel. You ought to know that by now" (Baldwin, *GTM,* 56).

35. Baldwin, *GTM,* 64.

36. The identity of a human being, Locke wrote, "consists . . . in nothing but a participation in the same continued life . . . [in] the same organized Body"; in this respect, human identity is "like that of other Animals" (*Essay on Human Understanding,* II, xxvii).

37. *Othello,* act 1, scene 3.

38. Ephesians 6:11–12.

39. Baldwin, *The Evidence of Things Not Seen,* 78; Baldwin, *Nobody Knows My Name,* 36; Baldwin, *Notes of a Native Son,* 165.

40. Baldwin, *GTM,* 38–39.

41. For Baldwin personally, spiritual paternity was a major theme, whether in relation to his stepfather or to Richard Wright (*Nobody Knows My Name,* 153, 160). It is significant, of course, that in *GTM,* Richard is John's biological father.

42. Baldwin, *Nobody Knows My Name,* 183. See also H. Richard Niebuhr, *Christ and Culture* (New York: Harper Brothers, 1951).

43. Ecclesiastes 3:1; Ephesians 5:16. See also Jacques Maritain, *Ransoming the Time* (New York: Charles Scribner, 1941). For those who would change the world, contra Marx, the first task is to understand it.

44. Revelation 6:9–11.

45. Baldwin's stepfather's mother, like the mother of Florence and Gabriel, had been born a slave and lived the last years of her life in Baldwin's home (Leeming, *James Baldwin,* 4).

46. Baldwin, *GTM,* 81–84.

47. Ibid., 72.

48. On the seductive quality of Baldwin's writing, see Balfour, *Evidence of Things Not Said,* 36; and Leeming, *James Baldwin,* 101.

49. The quotation, of course, is from Machiavelli, *The Prince,* chap. 15.

50. Baldwin, *GTM,* 77, 104.

51. Ibid., 110.

52. Alexis de Tocqueville, *Democracy in America* (New York: Knopf, 1980), 1:309–10. Hobbes put the "Fear of Death" first among the "Passions that conduce to Peace" (*Leviathan,* pt. 1, chap. 13).

53. Baldwin, *GTM,* 117.

54. Ibid., 113. His own stepfather, Baldwin wrote, saw himself as the "good friend of Great God Almighty" (*No Name in the Street,* 3–9). See also Baldwin, *Notes of a Native Son,* 87–92.

55. 2 Kings 20:1; Baldwin, *GTM*, 33. It is also, appropriately, a text that occurs to Florence (Baldwin, *GTM*, 78). It was the favorite text of Baldwin's stepfather, and one that Baldwin himself used in his own last sermon, where the "house" in question was a Western civilization (Leeming, *James Baldwin*, 31).

56. Baldwin, *GTM*, 178.

57. Genesis 21:10–13. The metaphor is strikingly inappropriate, since Gabriel's complaint—unlike Sarah's—is against John's paternity: Elizabeth is also the mother of Gabriel's "rightful heir."

58. Galatians 4:23. In fact, Paul describes himself as a mother—"in travail of birth until Christ be formed in you" (Galatians 4:19). Notably, Gabriel appeals to Paul's teaching in his first great sermon (Baldwin, *GTM*, 128).

59. By contrast, Baldwin saw his stepfather as his father "in every sense except the biological or literal one" (*The Devil Finds Work* [New York: Dial, 1976], 12–16).

60. Baldwin, *GTM*, 119.

61. Ibid., 58–59, 119.

62. Ibid., 126–31.

63. Isaiah 6:1.

64. 2 Chronicles 26:5, 16, 19.

65. The fact that lepers had to cover their lips because their breath might pollute the community (Leviticus 13:45) is an indication of the view that leprosy bespeaks an inner corruption.

66. Baldwin, *GTM*, 148–51.

67. On the necessities of political practice, see the account that follows Gabriel's text (2 Chronicles 19:1–8).

68. Baldwin, *GTM*, 200.

69. Ibid.

70. The citation of Augustine, of course, is from his *Confessions*, bk. 3, chap. 1.

71. Baldwin, *GTM*, 198.

72. Ibid., 203. Richard's response to Elizabeth's appeal to the love of Jesus is to "tell that puking bastard to kiss my big black ass" (ibid., 211).

73. Ibid., 216. The first-person italics underscore Richard's individualism: he resents the indignities of race, but his protest is personal, not political.

74. Ibid., 221.

75. Ibid., 211. Elizabeth, fearing to add to Richard's burdens, did not tell him that she was pregnant, leaving him ignorant of an obligation that just might have bound him to life (ibid., 226).

76. Ibid., 227.

77. Ibid., 245–46.

78. Ibid., 228.

79. Ibid., 246–47.

80. Ibid., 247.

81. Ibid., 252.

82. Ibid., 262–63.

83. 2 Corinthians 11:25–27; Baldwin, *GTM*, 263.

84. 2 Corinthians 11:30, 12:9–10.

85. Baldwin, *GTM*, 266. "The light and the darkness had kissed each other, and were married now, forever, in the vision of John's soul" (ibid., 266–67).

86. Baldwin, *Notes of a Native Son*, 44.

87. Baldwin, *GTM*, 265–66.

88. Ibid., 286–87; Jeremiah 31:8–12; compare the implicit contrast of Socrates's courage with that of Achilles in Plato's *Apology*, 28D–29A.

89. Baldwin, *GTM*, 267.

90. Leeming, *James Baldwin*, 89; Bertrand de Jouvenel, *Sovereignty*, trans. J. F. Huntington (Indianapolis: Liberty Fund, 1997), 317.

91. John's plea to Elisha is almost certainly Baldwin's own proclamation to his readers: "no matter what happens to me, where I go, what folks say about me, no matter what anybody says, you remember—please remember—I was saved. I was *there*" (Baldwin, *GTM*, 290). Leeming writes that Baldwin's early "salvation" was "the preface to a life of searching on the universal threshing floor of personal and societal pain" (*James Baldwin*, xiii). John's emphasis suggests that Baldwin's experience might better be described as a foundation for that life.

92. Baldwin, *GTM*, 271.

93. Job 16:22.

94. Baldwin, *GTM*, 26–27.

95. John 3:13; see also John 1:18.

96. John 3:20–21.

97. Defending himself against Florence's attack on his pretensions and misbehaviors, Gabriel declares that "God sees the heart." Florence responds that God "ought to see it" because "He made it. But don't nobody else see it, not even your own self. *Let* God see it—He sees it all right, and He don't say anything"; Gabriel, with unconscious irony, answers, "All you got to do is listen" (Baldwin, *GTM*, 280). Similarly, Sister McCandless, also a great talker, says that "all you got to do is *listen* to the Lord" (ibid., 272).

98. Ibid., 267.

99. James Baldwin and Margaret Mead, *A Rap on Race* (Philadelphia: Lippincott, 1971); G. K. Chesterton, *What I Saw in America* (New York: Dodd Mead, 1922), 18.

III

The Individual Life,
the Interior Life,
the Unexamined Life

8

Socrates in a Different Key

James Baldwin and Race in America

Joel Alden Schlosser

In his recent book *Democracy Matters,* Cornel West names James Baldwin as the "black American Socrates." "A blues-inflected, jazz-saturated democrat," Baldwin, in West's words, exercises "a powerful and poignant self-examination—always on the brink of despair, yet holding on to a tragicomic hope," bespeaking "a rare intellectual integrity and personal anguish." Like Socrates, Baldwin infects others with perplexity, forcing his readers to grapple with the difficulties of "trying to be a decent human being and thinking person in the face of the pervasive mendacity and hypocrisy of the American empire."[1]

Taking its cue from West, this essay explores how James Baldwin's essays and fiction continue and modify a kind of Socratic examination transposed to the context of racial domination and white supremacy. Recent work in political theory on Baldwin has paid particular attention to the usefulness of his work for democratic theory, emphasizing how Baldwin's essays can inform a "public discourse" about issues such as inequality, citizenship, power, identity, democratic authority, and the uses of history. For these scholars, Baldwin's writings lay "a critical groundwork," in Lawrie Balfour's words, for engaging these concerns while also, as George Shulman has put it, urging the cultivation of "practices of citizenship that defeat idealization but not aspiration."[2] Denying the possibility of realizing American democracy without confronting the history of oppression interwoven in the very fabric of the republic, Baldwin voices the claims of African American critics stretching from Douglass through Du Bois and West. Baldwin thus builds on the strand of African American political thought that aims to confront the history of race and white supremacy as the indispensable condition of any plausible vision of American democracy by providing theoretical resources for challenging power inequalities related to race, gender, sexuality, and class.[3] Elaborating Baldwin's work as a practice akin to Socrates's, this essay links these concerns of African American political thought to Socrates's influential model of the questioning philosopher or social critic dedicated to improving his or her fellow citizens through the collective pursuit of knowledge.[4] Recently, "Socrates" has come to serve as a trope for self-examination and the kind of "critical" or "philosophic" citizenship propounded by many as needful in twenty-first-century liberal democracies;[5] I argue that Baldwin takes up this Socrates in his original key by articulating and undertaking a practice of *examination:* the interrogation of self and world to recognize the delusions and blindness that contribute to persistent structures of oppression. Baldwin thus insists on the destructive reality of the "racial contract," as Charles Mills has put it, in its epistemological form, rejecting the ideological coercion propagated by a liberal democracy that insists on denying a racialized past.[6] As a "black American Socrates," Baldwin carries forward the provocative work of the gadfly by confronting the ignorance of those around him, seeking to bring his interlocutors to more truthful and just collective life through examination.[7]

Yet while Baldwin continues these aspects of Socrates's activity, I also argue that he transforms Socrates's project, enacting a Socrates "in a different key" by depicting how human beings struggle to practice this examination in their daily lives. In this sense Baldwin's work provides an opportunity for rethinking Socratic citizenship in ways that anticipate and extend work by contemporary feminists of color, critical race theorists, and theorists of gender and sexuality, highlighting the embodiment of examination and the necessity of social or collective forms of interrogation.[8] Here I show how Baldwin's fiction complements the essays by suggesting collective practices of selfcraft that involve a social process of working through the divisions wrought by a history of oppression.[9] Although the essays lay out a strategy of redress in familiar Socratic terms, the insistence on knowledge remains incomplete; one can pursue self-examination and remain defeated. Only when read alongside Baldwin's fiction can we understand the complications of examination and the necessity of a social practice of examination pursued with others.

Political theorists have largely ignored Baldwin's fiction, but I argue that his fiction transforms the enterprise of examination presented in the essays by confronting it with what Baldwin calls the "incoherence" of American life: the disparities produced and perpetuated by categorical exclusions. Here I propose seeing Baldwin's fiction as depicting the heterogeneous humanity beneath the stereotypes of race, gender, sexuality, and class and thus reflecting, albeit in a changed way, the problems Baldwin articulates with his own voice in his essays.[10] Political theorists may demand more philosophic or critical citizenship, but I read Baldwin's highly regarded third novel, *Another Country,* as showing how social positions constrained by power articulated along racial, sexual, gender, and class categories can prevent these undertakings from getting off the ground.[11] The novel focuses readers' attention on how struggle with others can realize Baldwin's call to examination and how society so often militates against such realization. In this way, Baldwin transforms "Socratic citizenship" by showing that any examination of reality depends on communication with differently situated bodies, who each have a distinct vantage point on a shared reality. While Baldwin's novel gives reasons to resist a simplistic commitment to liberation through examination, it nonetheless sketches the terms under which a complicated examination might take place.

Socrates's Original Key and Baldwin's Practices of Examination

"Socrates" has come to signify many different approaches to politics and philosophy, but a recent consensus has emerged about the potential for theorizing democratic citizenship in terms of Socrates's practice of philosophy.[12] Put in general terms, Socrates has been invoked as the exemplary critic of democracy who, through his criticisms, attempted to bring democratic Athens to a better version of itself. Although with varying (and sometimes conflictual) frames of approach, most recent commentators agree on three important elements of this Socrates: Socrates proceeds by critical examination of his fellow citizens; he subscribes to some kind of intellectualism, by which knowing the truth will lead to better action; and Socrates's ultimate task lies in bringing citizens to think what they are doing, entailing not political withdrawal but a new kind of informed political engagement. "Socrates" on this reading represents a gadfly dedicated to the productive unsettling of conventional opinions and the concomitant awakening of his fellow citizens to more thoughtful participation in collective life.

Baldwin's essays pick up this original key of Socrates and play it in in the context of racialized America. In the first place, Baldwin proceeds in his essays from a commitment to the value and importance of examination. Although Baldwin never explicitly names Socrates as influencing his approach, themes of examination and questioning pervade his work, and these themes frame Baldwin's task of inquiry as similar to Socrates's. "It is part of the business of the writer," Baldwin writes in the "Autobiographical Notes" that begin his first essay collection, *Notes of a Native Son,* "to examine attitudes, to go beneath the surface, to tap the source."[13] Baldwin seeks to "dig down to where reality is" and tell society the truth about itself: "The things that people really do and really mean and really feel," Baldwin writes, "are almost impossible for them to describe, but these are the very things which are most important about them. These things control them and that is where reality is." What Baldwin seeks to do is "show this reality" by plumbing "subterranean assumptions" and thereby "face the truth."[14]

Second, examination describes a necessary and urgent task for Baldwin. Everyone has the "right and necessity to examine everything," Baldwin writes in the *Saturday Review* in 1963.[15] The right to examine in a democracy is evident enough, but its *necessity* stems from the needfulness of finding better ways to live together. "Examination" for Baldwin does not just name a quest for truth and knowledge as intrinsic goods but offers America the only hope to overcome its delusions about itself and thereby realize its full promise and potential, or, in Baldwin's words, to "achieve its identity." The first clear allusion to Socrates in Baldwin's work underscores this connection between examination and living together well, in the introduction to Baldwin's second collection of essays, *Nobody Knows My Name:* "Havens are high-priced. The price exacted of the haven-dweller is that he contrive to delude himself into believing that he has found a haven. It would seem, unless one looks more deeply at the phenomenon, that most people are able to delude themselves and get through their lives quite happily. But I still believe that the unexamined life is not worth living: and I know that self-delusion, in the service of no matter what small or lofty cause, is a price no writer can afford."[16] Believing they inhabit a haven, Baldwin argues, most Americans live under the delusion of a world untarnished by racial hatred and the effects of white supremacy—they live unexamined lives. Moreover, this delusion pertains to both whites and blacks. In this passage and others, Baldwin emphasizes his *own* need to examine delusions, especially delusions of his own worthlessness perpetuated by a racist society. The examination Baldwin practices applies to every reader, regardless of race.[17]

The converse of this second feature of Baldwin's Socratic project is that life without examination is not worth living. Left unexamined, those who live under delusions about the reality of racism in America cannot recognize the suffering around them or their own implication in (and experience of) this suffering. "Fifth Avenue, Uptown: A Letter from Harlem," an essay later in *Nobody Knows My Name,* contrasts most Americans' lack of examination and their resulting delusions with Baldwin's project of uncovering and questioning through examination.[18] Baldwin describes the "fishhooks, the barbed wire" of "wide, filthy, hostile Fifth Avenue," so unlike the Fifth Avenue of Manhattan, just a few blocks south. "Immense human gaps" populate this stretch of the avenue, gaps where the shells of human beings, deadened by the false hopes of the "holy Roller sects" or "the hatred of the white world and all its works" haunt the stunted trees and looming projects. Those who do avoid these deaths "get up in the morning and go downtown to meet 'the man,'" working in the white man's world all day only to return to "this fetid block," struggling to keep a modicum of human dignity "in spite of the insults, the indifference, and the cruelty" they encounter in their working day.[19]

In other words, without examination and recognition of the actual effects of these projects, most Americans ignore their reality, denying a constitutive part of themselves in the process. Baldwin intensifies the Socratic call for an examined life, showing the urgency of questioning what previously lay unquestioned. Most Americans cannot endure the vertigo that critical examination of this system would induce, but Baldwin insists that only through such examination can we live well together. "The way to begin," Baldwin writes, "is through taking a hard look at oneself. Just as Socrates's questioning elicits the pain and dislocation of perplexity, or *aporia,* in his interlocutors, Baldwin recognizes the difficulty of the task he demands. Most Americans prefer to cling to an illusion of happiness that denies the reality around them, reinforcing their power in the process. "Why don't all the Negroes in the South move North?" someone asks Baldwin. He explains what has unfailingly happened: "They do not escape Jim Crow: they merely encounter another, not-less-deadly variety. They do not move to Chicago, they move to the South Side; they do not move to New York; they move to Harlem."[20] Baldwin seeks to unseat the delusion that all Americans have the freedom to choose where they live, to shop where they wish, to work hard for a better life—one of the great and unexamined myths of the republic. But this myth functions as another delusion, and recognizing this myth as false proves nearly impossible when one's illusions about the safety and security of power depend on it.

Following the third facet of Socrates's project, Baldwin also insists that examination will help lead his readers and fellow citizens to think what they are doing and thus reengage in collective life with others. The stakes of the needful examination for which Baldwin calls go beyond just knowing the facts. Baldwin argues that northerners "indulge in an extremely dangerous luxury" when they believe that having fought on the right side of the Civil War allows them to deplore what occurs in the South without turning a critical glance toward themselves. When human beings deny complexity, Baldwin writes in "Many Thousands Gone," they deny themselves and their common humanity: "Our dehumanization of the Negro then is indivisible from our dehumanization of ourselves: the loss of our own identity is the price we pay for our annulment of his."[21] One cannot justify the plight of blacks in the North by the worse situation in the South: "This perpetual justification empties the heart of all human feeling," writes Baldwin. "It is a terrible, an inexorable, law that one cannot deny the humanity of another without diminishing one's own: in the face of one's victim, one sees oneself. Walk through the streets of Harlem," Baldwin counsels dolefully, "and see what we, this nation, have become."[22] Delusions and the veil of innocence under which these delusions masquerade cost human beings their humanity and human community—these are the high prices of their havens.[23]

Examination, Acceptance, and Struggle: *Another Country*

Following Socrates in his original key, Baldwin's essays voice a powerful call for examination to address the dehumanizing delusions that persist in a society structured by categorical oppression. Yet as in the case of Socrates, this call for examination also assumes that people can change simply through knowing better, that recognition of the reality of racism could lead to ameliorating the destructive delusions under which most Americans live. This is not to say that Baldwin blithely repeats the paradox of Socratic intellectualism; on the contrary, he seems to recognize the dangers of such an assumption in *The Fire Next Time,* writing that "people find it very difficult to act on what they know," and in a speech five years later, Baldwin admits that people are always in great danger when they know what they should do, and refuse to act on that knowledge."[24] But in his essays Baldwin never directly offers a way of dealing with the problem that knowledge may not be enough to overcome an oppressive situation.[25] For this problem, *Another Country* offers an elaboration.

Another Country suggests the tragic possibility that knowing may not be sufficient, and for as much as Baldwin seems to promise in his essays that by interrogating myths and delusions one might illuminate some liberating truth about reality, *Another Country* moves against this by simultaneously insisting on an uncooperative and inert world, one resistant to the change inquiry might urge. The American experience, Baldwin admits, is "an enormous incoherence."[26] *Another Country* discloses this incoherence as rooted in the reality of racism in America and intertwined with gender, sexuality, and class in ways that constrain and resist questioning, forcing readers to recognize the harsh consequences of categorical oppression that even intensive examination might not alleviate. Reading Baldwin's novel alongside the essays thus deepens and complicates the question of how examination might lead to social change.

Whereas in his essays Baldwin often develops a "passage from Egypt" narrative that moves from denial to knowledge to redemption,[27] *Another Country,* like much of Baldwin's fiction,[28] circles the inescapability of conflict, of pain, and of suffering in a world marked forever by a history of oppression, eschewing plot for dialogue centering on its characters' struggles to achieve their identities. By discussing Baldwin's fiction as well as his nonfiction, I do not mean to elide the important differences between these genres; rather, I propose seeing Baldwin's fiction as reflecting, albeit in a changed way, the problems Baldwin articulates with his own voice in his essays. *Another Country* thus offers a way to claim the heterogeneous humanity of African Americans, as Roderick Ferguson has suggested, and to situate examination in the particular lives of its characters.[29] As they wander, intersect, and disperse, the characters of *Another Country* grope toward knowledge of themselves and recognition by those around them. The shapelessness of the novel reflects the characters' own shapeless existences and their limited power to fashion coherent lives despite their strident pursuit of self-knowledge, love, and connection.

The novel's characters crash again and again on the categorical barriers around them, but different responses emerge from this chaos of a world structured by racism, sexism, classism, and homophobia.[30] These different responses suggest how Baldwin transposes Socrates in the original key, bringing the project of examination to the embodied situations of particular characters and thus illustrating to his readers the singular ways in which the examined life is pursued. In the figure of Rufus, *Another Country* confronts the enterprise of examination with the conditions of its failure and thus with the chance that no hope of redeeming the horrific American past might persist. Yet the characters of Vivaldo and Ida display different ways in which examination might proceed, even in a society apparently intent on destroying them. Each of these characters complicates the original Socratic key of Baldwin's essays, showing how the problem of examination is less concerned with arriving at knowledge and changing one's life than with struggling through, in the company of others, the self-deluding myths that preclude connection and understanding. Complementing the strenuous labor of examination, acceptance and a commitment to struggle become thematic in *Another Country;* these frame the successes and failures of characters to "achieve their identities," moving Baldwin's "Socrates" into a distinctly different key.

Frustrated Examination: Rufus

If the essays suggest how examination might liberate all Americans from their racialized society, the character of Rufus complicates and ultimately denies such a possibility. *Another Country* begins with Rufus, and his character shadows all of the novel's other characters, containing within himself the most important motifs of the novel.[31] In the first few sentences many of these themes emerge: "He was facing Seventh Avenue, at Times Square. It was past midnight and he had been sitting in the movies, in the top row of the balcony, since two o'clock in the afternoon. Twice he had been awakened by the violent accents of the Italian film, once the usher has awakened him, and twice he had been awakened by caterpillar fingers between his thighs. He was so tired, he fallen so low, that he scarcely had the energy to be angry; nothing of his belonged to him anymore."[32] Rufus, like nearly all the novel's characters, faces a bleak and intimidating New York. While Rufus has tried to escape the streets to the movies, he cannot elude the threat of violence—both in the film and in sexual predations. Tired, low, angry, dispossessed: Rufus appears already beaten by the end of the novel's first paragraph.

Rufus's isolation marks one impediment to successful examination. His heterogeneity—his race, his sexuality, and his class—alienates Rufus from a world that pathologizes difference even while it produces it.[33] Rufus exists "entirely alone, and dying of it, . . . part of an unprecedented multitude."[34] As he "peddles his ass"—trying to pick up wealthy, white men who might buy him dinner in exchange for sex—Rufus feels the burden of the past looming like the skyscrapers around him. Still, Rufus examines himself and the world in which he finds himself. He remembers Leona, a white southern woman whom he had loved and yet beat violently until she was taken to Bellevue, the New York mental hospital. As Rufus recollects, we encounter the beginning of their relationship: after meeting at a Harlem club, Rufus takes Leona to a party of Charlie Parker music and marijuana where they have sex on the balcony overlooking Riverside Drive. But in this act Rufus loses his tenderness, overcome with aggression and inexplicable revenge that tear his character apart. Rufus loves Leona and yet he hates her: his love both represents the color-blind and affluent sophistication that the Riverside Drive party seems to symbolize and seems impossible in a society where "miscegenation" remained an indictable crime and Rufus will always be a poor black (and confused) boy. Rufus cannot endure this tension— "The price was too high."[35] Affection gives way to violence, and Rufus acts out the role society expects him to play over and against his knowledge and his desires. Despite recognizing the truth of his oppression and resentment, Rufus cannot escape his self-destructive character. He cannot accept what the world has made him.

As Rufus reflects and examines himself, it becomes clear that without the support of others he cannot face the horrible truths about himself and the world around him. Remembering this doomed affair from his nameless position on the street, Rufus recounts how his life became only worse with Leona. He and Leona begin to compete for the greatest unhappiness. Rufus brawls with Vivaldo in a bar when he thinks Vivaldo has flirted with Leona.[36] Leona later tries to reassure Rufus that "there's nothing wrong with being colored," sparking another round of violence.[37] Despite seeing it for what it is, Rufus cannot persist in a world that denies the possibility of his life with Leona, nor can he escape the terms in which he has been cast: "I'm your boy," he tells Leona. "You know what that means? . . . It means you've got to be good to me."[38] Rufus hears Bessie Smith's blues wisdom— "There's thousands of people, ain't got no place to go"—and it "speaks to his troubled mind," but only enough for him to wonder "how others had moved beyond the emptiness and horror which faced him now."[39] He cannot seem to find a way.[40]

The examination promised in the essays runs up against the reality of Rufus's situation; this reality overpowers the hopefulness of facing the truth about himself. Rufus's reflections build his backstory—the musical brilliance, the hatred, the wishes for love—and yet Rufus cannot escape a fatalistic awareness "that nothing would stop it, nothing: this was himself": "Rufus was aware of every inch of Rufus. He was flesh: flesh, bone, muscle, fluid, orifices, hair, and skin. His body was controlled by laws he did not understand. Nor did he understand what force within this body had driven him into such a desolate place. The most impenetrable of mysteries moved in this darkness for less than a second, hinting of reconciliation. And still the music continued, Bessie was saying that she wouldn't mind being in jail but she had to stay there for so long."[41] Rufus eventually finds an escape from this carceral regime by leaping from the George Washington Bridge to his death. Rufus's self-knowledge, won though the reflecting that takes the novel's first seventy pages, cannot save him. Knowing that the pain would never stop, that he could never make it this way, that the rules of the game all but decided the outcome, Rufus sees everybody, white and black, chained together, wishing they could escape from each other. "But we ain't never going to make it," Rufus thinks. "We been fucked for fair."[42]

Examination fails when it proceeds without the company of others and, apparently, when the life needing examination proves too incomprehensible through the lens of categorical difference. Struggling yet ultimately defeated, Rufus "goes under." Tragically, Rufus tries: he comes to know himself but ultimately cannot use this knowledge to create a better place for himself (or others) in the world. Thus while Rufus does not explicitly become

Baldwin's version of Richard Wright's *Bigger Thomas*—that is, as Baldwin describes him, one whose "life is controlled, defined by his hatred and his fear"—Rufus comes horribly close.[43] He recognizes his hatred and fear, but he can never fully accept the fate of his character—his masculinity, his color, his ambivalent sexuality, his being an American. Rufus wants to love Leona, but he cannot accept and struggle against the social condemnation of a love affair between a black man and a white woman even while he struggles with the heteronormative image of a black man foisted on him. Rufus examines and wonders, but he also resents all of those around him. Soon pain becomes Rufus's whole identity; the bitterness of generations concentrates in him. The truth of his condition, reached through the labor of examination, simply became too much for Rufus to bear.

Examination and Acceptance: Vivaldo

Rufus examines but cannot accept what he discovers: his isolation and the horrific truth of his situation seem to prevent it.[44] Yet *Another Country* offers another character to chronicle the struggles of examination, Vivaldo, Rufus's best friend and a poor Italian-Irish would-be novelist. Vivaldo offers an analogue to Rufus with one major exception: he is white. Vivaldo's whiteness, however, fundamentally changes his experience of the world: Vivaldo can express his love for men without being forced to sell it for sex; Vivaldo can frequent Harlem prostitutes without thinking of his sister; Vivaldo can, despite his poverty, pass as respectable, a future version of his former teacher Richard, who lives on Riverside Avenue. In other words, despite their being "up the same streets," Vivaldo and Rufus cannot know each other.[45] Vivaldo seeks to help Rufus, but he cannot yet understand the source of Rufus's rage and resentment. Hours before Rufus's death, Vivaldo still does not detect his pain.

Differently situated from Rufus, Vivaldo also develops quite differently in the novel, giving an alternative trajectory to examination. The loss of Rufus puts Vivaldo on the path of examination, and Vivaldo's connections with others provide a space for him to come to terms with himself and the world. Following Rufus's funeral, Vivaldo begins to ask questions. Sitting frustrated at his writing desk, Vivaldo feels as if he doesn't know his characters well enough to continue writing. He realizes, at this moment, that "the occurrence of an event is not the same thing as knowing what it is that one has lived through." Vivaldo's reflections continue: "Most people had not lived . . . through any of their terrible events. . . . They passed their lives thereafter in a kind of limbo of denied and unexamined pain. The great question that faced him this morning was whether or not he had ever, really, been present at his life. For if he had ever been present, then he was present still and his world would open up before him."[46] Without mentioning Rufus's death, Vivaldo seems to confront the crucial question for himself in the novel: whether or not he can become present to the death of Rufus, whether or not he can face and accept that pain and still struggle onward. As Vivaldo reflects on his incipient love affair with Ida, the younger sister of Rufus, his own insights begin to unfold. Vivaldo recollects his visits to prostitutes in Harlem while he also thinks fondly of first meeting Ida at Rufus's parents' apartment in the same area. The contradiction does yet appear in his mind, that is, that Vivaldo can treat some black Americans as less than human—he would not visit prostitutes in his own neighborhood, after all—while considering others his beloved friends. After his first night with Ida, Vivaldo still carries this tension between innocent delusion and reality: he is crazy about Ida, and he sees her face as a lover would, imbued with mystery as well as the possibility of torment; at the same time, however, making love with Ida, Vivaldo feels as if he is "traveling up a savage, jungle river," engulfed in her strange blackness.[47] Vivaldo still sees Ida as a poor black woman, yet he does not yet see his own complicity in these destructive definitions. Even while it seeks to connect despite their differences, his love remains structured by the gap between their positions and the different burdens this creates.

Vivaldo's examination proceeds and blossoms in the company of others as he encounters differences between himself and the world and begins to reflect. Although Vivaldo examines, he comes only slowly to accept his responsibility for the world in which he is a white man and Ida a black woman. At first Vivaldo cannot understand why Ida angrily identifies him with "white people" who have made her life miserable.[48] Nor can Vivaldo set aside his own jealousy toward the wealthy white producer Ellis to see how Ida has been drawn into a desperate affair in the hope of making it as a singer. But Vivaldo's own search for reality, anticipated by his insight at the writing desk, eventually brings him to confront and accept his own lack of knowledge. Among old friends in a workingman's bar, Vivaldo begins to recognize his own ignorance. "Love was a country," Vivaldo realizes as he reflects on his life with Ida, "he knew nothing about."[49] Not one of us knows this country well—or well enough to avoid the pain and suffering it inevitable incurs: "And now—" thinks Vivaldo, looking around himself, "now it seem that they were all equal in misery, confusion, and despair":[50] "Something in him was breaking; he was, briefly and horribly, in a region where there were no definitions of any kind, neither of color, nor of male and female. There was only the leap and the rending and the terror and the surrender."[51] For a moment, Vivaldo looks deeply into the chaotic equality of all human beings, the fact that regardless of color, gender, class, or sexuality, we all struggle to make our lives despite our limits, indeed to make lives out of such limits. Vivaldo wishes he could give up his differences for Ida so that she might take and love him, so that what held them apart—the immutable fact of each one's situation—might be overcome. Yet Vivaldo still does not know where this insight leads. As he listens to music with his now drunken friends, Vivaldo recalls the blues that Ida so often sings: "what in the world did these songs mean to her?" he wonders. Slowly the recognition awakens: an understanding of Ida's suffering, about the wound left by the loss of her brother, about the agonies wrought by a hostile world. Reflecting silently among these same, unknowing friends, Vivaldo envies their "deadly and unshakable innocence."[52] He cannot forget what his examination has won.

While Rufus's examination led him to the brink of an unacceptable reality, Vivaldo thus finds the strength to accept himself and the world that has made him. The Socratic project shifts to a different key, from the simple task of examination to the painful work of acceptance followed by the suffering of struggle. Accepting this reality, then, Vivaldo struggles against it. While an oppressive society threatens his love for Ida, Vivaldo, unlike Rufus, can persist in part because of his commitment to another. Displayed in public, the love affair between Vivaldo and Ida raises "clouds of hostility" that threaten to swamp them; the "entire shapeless, unspeakable city" seems to hover around their squalid apartment, oppressing them with its every noise and glance.[53] "Minefields accumulate" around and between Vivaldo and Ida.[54] Yet while Vivaldo never claims to know the depths of Ida's pain, he can commit to struggle alongside her, still haunted by his failure to do so for Rufus. Vivaldo recognizes the need to work for love and that, absent love, one cannot get through it all.[55] One must accept the pain, but, Vivaldo tells his friend Eric, "one's got to *try*."[56] Vivaldo resolves to take up his burden and love Ida despite the unfriendly world that refuses to acknowledge this love as legitimate.

Examination and Struggle: Ida and Vivaldo

Vivaldo shows how examination might proceed toward acceptance and struggle, but Vivaldo's struggle also requires another: Ida. Although Vivaldo's love appears in stark contrast to Rufus's isolation, the transposition of the Socratic project of the essays remains incomplete without an account of how the commitment to another human being can provide the space and the strength to pursue examination. Moreover, whereas Vivaldo provides a counterpoint to Rufus, Ida inhabits the space between them. Vivaldo appears better equipped to accept a reality absent Harlem's stunted projects and the violent prejudice faced by black, nonheteronormative Americans; this reality broke Rufus, whereas Vivaldo can bear up against it. But Ida lives with an awareness of both worlds; she is the "outsider-insider" of the novel. She has left the Harlem of her childhood behind and now lives in the Village with Vivaldo. The loss of Rufus haunts her, breeding resentment and anger toward a world that could allow such a thing to occur. Ida thus functions as the fulcrum for the argument of this essay: if Ida shows evidence of ameliorating the vicious effects of a racialized society through her own self-examination, the hopefulness of Baldwin's Socratic project of inquiry in the essays persists; if, however, Ida's character goes the way of Rufus, the novel at best shows how white people such as Vivaldo have overcome their delusions while bleakly admitting the impossibility of black people doing the same.

Ida's embattled situation initially appears to doom any project of examination. This bleak horizon emerges in stark contrast to the liberal innocence of Cass, the white and affluent wife of Richard, Vivaldo's teacher and friend. "There are other countries—have you ever thought of that?" Cass suggests to Ida: "Ida threw back her head and laughed. 'Oh yes! And in another five or ten years, when we get the loot together, we can pack up and go to one of those countries.' Then, savagely, 'And what do you think will have happened to us in those five years? How much will be left? . . . What you people don't know,' she said, 'is that life is a *bitch*, baby. It's the biggest hype going.'"[57] While Cass has just revealed her affair with Eric as an act of boredom, Ida confronts her with the bleak reality of a black woman striving to make it. For despite loving him, Ida feels unable to marry Vivaldo—love cannot change the reality of their disparate situation. Their differences, artificial as they may be, create an unbridgeable gap. Cass could never know "what it's like to be a black girl," just as Vivaldo could never understand what led Ida's brother, Rufus, to commit suicide. Vivaldo cannot understand the prison of Harlem that produced Ida and Rufus; he can accept his own responsibility, but he can never fully confront Ida's world, a world very similar to that which sent her brother off the George Washington Bridge.

Ida's circumstances do not bode well for the prospects of a "passage from Egypt" through examination. Throughout the novel, Ida appears hardened against those around her, impervious to hate as well as love. Ida acts distant and unfriendly: Vivaldo remembers her air of disdain when they met; "It doesn't pay to be too nice," she tells Eric.[58] Ida erupts at Cass for not seeing the pain that led her brother Rufus to his death. Everyone has to suffer, she tells Cass: "You don't have to experience paying your dues and it's going to be rough on you, baby, when the deal goes down."[59] Ida's inflexibility also seems to shadow any insights Vivaldo wins, suggesting that while he may examine and accept the world, Ida's resistance may prevent any overcoming of the distance between them.

The structure of the novel builds these questions around examination to a culmination at the novel's end. Up until that point, Baldwin never narrates the novel from Ida's point of view, thus refusing readers any knowledge about how Ida's self-examination has proceeded, that is, about how well she has come to terms with the reality of the world she and Vivaldo face. Throughout the novel, readers only see Ida from the outside. Whereas every other major character has a portion of the story told through his or her point of view, Ida's inner world remains unavailable; Ida speaks with other characters whose internal responses Baldwin describes, yet Ida remains closed. One cannot be sure if Ida has asked herself the questions asked by Rufus and Vivaldo, if Ida has undertaken to examine herself and her delusions about the world.[60]

The closed, enigmatic Ida dramatically reveals herself in the final scene with Vivaldo, a scene that adds a crucial facet to the development of examination, acceptance, and struggle—and thus to Baldwin's "Socrates in a different key." Vivaldo returns from a night with his friend Eric, and Ida confesses her desperate seduction of Ellis. Ida explains to Vivaldo how much difficulty she has had accepting the loss of Rufus and the fundamental unfairness of her beloved brother's ending up as he did. Ida had resolved to succeed in the white man's world and "settle the score" after her brother's death: she would "hit the A train" and make it downtown as her brother hadn't.[61] But the "love jive" confuses Ida: Ida's love for her brother Rufus leads her down a path of vengeance, but her love for Vivaldo also seems to draw her toward coherence and some kind of healing.[62] Thus being with Vivaldo makes her wonder about the idea of success behind her plans; her beliefs about "the way of the world" seem less than true when contrasted with the world she and Vivaldo have begun to create together. She recognizes that what she believed about the world had led her against herself: "It wasn't me. It wasn't me," she tells Vivaldo.[63]

This revelation leaves Vivaldo reeling, vertiginous; Ida's speech suddenly shifts the reality of his earlier resolution to love Ida despite the struggles it would entail. Vivaldo reaches out to find some grip: the coffeepot, the coffee cups, sugar, milk, cigarettes. Feeling these things, reminding himself of their existence, reconnects Vivaldo to the reality that had seemed to vanish with Ida's words. Ida had withheld the truth to protect Vivaldo, fearing he could not bear it. Vivaldo thinks to himself that he had at last found what he wanted, the "true Ida," but now he has no idea how he could live with it.[64] For a moment, it seems as if everything between them will fall apart, disintegrating beneath the weight of the truth.

Ida's dramatic revelation calls attention to her particularly fraught struggle in the novel. Ida lives with the most intimate knowledge of the murderous effects of an oppressive society; she has the most to confront in her task of examination. As a black woman, moreover, she has found herself forced to use her sexuality for advancement: Vivaldo sees her as a whore even in her moment of confession; when she seeks protection from Ellis, it can come only through her own subordination. As Baldwin later wrote, Ida was "an object of wonder and even some despair—and some distrust—to all the people around her, including people who were very fond of her."[65] Fearing further abandonment and disempowerment, Ida is reluctant to speak the truth to Vivaldo, saying that men wouldn't love women if they spoke truly and trying to attribute her lonely sadness to its being that "time of the month."[66] Ida's situation has led her to act against herself, to a self-destructive identity, which she has no choice but to struggle against—or else suffer the same fate as her brother.

Under these conditions, Ida's powerful speech indicates the degree of struggle required by Baldwin's project of examination. Ida must insist on her own self-definition and self-valuation, on a black female–centered understanding denied by Vivaldo and the world around him. Yet rather than define herself exclusively in opposition to Vivaldo, she also must seek connection. Ida must simultaneously reject the internalized psychic oppression of being but a "poor, ignorant, black girl" while articulating to Vivaldo what it means to be Ida, to be a subject worthy of recognition. Ida does this by speaking out, bringing herself to the fore and initiating the work of reconciliation on which both she and Vivaldo depend. She witnesses her oppression, in Kelly Oliver's term, making Vivaldo witness herself as well, to "enable working-through rather than merely the repetition of trauma and violence."[67]

This working-through happens in the context of a loving connection that Ida and Vivaldo forge during the course of the novel. The end of *Another Country* thus shows the interdependence of Vivaldo and Ida—and thus the importance of the pursuit of connection—as a final element alongside acceptance and struggle that constitute Baldwin's "Socrates in a different key." While each of them feels overwhelmed by the truth, Ida and Vivaldo do not despair. Vivaldo is stunned, but Ida asks not for understanding or kindness—just, it would seem (for Ida doesn't quite say it), that Vivaldo might stay. Ida and Vivaldo touch: "They stared at each other. Suddenly, he reached out and pulled her to him, trembling, with tears starting up behind his eyes, burning and binding, and covered her face with kisses, which seemed to freeze as they fell. She clung to him; with a sigh she buried her face in his chest. There was nothing erotic in it; they were like two weary children."[68] Ida and Vivaldo cleave to one another. Having examined and accepted the truths of their life together, now they must struggle forward in a world that seems intent on breaking them. The final section of *Another Country*, hopefully titled "Toward Bethlehem," seems to promise an alternative to the lonely logic of Rufus's examined, yet destroyed life as well as the incompleteness of examination when undertaken by Vivaldo alone. Needless to say, the life created by Ida and Vivaldo remains fraught and difficult: In their final scene, Ida admits that there may not be any hope for her, as if aware of being doomed to repeat her brother's history; Vivaldo, too, finds himself both afraid of Ida and overwhelmed by the "wilderness of anger, pity, love, and contempt and lust" that she provokes in him.[69] Yet when Ida and Vivaldo embrace like "weary children" in their final scene, Baldwin seems to emphasize their youth and the possibility it holds. Moving "toward Bethlehem," Ida and Vivaldo have begun a journey with their own miraculous actions. While Ida remains silent, the scene closes with Mahalia

Jackson's gospel filling the room, holding this same promise that Ida and Vivaldo hold within themselves: the possibility of bringing a changed world into being.[70]

Socrates in a Different Key: The Journey toward Coherence

"The principal action in the book," Baldwin said of *Another Country* in an interview with the *Paris Review,* "is the journey of Ida and Vivaldo toward some kind of coherence."[71] Writing elsewhere, Baldwin describes how the shapelessness of *Another Country* also reflects the "incoherence" of life in America. The novel's characters desperately seek the self-knowledge without which real love is impossible, but they find themselves unable to change and incapable of gaining real insight. By depicting this, Baldwin writes that *Another Country* suggests that "love is refused at one's peril."[72] While revealing the struggle to examine and change, *Another Country,* according to Baldwin, also demonstrates complicity, especially white innocence and the delusions that structure daily life.

The trajectory of Ida and Vivaldo "toward some kind of coherence" shows what it might mean to struggle against the incoherence of life in America, a struggle pursued through examination and acceptance and yet never finished, just as the final embrace of Vivaldo and Ida at the end of *Another Country* describes only one more step *toward* coherence, not its achievement. "The journey toward coherence" represents the path of examination chastened by the pain and suffering to which *Another Country* bears witness. This paradoxical moment of connection and looming disintegration encapsulates the unfolding of examination that has taken place in the novel. Rufus examines himself but cannot accept what he finds. Vivaldo, with his lighter burden, can accept the fruits of his examination, but that acceptance depends on his connection with Ida. Ida's pursuit of examination remains shrouded until the final scene, when she recounts it herself, yet this truth telling threatens to destroy the fragile bond she and Vivaldo had created. Still, Ida's fundamental opaqueness in the novel indicates the opaqueness at the core of every human being and thus the endlessness of all struggles to know and be known by others. Baldwin's "Socrates in a different key" has complicated the simple task of examination by depicting the work of acceptance, struggle, and connection in the characters of *Another*

Country; each character's particular embodiment delimits and conditions his or her ability to examine and overcome the oppressive structures of society. Moreover, the characters' connections to each other lend space and strength to the painful undertakings Baldwin acclaims in the essays. The journey is a struggle and, at least in the terms of the novel, an endless one.

The language of "incoherence" thus performs two important functions for Baldwin. First, in the essays, the confrontation with incoherence encompasses the task of examination as Baldwin describes it. Here is Baldwin's black American Socrates in Socrates's original key: just as Socrates confronts the incoherent beliefs and actions of his fellow Athenians to bring them to more truthful lives, Baldwin notes how the incoherence of the world in the face of question prods further examination. In an essay from 1961, "Notes for a Hypothetical Novel," Baldwin describes how "disparities" often produced by "the fact of color" lead to "incoherence."[73] This incoherence—what Baldwin calls the incoherence of the American experience—presents the largest obstacle to the writer in America: "to try and find out what Americans mean is almost impossible because there are so many things they do not want to face."[74] Incoherence, then, describes the product of delusions pervasive in American life, the resulting incongruity between mythic innocence and reality, between the illusions (and delusions) by which most people live and the actual conditions of collective life. Such incoherence is also born from inarticulacy about one's past and how it has formed the present; this is the inarticulacy Baldwin confronts with his essays.[75] As Baldwin writes in his review of Alex Haley's *Roots,* being deluded about one's origins creates incoherence: "They become incoherent because they can never stammer from whence they came."[76] To examine both ourselves and the world, we must confront the present state of incoherence as the first step.

The "journey toward some kind of coherence" depicted in *Another Country* adds a second layer to "coherence." Here Baldwin transposes Socrates to a different key, one of acceptance, struggle, and the pursuit of connection. As the final scene between Vivaldo and Ida powerfully demonstrates, coherence possesses a more basic meaning than logical compatibility. The coherence toward which Vivaldo and Ida journey describes, at the most basic level, the pursuit of mutuality, of sticking together, and thus the basis of their commitment to connection even as they struggle. They journey *toward* coherence. Just as Baldwin titles the final section of *Another*

Country "Toward Bethlehem," this coherence describes something on an ever-receding horizon, an object of pursuit never quite attained. Rufus fails to approach anything like this coherence: we encounter him alone on the streets from the beginning of the novel, and he seems incapable of sharing his burdens with others, as Vivaldo and Ida learn to do. Similarly, Vivaldo's love for Ida moves him from recognition to acceptance and struggle, but until he faces Ida and she witnesses his commitment, his inner reflection remains mere words. So, too, the powerful speech of Ida at the end of the novel underscores the obstacles to examination and the painfulness of the struggle that examination requires of her. Although Ida and Vivaldo come together at the novel's end, this promises only "a kind of coherence," in Baldwin's words, one that remains unachieved.

The movement toward coherence suggests how Baldwin's work brings together examination and the confrontation of an oppressive society into practices of embodied, collective examination. Baldwin's work suggests that examination alone is not enough to overcome incoherence. Recent accounts of Baldwin's politics have introduced the "problem of acknowledgement" to describe how knowledge alone is insufficient for addressing systems of oppression,[77] but adding a reading of *Another Country* shows how one must commit to examine, accept, and struggle *with others*. Acknowledgment becomes a collective task. Substituting coherence as an unreachable yet nonetheless imaginable object of human striving thus shifts discussions of democratic citizenship from simply a matter of diagnosis and prescription by Socratic social critics or philosophic citizens to a *process of engagement* with oneself and others, seeking not knowledge or enlightenment but self-understanding and self-possession through examination, acceptance, and struggle. The essays, as Balfour has suggested, provide a language for this process; *Another Country* shows the struggle of articulating this language, the messiness of its embodiment, and the costs exacted by the pursuit of understanding.[78]

Another Country furthers this shift from solitary to social examination by situating these practices into the particular lives of its characters. The struggle forward does not come to pass by individual decisions so much as by moments of cooperation, such as when Ida and Vivaldo fall into one another's arms, pledging with words and action their commitment to persevere. Selfcraft, in Edwina Barvosa's term, proves inadequate as a solitary practice because of the obstacles posed by existing identity schemes and social constructions; only an "intrapersonal politics" that engages both self and others can promise some kind of reconciliation.[79] The struggle of Ida and Vivaldo, moreover, dramatizes the pain and difficulty of moving toward coherence that Kelly Oliver calls "working through," showing how, as she puts it, "in order to imagine peaceful and compassionate relations, we must be able to imagine working-through whatever we might find threatening in relations to otherness and difference."[80] Ida and Vivaldo discover how they can act on what they know (and do not know) about each other; *Another Country* shows how each of their struggles to examine and understand the world around them requires the involvement of the other. The struggle becomes a messy, human wrestling within and among selves and world in Baldwin's novel, showing the range of shapes examination can take within the lives of those affected by (as well as perpetuating) categorical domination.

The necessity of this examination's being *social* stems not only from the need to include the perspectives of others to achieve some knowledge of one's situation but also by virtue of the deeper motivation for examination, acceptance, and struggle according to Baldwin: love. Here Baldwin's work usefully spans two strands of discourse emerging from feminists of color and others who have emphasized love and connection as a response to oppression. On one hand, Baldwin's work anticipates arguments by Maria Lugones and Merle Woo, among others, that have stressed love's function as a survival tool.[81] Here love inspires a new kind of "playful perception," in Lugones's words, that can identify with the other and motivate traveling to the other's perspective. Love enables mutuality by motivating commitment to the other. Love in this sense serves at least two functions in *Another Country:* it leads Ida to "hit the A train" and avenge the death of her brother; yet it also draws Vivaldo and Ida together and instigates their recognition of how mutual love can sustain the agony of struggling to understand themselves and one another. Shadowed by a hate that also drives Ida to use Ellis for her advancement, Ida's love also motivates her connection with Vivaldo and thus animates the hopeful spirit of reconciliation at the end of the novel.

On the other hand, Baldwin's work also anticipates love as a political practice of resistance.[82] In this form, love becomes the basis for resisting categorical oppression at large, articulating what Cynthia Willet has called the "erotic" power for social change.[83] From the basis of their love, Vivaldo and Ida have a position from which they can work through the oppressive structures of the world as they move toward coherence; love thus sustains examination, acceptance, and struggle and carries the potential to emancipate lovers from structures of oppression. Love becomes, in bell hooks's words, "a practice of freedom,"[84] the motive force that moves estranged and isolated individuals toward some kind of reconciliation. Whereas writings by Audre Lorde, Toni Morrison, Patricia Hill Collins, and others have called for a focus on the erotic and its value for resisting oppression, Baldwin's work links this political practice with the ethical disposition named by Lugones and others, illuminating how love can motivate political projects while being rooted in particular human beings.[85]

Although political theory has largely been reluctant to treat race and racial injustice as fundamental to the study of modern democratic life, James Baldwin's work joins a chorus of African American writers before him by powerfully articulating the necessity of not simply understanding but acting to overcome America's history of categorical oppression. Writing as a "Socrates in a different key," Baldwin distinctively transposes critical citizenship into the register of embodied collective inquiry, illuminating a mode by which we all might fight systems of oppression and the delusions such systems foster through collective examination, acceptance, and struggle. As Baldwin once put it: "I don't believe any longer that we can afford to say that it is entirely out of our hands. We made the world we're living in and we have to make it over."[86]

Notes

Originally published as Joel Alden Schlosser, "Socrates in a Different Key: James Baldwin and Race in America," *Political Research Quarterly* 66, no. 3 (2013). Reprinted by permission of Sage Publications, Inc.

An earlier version of this essay received the 2010 award for "Best Paper on Blacks and Politics" from the Western Political Science Association. The essay began with my participation in the "Contemplating James Baldwin" symposium held at Carleton College, April 13–18, 2008, and the faculty reading group led by Professor Harry Williams, to whom I owe great thanks for introducing me to the work of Baldwin. I would also like to thank the following people for their helpful readings and suggestions during the revision process: Libby Anker, Ali Aslam, Lawrie Balfour, P. J. Brendese, Winter Brown, Peter Euben, David McIvor, Susan McWilliams, George Shulman, Kim Smith, Chip Turner, Akira Yatsuhashi, and my three anonymous reviewers at *PRQ*. I am also grateful to Jennifer Rapp and Tim Henderson, both of Deep Springs College, for important conversations as this essay neared completion.

1. Cornel West, *Democracy Matters: Winning the Fight against Imperialism* (New York: Penguin, 2004), 79–80.

2. Lawrie Balfour, *Evidence of Things Not Said: James Baldwin and the Promise of American Democracy* (Ithaca, NY: Cornell University Press, 2001), 135; George Shulman, *American Prophecy: Race and Redemption in American Political Culture* (Minneapolis: University of Minnesota Press, 2008), 27.

3. For another example of this approach to Baldwin, see the recent discussion by Jason Frank in *Constituent Moments: Enacting the People in Postrevolutionary America* (Durham, NC: Duke University Press, 2010).

4. Some of this language comes from Ruby Blondell's description of the minimal reading of Socrates in *The Play of Character in Plato's Dialogues* (Cambridge: Cambridge University Press, 2002). On Socrates as a social critic, see Michael Walzer, *In the Company of Critics: Social Criticism and Political Commitment in the Twentieth Century*, new ed. (New York: Basic, 2002).

5. See the description of "Socratic citizenship" in Dana Villa, *Socratic Citizenship* (Princeton, NJ: Princeton University Press, 2001). See also John Wallach, "Socratic Citizenship," *History of Political Thought* 9 (1998): 393–418; and George Kateb, "Socratic Integrity," *Patriotism and Other Mistakes* (New Haven, CT: Yale University Press, 2006), 215–44.

6. Charles W. Mills, *The Racial Contract* (Ithaca, NY: Cornell University Press), 18, 88.

7. By discussing "race in America" I do not mean to deny that, as Baldwin once told an interviewer, "the racial question and the sexual question have always been entwined." Baldwin shows that there is no extricating questions of race from those of gender, sexuality, and class.

8. See, e.g., Patricia Hill Collins, *Black Sexual Politics* (New York: Routledge, 2005).

9. For "selfcraft," I draw on the work of Edwina Barvosa in *Wealth of Selves: Multiple Identities, Mestiza Consciousness, and the Subject of Politics* (College Station: Texas A&M University Press, 2008). For "working through," I am indebted to Kelly Oliver, *Witnessing: Beyond Recognition* (Minneapolis: University of Minnesota Press, 2001).

10. On "heterogeneous humanity" in African American literature, see Roderick A. Ferguson, *Aberrations in Black: Toward a Queer of Color Critique* (Minneapolis: University of Minnesota Press, 2004).

11. I use the term *categories* to refer to race, sexuality, class, and gender and *categorical oppression* to refer to oppression that occurs along any one or all of

these categories. This follows Lombardo: "It is not just our category mistakes but indeed the mistake of relying too heavily upon categories that prevent us from understanding ourselves. The means by which we may free ourselves from this mistake is not to dismiss but, rather, to critically interrogate the assumptions concerning who and what we are that we receive in and as 'common sense'" (see Marc Lombardo, "James Baldwin's Philosophical Critique of Sexuality," *Journal of Speculative Philosophy* 23 [2009]: 40–50, 44).

12. See, e.g., Martha Nussbaum, *Not for Profit: Why Democracy Needs the Humanities* (Princeton, NJ: Princeton University Press, 2010); Walzer, *In the Company of Critics*, 13; and Villa, *Socratic Citizenship*, 3, 15, 58. For a reading of Socrates along similar lines to Villa, see also Kateb, "Socratic Integrity." Herbert Marcuse invokes Socrates in terms similar to Walzer's as a critic connected to Athenian democracy (see Herbert Marcuse, *One-Dimensional Man* [Boston: Beacon, 1964]).

13. James Baldwin, *Collected Essays* (New York: Library of America, 1998), 7.

14. Ibid., 708, 587.

15. Ibid., 686.

16. Ibid., 135–36.

17. Ibid., 835.

18. Ibid., 170–79.

19. Ibid., 170–72.

20. Ibid., 177.

21. Ibid., 20. Note here that Baldwin's "we" applies to everyone, as Balfour has argued in *Evidence of Things Not Said*, 43–49.

22. Baldwin, *Collected Essays*, 178–79.

23. "Innocence" describes an important concept for Baldwin: a denial of the reality of the world and of others as well as of responsibility to others and the world (see Balfour, *Evidence of Things Not Said*, 43–49; and Shulman, *American Prophecy*, 134–35).

24. Baldwin, *Collected Essays*, 295, 752

25. This describes a problem different from the classic problem of "akrasia." Baldwin's concern is not with lack of will but rather with basic inability caused by structural constraints. His characters have the "taste for conflicts" that the akratic agent lacks (see Amélie Oksenberg Rorty, "Self-Deception, *Akrasia*, and *Irrationality*," in *The Multiple Self*, ed. Jon Elster [New York: Cambridge University Press, 1986], 115–31).

26. Baldwin, *Collected Essays*, 228.

27. Darryl Pinckney, "James Baldwin: The Risks of Love," *New York Review of Books* 47.6 (2000).

28. For the purposes of this essay, I focus on *Another Country*, but I refer to

points of intersection with other fictional works as they appear. Treatments of *Go Tell It on the Mountain* and *Giovanni's Room* appear in Wilson Carey McWilliams's contribution to this volume and in James Campbell, *Talking at the Gates: A Life of James Baldwin*, rev. ed. (Berkeley: University of California Press, 2002), respectively. By finding tension between Baldwin's essays and novels, my reading differs from that of Zaborowska, who identifies similar themes in the novel but does not touch on the earlier essays under analysis here (see Magdalena Zaborowska, *James Baldwin's Turkish Decade* [Durham, NC: Duke University Press, 2002]). Also, Baldwin's last three novels—*Tell Me How Long the Train's Been Gone, If Beale Street Could Talk*, and *Just above My Head*—turn away (at least in part) from confronting the senselessness of American life as illuminated by conflicts along lines of race, gender, and sexuality, and instead appear to seek some respite in the black family. For more on these three novels, see Lynn Orilla Scott, *James Baldwin's Later Fiction* (East Lansing: Michigan State University Press, 2002); and Trudier Harris, *Black Women in the Fiction of James Baldwin* (Knoxville: University of Tennessee Press, 1985).

29. Ferguson, *Aberrations in Black*, 24.

30. Here I show the interrelation of these four categorical inequalities (race, gender, sexuality, and class), following the suggestion of James McBridge that "whenever we are speaking of race, we are always already speaking about gender, sexuality, and class" (see James McBridge, "Straight Black Studies: On African American Studies, James Baldwin, and Black Queer Studies," in *Black Queer Studies: A Critical Anthology*, ed. E. Patrick Johnson and Mae G. Henderson [Durham, NC: Duke University Press, 2005], 68–89). However, other scholars have focused almost exclusively on race and sexuality in studies of *Another Country* (see Zaborowska, *James Baldwin's Turkish Decade*, 91–140; see also James A. Dievler, "Sexual Exiles: James Baldwin and *Another Country*," in *James Baldwin Now*, ed. Dwight McBride [New York: New York University Press, 1999], 161–83; Susan Feldman, "Another Look at *Another Country*: Reconciling Baldwin's Racial and Sexual Politics," in *Re-viewing James Baldwin: Things Unseen*, ed. Quentin Miller [Philadelphia: Temple University Press, 2000], 88–104; and Charles Toombs, "Black Gay Man Chaos in *Another Country*," ibid., 105–27).

31. Baldwin (*Collected Essays*, 709) discloses Rufus's important role for the entire novel in "Words of a Native Son," published in *Playboy* in 1984: "Rufus was the only way that I could make the reader see what had happened to Ida and what was controlling her in all her relationships, why she was so different, why she was so uncertain, why she suffered so."

32. James Baldwin, *Early Novels and Stories* (New York: Library of America, 1998), 367.

33. Ferguson, *Aberrations in Black*, 26.

34. Baldwin, *Early Novels and Stories*, 368.

35. Ibid., 389. See the powerful end of Baldwin's short story "Going to Meet the Man" (933–50), where the poisonous combination of racial hatred and sexual aggression creates Baldwin's fictional Bull Connor.

36. Baldwin, *Early Novels and Stories*, 394.

37. Ibid., 411.

38. Ibid., 401.

39. Ibid., 408–9.

40. In the same way, the protagonist of Baldwin's story "Sonny's Blues" finds himself at a dead end for his life despite his talents and possibilities. As his brother says of Sonny, "I didn't want to believe that I'd ever see my brother going down, coming to nothing, all that light in his face gone out, in the condition I'd already seen so many others" (ibid., 831).

41. Ibid., 413.

42. Ibid., 442.

43. Baldwin, *Collected Essays*, 18.

44. Perhaps Rufus could accept his situation, but it would amount to a death sentence. I would read his suicide, however, as a rejection rather than an acceptance.

45. Baldwin, *Early Novels and Stories*, 409, 411. Du Bois's "veil of race" renders each opaque to the other and structures their lives in radically different ways.

46. Baldwin, *Early Novels and Stories*, 480.

47. Ibid., 523.

48. Ibid., 599.

49. Ibid., 631.

50. Ibid., 635.

51. Ibid., 636.

52. Ibid., 646–47.

53. Ibid., 495, 650.

54. Ibid., 652.

55. Ibid., 670.

56. Ibid., 716.

57. Ibid., 679.

58. Ibid., 493–596.

59. Ibid., 679.

60. In an essay published in 1984, Baldwin describes this strategy of making the reader wonder about Ida by not having her describe her situation in her own words: "I had to put great lights around Ida and keep the reader at a certain distance from her. . . . What Ida thought had to remain for all of them [the other characters of *Another Country*] the mystery which it is in life, and had to be, therefore,

a kind of mystery for the reader, too, who had to be fascinated by her and wonder about her and care about her and try to figure out what was driving her to where she was so clearly going" (see "Words of a Native Son," *Collected Essays*, 709).

61. Baldwin, *Early Novels and Stories*, 741.

62. Ibid., 733.

63. Ibid., 748.

64. Ibid., 751.

65. Baldwin, *Collected Essays*, 709.

66. Baldwin, *Early Novels and Stories*, 732, 734.

67. Oliver, *Witnessing: Beyond Recognition*, 18.

68. Baldwin, *Early Novels and Stories*, 752.

69. Ibid., 748, 751.

70. Still, this promise is ambivalent: Vivaldo and Ida are young, but they are also, to some extent, innocent. For the purposes of length, I have omitted the other relationships—primarily those between Richard and Cass and between Eric and Yves—that continue variations on this theme.

71. James Baldwin, "James Baldwin, The Art of Fiction, no. 78," *Paris Review* 91 (March 1, 1984): 48–82.

72. David Leeming, *James Baldwin: A Biography* (New York: Knopf, 1994), 200. The quotes from this paragraph—and my account of the letter, which is not publicly available—come from 200–201.

73. Baldwin, *Collected Essays*, 227.

74. Ibid., 228.

75. Ibid., 723.

76. Ibid., 763.

77. See Shulman's *American Prophecy* and "Acknowledgement and Disavowal as an Idiom for Theorizing Politics," *Theory & Event* 14.1 (2011), retrieved from http://muse.jhu.edu/journals/theory_and_event/v014/14.1.shulman.html. See also Patchen Markell, *Bound by Recognition* (Chicago: University of Chicago Press, 2003); and Jack Turner, *Awakening to Race: Individualism and Social Consciousness in America* (Chicago: University of Chicago Press, 2012).

78. Balfour, *Evidence of Things Not Said*.

79. Barvosa, *Wealth of Selves*, 207–29. Barvosa focuses more on the integration of singular selves, but her conclusion points toward how these practices must be collective, especially in situations marked by categorical differences.

80. Oliver, *Witnessing: Beyond Recognition*, 10.

81. Maria Lugones, "Playfulness, 'World-Traveling,' and Loving Perception," *Hypatia* 2 (1987): 85–99; Merle Woo, "Letter to Ma," in *This Bridge Called My Back: Writings by Radical Women of Color*, ed. Cherríe Moraga and Gloria

Anzaldua (New York: Kitchen Table/Women of Color Press, 1981), 140–47; Chela Sandoval, *Methodology of the Oppressed* (Minneapolis: University of Minnesota Press, 2000), 139–84.

82. Here Stephen Marshall comments more generally that Baldwin offers "a political practice of love as provocation to be undertaken by lovers struggling with and on behalf of a beloved society" (see *The City on the Hill from Below: The Crisis of Black Prophetic Politics* [Philadelphia: Temple University Press, 2011]).

83. Cynthia Willet, *The Soul of Justice: Social Bonds and Racial Hubris* (Ithaca, NY: Cornell University Press, 2001).

84. bell hooks, "Love as a Practice of Freedom," in *Outlaw Culture* (New York: Routledge, 1994), 289–98.

85. Willet, *The Soul of Justice*, 177–80.

86. Baldwin, *Collected Essays*, 230.

9

Crossing Identitarian Lines

Women's Liberation and James Baldwin's Early Essays

Brian Norman

Reading James Baldwin's early essays in the fifties had stirred me with a sense that apparently "given" situations like racism could be analyzed and described and that this could lead to action, to change.

—Adrienne Rich, "Split at the Root"

Through an engagement with Baldwin's fiction and essays, with their ethical and transgressive elements focused in narratives of revised masculinity and rewritten relations between blacks and whites, a wide range of women readers of the fifties and sixties could reach beyond their own subaltern inscriptions in dominant sexuality and culture, acknowledging both directly and through analogy other scenes of social and sexual desire—"variant" lives of all kinds.

—Cora Kaplan, "A Cavern Opened in My Mind"

I think especially of watching William Buckley on his "Firing Line" television program in the sixties debate [with] the writer James Baldwin on segregation. Buckley was elegant and brilliant and *wrong;* Baldwin was passionate and brilliant and wore his heart on his sleeve—he was also right. But Buckley won the debate; Baldwin lost it. I'll never forget how much I learned from the confrontation: be Baldwin, not Buckley.

—Andrea Dworkin, *Heartbreak*

In 1970, celebrated black writer and political spokesperson James Baldwin met with renowned anthropologist Margaret Mead for "A Rap on Race." The following year, Baldwin sat down for "A Dialogue" with young activist poet Nikki Giovanni on the television show *Soul!* In each meeting, Baldwin doggedly maintained that the nation and all its divided groups must address their shared past of disenfranchisement and discrimination if the nation stood a chance at achieving its promises of full inclusion for all. The very public conversations evidence the tensions between white liberalism, integration projects, and a newly militant generation calling for self-determination and a radical rethinking of race, gender, and experiences of exclusion. As a famed civil rights spokesperson insistent upon meaningful integration, Baldwin's attempts to address various segments of the post-1960s fractured Left testify to the difficulty of his quest to navigate the identitarian concerns that define twentieth-century literature and politics.

When Black Power eclipsed integration politics in the late 1960s, Baldwin was famously and viciously cast out of the role of black male spokesperson by Eldridge Cleaver in *Soul on Ice*.[1] Baldwin's subsequent conversations with Mead and Giovanni were largely ignored while Baldwin's readership and detractors awaited a more direct response[2] to Cleaver's inflammatory charges that Baldwin's homosexuality stood for a pathological love of white men, thereby undercutting the political ideal of integration. Rather than seeing this period as a delayed response, however, it is important to understand that Baldwin's turn to women in his discussions of black masculinity may also respond to—and ally with—the rise of a women's liberation movement (ca. 1967–1975), a movement that also emerged partly from Black Nationalist dismissals of women's participation.[3] The epigraphs attest to the ways in which Baldwin as a literary and political figure informed women's liberation, even if Baldwin himself did not participate directly in that social movement. By examining how and why Baldwin played a key role in the development of many women's liberationists, we can appreciate how he is able to travel across sharp lines within twentieth-century literary and political identitarian traditions. Whereas feminist theorist Cora Kaplan focuses in her epigraph on the significance of Baldwin's early fiction for women readers of the 1950s and 1960s, I am interested in how Baldwin's essays do this work.

In his role as best-selling essayist confronting issues of race and national belonging, Baldwin is an excellent case study in how literary figures can travel across stark political and identitarian lines. As such, we can see how twentieth-century literature accommodates the twin pulls of national collectivity and group identity. This chapter seeks to understand how and why Baldwin's early essays forge a connection with his women readers, especially white women who would come to identify with the feminist movement. In the late 1960s, women's liberation offered *woman* as a category of analysis through which to forge a *sisterhood* among those dispersed differently by systems of patriarchal power. Contemporary dismissals of the Second Wave often characterize the movement as only offering *woman* as an exclusive, monolithic category of analysis geared toward white middle-class women and insufficiently concerned with race and ethnic identity.[4] However, recent historical and archival studies of women's liberation question easy juxtapositions of race-consciousness and the Second Wave.[5] Within this exciting move to reconsider race-consciousness in the Second Wave, the rich connections between Baldwin's essays and his women readers, especially white feminists, represent one location where women's liberation and race-consciousness are mutually present. By analyzing personal experiences of disenfranchisement, Baldwin offered women's liberation a model for addressing division within a nation that announces inclusion and enacts exclusion. I propose three related explanations for how and why Baldwin arises as an important figure to (white) American feminist traditions: (1) As a masterful essayist and celebrated literary figure, Baldwin incorporates (white) women as key figures in his literary depictions of the experience of race in America, thereby offering an entry point for real women into such conversations; (2) As a ubiquitous racial spokesperson, Baldwin offers a protofeminist model of personal politics in which his women readers could analyze their personal experience in race-conscious theories of oppression and exclusion from full social participation; and (3) As a brilliant polemicist, Baldwin offers a model for building collectivity based in personal experience and what I will call "imperfect analogies," a model readily adapted to the women's liberation project of *sisterhood*.

Figures of (White) Women in Baldwin's Essays

Baldwin's status rests on his ability to examine race in America, but his early essays also invite feminist analysis of gender by offering a space for women to enter national conversations about social inclusion and personal identity.

In *Notes of a Native Son, Nobody Knows My Name,* and *The Fire Next Time,* Baldwin offers extended personal examinations of race in America, or as he framed it in his 1984 introduction to *Notes,* what America looks like from the vantage of a black citizen "captive in the promised land."[6] Though the merits of Baldwin's fiction are often subject to debate, Baldwin's early essays are almost universally celebrated. Esteemed literary critic Irving Howe praised Baldwin's "brilliant, nervous essay."[7] In one of the more famous reviews of *Notes,* Langston Hughes writes, "Few American writers handle words more effectively in the essay than James Baldwin," even though both questioned Baldwin's novelistic talents.[8] Due to the success of his essays, Baldwin was catapulted to fame as a racial spokesperson, and he appeared in numerous television and radio programs and on the covers of magazines, including *Time,* throughout the 1950s and 1960s. In 1964, literary critic David Levin noted: "The world and James Baldwin's place in it have changed drastically since the publication of [*Fire*] a year ago. . . . Now, of course, Baldwin has come to represent for 'white' Americans the eloquent, indignant voice of an oppressed people, a voice speaking in print, on television, and from the public platform in an all but desperate, final effort to bring us out of what he calls our innocence before it is (if it is not already) too late."[9] The urgency with which Baldwin's readers approach his essays is intense, and his readers felt uniquely invited to question the very tenets of race and democracy in America.

Within this bright spotlight of fame as a racial spokesperson, few critics then or now have noticed the critical role that women play within Baldwin's famous essays, and the resultant gender critique embedded in—if not fully explored in—his essays. In *Fire,* Baldwin examines the full challenge of integration as he devastatingly denounces both the Nation of Islam and American society for their self-delusions about race. In one of the more famous passages, Baldwin invests integration with some self-determination ideology as he famously asks, "Do I really want to be integrated into a burning house?"[10] But he also frames the question in gendered terms in the subsequent passage by addressing the sexual underpinning of racial anxiety and asking, "Why, for example—knowing the family as I do—I should *want* to marry your sister is a great mystery to me."[11] Baldwin calls attention to the sexist assumptions placed equally upon both white women and black men in the resistance to integration and the specter of miscegenation. Though one might look at this passage as a gay writer divesting from heterosexist institutions, Baldwin also highlights—ever so briefly—the way (white) women's rights and identities are curtailed because "your sister and I have every right to marry if we wish to."[12] Baldwin invests potentially abstract debates about integration with the language of the personal and the language of civil rights. If he does not fully examine—or even acknowledge—the need for a women's liberation movement, he has created the space for one in high-profile civil rights conversations.

Baldwin's use of (white) women in his introspective, meditative analyses of his personal experiences with American racial delusions appeared as civil rights activities in the South swelled to a national movement in the 1950s, following especially *Brown v. Board of Education* and the brutal lynching of Emmett Till in 1955. This paired Baldwin's devastating critiques of the racial nightmare in America with the end of official Jim Crow policies. The resultant American fears that social relations were crumbling often crystallized in the specter of a white woman willingly having sex with a black man. This was not a new anxiety. This is the fuel to the deep anxieties of William Faulkner's *The Sound and the Fury*, and this is the formidable power of Richard Wright's *Native Son*. In fact, Wright reported that he created Bigger Thomas specifically to confirm that white Americans' worst fears were, in the end, true.[13] But the painful irony of *Native Son* lies in the fact that Bigger Thomas did not, after all, sleep with the young white heiress of southern fortune; nor did he even, really, covet her. There are no textual clues of his coveting similar to, say, Emmett Till's alleged and fatal whistle in the direction of a white woman. The only evidence is his black masculinity: defined in white fantasy as the desire for, and inability to have, a white woman. The obscuring power of this specter of black male-white female coupling is perfectly captured in the trial of Bigger Thomas. In the trial, the body of Bessie, a black woman raped and mutilated by Bigger, is wheeled into the shocked white courtroom in order to provide incriminating evidence of the fantasized rape of the absent Mary Dalton, Bigger's white victim. The brutalization of a black woman is acknowledged only insofar as it helps to elucidate the relationship between white women and black men. When Black Nationalism emerged in the late 1960s and 1970s on a large scale, the purging of internalized whiteness, especially following Cleaver, was represented by a casting off of desire for the ultimate prize—a white woman—and replacing her with a black woman as helpmeet, a move that reinscribes dominant versions of heterosexuality.[14]

In Baldwin's early essays, however, white women often play a central—but underrecognized—role in the formation of a consciousness ready to question and change reality. Feminist critic Cora Kaplan revisits Baldwin's early work as a means of reexamining the complexities of Baldwin's explorations of black masculinity before the rise of identity politics, Second Wave feminism, and the gay and lesbian liberation movements. Before these movements exploded, Kaplan notes, many women writers and feminists found in Baldwin's central and messy depictions of sexuality a new language outside the rigidity of the New Left. For Kaplan, a self-described red-diaper baby, the promises and limits of Baldwin's racial and gendered explorations lie precisely in his use of women characters as embodiments of pained knowledge in contrast to a dangerously unexamined innocence of prelapsarian whiteness. But, like most feminist readings of Baldwin's fiction (e.g., Harris), Kaplan argues that these women are ultimately pawns in a male project and that Baldwin was never able to extend his criticism from *A Dialogue* that white people invented black people, or that straight men invented faggots to a fully feminist argument that men invented women as a fantasy to procure their own safety.[15]

In response to Kaplan's frustrations with the limits of the women in Baldwin's fiction, I suggest Baldwin's essays as an alternate avenue toward his gender critique. In his formative 1949 essay "Everybody's Protest Novel," Baldwin launches his writing career by disidentifying with Wright and Harriet Beecher Stowe. For the young Baldwin, America's refusal to deal truthfully with the complexities of race lay precisely in the fantasies it projected onto its citizens, especially black men and white women. Baldwin argues that the problem in the best-selling protest novels of Stowe and Wright is that they share the same underquestioned reality, that they are "a mirror of our confusion, dishonesty, panic, trapped and immobilized in the sunlit prison of the American dream."[16] If a protest novel can only reflect back an unchanged social order, Baldwin contends, the novels can only reinforce that dream as reality. Further, the trope of black male-white female coupling lies at the epicenter of America's racial self-delusions. In Baldwin's polemic, Wright and Stowe enter into a textually brokered sexual-historical union where "the contemporary Negro novelist and the dead New England woman are locked together in a deadly, timeless embrace."[17] For the young Baldwin, America's protest tradition is unable to move us past sexually inscribed racial fantasies into experience-based self-examination for which

Baldwin never ceased calling. And in Baldwin's essays that followed, white women and black men meet in complex interracial experiential anecdotes, which promises an alternative where black male antiracists and white female feminists share a common project. To do this, Baldwin turns to personal experience in order to account for the internalization of America's shared racial—and gender—delusions.

In the early criticism of Baldwin, the appearance of complex and even sympathetic white characters is seen as a "problem of identity" because they do not align neatly within a self-determination ideology.[18] Many have convincingly expressed anxiety at the fact that in "Notes of a Native Son" it is a *white* woman schoolteacher who brings Baldwin salvation by helping him to escape his preacher father's bitter religion, a religion that urged total separatism from white culture. Others have cited Baldwin's biographical history to wonder at the seminal role of white women in Baldwin's early development. David Leeming cites Orilla Miller as the schoolteacher from "Notes," and he cites Bette Davis as an image with whom Baldwin identified on the basis that she, too, had "frog eyes" like him. But in this case, as Baldwin transfers his awe of Davis to an allegiance with his mother, it is a white woman's body that stands in for a black woman's—the polar opposite of Bigger Thomas's trial. According to Jane Gaines, Baldwin's "relationship to race was unorthodox, if not ambivalent. What he did was quite extraordinary: making out of [the figure of Davis] something like and not like himself, something to aid identification as well as to prevent it absolutely by warding it off."[19] Baldwin's "ambivalent" and "extraordinary" use of figures of white women is not merely a chapter in Baldwin's psychological development. White women are central to Baldwin's call to examine personal experience and identity in order to change the reality of race in America.

The key difference between the plot of Baldwin's subsequent protest essays and that of Wright's protest novel is the direction of black male violence. Baldwin's major attack on Wright is that Bigger Thomas, unlike Wright himself, is an unthinking man without a community. In response, Baldwin wrote the seminal essay "Notes of a Native Son," wherein he encompasses Bigger Thomas's story within a psychologically complex autobiographical exploration of race and community. Baldwin does not dismiss Wright's Bigger Thomas; he incorporates Bigger Thomas into his larger project of a psychological analysis of race. In that essay, instead of Wright's mutilated black woman and charred white woman, Baldwin's exploration of violence dramatizes the restraint of fantasized violence toward a female character, a figure who serves as a proxy for the violent political struggle between white and black men. When a white waitress refuses to serve Baldwin in a New Jersey diner, his immediate reaction is not a "conscious plan."[20] Reminiscent of Bigger Thomas, Baldwin explains, "I wanted to do something to these white faces that were crushing me."[21] Instead of instinctual violence, however, the white waitress provides Baldwin with a crucial opportunity for psychological reflection: "I frightened the waitress who shortly appeared, and the moment she appeared all my fury fled toward her."[22] But Baldwin *misses* when he throws a coffee cup at her head. If the white waitress serves only as the messenger of racism deployed through a policy of racial segregation in a service economy, the target of Baldwin's fury cannot be the waitress herself. In order to complete the second half of the essay, Baldwin implants psychological reflection where there was none in Wright's story. Baldwin does not kill the white waitress; he reflects.

The confrontation with the face of the white waitress not only saves the physical life of the speaker, but it also serves as a catapult into characteristic Baldwinian self-examination of racial roles. After the coffee cup misses, Baldwin writes, "I returned from wherever I had been, I *saw,* for the first time, the restaurant, the people with their mouths open, already, as it seemed to me *rising as one man,* and I realized what I had done, and where I was, and I was frightened" (emphasis mine).[23] Baldwin escapes the narrowness of the black male–white female specter that diverts attention from and exculpates white men and real political power. Instead, Baldwin recognizes the communal and masculinist aspect of racism and the deployment of white women as complicit pawns. Although this may easily be read as "the man" of Black Nationalist rhetoric in the context of Baldwin's autobiographical mode, "the man" rising to oust Baldwin from the diner is closer to the patriarchal man so central to the writings and political analysis of women's liberation. The essayist emerges (alive!) with a sharpened and grounded critical consciousness not unlike the rigorously self-reflexive consciousness demanded by a women's liberation movement a decade or so later.

Baldwin further notes that this newly conscious speaker takes its cues from a news story about "six Negro girls who set upon a white girl in the subway because, as they all too accurately put it, she was stepping on their toes. Indeed she was, all over the nation."[24] The misogynist slippage in the metonymic use of "she" for the nation's racism is problematic. But, in the context of Baldwin's racial exploration, white women are not merely patsies for white racism; Baldwin examines white women as gendered pained participants in a nation multiply divided. Baldwin forges a black masculinity not through a distinction from/against a female Other. Rather, Baldwin enters a transformed consciousness by recognizing the costly chasm of otherness (both sexual and racial) itself.[25] Where Bigger Thomas's fear of racist violence results in the murder of a white woman, fear in Baldwin's essay is the catalyst pulling him *toward* critical analysis of race and gender and *away* from violence against women. There is no convenient black woman upon whose body masculinity reasserts itself. There is only survival by self-examination, which leads to systemic examination. In his essays, Baldwin offers his readers a speaker that can enter into large-scale political analysis when personal experience is understood as a manifestation of a *collective* experience of oppression. Baldwin's essays bear kinship to the collective subjectivity central to women's liberation, especially in the consciousness raising (CR) group. With a focus on personal politics and collective subjectivities, Baldwin's early essays offer a possible location of true political interaction and solidarity among black male antiracists and (white) women.

Personal Politics and Baldwin's Protofeminism

Baldwin's early essays employ a "personal politics" whose model of recounting personal experience as a starting point of systemic analysis looks a lot like that of women's liberation, even if the subject of the recounted personal experience may not. Though Baldwin is famous for his brilliant and insightful analyses of the social experience of race in America, and though *Fire* remains one of the most important writings on civil rights and Black Nationalism, scholars have not yet adequately explored the intricate relationships between black men and white women, or between feminism and black masculinity, in Baldwin's early essays. In *Fire*, Baldwin addresses a nation mired in violent conflicts over integration as the latest manifestation of that nation's long-standing race problem. Baldwin asserts simply, "Color is not a human or a personal reality; it is a political reality."[26] I suggest that it is this American-specific insight—as much as Simone de Beauvoir's famous dictum that "one is not born a woman, but becomes one"—that offered a model for how personal experience could form a basis for political organizing, which presents an important alternative to the more abstract theories of oppression coming out of the New Left and black liberation. This importance that many women's liberationists like Rich and Kaplan attach to Baldwin continues to influence the next generation of feminists and political activists. Political theorist Lawrie Balfour, for instance, writes, "Baldwin's words captured me, immediately and insistently. [*Fire*], in particular, enabled me to think through the complicated interrelation between democratic and American racial history in a way that the resources of the political theory curriculum had not."[27]

Baldwin offered a project that begins in meditations on seemingly personal experience as the necessary starting point for critiques of unacceptable "political realities" such as white supremacy and black second-class citizenship. Baldwin explains in an essay about segregation in the South, "It is not an easy thing to be forced to re-examine a way of life and to speculate, in a personal way, on the general injustice."[28] To a nation—and even a New Left—grown comfortable with abstractions like "the Negro problem" (or "the woman question"), Baldwin insists upon the personal. For Baldwin, changing "political realities" necessitates seeing things anew, seeing how one's personal experience includes or excludes one from the hopeful "we" of integration, of citizenship. If, as Baldwin proclaims, "We cannot be free until they are free," each person must recognize, examine, and change the psychological myths that ensnare us and determine our personal experience.[29] For Baldwin, individual destinies and identities were inextricably linked with others' and with a national imaginary. For Baldwin, in order to salvage the inclusive project of the nation, his readers must raise their consciousnesses through rigorous analysis of personal experience.

Baldwin's "personal politics" provide a blueprint for political analysis in accord with that developed most powerfully by the women's liberation movement a decade later. Yet Baldwin's contribution to that movement has gone relatively unnoticed. In order to construct discrete, identity-based trajectories of social movements, scholars may focus on those moments when specific groups offer something new from previous or proximate protest movements. Specifically, women's liberation in the United States marks a point when the experience of sexual difference itself became a fulcrum for organizing and working toward radical social change. Put in the most succinct terms, the New York Radical Women (NYRW) proclaim in their 1968 manifesto, "We take the woman's side in everything."[30] We remember the rise of women's liberation as the moment when sexual difference, and actual women, first occupied the center of political collectives in a modern social movement. Whereas Baldwin's "we" addresses difference in a universal national project, the NYRW demand a much more specific "we" to counteract the exclusion of women from political and social power. Nonetheless, Baldwin's attention to personal experience and collectivity resonates throughout statements like that of the NYRW. What is deemed feminist just before sexual difference became a prime location for political organizing in the United States, however, has always been, and remains, a site of contention within feminist studies. By looking at the "protofeminist" personal politics in Baldwin's essays before the rise of a fully fledged feminism (ca. 1968), we recover and appreciate the quiet but important contribution of Baldwin's essays to the rise of women's liberation.

Many feminist and black queer studies scholars have described the early work of Baldwin's as "protofeminist."[31] Thereby they offer a productively blurry genealogy of a feminism that arises out of the experiences of African Americans, including men. This move is exciting because it gestures toward a (literary) history that straddles rifts in earlier criticism of Baldwin's work in particular, and feminist history in general: between Second Wave feminism and Black Nationalism, between critical race theory and gender studies, between Black Arts and queer studies, and between liberal humanist projects of integration/inclusion and radical moves toward self-determination. Taking others' peripheral claims of Baldwin's protofeminism as central, we can appreciate the protest strategies Baldwin delivered to a nascent women's liberation movement. Baldwin offered analyses of personal experience as a means of challenging national fantasies of gender and race that could not weather sustained interrogations of the evidence of personal Baldwin's experience. Yasmin De Gout, for example, locates protofeminism in his fiction's self-conscious representation of masculinity and gender that "reveals him to be progenitor of many of the theoretical formulations currently associated with feminist, gay, and gender studies."[32] Scholars like De Gout place Baldwin in feminist trajectories by capitalizing on the presence of sophisticated analyses of gender as a political reality in his work before 1960. In short, Baldwin employs gender analysis before our narratives of feminism tell us such analysis should exist fully formed. When Baldwin becomes a protofeminist claimed by women's liberationists and later feminists, we must look at how Baldwin's influence permeates women's liberation be-yond his use of (white) women figures within his essays and fictions.

Baldwin places personal experience at the center of his 1950s and early 1960s calls for radical social change. In "Notes," he chronicles his experi-ence of segregation in New Jersey because, "I learned in New Jersey that to be a Negro meant, precisely, that one was never looked at but was simply at the mercy of the reflexes the color of one's skin caused in other people."[33] The essay marks and analyzes the effects of American self-delusions, as well as enables and enacts the way forward: looking directly at the speaker's ex-perience, not at the racial myths that could prematurely explain it. When we understand Baldwin's movement from the personal to the political, we can see an essayistic technique that deduces patterns by recounting illustrative personal experiences that lead to epiphanic understandings of the larger society. Within a specifically feminist context, Linda Nicholson calls these "aha" moments where social patterns are deduced through personal experi-ence.[34] For essay scholar James Cunningham, "the real subject matter" of a Baldwinian essay "turns out to be the business of acquiring a personal perspective on both the self and the world."[35] So, while each reader will have a different set of personal experiences—which Baldwin taught them to insist upon and analyze—the work for the reader is to follow Baldwin's blueprint for self-reflection so that each reader maps her experiences onto the national imaginary described by Baldwin. Otherwise, as Baldwin's essay "A Question of Identity" warns, without such reflection, even when assumed to be common, there arises the "disturbing possibility that experience may perfectly well be meaningless."[36]

In one of the epigraphs to this essay, celebrated feminist writer and ac-tivist Adrienne Rich credits Baldwin's essays for providing the model, if not the content, for early women's liberation. This early move supports current scholarly efforts to reconsider the relationship between women's liberation and proximate movements of race-consciousness. In *Personal Politics*, Sara Evans provided the most influential story of the origins of women's liber-ation by chronicling participation and disillusionment of both white and black women in key 1960s social movements. Evans pointed to the rise of a masculinist Black Nationalism and a sexist New Left as the major catalysts igniting an organized push for radical women's liberation, a movement with women and women's experience at the center of analysis. That is, women's liberation forged an unsteady coalition between white and black women as a reaction against the unwillingness to examine fully gendered oppression within existing opposition movements dominated by men. Evans cited the notorious 1964 Student Nonviolent Coordinating Committee (SNCC) conference at which Ruby Doris Smith Robinson, an African American civil rights worker, was ridiculed for presenting a paper (anonymously co-authored with three white women) on the problematic status of women in SNCC. For many African American men in SNCC, the coalition between white and black women through feminist analysis ignited accusations of treason aimed in particular at black women. In *Sisterhood Is Powerful*, the most influential collection of writings from women's liberation, Robin Morgan also cited Robinson's SNCC paper and framed the emergence of an independent women's movement as a necessary response to the sidelining of women and women's issues on the left, such as when "women who demanded that a plank on women's liberation be inserted in the [1966] Students for a Democratic Society (SDS) resolution . . . were pelted with tomatoes and thrown out of the convention."[37]

If women's liberation arises as a response to the exclusion of women within the New Left and Black Power movements, how do we account for the status that a wide array of women's liberationists, including Rich, Kaplan, Andrea Dworkin, and many others since, now accord Baldwin? Echoes of, and responses to, Baldwin permeate foundational collections of women's liberation, especially in his critique that America created the Negro as much as it created white identity. One of the political analogies buttressing the rhetoric of women's liberation is the comparison of the status of women to that of African Americans. Though the analogy has since been widely critiqued, women's liberation theorists like Shulamith Firestone consistently used it, and it was put most bluntly in Naomi Weisstein's essay "Woman as Nigger," included in the popular anthology *Voices from Women's Liberation*. Just after Morgan framed women's liberation as a break from SNCC and male chauvinism, Weisstein echoes Baldwin's insistence upon connecting disparate identities into shared futures ("we cannot be free until they are free") by explaining the position of black women's liberationists within Black Power movements: "We share a common root as *women*, much more natural to both groups [SNCC and Black Panthers] than the very *machismo* style of male-dominated organizations, black, brown, and white."[38] Though most of the reclamations of Baldwin have happened after the rise of identity politics in feminism, in 1972 young critic Jennifer Jordan defended

Baldwin in *Black Books Bulletin,* a publication of the Institute for Positive Education. Jordan celebrated Baldwin's critique of Norman Mailer's writing as mere "verbal masturbation" that had "seduced" Cleaver, who, she reminded her readers, is a rapist psychopath and who may be "guilty of the crime of which he accuses brother Baldwin."[39] The crime ostensibly being homosexuality, which serves as red herring in the battle for the mantle of spokespersonship. It was his women readers who were more likely to come to beleaguered Baldwin's defense. As a comparison, key Black Arts theorist Addison Gayle came to Baldwin's defense even before Cleaver's attacks to argue rather tepidly, "The day is quite distant when Negroes will be found engaging in sit-ins for the rights of homosexuals."[40] Baldwin's personal politics seem to resonate more within a feminist sensibility so that his essays are able to cross identitarian lines into women's liberation more so than into Black Power.

Personal Protest and Imperfect Analogies

> After the Senate Judiciary Committee hearings on Clarence Thomas' nomination to the Supreme Court, I said, "Lord, we really need James Baldwin now." . . . *Lord, Lord, we really need James Baldwin now.* He would have put it all into perspective; of that I was sure. He might have even made sense of it.
>
> —Gayle Pemberton on the Thomas-Hill Hearings

> We call on all our sisters to unite with us in struggle.
> We call on all men to give up their male privileges and support women's liberation in the interest of our humanity and their own.
>
> —Redstockings, "Manifesto," 1969

The white women in "Notes of a Native Son" that I discussed in the first section may be central to the formation of a black male speaker with a raised consciousness formed by the personal politics of experiential analysis I discussed in second section. But the central subject of the essays—Baldwin himself—cannot speak directly to women and women's liberation concern. Kaplan solves this problem by turning to the women, one white and one black, in Baldwin's novel *Another Country.* Kaplan demonstrates and applauds the ways in which these female characters consciously navigate the fantastical projections placed upon them by male culture. The two incendiary personal essays in *Fire* also illustrate how Baldwin offers personal experience as a starting point to the creation of a collective "we," a site of collective subjectivity that holds the promise and power to transform a nation. In *Fire*, Baldwin recounts his autobiographical experiences with the Black Church, first as a storefront preacher in Harlem at the age of fourteen, then as a black writer courted by the Prophet Elijah Muhammad at the age of thirty-seven. Baldwin's meditations on his personal experience are pathways into national fantasies and racial self-delusions that are held with fundamentalist fervor. Without this roadmap, Baldwin warned, total destruction of the nation was imminent. Further, central to this roadmap is the ability to forge connections across experience and lines of identity. In her studies of politics and the postmodern in the American 1960s, Marianne DeKoven locates the ability to cross identitarian lines in the notoriously shifting pronouns in Baldwin's most famous protest essay, *Fire*. She argues that for Baldwin, "the essay, even when it has clear and ascendant political agendas, is a literary genre."[41] And she argues that Baldwin's mastery is evident in the "multiple, contradictory fluidity of the subject positions Baldwin uses [the essay] to construct."[42]

Fire has been awarded central status in our studies of the hopeful protest movements of the 1960s. At the same time, *Fire* has been largely overlooked for its role as a document central to the rise of feminism because, though women appear in the essay, *woman* is not the category through which Baldwin analyzes his experiences of American political realities. Although feminist scholars deem Baldwin's early work protofeminist, most abandon his work to finish the project of a radical critique of gender itself. For instance, Kaplan looks for a more direct path to a radical gender critique in the promise of queer theory's troubling of the very definitions of sex and sexuality, which solves the problem she describes as a "static androgyny" in Baldwin's early fiction. Kaplan argues regarding Baldwin's tardy theorizing of sexuality in 1985's "Here Be Dragons," "The fall into that category of the grotesque is 'hell,' and this hell is narratively, syntagmatically linked with the painful inversions of power relations between two incommensurably subordinated groups, black men and white women, inversions that, like the blurring of boundaries and binaries in the grotesque, threaten masculinity."[43] At the heart of the limits of Baldwin's protofeminism, for Kaplan, lies the incommensurability of analyses of personal experience across lines identity-based difference. In one of this essay's epigraphs, Kaplan praises the "analogies" of oppression that women readers were able to take from Baldwin's fiction, but she insists that these analogies are finally imperfect.

I suggest that it is the imperfectness itself of the analogies between personal experiences that might, paradoxically, account for the considerable distances that Baldwin's influence travels. There is a critical tradition of simultaneously praising and dismissing Baldwin as ultimately failing feminism by offering fictional female characters who are interesting but, as Trudier Harris and Kaplan contend,[44] ultimately secondary to a masculine project. By focusing on fiction and its readership, Harris, Kaplan, and many other feminists who hesitantly claim Baldwin's work as protofeminist rely on a politics of identification. Baldwin fails this identitarian analysis of oppression if the images and stories he offers do not tell exactly the story of the reader. But Baldwin's personal politics and, later, the CR groups of women's liberation and the identitarian concerns of critical race theory *rely on* analogy as constitutive of Baldwin's heterogeneous "we" that will transform the nation. In his incendiary and hopeful document of the project of integration, Baldwin drew a political analysis explicitly from his personal experience situated between two poles: Black Nationalist ideologies and white liberal dreams of unity. Indeed, Baldwin conceives America's political landscape as a series of poles the speaker must simultaneously address: "I knew the tension in me between love and power, between pain and rage, and the curious, the grinding way I remained extended between these poles—perpetually attempting to choose the better rather than the worse. But this choice was a choice in terms of a personal, a private better (I was, after all, a writer); what was its relevance in terms of a social worse?"[45] In the context of a nation polarized by "political realities" of race, Baldwin presents the essayistic speaker as a means of both analyzing polarization and moving beyond it. Baldwin stands firmly between poles: white and black, self-determination and integration, and between his generation and that of his nephew James. Rather than serve as a homogeneous social subject, Baldwin's speaking self serves as a rhetorical space that allows entrance into national critiques that move beyond the autobiographical, the personal, or the private precisely by grounding political analysis in experience and thereby avoiding meek abstraction.

The experiential self from which Baldwin writes is never merely autobiographical because he recounts experience only insofar as it represents a collective experience testifying against the fantasies the nation tells itself about already-achieved universal equality, about naturalized differences, or about the irrelevance of groups like the Nation of Islam. Through imperfect analogy of their own experiences, Baldwin's readers can follow him toward national political critique. Cunningham argues that in the autobiographical mode, Baldwin's "recollections are at once public and private, expressive and intellectual"[46] and the perspective is both "introspective and retrospective."[47] For Cunningham, the poles between which Baldwin moves are his audience on the South Side, many of whom could not read, and his affluent readers who "merely bought books in order to devour them."[48] The poles Baldwin navigates are also those of public and private: political constructs that would become a main target of women's liberation. Rich testifies in the epigraph that Baldwin's essays provided the rhetorical ability to negotiate between "private" experience of "political" realities so that they could be analyzed so as to be changed. If, for Baldwin, the space between the poles of public and private, or between autobiography and social commentary, lay mostly within the category race, the lessons of making the private public for women's liberationist readers did not have to be so confined. In fact, Baldwin also addresses systems of gender polarization. When Baldwin recounts the prophet Elijah Muhammad's dinner table, he depicts the poles of gender as so stylized that they are overdeterminedly marked, like race, as no more than political theater: "On one side of the room sat a half dozen women, all in white; they were much occupied with a beautiful baby. . . . On the other side of the room sat seven or eight men, young, dressed in dark suits, very much at ease, and very imposing."[49] The terrain of gender, as polarizing as the terrain of race in the 1960s, is subject to Baldwin's analysis of changeable political realities. The key to widespread national change for Baldwin, prescient of the language of women's liberation, lies in his oft-cited invocation of a national collective subjectivity: "If we—and now I mean the relatively conscious whites and the relatively conscious blacks, who must, like lovers, insist on, or create, the consciousness of the others—do not falter in our duty now, we may be able, handful that we are, to end the racial nightmare, and achieve our country, and change the history of the world."[50] In *Fire,* a protest essay addressed directly to the nation at large, Baldwin offers personal experience as the beginning of a "better solution" to political realities. Baldwin articulates the political solution within the seemingly private language of lovers. For Kaplan, Baldwin's fictional representation of homosexuality in *Giovanni's Room* remains ultimately unsatisfying to a feminist politicization of gender and sexuality because of Baldwin's resolute understanding of race as a political reality and of homosexuality as a poetic or personal reality. In Baldwin's essays, however, it is precisely in the most intimate spaces—the psyche, sexual interaction, personal experience— where political change is possible. *Fire* creates a "we" into which any reader is propelled toward rigorous self-examination. Yet the ambiguity of the "we" at the end of *Fire* may harbor limits at the same time that it opens up the possibility of an integrated subjectivity. Baldwin has been marked as protofeminist in part because women do not occupy the center of his analysis. Though a nongendered "we" might solve the problem of Baldwin's potential masculine bias, the "we" can also be read as prematurely announcing a raised consciousness about gender. At the beginning of the essay, in a letter to his nephew, Baldwin proclaims, "If the word integration means anything, this is what it means: that we, with love, shall force our brothers to see themselves as they are, to cease fleeing from reality and begin to change it."[51] At the outset, Baldwin casts his program for changing political realities via personal politics as a "brotherhood." Like so much of Baldwin's political capital, it depends on the reactions of his readership if the hopeful "we" that ends the essay is able to move beyond this initial scene of patrilineage. In other words, women can only access through analogy the inclusive "we" that concludes an essay that begins in brotherhood. And with the advent of women's liberation and the creation of a political subjectivity by, for, and about women, Baldwin's collective subjectivity becomes increasingly susceptible to charges of an underanalyzed masculine bias, despite Baldwin's best intentions or initial reception. Regardless, if Baldwin's "brotherhood" does not or could not yet fully account for women's experience, his essays nevertheless provide a blueprint for women's liberation interested in analyzing gender so as to change it. Even if Baldwin's own recounted experiences may not cross the chasm between gendered poles, the experiences and imperfect analogies of his women readers can meet that brotherhood on the other side of an "achieved country." Though women's liberation may have generated a political subjectivity of woman from which to speak collectively, the "we" of women's liberation functioned outside the boundaries and experiences of the specific women it sought to represent. In her examination of the women's liberation, Elisabeth Armstrong notes that, contrary to Second Wave anthologies, "third wave" anthologies contain essays "written, almost exclusively, in the first person."[52] But it is important to understand that the "we" at the heart of the project of sisterhood results from a process of bringing together potentially incongruent narratives of personally or ethnically specific experience. Likewise, Baldwin's call for a collective "we" at the end of *Fire* is only possible once the speaking "I" has recounted his experience for one hundred pages. Whereas Baldwin's personal essays provide a blueprint for how the personal "I" works diligently toward a collective "we" that culminates works like *Fire*, women's liberation often begins in this "we" as a way to validate and analyze women's experiences. By bringing the tenets of women's liberation into conversation with Baldwin's protofeminist personal politics, we can better understand the diverse collectives forged by women's liberation groups in the context of other protest movements and writings. At the advent of women's liberation in the 1960s, Baldwin's personal politics in his protest essays remained a crucial rhetorical model even when the grand theories of earlier political generations and movements lost their usefulness in a shift to the authority of personal experience. In her foundational 1970 anthology *The Black Woman*, Toni Cade writes, "When the experts (white or Black, male) turn their attention to the Black woman, the reports get murky, for they usually clump the men and women together" and disregard black experience.[53] That may be so, but Baldwin's model instead seeks collectivity by addressing individual experience and difference. So too, Kathie Sarachild, founding Redstockings member and originator of the phrase "sisterhood is powerful," explains regarding the principles of CR: "They are the basic radical political principles of going to the original sources, both historic and personal, going to the people—women themselves, and going to experience for theory and strategy."[54] Though the roots of women's liberation and CR in particular are numerous and complex, it is important to hear the echo of Baldwin's protofeminist influence.

Notes

Originally published as Brian Norman, "Crossing Identitarian Lines: Women's Liberation and James Baldwin's Early Essays" *Women's Studies* 35, no. 3 (2006). Reprinted by permission of Taylor and Francis.

First epigraph: Adrienne Rich, "Split at the Root: An Essay on Jewish Identity," *Blood, Bread, and Poetry: Selected Prose 1979–1985* (New York: Norton, 1986), 118.

Second epigraph: Cora Kaplan, "'A Cavern Opened in My Mind': The Poetics of Homosexuality and the Politics of Race in James Baldwin," in *Representing Black Men*, ed. Marcellus Blount and George P. Cunningham (New York: Routledge, 1996), 31.

Third epigraph: Andrea Dworkin, *Heartbreak: Political Memoir of a Militant Feminist* (New York: Basic, 2002), 71–72.

Fourth epigraph: Gayle Pemberton, "A Sentimental Journey: James Baldwin and the Thomas-Hill Hearings," in *Race-ing Justice, En-gendering Power*, ed. Toni Morrison (New York: Pantheon, 1992), 173.

Fifth epigraph: Redstockings, "Manifesto," in *Dear Sisters: Dispatches from the Women's Liberation Movement*, ed. Rosalyn Baxandall and Linda Gordon (New York: Perseus, 2000), 90–91.

1. For examinations of the homophobic attacks on Baldwin following Cleaver, see Douglass Field, "Looking for Jimmy Baldwin: Sex, Privacy and Black Nationalist Fervor," *Callaloo* 27 (Spring 2004): 457–80; Dwight A. McBride, "Can the Queen Speak? Racial Essentialism, Sexuality and the Problem of Authority," *Callaloo* 21 (1998): 363–79; Robert Reid-Pharr, "Tearing the Goat's Flesh: Crisis, Abjection, and Homosexuality in the Production of a Late-Twentieth-Century Black Masculinity," in *Novel Gazing: Queer Readings in Fiction*, ed. Eve Sedgwick (Durham, NC: Duke University Press, 1997), 353–76; and Kendall Thomas, "'Ain't Nothin' Like the Real Thing': Black Masculinity, Gay Sexuality, and the Jargon of Authenticity," in *Representing Black Men*, ed. Blount and Cunningham, 55–69.

2. *No Name in the Street* (1972) is generally considered Baldwin's tardy response. Further, Thomas suggests that Baldwin's embrace by Black Nationalism might not have happened until 1987—at Baldwin's funeral.

3. I use Echols's and Evans's approximate dates (see Alice Echols, *Daring to Be Bad: Radical Feminism in America, 1967–1975* [Minneapolis: University of Minnesota Press, 1989]; and Sara Evans, *Personal Politics: The Roots of Women's Liberation in the Civil Right Movement and the New Left* [New York: Knopf, 1979]).

4. For recent examples, see Louise Michele Newman, *White Women's Rights: The Racial Origins of Feminism in the United States* (New York: Oxford University Press, 1999); Kimberly Springer, "Third Wave Black Feminism?" *Signs* 27 (2002): 1059–82; and Becky Thompson, "Multiracial Feminism: Recasting the Chronology of Second Wave Feminism," *Feminist Studies* 28 (Summer 2002): 337–60. For responses to generational claims about black feminism amid white feminism, see Wini Breines, "What's Love Got to Do with It?: White Women, Black Women, and Feminism in the Movement Years," *Signs* 27 (2002): 1095–134; Beverly Guy-Sheftall, "Response from a 'Second Waver' to Kimberly Springer's 'Third Wave' Black Feminism?" *Signs* 27 (2002): 1091–94; and Sheila Radford-Hill, "Keepin' It Real: A Generational Commentary on Kimberly Springer's 'Third Wave Black Feminism?'" *Signs* 27 (2002): 1083–90.

5. See Elisabeth Armstrong, *The Retreat from Organization: U.S. Feminism Reconceptualized* (Albany: State University of New York Press, 2002); Rosalyn Baxandall, "Re-visioning the Women's Liberation Movement's Narrative: Early Second Wave African American Feminists," *Feminist Studies* 27 (2001): 225–45; Jean Curthoys, *Feminist Amnesia: The Wake of Women's Liberation* (New York: Routledge, 1997); Rachel Blau Duplessis and Ann Snitow, eds., *The Feminist Memoir Project: Voices from Women's Liberation* (New York: Three Rivers, 1998); Benita Roth, *Separate Roads to Feminism: Black, Chicana, and White Feminist Movements in America's Second Wave* (New York: Cambridge University Press, 2004); and Evans, *Daring to Be Bad.*

6. James Baldwin, *Notes of a Native Son* (New York: Beacon, 1984), xv.

7. Irving Howe, "James Baldwin: At Ease in the Apocalypse," in *James Baldwin: A Collection of Critical Essays*, ed. Kenneth Kinnamon (Englewood Cliffs, NJ: Prentice Hall, 1974), 97.

8. Langston Hughes, "From Harlem to Paris," in *James Baldwin: A Collection of Critical Essays*, ed. Kinnamon, 9.

9. David Levin, "James Baldwin's Autobiographical Essays: The Problem of Negro Identity," *Massachusetts Review* 5 (1964): 239.

10. James Baldwin, *The Fire Next Time* (New York: Dial, 1963), 94.

11. Ibid., 97.

12. Ibid.

13. See Wright's introduction to *Native Son*, "How Bigger Was Born." Wright describes Bigger Thomas as an enlarged version of the black man in white America's mind. Wright describes Bigger as a body part (no specific reference is given, but a phallus is certainly implied) placed in a jar of formaldehyde that Wright is able to study because of its grotesque largeness. For Wright, fiction is the petri dish of character studies (New York: Harper and Row, 1987), vii–xxxiv.

14. For a foundation text of this criticism, see Michelle Wallace, *Black Macho and the Myth of the Superwoman* (New York: Dial, 1979). For a reading of a white woman as protofeminist in Baldwin's 1972 Malcolm X screenplay, *One Day When I Was Lost*, see Brian Norman, "Reading a 'Closet Screenplay': Hollywood, James Baldwin's Malcolms and the Threat of Historical Irrelevance," *African American Review* 39 (2005): 103–18.

15. Kaplan, "A Cavern Opened in My Mind," 38. Kaplan cites Baldwin's dialogue with Giovanni for this point. See James Baldwin and Nikki Giovanni, *A Dialogue* (Philadelphia: Lippincott, 1973).

16. Baldwin, *Notes of a Native Son*, 19.

17. Ibid., 22.

18. Sam Bluefarb, "James Baldwin's 'Previous Condition': A Problem of Identification," *Negro American Literature Forum* 31 (1969): 26.

19. Jane M. Gaines, "Green Like Me," in *Hollywood Spectatorship*, ed. Melvyn Stokes and Richard Maltby (London: British Film Institute, 2001), 111.

20. Baldwin, *Notes of a Native Son*, 96.

21. Ibid.

22. Ibid., 97.

23. Ibid.

24. Ibid., 99.

25. This is the argument of much contemporary criticism on Baldwin. Henderson, for example, argues that David in *Giovanni's Room* denies problematically his sexual desires by rejecting the dirtying influence of fairy figures. Giovanni dies as a result. Not incidentally, Henderson describes *Giovanni's Room* as a novel in which "race is present, but blackness is erased" (see Gwendolyn Mae Henderson, "James Baldwin: Expatriation, Homosexual Panic, and Man's Estate," *Callaloo* 23 [2000]: 313–27, 313).

26. Baldwin, *The Fire Next Time*, 118.

27. Katharine Lawrence Balfour, *The Evidence of Things Not Said: James Baldwin and the Promise of American Democracy* (Ithaca, NY: Cornell University Press, 2001), xi.

28. Baldwin, *Nobody Knows My Name: More Notes of Native Son* (New York: Dial, 1961), 97.

29. Baldwin, *The Fire Next Time*, 24.

30. New York Radical Women, "Principles," in *Sisterhood Is Powerful: An Anthology of Writings from the Women's Liberation Movement*, ed. Robin Morgan (New York: Vintage, 1970), 585.

31. See Kaplan, "A Cavern Opened in My Mind"; Yasmin DeGout, "Dividing the Mind: Contradictory Portraits of Homoerotic Love in Giovanni's Room," *African American Review* 26 (1992): 425–35; Trudier Harris, *Black Women in the Fiction of James Baldwin* (Knoxville: University of Tennessee Press, 1985); Henderson, "James Baldwin: Expatriation, Homosexual Panic, and Man's Estate"; Dwight A. McBride, *Why I Hate Abercrombie & Fitch: Race and Sexuality in America* (New York: New York University Press, 2004); Dwight A. McBride and Jennifer Devere Brody, introduction to "Plum Nelly: New Essays in Black Queer Studies," special issue, *Callaloo* 23 (2000): 286–68; Kevin Ohi, "'I'm Not the Boy You Want': Sexuality, 'Race,' and Thwarted Revelation in Baldwin's Another Country," *African American Review* 33 (1999): 260–81; Amy Ongiri, "We Are Family: Miscegenation, Black Nationalism, Black Masculinity, and the Black Gay Cultural Imagination," in *Race-ing Representation*, ed. Kostas Myrsiades and Linda Myrsiades (Lanham, MD: Rowman and Littlefield, 1998), 231–46; and Barbara Shin and Andrew Judson, "Beneath the Black Aesthetic: Baldwin's Primer of Black American Masculinity," *African American Review* 32 (1998): 247–61. Generally,

scholars claim that Baldwin's discussions of identities (like "race," "gender," "sexuality") predate later sociopolitical movements and theoretical schools that place "identity" at their centers and that can now better value his work.

32. Yasmin De Gout, "'Masculinity' and (Im)maturity: 'The Man Child' and Other Stories in Baldwin's Gender Studies Enterprise," in *Re-Viewing James Baldwin: Things Not Seen*, ed. D. Quentin Miller (Philadelphia: Temple University Press, 2000), 134.

33. Baldwin, *Notes of a Native Son*, 93.

34. Linda Nicholson, *The Second Wave* (New York: Routledge, 1997), 3. For Nicholson, this women's liberation CR model tends to downplay differences among women. But for women reading Baldwin, the difference between personal experiences may actually be highlighted.

35. James Cunningham, "Public and Private Rhetorical Modes in the Essays of James Baldwin," in *Essays on the Essay: Redefining the Genre*, ed. Alexander J. Butrym (Athens: University of Georgia Press, 1989), 199.

36. Baldwin, *Notes of a Native Son*, 124.

37. Morgan, ed., *Sisterhood Is Powerful*, xxix–xxx.

38. Ibid., xxiv.

39. Jennifer Jordan, "Cleaver vs. Baldwin: Icing the White Negro," *Black Books Bulletin* (Chicago: Institute for Positive Education) 1, no. 2 (Winter 1972): 14.

40. Addison Gayle Jr., "A Defense of James Baldwin," *CLA Journal* 10 (1967): 205.

41. Marianne DeKoven, *Utopia Limited* (Durham: Duke University Press, 2004), 233.

42. Ibid., 234.

43. Kaplan, "A Cavern Opened in My Mind," 36.

44. Whereas Kaplan focuses mainly on White female characters, Harris focuses exclusively on black female characters. Their conclusions, however, are uncannily similar.

45. Baldwin, *The Fire Next Time*, 74–75.

46. Cunningham, "Public and Private," 195.

47. Ibid., 198.

48. Baldwin, *The Fire Next Time*, 75.

49. Ibid.

50. Ibid., 119.

51. Ibid., 23–24.

52. Armstrong, *The Retreat from Organization*, 11.

53. Toni Cade, ed., *The Black Woman* (New York: Signet, 1970), 8.

54. Kathie Sarachild, "Consciousness-Raising: A Radical Weapon," *Feminist Revolution* (New York: Random House, 1978), 147–48.

10

"Where the People Can Sing, the Poet Can Live"

James Baldwin, Pragmatism, and Cosmopolitan Humanism

Ulf Schulenberg

What is the legacy of James Baldwin? From today's perspective, there are numerous possibilities for answering this question. One could, for instance, consider his impact on black studies, cultural studies, gay and lesbian studies, diaspora studies, and American studies. Or one might feel inclined to contend that his version of a radical humanism is particularly useful for postidentity politics at the beginning of the twenty-first century. Another possibility for confronting the question of Baldwin's legacy would be to call attention to his understanding of the function of the writer as a public intellectual. According to Baldwin, the poet's responsibility "is to defeat all labels and complicate all battles."[1] This insistence upon the necessity of complicating all battles can be found at the center of his work. Baldwin, as essayist, novelist, dramatist, and public intellectual, depicts a world in which nothing is static and stable, a world governed by contingency, the unpredictability of experience, and the instability of all categories. Self-creation, as he repeatedly makes clear, entails the moral responsibility to change the world. Thus, the endeavor of self-fashioning also directs attention to the impossibility of separating the private from the public sphere. The idiosyncrasies of black self-creation must not be analyzed in isolation. They are, on the contrary, political gestures that have an impact on the public sphere.

As a radical historicist and fallibilist, and as a lover of complexity, particularity, and plurality, Baldwin seems useful in the attempt to make the idea of a postmetaphysical culture look attractive. Baldwin's worldliness puts an emphasis on the idea that one should reach a point where one no longer needs the certainty, reliability, immutability, and purity of what would be more than another human creation. His humanism urges one to understand that the world is man-made and that it thus can also be changed by man. Undoubtedly, there are still traces of metaphysics in Baldwin's thought. Like John Grimes, the protagonist in *Go Tell It on the Mountain*, Baldwin sometimes seems torn between the desire for transcendence and the need for worldliness.[2] Yet I think most of the time he appears as a protean and cosmopolitan humanist who takes nothing for granted and who is fascinated by the confrontation between the unpredictability of the human being and the demands of life.

Since the 1990s there has been a Baldwin renaissance.[3] His texts have been analyzed from various perspectives, by means of different theoretical approaches (from queer theory to postcolonial theory), and most of these authors have underscored the contemporary significance of Baldwin's oeuvre. However, it is important to note that so far Baldwin has played almost no role in discussions of American pragmatism. This is regrettable insofar as there are many aspects of his thinking that support the argument that, at least to a certain degree, he is part of a genealogy of black pragmatism that runs from W. E. B. Du Bois and Alain Locke to Cornel West. A discussion of Baldwin as part of a genealogy of black (cosmopolitan) pragmatism, I submit, offers an interesting and stimulating perspective on this writer, as well as on the much-debated revival of pragmatism. In this chapter, I will discuss Baldwin's essays in order to elucidate the significance of a middle ground between Cornel West's prophetic pragmatism as a decidedly leftist critique of late capitalism and Richard Rorty's liberal version of neopragmatism and his notion of a poeticized culture. This chapter also seeks to contribute to Baldwin studies by using his insights and arguments for a discussion of the question of pragmatism and race.

In the first part of this chapter, I discuss West's prophetic pragmatism as he developed it in the 1980s. Furthermore, I emphasize the significance of Marxism for this American pragmatist. In this context, it is interesting to see that although West turned into a proponent of left-liberal progressivism in the 1990s and 2000s, he returned to a more radical position with *The Rich and the Rest of Us: A Poverty Manifesto* (2012, coauthored with Tavis Smiley). In the second part, I discuss Rorty's neopragmatism and his notion of a postmetaphysical and poeticized culture that puts a premium on self-creation and the creativity of redescriptions. In the third and final part, I do three things. First, I discuss the pragmatist aspects of Baldwin's thought (for instance, his antiessentialism, his appreciation of contingency, his historicism, his critique of traditional moral philosophy, and his aversion to theories and systems). Second, I argue that in Baldwin's texts moral commitment, the notion of political and social change, the idea of (black) self-creation, and an understanding of the task of the poet are combined in a manner that indirectly critiques radical politics, on the one hand, and nonchalant liberal gestures of self-transformation and self-renewal, on the other. Finally, I illuminate the implications of the term "cosmopolitan humanism" in a discussion of Baldwin's essays.

Cornel West, Prophetic Pragmatism, and Marxism

Both Baldwin and West are protean authors whose political positions are difficult to define. Moreover, both are organic intellectuals in the Gramscian sense. Both have constantly sought to mediate between theory and practice—that is, as black public intellectuals one of their *bêtes noires* has been the idea of an anemic and otherworldy formalism that promises to govern practice from an outside to practice. With the publication of *The Rich and the Rest of Us,* West has once more changed his position. To a certain degree, this monograph recalls the political radicalism dominating his texts of the late 1970s and 1980s. The picture that West and Smiley are painting in *The Rich and the Rest of Us* is a rather bleak one. What they argue against is, of course, the ideology of the American Dream and the notion of American exceptionalism, both of which are grounded in the foundational myth that the United States is a classless society. Furthermore, the "rags-to-riches" myth implies that poverty is something one can leave behind if one is willing to work hard and pursue one's aims with all one's energy. According to West and Smiley, it "took the Great Recession to make poverty a real threat to the American psyche."[4] Yet at the same time they underscore that poverty "is not the stepchild of the Great Recession; poverty has always been a part of American life. It is a state of being that this country has valiantly faced at times, but, more frequently, recoiled from in fear and condemnation."[5] For millions, the American Dream has turned into a nightmare, leaving them to struggle in an indifferent society. West and Smiley maintain that the Occupy Wall Street movement was only the most visible recent example of moral outrage and resistance directed against US late capitalism: "Because economic injustice in America has been overshadowed by greed, because unequal taxation benefits the rich at the expense of everyone else, because our political system has become so paralyzed and acquiescent to the culture of greed and moral decay—the poor are fighting back."[6]

West's radical critique of the excesses of late capitalism could not be found in the 1990s, a decade in which he developed a left-liberal progressivism that culminated in his book with Roberto Unger, *The Future of American Progressivism* (1998). In this book, West's former notion of radical political and social change has been toned down to the tame wish for reform programs, and it also becomes obvious that he has accepted (American) capitalism as the framework within which to develop his idea of the democratization and diversification of the market, his notion of greater social mobility, and his understanding of democratic and institutional experimentalism. Moreover, his policy proposals are mostly reformist gestures intended to contribute to the reinvention, or final realization, of the American Dream.

In the 1980s, by contrast, West's primary concern was to develop an oppositional cultural criticism. He did this by mediating between pragmatism, Marxism, and black liberation theology.[7] For our purposes, his most important text is *The American Evasion of Philosophy: A Genealogy of Pragmatism* (1989), which is still one of the most stimulating books on pragmatism. In the introduction, West stresses the Americanness of pragmatism: "I understand American pragmatism as a specific historical and cultural product of American civilization, a particular set of social practices that articulate certain American desires, values, and responses and that are elaborated in institutional apparatuses principally controlled by a significant slice of the American middle class."[8] On West's account, the American evasion of philosophy, that is, the pragmatists' radical critique and evasion of epistemology-centered philosophy, has led to a profound change in the conception of philosophy. Because of this evasion, philosophy has slowly but steadily turned into a kind of cultural criticism in which the meaning of America is continually questioned and debated. What this means is that this swerve from epistemology or abstract pure philosophy in general has led not to a radical dismissal of philosophy but to its reconception as a form of cultural criticism that is politically engaged and that, at least in its Westian version, can be understood as a kind of American leftist critique. As West puts it: "In this sense, American pragmatism is less a philosophical tradition putting forward solutions to perennial problems in the Western philosophical conversation initiated by Plato and more a continuous cultural commentary or set of interpretations that attempt to explain America to itself at a particular historical moment."[9]

By emphasizing the political and moral aspects of American pragmatism, West illustrates that he regards his genealogical account as an explicitly political endeavor. His cultural commentary wants to explain America to itself from a decidedly leftist vantage point, and *The American Evasion of Philosophy* is supposed to resuscitate leftist politics in the United States. West offers an admittedly idiosyncratic interpretation of one of the major progressive traditions in the United States, and by doing so not only does he address the profound crisis of the 1980s American Left, but also he hopes to "inspire and instruct contemporary efforts to remake and reform American society and culture."[10] His gesture of hope and resistance insists on the fact that pragmatism should be considered an indigenous and rich source of leftist politics in the United States, and this leads to his suggestion that his conception of prophetic pragmatism "serves as the culmination of the American pragmatist tradition; that is, it is a perspective and project that speaks to the major impediments to a wider role of pragmatism in American thought."[11] This is certainly not a modest proposal, but one ought to note that pragmatist ideas were already central to *Prophesy Deliverance!* West's preoccupation with pragmatism therefore has a longer history. Although the latter book's primary concern was the establishment of a fruitful dialogue between black liberation theology and progressive Marxism, it was also informed by pragmatism's notions of historicism, antifoundationalism, and fallibilism. Pragmatism, as West put it, "provides an American context for Afro-American thought."[12]

Like Deweyan pragmatism, West's conception of prophetic pragmatism can be considered a continuation, and creative revision, of Emerson's evasion of epistemology-centered philosophy. In a Deweyan manner, the radical historicist and fallibilist West rejects a spectator theory of knowledge, the quest for certainty, and the search for immutable foundations, and he attempts to contribute to the promotion of an Emersonian culture of creative democracy. It is crucial to see, however, that West's neopragmatism strives to go beyond the tradition of pragmatism, that is, it builds on the tradition that runs from Emerson to Rorty, and at the same time it radicalizes it. Combining insights of theorists as varied as Emerson, James, Dewey, Du Bois, Sidney Hook, C. Wright Mills, Reinhold Niebuhr, and Lionel Trilling, West contends that his prophetic pragmatism makes the "political motivation and political substance of the American evasion of philosophy explicit."[13]

West's prophetic pragmatism presents itself as a philosophy of struggle, a philosophy of praxis. As we have seen, it ought to be regarded as a cultural criticism that draws its strength from an American and African American tradition of leftist resistance. As regards the notion of struggle, West points out: "Human struggle sits at the center of prophetic pragmatism, a struggle guided by a democratic and libertarian vision, sustained by moral courage and existential integrity, and tempered by the recognition of human finitude and frailty."[14] As far as the utopian and revolutionary gestures underlying prophetic pragmatism are concerned, West maintains: "It calls for utopian energies and tragic actions, energies and actions that yield permanent and perennial revolutionary, rebellious, and reformist strategies that oppose the status quos of our day." West drives his point home when he concisely explicates that "the praxis of prophetic pragmatism is tragic action with revolutionary intent, usually reformist consequences, and always visionary outlook."[15] The vehemence and intensity of West's sentences remind one of his most radical book to date, *Prophesy Deliverance!* Although he speaks of "reformist consequences" in the last quotation, these passages unequivocally indicate that pragmatism and liberalism do not necessarily have to go hand in hand, that they do not always have to be intimately interwoven. What we read here are not the words of a nonchalant bourgeois pragmatist who tries to rhetorically convince us that we had better refrain from wanting anything other than a late-capitalist liberal bourgeois society. Rather, it becomes increasingly obvious in his text that West intends to build leftist coalitions that involve various oppositional social movements ranging from racial, ethnic, religious, class, and gender to gay and lesbian movements.

In the 1970s and 1980s, West saw it as one of his primary tasks to contribute to the rewriting of Marxism in the American context.[16] Since his early articles, Marxism had played a crucial role in the development of his theoretical framework. In those decades, it was impossible to imagine his thought without considering the impact Marxism had had on it. On the other hand, West's attitude toward Marxism has mostly been ambivalent. There have always been aspects of Marxism that he radically dismissed as useless, dogmatic, or as belonging to an obsolete orthodox version of Marxist thinking. Furthermore, West has increasingly distanced himself from Marxism in general. Although Marxism was central to *Prophesy Deliverance!*, it no longer plays a role in *The War against Parents* (1998, with Sylvia Ann Hewlett) and *The Future of American Progressivism*. In *Prophesy Deliverance!*, West openly admits that his reading of modernity through an African American lens would not have been possible without Marxist theory. Pragmatism and its notions of antifoundationalism and fallibilism, as well as a profoundly tragic sense of life, function as a background to the story he tells in this book. His central concern, however, is the alliance between prophetic Christianity or black liberation theology and progressive Marxism. According to West, in this alliance "lies the hope of Western civilization."[17] Moving within the framework of his revolutionary socialist politics, he underscores that what is needed is "a clear-cut social theory" that clarifies our situation and helps us change it. On West's account, it is Marxism that offers "the most powerful and penetrating social criticism in modern times."[18] The Westian gesture in his early texts is radical insofar as he clearly intends to overthrow the capitalist system (US capitalism and global capitalism), propagates the public ownership and democratic control of productive property as well as the democratic planning of societal development, vehemently attacks the dual oppression of racism and classism, and relentlessly argues for the creation of an anticapitalist, anti-imperialist, and internationalist theoretical and political perspective. We will see in the third part of this chapter that this Westian critique of late capitalism is much more radical than that of Baldwin (who never—or only very briefly— saw the necessity of abolishing capitalism).

Marxism, for West, is useful as a social theory that offers concrete historical analyses and focuses on aspects of social misery under the rule of capitalism. It allows the theorist to illustrate the existential struggles of people who are forced to confront the powers of commodification and reification on a daily basis. Marxism is capable of elucidating the operation of power in modern and postmodern society, and it attempts to draw attention to the necessity of empowering the people who suffer under capitalist conditions. In other words, it puts a premium on the agency of those people, on their specific and particular struggles of resistance. Marxist theory enables one to keep track of the evil effects of monopolies, oligopolies, and plutocracies, which often take the form of transnational powerful corporations in the age of globalization. Sophisticated Marxist theory—and West has explicated this numerous times—must not be seen as a kind of master discourse but rather as an indispensable and at the same time insufficient or inadequate intellectual tool or weapon in the struggle for freedom, justice, equality, democracy, and individuality. West has constantly tried to rewrite Marxist theory in order to make it relevant to present realities and necessities. Marxism is not static to him. On the contrary, it has to present itself as nondogmatic and dialogical, that is, it ought to be open to the ideas and demands of the new social movements and other non-Marxist leftist or progressive groups. It is perfectly legitimate to use Marxism for specific and clearly defined purposes: "I don't see how, in fact, we can understand the market forces around the world and the fundamental role of transnational corporations, the subordination of working people, the tremendous class conflicts going on around the world at the marketplace between management and labor without understanding some of the insights of the Marxist tradition."[19]

West in the 1980s wants to rework and rewrite Marxism as a critical social theory that opposes the forces of exploitation, oppression, commodification, and reification in late-capitalist America, and by doing so he can embed this theoretical approach within the broader framework of his black liberationist Christian perspective. Just as his reading of the pragmatist tradition has resulted in his own version of pragmatism, which can be termed a more moderate (prophetic) pragmatism in comparison with radically antifoundationalist and antiessentialist (anti)theories, his rewriting of the Marxist tradition has produced a moderate Marxism that can function as an effective local theory, that is, as a tool for specific purposes. One ought to see that this is a pragmatist way of employing Marxism as a useful social theory in the struggle for liberation.

The Westian endeavor to mediate between pragmatism, Marxism, and black Christian thought resulted in the development of one of the most interesting and promising theoretical approaches of the 1980s. However, West's leftist cultural criticism refrained from answering a crucial question: Where is the poet's place in this framework? Rorty and Baldwin answered this question in different but equally stimulating ways.

Poets and Metaphysicians: Richard Rorty and the Idea of a Poeticized Culture

In "Many Thousands Gone," Baldwin uses an almost Deweyan formulation when he speaks of "that dense, many-sided and shifting reality which is the world we live in and the world we make."[20] It is precisely this complex, multilayered, unstable, and unpredictable reality, which is in the Jamesian sense constantly in the making, that is of primary interest to the pragmatist. We live in this world, have to cope with it by means of our intelligent and creative actions, and it is legitimate to state that to a high degree we make this world.[21] Since its inception, pragmatism has often been governed by a fruitful tension between ontological materialism (or minimalist realism) and physicalism, on the one hand, and epistemological nominalism, on the other. However, the question of what role the poets play as far as this idea of intelligently and creatively shaping the world is concerned has too often been ignored. It is crucial to note that for Baldwin and Rorty the work of the poet is of the utmost importance. Both hold that the poet plays a central role as regards the idea of changing the way people speak. Moreover, both contend that the poet's words might eventually lead to future political and social changes. However, there is a profound difference between Baldwin and Rorty regarding the question of whether the poet's task necessarily is political or not. Rorty wishes to restrict the work of the poet or creative redescriber to the private sphere and underlines that any influence of the poet on the public sphere is purely contingent, whereas Baldwin suggests that the work of the poet, especially the black poet, has to be regarded as political and public.

It is interesting to see that both Baldwin and Rorty use the word "poet" in the generic sense. Although Rorty's use of "poet" is well known by now, Baldwin also makes clear that when he speaks of poets he means "all artists." These artists, as he avers, "are divorced from and even necessarily opposed to any system whatever."[22] Moreover, as he maintains in "The Creative Process," the artist is an "incorrigible disturber of the peace," and his war with society "is a lover's war." Stressing that the artist's responsibility to his society is "that he must never cease warring with it," Baldwin makes it difficult for his readers to ignore the poet's political mission.[23] At the same time, however, it would be too simplistic to claim that Baldwin concentrates exclusively on the political nature of art. One only has to think of his devastating critique of Richard Wright's *Native Son* (1940) and of the protest novel in general in order to realize that he was aware of the vulgarity and disenchanting predictability of many forms of politicized art and literature. Baldwin was a black aesthete, a lover of form and the idiosyncrasies of style, who understood that as a fighter for black emancipation and civil rights he must never allow the realm of form to be separated from the realm of politics or political activism.[24] This adds to his contemporary significance. Concerning his understanding of the role of the poet, the following sentences are particularly suggestive: "Where the people can sing, the poet can live—and it is worth saying it the other way around, too; where the poet can sing, the people can live. When a civilization treats its poets with the disdain with which we treat ours, it cannot be far from disaster."[25]

One could use these Baldwinian sentences to characterize Rorty's notion of a literary or poeticized culture. This cannot be the place to explain this Rortyan notion, which became one of his central ideas in the last two decades of his life, in detail.[26] But I wish to mention some aspects of it in order to prepare my discussion of Baldwin. Combining atheism, antifoundationalism, anti-essentialism, antirepresentationalism, and anti-authoritarianism, Rorty's humanist ideal culture is radically anthropocentric in a Protagorean, Nietzschean, and Deweyan sense, and it illustrates the centrality of the subject's creativity of action for the completion of the process of enlightenment. Instead of seeking metaphysical comfort in the confrontation with contingency and instead of insisting on continuing to use terms and expressions like representation, imitation (or mirroring), discovery (or metaphors of finding), and being adequate, the ideal member of a Rortyan literary or poeticized culture will gladly accept the instability and historicity of our vocabularies, the contingency of our ways of speaking and moral standards, as well as the unpredictability of the consequences of our actions. Moreover, she will not hesitate to acknowledge her finitude. Having taken the final step from the idea of finding to that of making, she will understand "that there is nothing deep down inside us except what we have put there ourselves, no criterion that we have not created in the course of creating a practice, no standard of rationality that is not an appeal to such a criterion, no rigorous argumentation that is not obedience to our own conventions."[27] It is crucial to note that Rorty seems to hold that only in his ideal poeticized culture man would achieve full human maturity and dignity.

What story does Rorty tell regarding the origin of his literary or poeticized culture? In his opinion, this kind of culture is "unlike anything that has existed in the past." Desiring "a new intellectual world" and "a new self-image for humanity," Rorty tells a story that is full of replacements and transitions.[28] Religion was replaced by philosophy; Kant's transcendental idealism and its ideal of philosophy-as-science was replaced by Hegel's historicism; romanticism was replaced by pragmatism; and philosophy has finally been replaced by literature. Underscoring the humanistic character of a literary culture, Rorty contends that this sort of culture "drops a presupposition common to religion and philosophy—that redemption must come from one's relation to something that is not just one more human creation."[29] In one of his last pieces, "Philosophy as a Transitional Genre," he states a thesis that is central to many of his texts: "The intellectuals of the West have, since the Renaissance, progressed through three stages: they have hoped for redemption first from God, then from philosophy, and now from literature."[30] In a genuinely antifoundationalist, nominalist, and dedivinized culture, a culture that is humanist and historicist, one must no longer strive to enter into a relation with a nonhuman entity or power; instead, one should try to get in touch with the present limits of one's imagination. The profoundly romantic character of a Rortyan literary culture becomes clear when he points out: "It is a premise of this culture that though the imagination has present limits, these limits are capable of being extended forever. The imagination endlessly consumes its own artifacts. It is an ever-living, ever-expanding, fire."[31]

In order to understand Rorty's narrative about the rise of a literary culture, one has to consider the role this idea plays in *Contingency, Irony, and Solidarity*. At the beginning of the first chapter ("The Contingency of Language"), Rorty advances the argument that what unites the German idealists, the French revolutionaries, and the romantic poets is that they understood, at the end of the eighteenth century, "that anything could be made to look good or bad, important or unimportant, useful or useless, by being redescribed."[32] Furthermore, what the German idealists, the utopian revolutionaries, and the romantic poets had in common was "a dim sense that human beings whose language changed so that they no longer spoke of themselves as responsible to nonhuman powers would thereby become a new kind of human beings."[33] At the end of the eighteenth century, redescriptions became ever more radical in nature, European linguistic practices changed at an increasingly fast rate, and more and more people seemed willing to accept the romantic idea that truth is made rather than found. This suggestion has to be seen in connection with the idea that a human self is not adequately or inadequately expressed in a vocabulary but that it is rather created by the use of a vocabulary. By introducing new sets of metaphors, and by making the idea of constant gestalt switches look attractive, the romantic poets initiated a new way of speaking that no longer had use for notions like "foundation," "reality," "real essence," "intrinsic nature," "fitting the world," and "correspondence of language to reality."

Rorty introduces his idea of a poeticized culture in chapter 3 of *Contingency, Irony, and Solidarity*. It becomes clear from his elaborations on his notion of a poeticized culture that he intends this kind of culture to be the final, and most exciting, stage of the process of secularization. His antifoundationalist story of progress ends here. In other words, Rorty wants us to no longer deify anything and to continue the process of emancipation and secularization that ought to eventually culminate in a postmetaphysical poeticized culture. He wants us to "try to get to the point where we no longer worship *anything*, where we treat *nothing* as a quasi divinity, where we treat *everything*—our language, our conscience, our community—as a product of time and chance."[34] This is undoubtedly one of the most important sentences Rorty ever wrote.

In Rorty's poeticized culture strong poets, creative redescribers, nominalist historicists, and other anti-Platonists would delight in the stimulating plurality of new ways of speaking that do not pretend to offer a single, firm, unequivocal, and transhistorical truth and that contribute to the critique of the idea that there is a permanent reality to be found behind the many temporary appearances. For the members of the literary culture, the literary intellectuals, "a life that is not lived close to the present limits of the human imagination is not worth living."[35]

Many have pointed out that one of Rorty's most provocative ideas is that of a private-public split. For an understanding of the Rortyan notion of a literary or poeticized culture this private-public dichotomy is of great importance. Rorty writes: "My 'poeticized' culture is one which has given up the attempt to unite one's private ways of dealing with one's finitude and one's sense of obligation to other human beings."[36] Although we can be playful and creative ironists or strong poets at home, Rorty wants to persuade us that it is crucial to concentrate all our energies on the attempt to establish a liberal consensus in the public realm. The Rortyan emphasis on the necessity of strengthening the relation between liberal democracy and harmony, and between late-capitalist free-market economies and the development of more tolerant attitudes, completely neglects the highly productive dialectical tension between consensus and dissent. Rorty's notion of liberal democracy and his understanding of reformist piecemeal social engineering, I propose, do not leave room for dissent, resistance, antagonism, and the desire for radical social change, or at least for the radical questioning of liberal institutions and practices. Rorty's "we liberals," longing for the establishment of a powerful liberal consensus in the public sphere and constantly advocating the beauty of shared vocabularies, do not want to see the importance of conflicting interests, desires, and values for democratic politics. Consigning sublimity and the dark forces of radical redescription and theory to the private sphere, the public sphere in its liberal version will finally present itself as governed by harmony, tolerance, and undistorted communication. It can never be more than beautiful.

For our reading of Baldwin it is crucial to see that Rorty contends that "poetic, artistic, philosophical, scientific, or political progress results from the accidental coincidence of a private obsession with a public need."[37] He also speaks of "idiosyncrasies which just happen to catch on with other people—happen because of the contingencies of some historical situation, some particular need which a given community happens to have at a given time."[38] What would Baldwin make of this Rortyan idea of an "accidental coincidence"? What would have been his reaction, as a public intellectual fighting for black civil rights, to the idea that the relation between the private and public sphere is governed by contingency? This Rortyan idea questions the possibility of radical energies becoming immediately effective in the public sphere. In this context the question arises as to whether there is a possibility of demarcating a space between radical leftist politics, on the one hand, and Rorty's liberal version of neopragmatism and his attempt to depoliticize the work of the poet and creative redescriber, on the other. In the next part, I will argue that Baldwin's texts help us answer this question.

James Baldwin, Pragmatism, and Cosmopolitan Humanism

In discussions of the renaissance of pragmatism, Baldwin has played hardly any role. Furthermore, his name also is rarely mentioned in discussions centering on the problematics of pragmatism and race.[39] Scholars like Eddie Glaude Jr., Walton M. Muyumba, Ross Posnock, and Cornel West have offered illuminating readings of Baldwin as belonging to a genealogy of black pragmatism. However, a more detailed discussion of Baldwin's pragmatism is still a desideratum. Rorty notoriously only mentions Baldwin en passant in *Achieving Our Country* (1998), taking the title from Baldwin's *The Fire Next Time* (1963) and counting him among the members of the old democratic Left that Rorty opposes to the disorientations of what he terms the cultural Left. Concerning the relation between pragmatism and race, Glaude's *In a Shade of Blue: Pragmatism and the Politics of Black America* (2007) is an important text. Binding pragmatism and African American politics together, according to Glaude, might "open up new avenues for thinking about both."[40] As a scholar and public intellectual, and as a former student of Cornel West, he has invoked his "pragmatic commitments as a basis for reimagining African American politics—to reject specious conceptions of black identity, facile formulations of black history, and easy appeals to black agency."[41] The attempt to color pragmatism, on Glaude's account, ought to consider the necessity of "a return to Baldwin."[42] In his study, Glaude seeks to rehabilitate and reactivate the philosophy of John Dewey. In order to do this, he has to teach Dewey the blues, as it were. Whereas West, in "Pragmatism and the Sense of the Tragic" (1993) and in *Democracy Matters* (2004), argued that Dewey was incapable of grappling seriously with tragedy and the problem of evil, Glaude proposes that a contemporary black Deweyan philosophy that wants to confront the dark aspects of life can profit enormously from Baldwin's work. The aspects of Baldwin's thought that are important for Glaude are his insistence that the realization that life is "inescapably tragic" must not lead one to engage in various quests for certainty in order to escape from the precariousness and threatening contingency of life; his antiessentialism and his grasp of the complexity of color; his future-orientation; his insistence upon the significance and complexity of black self-creation; his emphasis on intelligent action; and his aversion to theories, systems, and principles.[43]

In *The Shadow and the Act: Black Intellectual Practice, Jazz Improvisation, and Philosophical Pragmatism* (2009), Walton M. Muyumba discusses Baldwin, Ralph Ellison, and Amiri Baraka as members of the genealogy of black pragmatism. According to Muyumba, these writers' close examinations of black culture (especially music) and experience led them to develop what we would term pragmatist attitudes. These writers, as Muyumba contends, argued that "the very tools for escaping race were available in African American aesthetic experimentalism. That is, the very traits attributed to classical pragmatism—the rejection of foundationalism, the critique of belief and truth, and experimentalism—are always already at work in African American culture and aesthetic practices."[44] Muyumba goes on to emphasize that the best way to fully grasp the pragmatist aspects of these three writers "is to examine their use, theoretical and metaphorical, of blues idiom musical forms like jazz."[45] He explicitly speaks of "Baldwin's pragmatist vision and his willingness to fight for improvisational space," and he proposes that "in his cultural criticism Baldwin recontextualizes key terms of American discourse by creating narratives that either redescribe identity, redescribe community, or redescribe the relation of the two. These redescriptions illustrate the process of replacing inherited contingencies with self-made contingencies."[46] While Muyumba uses a Rortyan terminology in this passage, he is well aware that it is precisely Baldwin's need to redescribe the relation between identity (or his ethics of self-invention) and community (or forms of black political activism and solidarity) that differentiates him from Rorty.

From William James's critique of British neo-Hegelians like F. H. Bradley and T. H. Green to West's critique of Fredric Jameson's neo-Marxism and Rorty's attack on the American cultural Left, pragmatists have always rejected grand theory in the sense of abstract and totalizing theories that are divorced from the world of practice.[47] It is interesting to see that right at the beginning of his first volume of essays, *Notes of a Native Son* (1955), Baldwin radically critiques the abstraction of theory and principles and confronts them with the priority of practice (here: "the demands of life"): "I think all theories are suspect, that the finest principles may have to be modified, or may even be pulverized by the demands of life, and that one must find, therefore, one's own moral center and move through the world hoping that this center will guide one aright."[48] Abstraction can only fail since it is incapable of grasping the complexity, ambiguity, irony, and paradox of black life in the United States. Moreover, theory ought to be understood as critique in the sense of theoretical practice. This kind of practice longs for consequences of theory in history. One might feel tempted to advance the argument that the quoted sentence does not imply a total rejection of theory and that Baldwin's texts rather show that, in a Jamesian and Westian manner, fallibilism, tentativeness, *and* antiskepticism come together and urge one to revise one's understanding of the task theory has to fulfill. However, at the same time one should note that throughout his essays Baldwin puts an emphasis on precisely that which escapes the grasp of theories, abstractions, and principles: the singularity of all human experience, the particularity of pain (the horrors of black life), the power of individual resistance, the fragmentary and contingent character of human life, the possibilities of individual self-creation, human finitude (the tragedy and reality of death), and individual moral commitment in the face of uncertainty, absurdity, and paradox.

We have already seen that Baldwin, in a Jamesian manner, calls attention to "that dense, many-sided and shifting reality which is the world we live in and the world we make."[49] Undoubtedly, it often seems as if Baldwin were striving to penetrate through the veil of appearances, myths, misjudgments, and distorting prejudices to the really real or the Truth. In other words, the appearance-reality distinction, which Rorty criticized at least since *Philosophy and the Mirror of Nature* (1979) and which is central to metaphysical thought, often governs Baldwin's essays.[50] Nonetheless, Baldwin's aforementioned description of the world we live in, the world we *make,* could also be used to characterize an antifoundationalist and anti-essentialist culture that no longer needs the certainty and reliability of what is more than another human creation. Simply put, Baldwin is of course not a postmetaphysical writer, yet he often prefers making to finding or discovering. We make our world, constantly change and redescribe it in creative and innovative ways, and we also have to embrace our responsibility, as far as the question of political and moral commitment is concerned, in the confrontation with contingency and uncertainty. According to Lawrie Balfour, Baldwin's essays reorient "the focus from the level of principle to the murky region between principle and practice."[51] Balfour expands on this point as follows: "The dual conviction that principles cannot be conceived or elaborated apart from human experiences and that those experiences repeatedly undermine the possibility that the principles will be realized lends an indispensable ambivalence to Baldwin's writing. The ferocity of his moralizing stems from an acute awareness of the distance between principles and practice, and yet his appreciation of human finitude makes him suspicious of the meanings of the principles themselves."[52] In this "murky region between principle and practice," which is indeed a realm of "ambivalence" and the realm of writing, Baldwin manages to radically question transcendence and metaphysics without being able to leave metaphysical thinking completely behind. Baldwin, it seems, needs the tension of the in-between, the interplay of theory and practice, in order to sketch the possibility of establishing a new practice. In this new practice, as he made notoriously clear in his essays on Richard Wright, it would no longer be possible to make an abstraction of the individual black man or woman. I do not intend to discuss Baldwin's critique of Wright's naturalism in detail here, but some aspects of this critique are important for our purposes. Insisting on the fact that "literature and sociology are not one and the same," Baldwin argues that the protest novel, far from disturbing American society, "is an accepted and comforting aspect of the American scene, ramifying that framework we believe to be so necessary."[53] Baldwin's "Everybody's Protest Novel" concentrates on Harriet Beecher Stowe's *Uncle Tom's Cabin*, but it ends with a severe critique of Wright's *Native Son*. According to Baldwin, Wright's novel does not pay sufficient attention to the aforementioned "demands of life." It rejects life and denies the complexity and ambiguity of black existence. In other words, the Wrightian protest novel succumbs to the temptation of simplifying abstractions and categorizations. As Baldwin writes: "The failure of the protest novel lies in its rejection of life, the human being, the denial of his beauty, dread, power, in its insistence that it is his categorization alone which is real and which cannot be transcended."[54] Abstract categorizations, if one follows Baldwin's line of argument, belong to the field of sociology and its theoretical approaches; when applied to literature they can only lead to stasis and the depiction of one-dimensional characters. In "Many Thousands Gone," he suggests that in *Native Son* a crucial dimension of black life has been ignored or omitted. This dimension, as he underlines, is "the relationship that Negroes bear to one another, that depth of involvement and unspoken recognition of shared experience which creates a way of life. What the novel reflects—and at no point interprets—is the isolation of the Negro within his own group and the resulting fury of impatient scorn."[55] The climate of anarchy, fury, and violence thus created "has led us all to believe that in Negro life there exists no tradition, no field of manners, no possibility of intercourse."[56] Bigger Thomas appears as an utterly isolated and atomized character without a past and without any kind of cultural tradition that he might use as a source of strength and resistance. Furthermore, he is depicted as a young man who has never been offered the possibility of grasping the meaning of racial solidarity and who also seems to be without any kind of future possibility (the element of utopia). Hence, Bigger appears as trapped in a static present, deprived of the possibility of change. In the context of our argumentation, one might claim that what Baldwin primarily criticizes is that Bigger is never given the possibility of creating a self. In the protest novel, in other words, blacks are represented as helpless victims of white supremacy, giving in to the enormous pressures of white society, and self-creation is a goal utterly out of reach. In confronting the complexity of contingency, the demands of life, and the potential of change, a black redescriber may develop new forms of self-creation and thereby sketch new kinds of solidarity and innovative forms of resistance that may eventually lead to future social change. This scenario, or so Baldwin seems to hold, is incompatible with the depiction of black life in Wright's *Native Son*.

It should be obvious by now that Baldwin's understanding of self-creation, or his ethics of self-invention, is another crucial aspect when one wants to demonstrate his significance for a genealogy of pragmatism. A discussion of his notion of self-creation inevitably leads to the anti-essentialism of his concept of identity. Identity, as Baldwin demonstrates, is not fixed, not accomplished, not permanent; that is, it is to be understood as impure, transient, profoundly unstable, and plural.[57] In Baldwin's texts there can be found many Nietzschean, Bloomian, or Rortyan gestures of self-creation, and idiosyncratic metaphors of self-creation are clearly given priority over metaphors of discovery (here: discovering the real and authentic self). As a self-reliant redescriber who desires self-creation, self-trust, and self-overcoming, Baldwin must never accept somebody else's description of himself. Longing for self-creation and self-renewal, and the creative invention of a new language, new vocabularies, or a new set of metaphors, he vehemently underscores the particularity of his independent black self and voice. He creates himself as a writer: "Well, I had said that I was going to be a writer, God, Satan, and Mississippi notwithstanding, and that color did not matter, and that I was going to be free. And, here I was, left with only myself to deal with. It was entirely up to me."[58] Like Rorty, Baldwin seems to hold that the United States is the ideal country for self-creation and self-renewal. American society is not fixed, and this fact is especially attractive to writers: "American writers do not have a fixed society to describe. The only society they know is one in which nothing is fixed and in which the individual must fight for his identity. This is a rich confusion, indeed, and it creates for the American writer unprecedented opportunities."[59] US immigrants, on Baldwin's account, had "to make themselves over in the image of their new and unformed country." This creation of a new self, in the confrontation with a new culture, was difficult insofar as there "were no longer any universally accepted forms or standards" and "all the roads to the achievement of an identity had vanished."[60] At the end of "In Search of a Majority," Baldwin argues that "the one thing that all Americans have in common is that they have no other identity apart from the identity which is being achieved on this continent."[61] Although this may sound as if it comes dangerously close to another version of American exceptionalism, one ought to see that Baldwin considers the possibilities of (American) self-creation as indispensable in the attempt to radically question American ideology, as well as American myths. Fighting white supremacy, black self-creation creatively redescribes American ideology. However, one might feel tempted to advance the argument that all this talk about self-creation seems too playful, frivolous, and even cynical in view of the history of blacks in the United States. Black self-creation might be a stimulating endeavor for bookish intellectuals, but the majority of blacks has neither the time nor the money for such attempts at self-renewal and self-overcoming. Baldwin is perfectly aware of this problem. In *No Name in the Street* he stresses that the question of black self-creation is of an almost existential nature. According to Baldwin, "to be born black in America is an immediate, a mortal challenge."[62] Moreover, "a people under the necessity of creating themselves must examine everything, and soak up learning the way the roots of a tree soak up water."[63] What this signifies is that self-creation is a means of fighting white supremacy; it is a necessary part of the black battle against discrimination and injustice. Blacks have to create themselves in order not to perish. Questioning everything, from his own identity as a black and a gay to the foundations and structures of American society, Baldwin was "free only in battle, never free to rest."[64]

Throughout his texts, Baldwin draws attention to the fact that, as far as self-creation is concerned, there are obvious limits for blacks. In "My

Dungeon Shook," a letter to his nephew James, Baldwin explicates to the teenager that white society has set limits to his ambition, that is, it will be very difficult for this young black to create himself in view of various obstacles: "You were born where you were born and faced the future that you faced because you were black and *for no other reason*. The limits of your ambition were, thus, expected to be set forever. You were born into a society which spelled out with brutal clarity, and in as many ways as possible, that you were a worthless human being."[65] A visit to the ghetto of Chicago's South Side leads Baldwin to the following reflection: "Here was the South Side—a million in captivity—stretching from this doorstep as far as the eye could see. And they didn't even read; depressed populations don't have the time or energy to spare."[66] What all this boils down to is that the question of self-creation in Baldwin does not necessarily have to be seen in connection with the advantages of an antifoundationalist and anti-essentialist literary or poeticized culture. Rather, Baldwinian self-creation is primarily part of a political endeavor, a cultural criticism that critiques US society and white supremacy and that in a Westian manner eventually leads to moral responsibility and commitment in the face of contingency, absurdity, and tragedy. In his conversation with Margaret Mead, Baldwin states that he considers people "to be responsible, moral creatures who so often do not act that way. But I am not surprised when they do."[67]

Seeking to become "a truly moral human being," Baldwin contends that white people who rob blacks of their rights and their liberty have "no moral ground on which to stand."[68] This last metaphor is somewhat misleading as Baldwin in general does not favor the idea of a common ground in the form of a shared human attribute. He does not think that there is something like an ahistorical nature that unites us human beings and that the existence of this ahistorical nature as our real core forces us to recognize the importance of our steadily increasing moral knowledge and thus calls attention to the fundamental nature of firm moral principles. In contrast to foundationalists and metaphysicians, Baldwin does not hold that we are morally lost without the acceptance of the idea that deep down inside us there is something that unites us as human beings, a kind of ahistorical, transcultural, and noncontingent core, and he moreover critiques the notion that we need a moral reference point and that in order to achieve moral progress we need moral principles.

Is there a moral way the world is? Do we have to be adequate to something in moral matters? Do we need firm and transhistorical standards, laws, or principles when deciding moral questions? Do those laws and principles reflect something of our inner selves? Is it necessary to turn those firm laws and principles into a system, a moral theory, in order to make moral deliberation possible? Does moral theory moreover need immutable and indubitable foundations? Dewey would of course answer "no" to all these questions. His brand of pragmatism, as radical empiricism or naturalistic humanism, vehemently critiques traditional versions of moral philosophy. Dewey not only called attention to the weaknesses and shortcomings of Aristotelian virtue ethics, utilitarian ethics, and Kantian deontological ethics, but he also illuminated that there are important parallels between the quest for certainty in epistemology and the search for firm rules and fixed ideals in morality. These quests in epistemology and morality are a hindrance to man's progress and self-realization. Whereas philosophers in the field of epistemology have advanced the idea that without certainty there will never be real (pure) knowledge, moral philosophers have claimed that without firm laws and fixed ideals there will be moral chaos. Both approaches are grounded in the theory-practice dichotomy; both strive to free themselves of the messy and contingent world of everyday life; and both long for the certainty, reliability, immutability, and purity of what would be more than another human creation. Criticizing the quest for certainty in moral philosophy, Dewey introduces his pragmatist ethics that radically rejects theoretical approaches using a priori categories and mechanical decision procedures.

Like Dewey's ethics, Baldwin's notion of moral commitment and his ethics of self-invention start with, always come back to, and end with, human beings' practical life, that is, their lived experience in a particular situation under specific conditions. Authors as varied as James, Dewey, Rorty, and Baldwin teach one the primacy of the philosophical endeavor to fully appreciate the implications of human beings' attempts to cope with the world, including their needs and desires, the consequences of their actions, the importance of alternative possibilities, and the power of the imagination to shape a different future. The live creature's lived experience in society, in a particular environment and under particular historic conditions, necessitates a redescription of traditional moral philosophy since the latter appears too static and governed by absolutism and universalism.

Baldwin's aforementioned anti-essentialism plays a crucial role in Ross

Posnock's discussion of his work. One of Posnock's primary concerns in *Color & Culture: Black Writers and the Making of the Modern Intellectual* (1998) is to illuminate the importance of pragmatism for the careers of twentieth-century black intellectuals, specifically W. E. B. Du Bois and Alain Locke. Du Bois and Locke, as Posnock suggests, were profoundly influenced by William James's pragmatist pluralism, by his openness to the excluded and marginalized, and by his critique of traditional notions of identity. Regarding Locke's understanding of identity, for instance, Posnock writes: "In emphasizing the primacy of use rather than identity, Locke makes the pragmatist move that conceives identity not as antecedent essence but as an effect of action."[69] Situating Baldwin within what he terms "the miscegenated lineage of pragmatist pluralism," Posnock argues that Baldwin strove to substitute a cosmopolitan nationalism for a racial essentialism.[70] Posnock reads Baldwin as a "prophet of post-ethnicity" who demonstrated that black and white were obsolete and useless terms and who desired to contribute to the creation of a color-blind society.[71] His "dialectical cosmopolitanism" or "maverick cosmopolitanism" was strongly opposed to ideologies of authenticity and purity and instead favored impurity, intermixture, miscegenation, creative invention, deracination, and the dispersal of identity.[72] According to Posnock, Baldwin had to confront "the task faced by all pragmatist pluralists—turning identity from an accomplished fact that excludes and forecloses to a continuing practice of skepticism."[73] Posnock is right in underlining that Baldwin often criticized America for being insufficiently motley, not plural and heterogeneous enough. America had not yet used its potential for otherness to a satisfying degree. Baldwin's self-creation wanted to draw attention to the complexity of this potential, and at the same time he intended for others to realize the possibility of creative self-renewal and self-overcoming for themselves. Posnock describes Baldwinian self-creation as follows: "Baldwin performs an act of flagrant artifice, as he blends black and white, Europe and America, high and popular culture, into an assemblage designed to catalyze his artistic birth. The 'specialness' that emerges—the creation called James Baldwin—embodies what he calls 'enormous incoherence' and Henry James calls a 'hotch-potch.' Which is to say he is utterly American."[74] Although Posnock speaks of Baldwin's cosmopolitan nationalism, I would prefer to read his version of black pragmatism as a cosmopolitan humanism.[75] As we have seen, Baldwin is not only a truly transnational, transatlantic, and displaced writer ("my diaspora continues") who never accepted firm geographical boundaries but who at the same time was genuinely American, but also an author who helped prepare the establishment of a detranscendentalized and postmetaphysical culture.[76] I think what Baldwin offered in his best pieces was a cosmopolitanism without transcendence, or rather, a radical cosmopolitan humanism that illuminated how humanism, pragmatism, historicism, antifoundationalism, postmetaphysics, and cosmopolitanism are linked.

For our purposes it is important to see that Baldwin's desire for political and social change became more intense and explicit in his later texts.[77] Especially in *No Name in the Street* this reorientation is obvious. Influenced by Malcolm X and later on by the Black Panthers around Huey Newton, Baldwin presents himself as a black socialist writer and partly even as a black radical and revolutionary who seeks to justify the use of arms in the fight for black freedom.[78] The intensity of Baldwin's proposals in the early 1970s reminds one of Cornel West in the 1980s. As regards the question of socialism in the United States, Baldwin states: "Huey believes, and I do, too, in the necessity of establishing a form of socialism in this country—what Bobby Seale would probably call a 'Yankee Doodle type' socialism. This means an indigenous socialism, formed by, and responding to, the real needs of the American people."[79] He justifies his decision to call for the establishment of an indigenous socialism by directing attention to a broader context: "The necessity for a form of socialism is based on the observation that the world's present economic arrangements doom most of the world to misery; that the way of life dictated by these arrangements is both sterile and immoral; and, finally, that there is no hope for peace in the world so long as these arrangements obtain."[80] Baldwin makes unequivocally clear that he is not talking about liberal piecemeal reform here but rather about radical political and social change. A real commitment to black freedom in the United States, as he maintains, "would have the effect of re-ordering all our priorities, and altering all our commitments."[81] Speaking "out of the most passionate love" for the United States, and never faltering in the attempt to achieve his country, Baldwin throughout his career demonstrated that his idiosyncratic self-creation and the fate of his native country were inextricably entwined.[82]

"We do not seem to want to know that we are *in* the world."[83] Throughout his life as a writer and public intellectual James Baldwin tried to draw his readers' attention to the consequences of the inescapable fact that man is *in* the world and that this world is *his* world because he has made it and hence can change it.[84] In this chapter, I have argued that Baldwin, to a certain extent, can be considered part of a genealogy of black pragmatism (or black cosmopolitan pragmatism). His thought, as we have seen, contains pragmatist elements: his aversion to theory, systems, and firm and first principles; his anti-essentialism and ethics of black self-creation; his antifoundationalism and historicism; his critique of traditional moral theory; as well as his cosmopolitan humanism. Moreover, I have suggested that in Baldwin's texts the idea of black self-fashioning, moral commitment, the notion of political and social change, and an understanding of the task of the poet are linked in a manner that allows one to situate it between Cornel West's and Richard Rorty's versions of pragmatism. It would certainly be pointless to claim that Baldwin is a radically postmetaphysical author and thus an ideal member of a pragmatist literary or poeticized culture. But his politicized version of self-creation seems to legitimize advancing the idea that one can regard him as part of a left-liberal tradition of worldly pragmatism that sees the work of the strong poet or creative redescriber as contributing to political and social change. Like Du Bois, Baldwin was a black aesthete *and* a fighter for black emancipation and civil rights who understood that the realm of form must not, and cannot, be separated from the political sphere. Baldwin was a transnational writer who lived in the United States, France, Switzerland, Turkey, and other countries, and his texts illuminate the emancipatory potential of a cosmopolitan humanism. This also implies that these texts address the question of political emancipation in a postmetaphysical culture.

If there is a characteristic that unites pragmatists as varied as James, Dewey, Rorty, and West, apart from their critique of Platonist and Kantian epistemology and of traditional moral philosophy, it is their strong emphasis on the democratic potential of America.[85] The significance of pragmatism cannot be adequately grasped without considering the gesture of holding on to this democratic potential. Pragmatism accentuates and strives to expand democratic possibilities in the United States. In *Democracy Matters: Winning the Fight against Imperialism* (2004), West illustrates the importance of Baldwin's thinking in this context. According to West, Baldwin was "the most fully Emersonian of democratic intellectuals" in US history.[86] Furthermore, Baldwin's "artistic eloquence, dramatic insights, and prophetic fire put him at the center of democracy matters for over thirty years."[87] It is crucial to note that West claims that on Baldwin's account it is the conception of democracy developed by blacks that is the best means of confronting the crisis of moral decay in the United States. Baldwin offers a hitherto neglected perspective from which to analyze the current dilemma: "Baldwin contends that the crisis of the moral decay of the American empire is best met by turning to the democratic determination of black people—looking at America's democratic limits through the lens of race in order to renew and relive deep democratic energies."[88]

Complicating all battles, Baldwin was a poetic prophet who saw the necessity of holding on to the concept of truth but who at the same time realized that one should rather speak of a plurality of truths: "The multiple truths about a people are revealed by that people's artists—that is what the artists are for."[89] Baldwin, I think, would have liked Rorty's pragmatist humanism and his notion of a poeticized culture. A political and worldly strong poet or creative redescriber, Baldwin was a determined fighter for black freedom and emancipation, and at the same time his version of cultural criticism can be used to help prepare the establishment of a postmetaphysical culture. However, he certainly would have disapproved of Rorty's liberal private-public split. Confronting the demands of life, Baldwin made clear that the work of the poet must not be confined to the private sphere and that the realm of art and form must never be separated from the realm of political activism. Where the people have the freedom to sing, the poet can live, and where the songs of the poet can be heard and enjoyed, the people can live. It is this dialectics that is a crucial part of Baldwin's legacy.

Notes

1. James Baldwin, "'This nettle, danger . . . ,'" in *James Baldwin: Collected Essays*, ed. Toni Morrison (New York: Library of America, 1998), 687–91.

2. Developing his version of pragmatism as humanism, it was the British pragmatist F. C. S. Schiller who radicalized the Protagorean dictum that "man is the measure of all things" and who contended that a pragmatist humanism drew attention to the idea that in a fully realized detranscendentalized culture man would appear as a maker. Man as the maker of (his) truths, principles, laws, and the sciences refuses to accept the alleged authority of something nonhuman and absolute, something that presents itself as more than another human creation. In this context, see Schiller's two collections of essays, *Humanism* (1903) and *Studies in Humanism* (1907).

3. See the following collections of essays: Dwight A. Bride, ed., *James Baldwin Now* (New York: New York University Press, 1999); Quentin D. Miller, ed., *Re-Viewing James Baldwin: Things Not Seen* (Philadelphia: Temple University Press, 2000); Lovalerie King and Lynne Orilla Scott, eds., *James Baldwin and Toni Morrison: Comparative Critical and Theoretical Essays* (New York: Palgrave Macmillan, 2006); Douglas Field, ed., *A Historical Guide to James Baldwin* (New York: Oxford University Press, 2009); and Cora Kaplan and Bill Schwarz, eds., *James Baldwin: America and Beyond* (Ann Arbor: University of Michigan Press, 2011).

4. Tavis Smiley and Cornel West, *The Rich and the Rest of Us: A Poverty Manifesto* (New York: Smiley Books, 2012), 171.

5. Ibid., 7.

6. Ibid., 9. The idea that "the poor are fighting back" is also central to Michael Hardt and Antonio Negri's *Empire* (2000) and *Multitude* (2004). It would be interesting to analyze the similarities and differences between Smiley and West's materialist manifesto and Hardt and Negri's neo-Marxist critique of late or multinational or postmodern capitalism.

7. For a more detailed discussion of the development of West's thought, see the chapter "Love and Resistance: Cornel West's Prophetic Pragmatism as Oppositional Cultural Criticism," in Ulf Schulenberg, *Lovers and Knowers: Moments of the American Cultural Left* (Heidelberg: Winter, 2007), 187–221. In addition, see Rosemary Cowan, *Cornel West: The Politics of Redemption* (Cambridge: Polity, 2003); and George Yancy, ed., *Cornel West: A Critical Reader* (Malden, MA: Blackwell, 2001). See also West's memoir, *Brother West: Living and Loving Out Loud, A Memoir* (New York: Smiley Books, 2009).

8. Cornel West, *The American Evasion of Philosophy: A Genealogy of Pragmatism* (Madison: University of Wisconsin Press, 1989), 4–5.

9. Ibid., 5.

10. Ibid., 7.

11. Ibid.

12. Cornel West, *Prophesy Deliverance!: An Afro-American Revolutionary Christianity,* anniversary edition with a new preface by the author (Louisville: Westminster John Knox Press, 2002), 21.

13. West, *The American Evasion of Philosophy,* 213.

14. Ibid., 229.

15. Ibid.

16. For a decidedly Marxist critique of West's theoretical approach, see Mark David Wood, *Cornel West and the Politics of Prophetic Pragmatism* (Urbana: University of Illinois Press, 2000). For a discussion of the relation between Marxism and pragmatism, see Ulf Schulenberg, "Marxism, Pragmatism, and Narrative," *New Literary History* 48, no. 1 (2017): 149–70.

17. West, *Prophesy Deliverance!*, 23.

18. Ibid., 111–12.

19. Cornel West, *The Cornel West Reader* (New York: Basic Civitas, 1999), 27.

20. James Baldwin, *Notes of a Native Son* (1955; Boston: Beacon, 1984), 44.

21. That West's rhetoric in *The Rich and the Rest of Us* at least partly reminds one of the radical gesture governing his texts of the late 1970s and 1980s becomes obvious in the following passage: "If we don our historical lens, we'll see a once-democratic vision now compromised and corrupted by materialism and greed that has morphed into an insatiable, capitalist monster that threatens our very existence" (34). This sentence could also be taken from *Prophesy Deliverance!*

22. James Baldwin, "The Artist's Struggle for Integrity," in *James Baldwin: The Cross of Redemption*, ed. Randall Kenan (New York: Vintage, 2010): 50–58, 51.

23. James Baldwin, "The Creative Process," in *James Baldwin: Collected Essays*, ed. Toni Morrison (New York: Library of America, 1998), 669, 670, 672.

24. In this context, see Monica L. Miller's interesting study *Slaves to Fashion: Black Dandyism and the Styling of Black Diasporic Identity* (Durham: Duke University Press, 2009).

25. James Baldwin, "Nothing Personal" in *James Baldwin: Collected Essays*, ed. Morrison, 692–706, 695.

26. For a more detailed discussion of Rorty's idea of a poeticized culture, see Ulf Schulenberg, *Romanticism and Pragmatism: Richard Rorty and the Idea of a Poeticized Culture* (Basingstoke and New York: Palgrave Macmillan, 2015); see also Schulenberg, "From Redescription to Writing: Rorty, Barthes, and the Idea of a Literary Culture," *New Literary History* 38 (Spring 2007): 371–85.

27. Richard Rorty, *Consequences of Pragmatism: Essays 1972–1980* (Minneapolis: University of Minnesota Press, 1982), xliii.

28. Richard Rorty, "Philosophy as a Transitional Genre," in *Pragmatism, Critique, Judgment: Essays for Richard J. Bernstein*, ed. Seyla Benhabib and Nancy Fraser (Cambridge, MA: MIT Press, 2004): 3–28, 4.

29. Ibid., 11.

30. Ibid., 8.

31. Ibid., 12.

32. Richard Rorty, *Contingency, Irony, and Solidarity* (New York: Cambridge University Press, 1989), 7.

33. Ibid., 7.

34. Ibid., 22.

35. Rorty, "Philosophy as a Transitional Genre," 12.

36. Rorty, *Contingency, Irony, and Solidarity*, 68.

37. Ibid., 37.

38. Ibid.

39. Concerning the renaissance of pragmatism, see Morris Dickstein, ed., *The Revival of Pragmatism: New Essays on Social Thought, Law, and Culture* (Durham: Duke University Press, 1998). For a discussion of the question of pragmatism and race, see Bill E. Lawson and Donald F. Koch, eds., *Pragmatism and the Problem of Race* (Bloomington: Indiana University Press, 2004); and George Hutchinson, *The Harlem Renaissance in Black and White* (Cambridge: Harvard University Press, 1995).

40. Eddie S. Glaude Jr., *In a Shade of Blue: Pragmatism and the Politics of Black America* (Chicago: University of Chicago Press, 2007), x.

41. Ibid., xi.

42. Ibid., 11.

43. Ibid.

44. Walton M. Muyumba, *The Shadow and the Act: Black Intellectual Practice, Jazz Improvisation, and Philosophical Pragmatism* (Chicago: University of Chicago Press, 2009), 5.

45. Ibid., 5.

46. Ibid., 93, 97.

47. In *Lovers and Knowers: Moments of the American Cultural Left* (Heidelberg: Winter 2007), I discuss the development of the American cultural Left in the twentieth century by focusing on the relation between antifoundationalists and foundationalists, antitheorists and theorists, and ironists and metaphysicians.

48. Baldwin, *Notes of a Native Son*, 9.

49. Ibid., 44.

50. As far as Baldwin's desire to penetrate through the veil to the really real is concerned, the following passage from "The Creative Process" is particularly illuminating: "Society must accept some things as real; but he [the artist] must always know that the visible reality hides a deeper one, and that all our action and all our achievement rests on things unseen. A society must assume that it is stable, but the artist must know, and he must let us know, that there is nothing stable under heaven" (see "The Creative Process," in *Collected Essays*, ed. Morrison, 669–72, 670). In "Words of a Native Son," Baldwin claims that "every artist is involved with one single effort, really, which is somehow to dig down to where reality is. We live, especially in this age and in this country and at this time, in a civilization which supposes that reality is something you can touch, that reality is tangible. The aspirations of the American people, as far as one can read the current evidence, depend very heavily on this concrete, tangible, pragmatic point of view. But every artist and, in fact, every person knows, deeper than conscious knowledge or speech can go, that beyond every reality there is another one which controls it" (see "Words of a Native Son," in *Collected Essays*, ed. Morrison, 707–13, 708). In passages like these Baldwin comes close to presenting himself as a Platonist

metaphysician who prefers the discovery of the really real to the act of making or redescribing.

51. Lawrie Balfour, *The Evidence of Things Not Said: James Baldwin and the Promise of American Democracy* (Ithaca, NY: Cornell University Press, 2001), 20.

52. Ibid., 17.

53. Baldwin, *Notes of a Native Son,* 19.

54. Ibid., 23.

55. Ibid., 35.

56. Ibid., 35–36.

57. Regarding Baldwin's notion of identity, consider the following passage from "The White Problem," in which he speaks of an "invented reality": "The crucial element I wish to consider here is that element of a life which we consider to be an identity; the way in which one puts oneself together, what one imagines oneself to be; for one example, the invented reality standing before you now, who is arbitrarily known as Jimmy Baldwin. This invented reality contains a great number of elements, all of them extremely difficult, if not impossible, to name. . . . The truth, forever, for everybody, is that one is a stranger to oneself, and that one must deal with this stranger day in and day out—that one, in fact, is forced to create, as distinct from invent, oneself" (see "The White Problem," in *The Cross of Redemption,* ed. Kenan, 88–97, 89). Throughout his texts, Baldwin stresses that "everything must be re-examined, must be made new; . . . nothing at all can be taken for granted" (see "Notes on the House of Bondage," in *Collected Essays,* ed. Morrison, 799–807, 806). This also applies to the concept of identity. In "Every Good-Bye Ain't Gone," his contention is "that all identities, in short, are in question, are about to be made new" (see "Every Good-Bye Ain't Gone," in *Collected Essays,* ed. Morrison, 773–79, 778). The fragility of identity and the constant need to redescribe one's character are central aspects of what is probably Baldwin's best novel (although it is not a good novel), *Another Country* (1962).

58. James Baldwin, *Nobody Knows My Name: More Notes of a Native Son* (1961; New York: Vintage, 1993), xiii.

59. Ibid., 11.

60. Ibid., 131.

61. Ibid., 137.

62. James Baldwin, *No Name in the Street* (London: Michael Joseph, 1972), 114.

63. Ibid.

64. Ibid., 112.

65. James Baldwin, *The Fire Next Time* (1963; New York: Vintage, 1993). 7.

66. Ibid., 61.

67. Margaret Mead and James Baldwin, *A Rap on Race* (Philadelphia: Lippincott, 1971), 143.

68. Baldwin, *The Fire Next Time*, 47, 23.

69. Ross Posnock, *Culture & Color: Black Writers and the Making of the Modern Intellectual* (Cambridge: Harvard University Press, 1998), 11–12.

70. Ibid., 223.

71. Ibid., 224.

72. Ibid., 226, 235.

73. Ibid., 227.

74. Ibid., 237.

75. For a discussion of Baldwin's cosmopolitanism, see the volume edited by Cora Kaplan and Bill Schwarz, *James Baldwin: America and Beyond* (Ann Arbor: University of Michigan Press, 2011). In addition, see the essays in "Part III: Baldwin and the Transatlantic," in *James Baldwin Now*, ed. Dwight A. McBride (New York: New York University Press, 1999); and Magdalena J. Zaborowska, "'In the Same Boat': James Baldwin and the Other Atlantic," in *A Historical Guide to James Baldwin*, ed. Douglas Field (New York: Oxford University Press, 2009), 177–211. Zaborowska's study *James Baldwin's Turkish Decade: Erotics of Exile* (Durham: Duke University Press, 2009) also is illuminating. Regarding Baldwin's years in France and the influence of this time on his work, see James Campbell, *Exiled in Paris: Richard Wright, James Baldwin, Samuel Beckett, and Others on the Left Bank* (New York: Scribner, 1995). In this context it is interesting to see that Baldwin plays no role for Giles Gunn's recent attempt to develop a "pragmatic cosmopolitanism" (see *Ideas to Die For: The Cosmopolitan Challenge* [New York: Routledge, 2013], 9). Seeking to link cosmopolitanism, pragmatism, and humanism, Gunn completely ignores the work of authors like Du Bois, Wright, and Baldwin. For a stimulating discussion of cosmopolitanism from the perspective of social and political theory, see Gerard Delanty, *The Cosmopolitan Imagination: The Renewal of Critical Social Theory* (New York: Cambridge University Press, 2009).

76. James Baldwin, "The Price of the Ticket," in *Collected Essays*, ed. Morrison, 830–42, 841.

77. Concerning Baldwin's socialism, one should take into consideration his retrospective comment in his late piece "The Price of the Ticket." In the following passage he comments on his membership in the *Young People's Socialist League* when he was nineteen and interested in Trotskyism. However, I think this harsh judgment can also be seen on a more general level: "My life on the Left is of absolutely no interest, It did not last long. It was useful in that I learned that it may be impossible to indoctrinate me; also, revolutionaries tend to be sentimental and I hope that I am not" ("The Price of the Ticket," in *Collected Essays*, ed. Morrison, 834).

78. Baldwin, *No Name in the Street*, 163–64. As regards the attitude of African Americans toward Marxism, W. E. B. Du Bois's insights are still crucial. In essays such as "Socialism and the Negro Problem" (1913), "The Class Struggle"

(1921), "The Negro and Communism" (1931), and "Marxism and the Negro Problem" (1933), he contemplated the problematical nature of the relationship between African Americans (or "colored labor") and Marxism. His perspective seemed rather bleak. He repeatedly made clear in these texts that he thought there was no common ground for black labor and white labor. Race antagonisms and labor group rivalry were omnipresent. Hence, he held that there was no possibility of establishing something like a united proletariat driven by a working-class class consciousness. Du Bois explicitly stated that there was a clear separation between the black and the white proletariat, that the black proletariat had never been a part of the white proletariat. In this context, see Cedric J. Robinson's classic study *Black Marxism: The Making of the Black Radical Tradition*, with a new preface by the author (1983; Chapel Hill: University of North Carolina Press, 2000).

79. Baldwin, *No Name in the Street*, 150.

80. Ibid.

81. Ibid., 153.

82. Ibid., 166.

83. James Baldwin, "Mass Culture and the Creative Artist: Some Personal Notes," in *James Baldwin: The Cross of Redemption*, ed. Randall Kenan, 3–7, 6.

84. As far as this idea of a man-made world is concerned, William James's version of pragmatism is particularly suggestive. Consider the following famous passage from *Pragmatism:* "In our cognitive as well as in our active life we are creative. We *add*, both to the subject and to the predicate part of reality. The world stands really malleable, waiting to receive its final touches at our hands. Like the kingdom of heaven, it suffers human violence willingly. Man *engenders* truths upon it" (see William James, *Pragmatism and Other Writings*, ed. Giles Gunn [New York: Penguin, 2000], 112). For our discussion, the term "man-made world" refers primarily to society. At the end of "The White Problem," Baldwin writes: "I prefer to believe that since a society is created by men, it can be remade by men" ("The White Problem," in *The Cross of Redemption*, ed. Kenan, 97).

85. In this context, see Robert Westbrook, *Democratic Hope: Pragmatism and the Politics of Truth* (Ithaca, NY: Cornell University Press, 2005).

86. Cornel West, *Democracy Matters: Winning the Fight against Imperialism* (New York: Penguin, 2004), 78.

87. Ibid., 79.

88. Ibid., 85.

89. James Baldwin, "As Much Truth As One Can Bear," in *The Cross of Redemption*, ed. Kenan, 34–42, 37.

11

Baldwin's Individualism and Critique of Property

Jack Turner

James Baldwin's critique of white supremacy is largely existential. In addition to being a moral atrocity, white supremacy is a system of self-delusion, preventing its adherents from facing reality and taking responsibility for their freedom. In *The Fire Next Time* (1963), Baldwin speculated that fear of death was one of the wellsprings of not only white supremacy but all forms of racial, religious, and national chauvinism: "Perhaps the whole root of our trouble, the human trouble, is that we will sacrifice all the beauty of our lives, will imprison ourselves in totems, taboos, crosses, blood sacrifices, steeples, mosques, races, armies, flags, nations, in order to deny the fact of death, which is the only fact we have."[1] Fear of death drives us to lose ourselves in group identities—in religions, races, and nations that seek divine favor or worldly glory, that in their quest for eternal life or historical grandeur offer a faint promise of immortality. The price, however, is conformity. When people submit to chauvinist ideology, they surrender the chance to achieve an honest sense of self and experience an honest encounter with the world. Baldwin's ideal of moral maturity, writes Molly Farneth, requires "the abandonment—or, at least, the critical interrogation—of fixed or given identities."[2] Baldwin's critique of white supremacy is rooted in his conviction that every person is obliged to interpret for himself and become individual.

This is not to say that that individual should blind himself to the ways he has been shaped by his culture and by ascribed identities not of his own making. It is to say, however, that the individual must not reduce himself to ascribed identities or leave self-definition to others. Doing so would obscure the ways each individual is "absolutely unique in the world because [he] has never been here before, and never will be again."[3]

This chapter explores the distinguishing qualities of Baldwin's individualism. First, I show how Baldwin conceives of individuality as "novel creative energy," and how this conception of individuality underwrites his theory of political responsibility. Second, I analyze Baldwin's critique of American liberalism: against those who argue that Baldwin's critique of liberalism automatically entails a critique of individualism, I reveal that Baldwin in fact seeks to redeem individuality from liberalism, partly by driving a wedge between the rights to life and liberty, on the one hand, and the right to property, on the other. Third, I detail Baldwin's critique of property and his call for the wholesale reconstitution of the American polity. Fourth, I explain Baldwin's idea of self-trust and its relationship to the agency of the oppressed.

Interpreting Baldwin as an individualist brings the foundations of his democratic commitments into sharper relief. Nancy Rosenblum's summary of Thoreau's justification for democracy encapsulates Baldwin's: democracy is "the political order that best corresponds" to each individual's "infinite" (hence equal) "potentiality."[4] This is not to downplay Baldwin's equally strong conviction that individuals are historical, limited, and mortal: "Not everything that is faced can be changed; but nothing can be changed until it is faced."[5] Yet a creativity lies within us whose limits it would be presumptuous to estimate. Incalculable creativity holds the promise of (at least partial, inevitably partial) self-redemption. Through our creative faculties, we bend history to our purposes and produce art that secures us a place in human memory. Art should be interpreted broadly, for it encompasses democracy: creating a political order that accords "equal power" to each and every individual.[6]

Creative Individuality, Radical Responsibility

Baldwin conceives of individuality as a miraculous eruption of new creative energy, most poignantly signified by birth, marking a new beginning:

"Every human being is an unprecedented miracle."[7] His representation of individuality in the idea of birth distances him from those who would figure the self as fundamentally independent; human beginnings actually highlight the self's dependence:

> A newborn baby is an extraordinary event; and I have never seen two babies who looked or even sounded remotely alike. Here it is, this breathing miracle who could not live an instant without you, with a skull more fragile than an egg, a miracle of eyes, legs, toenails, and (especially) lungs. . . . You watch it discover a hand; then it discovers it has toes. Presently, it discovers it has *you*, and since it has already decided it wants to live, it gives you a toothless smile when you come near it.[8]

Baldwin's emphasis on the self's dependence does not lead him to endorse a communitarianism hostile to self-assertion. He places a high premium on intellectual independence[9] and demands that his fellow citizens buck complacency and conformity and "*be*—not seem—outrageous, independent, anarchical."[10] Baldwin's emphasis on the self's dependence reflects, rather, his conviction that individuality cannot flourish without a foundation of love and social support. Individuality emerges within human connection. We are partly defined by our concern for others. "Baldwin views the quality of an individual's attachments as the measure of that individual's integrity," writes Lawrie Balfour.[11] The quality of one's relationships reveals the self one has chosen to become.

One logical consequence of Baldwin's conceptualization of individuality as novel creative energy is a radical conception of personal responsibility—an idea of personal responsibility for the social world. "The world in which we live is, after all, a reflection of the desires and activities of men," he says in *No Name in the Street* (1972); "We are responsible for the world in which we find ourselves, if only because we are the only sentient force which can change it."[12] This far surpasses the ethics of noncomplicity.[13] It is not enough to extricate oneself from all the injustice that one personally authorizes or enables; one should attend to all injustice within one's capacity to change. So long as injustice exists, one must act against it. Complicity in injustice may compound the obligation to correct it, but noncomplicity does not by itself fulfill that obligation.

The demanding nature of Baldwin's idea of personal responsibility creates tensions within his ethics. He himself acknowledges that his vocation as writer requires occasional withdrawal from street-level democratic politics. In the very same book in which he specifies his radical notion of responsibility, Baldwin also reflects on how often in his life he needed to retreat to Europe: "In America, I was free only in battle, never free to rest—and he who finds no way to rest cannot long survive the battle."[14]

Baldwin's practice of responsibility is more sustainable than his theory. The practice acknowledges that the individual has the right to withdraw periodically from the public sphere to recover one's energy and one's sense of oneself. The model is *rotating citizenship:* citizens taking turns in and out of political battle.[15] Periods away from battle are essential because of the ethical and political value of withdrawal: in private conversation and personal solitude, one can refresh one's sense of one's commitments and replenish one's capacities for critical thinking and perception.[16] No less a political actor than Martin Luther King Jr. attests to the need for time "to retreat, concentrate, and reflect."[17] In the years following the Montgomery Bus Boycott, King felt frustrated over the fact that political struggle consumed his life: "My whole life seemed to be centered around giving something out and only rarely taking something in. My failure to reflect would do harm not only to me as a person, but to the total movement." King henceforward set aside time for "silence and meditation." Personally replenishing, these periods of withdrawal also allowed him to "think through the total struggle ahead."[18] Rotating citizenship befits democratic individualism. It preserves space for self-cultivation and self-recovery, even as it sustains the struggle for universal freedom.

Though Baldwin sensed tension between the personal and the political, he also exposed the error of overdrawing the distinction. Self-examination and self-transformation, in his eyes, were inescapably political. Baldwin would have agreed with Wilson Carey McWilliams when the latter claimed that "democratic theory must always be primarily a theory about a *demos,* about the character and relations of citizens."[19] Institutions and social structures emanate from the conscious and unconscious designs of women and men: "Though we do not wholly believe it yet, the interior life is a real life, and the intangible dreams of people have a tangible effect on the world."[20] Americans mistakenly divide the work of constituting the polity from that of constituting a self. Treating democratic self-governance as a kind of mechanical engineering—requiring only the discernment and mastery of external forces—masquerades as political sophistication. These so-called political sophisticates then treat the idea of democratic soulcraft as poetic bosh. The result is socially sanctioned flight from self and world in their interdependence.

Baldwin's idea of innocence is the most important way he implicates the personal in the political. Elsewhere in this volume, Lawrie Balfour and George Shulman brilliantly explicate the centrality of innocence in Baldwin's work. "By innocence," Balfour writes, "Baldwin means a willful ignorance, a resistance to facing the horrors of the American past and present and their implications for the future."[21] Baldwin's idea of innocence, says Shulman, denotes "a denial of the reality of others and a disclaiming of this refusal."[22] Building on Balfour and Shulman, I would like to sharpen the focus on how Baldwin conceives of late twentieth-century American liberalism as essentially innocent. This will allow me to disentangle Baldwin's democratic individualism from the liberalism he criticized.

The White Innocence of American Liberalism

"I don't trust people who think of themselves as liberals," Baldwin said in 1969; "What I am saying is that I don't trust missionaries."[23] Baldwin's association of liberals with missionaries is telling. The gaze of the missionary is outward. He is certain that he possesses the truth and that he is duty-bound to spread it. He regards the objects of his mission as equal to him in the eyes of God but inferior to him in knowledge of the Word. He is egalitarian in principle, hierarchical and condescending in practice.[24] The late twentieth-century American liberal, in Baldwin's eyes, shares the missionary's basic assumption: "The black man, to become truly human and acceptable, must first become like us."[25]

Baldwin saw American liberalism as "chicken-shit" from the time he witnessed liberals cave to Joseph McCarthy in the early 1950s until the collapse of the New Deal Coalition at the end of Baldwin's life in the mid-1980s.[26] He said in 1982 that "blacks have never had a President, in these yet to be United States, who cared whether they lived or died."[27] Liberal idols such as Roosevelt and Kennedy, according to Baldwin, defended black humanity only when doing so cost them little or nothing.[28] They proved his contention that "it is not necessary for people to be wicked" for a civilization to be destroyed, "but only that they be spineless."[29] Democracy, for

Baldwin, is the measure of civilization, and society's vigilance in defending its weakest member is the measure of democracy.[30] By these standards, America was neither democratic nor civilized.[31] American liberals persisted nevertheless in seeing incidents of American barbarity as abnormal deviations from American historical identity rather than as reflective of America's essential nature.[32] Baldwin's critique is all the more instructive given that so many of the liberals he debated—Norman Podhoretz, for example—went on to become neoconservatives calling for an end to race consciousness.[33]

Baldwin invariably condemns "liberals," not liberal*ism*. I have not found a single instance in Baldwin's essays where he refers to liberalism as a doctrine or philosophy. It is thus tempting to say that Baldwin objects not to liberalism per se but to the imperfect ways that Americans enact it. The predictable implication of such a formulation is that the problem is not liberalism itself but a shortfall in its practice. Baldwin himself impersonates this line of argument: "Though there are whites and blacks among us who hate each other, we will not; there are those who are betrayed by greed, by guilt, by blood lust, but not we; we will set our faces against them and join hands and walk together into that dazzling future when there will be no black or white. This is the dream of all liberal men."[34]

But to say that the solution is not the abandonment of liberalism but the more perfect practice of it—which frames the problem as exclusively one of willpower—is to pretend that there is neat bifurcation between principles and practice. Baldwin resists this notion: our actions reveal the principles we live by (versus the principles we avow), and the principles we avow often camouflage the principles we live by.[35] Given the complex relationship between lived and avowed principles, we cannot reform the former without transforming our understanding of the latter. Taking comfort, for example, in our abstract commitment to equality—without rigorously examining our own investments in superiority—is a form of innocence, an attempt to escape "the heat, and horror, and pain of life itself where all men are betrayed by greed and guilt and blood-lust and no one's hands are clean."[36] Moral reform, for Baldwin, is not just intellectual but sensual.[37] It requires one to attend to one's existence as not just mind but flesh. Where does one sleep? Who does one love? What does one desire? The answers to these questions reveal our basic commitments. The liberal tendency to treat abstract principles as fundamental—to run away from the "heat, and horror, and pain" of embodiment—exposes liberalism's "thin, passionless, strident" nature.[38]

American liberalism, according to Baldwin, is also bound up with a set of comforting myths. The most pervasive of these myths is that racism is always elsewhere. In the mid-twentieth century, this took the form of identifying the "race problem" as primarily a southern problem. As Baldwin recounts in "Fifth Avenue, Uptown: A Letter from Harlem" (1961): "I once tried to describe to a very well-known American intellectual the conditions among Negroes in the South. My recital disturbed him and made him indignant; and he asked me in perfect innocence, 'Why don't all the Negroes in the South move North?' I tried to explain what *has* happened, unfailingly, whenever a significant body of Negroes move North. They do not escape Jim Crow: they merely encounter another, not-less-deadly variety. They do not move to Chicago, they move to the South Side; they do not move to New York, they move to Harlem."[39] The intellectual's assumption that moving north would free blacks from racism bespeaks, according to Baldwin, a larger liberal tendency to externalize racism, to see it as existing only in other places, only in other people.[40] Baldwin thought that liberals "much prefer to discuss 'the Negro problem' than to try to deal with what this figure of the Negro really means personally to them."[41] No one could legitimately call herself antiracist, however, until she had taken the step of delving into herself and examining how pathological visions of black people shaped her own identity and behavior.[42]

A contemporary form of locating racism elsewhere is the tendency of both conservatives and liberals to view the Civil Rights Act of 1964 and the Voting Rights Act of 1965 as cathartic events that purged America of the worst forms of racism and marked the beginning of our first "postracial" era.[43] Baldwin resisted this Whig interpretation from the very beginning. "We have a civil rights bill now. We had the 15th Amendment nearly 100 years ago," he said in 1965. "If it was not honored then, I have no reason to believe that the civil rights bill will be honored now."[44] In 1985, Baldwin still contested the liberal error of thinking that once southern segregation was broken, the struggle for racial justice could conclude:

> It is not enough to be a liberal, to have the right attitudes or even to give money to the right causes. . . . You have to be prepared to risk more than that. I am telling you this because I have watched what happened to many of my liberal friends when the civil rights movement was in Alabama, let us say, in the Deep South, they were . . . very indignant.

And then I watched what happened imperceptibly but fatally when the same movement moved north to Brooklyn, to Pittsburgh, Detroit, and New York. . . . Their attitudes changed because they began to feel more threatened, and a liberal façade or even a liberal attitude was not enough to deal with the speed with which the movement was moving and the complications of American life as revealed in the fact by the interracial tensions in every major city.[45]

Baldwin's interpretation of the pre- and post-1965 American racial situation as essentially continuous has important implications for how we interpret the earlier work: his pre-1965 indictments of American society are just as applicable to post-1965 America.[46] We must therefore resist interpreting his 1961 declaration that *"Negroes want to be treated like men. . . . People who have mastered Kant, Hegel, Shakespeare, Marx, Freud, and the Bible find this statement utterly impenetrable"* as dated.[47] There is a reason he never retracted that statement: he thought its truth held to the end of his life.[48]

A second liberal myth is that achieving racial justice does not require white people to fundamentally transform the way they live. The postwar experiment in "urban renewal" epitomized the white liberal desire to assuage their (semiconscious) guilt over the condition of black Americans without paying the price of change. In "Fifth Avenue, Uptown," Baldwin analyzed how Metropolitan Life Insurance Company's construction of the Riverton housing project in early-1950s Harlem exemplified the white fantasy of getting racial justice cheap. Metropolitan Life erected the project after a number of black veterans had tried to secure middle-income apartments in Met Life's all-white Stuyvesant Town facility. Met Life denied the veterans' applications, and as an interracial grassroots resistance movement arose on the veterans' behalf, Met Life announced the Riverton Project in the hope of easing pressure for integration.[49] Of Riverton, Baldwin wrote:

Harlem watched Riverton go up . . . in the most violent bitterness of spirit. . . . They began hating it at about the time people began moving out of their condemned houses to make room for this additional proof of how thoroughly the white world despised them. And they had scarcely moved in, naturally, before they began smashing windows, defacing walls, urinating in the elevators, and fornicating in the playgrounds. Liberals, both white and black, were appalled at the spectacle. I was appalled at the liberal innocence, or cynicism, which comes out in practice as much the same thing.[50]

Baldwin interprets the residents' defacement of Riverton as political protest, as a refusal to accept Riverton as a sign of racial progress or as proof of whites' good intentions. Liberal shock at the defacement betrays liberals' tacit assumption that blacks should welcome any form of improvement, even if that improvement falls short of equality: "The people in Harlem know they are living there because white people do not think they are good enough to live anywhere else. No amount of 'improvement' can sweeten this fact."[51] What liberals cannot bring themselves to admit is that a "ghetto can be improved in one way only: out of existence."[52] Yet the prospect of either relentless financial investment in the ghetto until it is no longer a ghetto, or of rearranging the geography of the city so that the benefits and burdens of political life are equally shared, is too much for most liberals to accept: "The tragedy of this country now is that most of the people who say they care about [racial justice] do not care. What they care about is their safety and their profits. What they care about is not rocking the boat. What they care about is the continuation of white supremacy, so that white liberals who are with you in principle will move out when you move in."[53] Baldwin interprets "white flight" as an expression of liberals' lack of commitment. This does not mean that he exempts nonliberals from his ire. Nonliberal racism, however, is less tainted by hypocrisy. Innocence shields liberals from confronting their hypocrisy.[54]

A third liberal myth is that achieving racial justice does not require a revolution in moral and political standards. One constituent of this myth is the idea that racial justice is simply a matter of inclusion, of incorporating the excluded into a preexisting "mainstream" whose basic structure and values go unchanged.[55] Black citizens should avoid such inclusion, Baldwin argues, for the sake of both morality and self-preservation. On the count of morality, liberal inclusion is deficient because it makes one complicit in a fundamentally exploitative society. On the count of self-preservation, societies built on exploitation ultimately explode from their own internal pressure; being "included" in such a society is tantamount to being "integrated into a burning house."[56] Instead of inclusion, black citizens should seek wholesale social reconstitution—starting with some of American society's basic values and habits of mind.[57]

One mental habit Americans must overcome, Baldwin suggests, is thinking of life, liberty, and property as a holy triumvirate, wherein property is a direct extension of the self and therefore shares the self's moral inviolability. Baldwin is sympathetic to the nineteenth-century American slave's desire to "own" himself. Yet he is suspicious of the American tendency to figure the rights to life and liberty as a right to "property in oneself," as if one can buy, lease, or sell one's self, as if life and liberty are as alienable as property.[58] Understanding freedom in terms of ownership is the outgrowth of the modern West's decision to practice slavery and convert persons into things, which turned the question of freedom into the question, Do you own yourself or does someone else own you?[59] Yet this transformation in the grammar of freedom normalized the assumption that persons and things are commensurable. Treating persons and things as commensurable, in Baldwin's eyes, indicates a disconnection from reality so deep that it is akin to a living death. The value of individual lives—with their wondrous capacities for freedom, self-definition, and creativity—differs from the value of property not in degree but in kind. Baldwin exhorts his readers to see human beings as occupying an entirely different order of existential magnitude: "When I say 'reality' I mean the reality of another human being—another human being!"[60] To suggest that property is of comparable significance to life and liberty is to misunderstand the latter two's existential magnitude.

In "An Open Letter to My Sister Angela Y. Davis" (1970), Baldwin argues that the proper valuation of persons requires the desanctification of property: "We know that man is not a thing and is not to be placed at the mercy of things. We know that air and water belong to all mankind and not merely to industrialists. We know that a baby does not come into the world merely to be the instrument of someone else's profit. We know, finally, that democracy does not mean the coercion of all into a deadly—and finally, wicked—mediocrity but the liberty for all to aspire to the best that is in him, or that has ever been."[61] An individual's right to life and liberty—and to the livelihood necessary to escape hand-to-mouth existence—must take precedence over the rights of industrialists and financiers to protect and grow their fortune. When he says, "We know that a baby does not come into the world merely to be the instrument of someone else's profit," he suggests that American society is currently organized to raise children into workers, to make persons into instruments of capital accumulation. Against this "coercion of all into a deadly, and finally wicked, mediocrity," he insists that society should be organized not to optimize economic efficiency and growth but to guarantee each person's liberty "to aspire to the best that is in him, or that has ever been." This drives a wedge between life and liberty, on the one hand, and property, on the other, by suggesting that society's economic institutions—including its positive rights of property—must be subordinated to the goal of both equalizing and maximizing opportunities for self-development. We must no longer think of property as a natural right with sacred value but rather as a social institution whose value depends on the degree to which it actually secures individuals' freedom. Here we begin to get a sense of what political change means for Baldwin: the institution of new standards and the reconstitution of society according to them, "no matter what the risk."[62]

Democratic Reconstitution and the Divestment of Property

Toward that end, it is helpful to analyze Baldwin as a theorist of democratic reconstitution. Baldwin does not offer specific institutional or policy proposals. He seeks, rather, to reconcile citizens to their power to constitute society anew, to exercise democratic sovereignty. Baldwin works to bring Americans up to the point where they are willing to begin political society over again using justice as their guide. He defers institutional and policy questions until the moment of constitutional deliberation, when the people collectively decide.

Here I place Baldwin in the tradition of Thomas Jefferson and Thomas Paine, but only in order to show how Baldwin takes their ideas in a new direction. In a letter to Samuel Kercheval dated July 12, 1816, Jefferson argued that every generation had the right to reconstitute its government. He even suggested that periodic reconstitution would be politically prudent—for it would remind the people of their political sovereignty and allow them to repurpose government to the needs of the time:

> Some men look at constitutions with sanctimonious reverence, and deem them like the arc of the covenant, too sacred to be touched. They ascribe to the men of the preceding age a wisdom more than human, and suppose what they did to be beyond amendment. . . . Laws and in-

stitutions must go hand in hand with the progress of the human mind. As that becomes more developed, more enlightened . . . institutions must advance also, and keep pace with the times. . . . Each generation is as independent as the one preceding. . . . It has then, like them, a right to choose for itself the form of government it believes most promotive of its own happiness. . . . It is for the peace and good of mankind, that a solemn opportunity of doing this every nineteen or twenty years, should be provided by the constitution; so that it may be handed on, from generation to generation, to the end of time.[63]

Periodic reconstitution keeps the spirit of revolution alive, reminding people that they always have it in their power, in Paine's words, "to begin the world over again."[64]

Baldwin agrees with Jefferson and Paine that each generation has the right to reconstitute its world. He grounds this right not in the authority of illustrious founders but in the principles of human equality and creative individuality as he interprets them. To know ourselves, we must know our ancestors.[65] But we pay gratitude to our ancestors not by perpetuating the world that they co-created (or were denied the opportunity to co-create) but by re-creating the world to make both it and us "larger, freer, and more loving."[66] Baldwin's allusions to reconstitution are indirect. They consist of those moments when he calls upon us to take a "hard look" at ourselves and "dare everything" in the effort "to achieve our country."[67] "Everything now, we must assume, is in our hands," he writes in *The Fire Next Time* (1963); "we have no right to assume otherwise."[68] "The obligation of anyone who thinks of himself as responsible," he says in "A Talk to Teachers" (1963), "is to examine society and try to change it and to fight it—at no matter what risk."[69]

What might a Baldwinian moment of democratic reconstitution look like? As a thought experiment, let us take the idea of a democratic moment of reconstitution literally—as a week or a month when United States citizens (and perhaps noncitizen residents and even undocumented workers)[70] suspend their normal activities and meet in caucuses of fifty for eight hours a day to discuss how to reconstitute the polity. Each of the caucuses would have to be made up of people of diverse ages, racial groups, religious and ethical outlooks, and economic backgrounds. (The deep segregations of American life would make this inordinately difficult, but for the sake of argument, let us assume it practicable). The caucuses would report up to the precinct and regional level, which would in turn report up to the national level (I refrain from saying county and state level, for Baldwinian reconstitution would throw open the question of whether America's current organization into counties and states makes sense). Out of the process a new national constitution would emerge.[71]

Two questions arise. First, what would take place in the caucuses? Second, what must occur beforehand for the caucuses to succeed? Baldwin leaves the first question open. This is fitting given his dedication to democracy. Commitment to democratic reconstitution, in Balfour's words, requires "an openness to a new order whose parameters cannot be specified in advance."[72] To the second question, Baldwin has a definite answer—the surrender by each participant of "the dream of safety":

> Any real change implies the breakup of the world as one has always known it, the loss of all that gave one an identity, the end of safety. And at such a moment, unable to see and not daring to imagine what the future will now bring forth, one clings to what one knew, or thought one knew; to what one possessed or dreamed that one possessed. Yet it is only when a man is able, without bitterness or self-pity, to surrender a dream he has long cherished or a privilege he has long possessed that he is set free—he has set himself free—for higher dreams and greater privileges.[73]

Reconstitution can only meaningfully occur if citizens are willing to divest themselves of the privileges they possess under the standing order. Everything beyond the lives, liberty, and equal status of the participants is subject to negotiation. Most provocatively, the surrender of safety would require at least the partial surrender of a vested right to property—that is, of a right to goods beyond what one needs to lead a life of equal freedom.[74]

This last conclusion may seem far-fetched—especially given that nowhere in Baldwin's essays does he directly state that democracy requires citizens to divest themselves of property. Yet the conclusion follows, first, from his conceptualization of democracy as a form of common life aiming to provide *everyone* the freedom "to aspire to the best that is in him, or that has ever been";[75] material subsistence and leisure time are preconditions of this right's exercise. If a person is unable to provide these for himself or herself, then the democratic community must, through redistribution if necessary.

The conclusion follows, second, from Baldwin's insistence that the rights to life and liberty trump the right to property. Baldwin disconnects freedom from property when he argues that freedom is *not* "a matter of keeping everybody else out of your backyard."[76] Baldwin's target here is the right to exclude, a right essential to property as an institution.[77] What makes my backyard "mine" is my legally sanctioned authority to exclude you from it. The right to exclude is, in this way, integral to the right to property. Denying that there is a right to property in material goods superfluous to one's freedom enables Baldwin to envision a world where people are not "placed at the mercy of things,"[78] where my right to dispose of my wealth as I see fit is not an obstacle to the community guaranteeing your rights to food, clothing, shelter, education, and employment. Baldwin wants to enable the community to ensure everyone the material underpinnings of freedom, and this means reconceiving property as a contingent and malleable political institution rather than a prepolitical right.

The conclusion follows, third, from Baldwin's imperative that we risk and dare everything, including our possessions. In contemporary American society, homes, vehicles, and money afford a large measure of security against the vagaries of capitalism and the claims of the hungry and desperate. Risking everything, daring everything, means surrendering that security in pursuit of more just arrangements, which means surrendering our claims to our homes, vehicles, and money as we know them. This does not mean that we will not reacquire homes, vehicles, and money under new arrangements. We should each receive a just portion. But the distribution of material goods will no longer be decided by inheritance, luck, and the social reproduction of privilege. It will instead be decided by the democratic community according to a standard of equal freedom for all.

The conclusion follows, fourth, from Baldwin's association of freedom with voluntary disinvestment, voluntary dispossession: freedom partly means for Baldwin deciding what one "will *not* have," for our possessions exhibit an uncanny ability to possess us.[79] One of the perversities of contemporary American culture is our tendency to stake so much of our identities in our property. We confuse material comfort and financial security with personal flourishing, and when that comfort and security are threatened, our self-respect is "shaken to [its] foundations."[80] Divesting one's self from one's property is therefore one way of practicing freedom. In surrendering our property, we may achieve the "lightness of being" that George Kateb—

following Milan Kundera—sees at freedom's heart.[81] Achieving lightness of being requires relinquishing our possessive tendencies, our reflexive propensity to "guard and keep" instead of "give."[82]

Baldwin's call to his readers to divest themselves of current privileges applies especially to whiteness. Baldwin conceives of whiteness not as a biological trait but as a political condition. In the American racial order, whiteness is a "moral choice" by people of certain ancestry and/or appearance to accept the privileges conferred on people of such ancestry and/or appearance[83]—the choice, for example, to take an apartment in a building that steers black and Latino apartment-seekers toward lower-grade housing; the choice to take a job for which well-qualified nonwhite candidates are routinely passed over; the choice to stay silent when one sees police stop black male pedestrians in one's neighborhood who look like "they don't fit in"; the choice to assume innocently that racial discrimination no longer occurs. Divesting oneself of white privilege is more complicated than giving up material wealth: it requires positive action against social structures.[84] Baldwin's call to the privileged to divest themselves of privilege is a call to initiate and sustain structural transformation, to abolish undeserved privilege in democracy's pursuit.

Baldwin leaves many important details in this theory of divestment unspecified. Must democracy try to ensure something approaching absolute social and material equality? Or must it only ensure that there is social and material equality sufficient for roughly equal autonomy? To what extent may the state use force to redistribute property and abolish white privilege? Baldwin's failure to answer these questions will frustrate professional political theorists. But what Baldwin invaluably pinpoints—which many professional political theorists fail to pinpoint—is the personal disposition required to make democratic reconstitution work: detachment from the things we think guarantee our safety, a willingness to surrender to others what their effectual freedom requires.[85] Proprietary divestment, however, is only the first step toward democratic reconstitution. A second—and just as important step—is reconstitution of both individual and collective self-understandings.

An ethics of democratic conversation pervades Baldwin's work—an ethics, that is, of how democratic citizens should address each other if they are to figure out how to solve political problems together. Baldwinian conversation rests on two principles: honesty and love.[86]

Baldwin is amazed at the dishonesty of American public discourse. That dishonesty reveals itself in both the lies we tell ourselves and the truths we fail to tell ourselves. Baldwin does not wish to deny that the Declaration of Independence and its proposition that "all men are created equal; that they are endowed by their creator with certain unalienable rights; that among these are life, liberty, and the pursuit of happiness" was an important and defining moment in American history, a profound articulation of a worthy ideal.[87] But he also does not wish celebration of that moment to displace America's mass slaughter of Native Americans and enslavement of Africans from political consciousness.[88] Honesty requires keeping both realities in one's mind's eye and not privileging either as America's historical essence. Honesty furthermore requires seeing both the ideal and the slaughter and enslavement as constitutive of the present. Baldwin's America is a prosaic nation among prosaic nations, unexceptionally capable of both good and evil.[89] At the same time, Baldwin believes we have it in our power to create a redeeming future if we admit that redemption has yet to occur.[90] American history is not providential, but a human co-creation. The passage of time cannot by itself diminish the effect of slavery and conquest on American character. Only political action will.[91] But intelligent action first requires honest conversation.

Baldwin's ethics of conversation intersects with his politics of reconstitution. For reconstitution to work, white citizens must sit face to face with black citizens and listen to black citizens tell their stories of America. White citizens must listen both critically and self-critically—critically because black citizens, like white citizens, are susceptible to error, but self-critically because it is a long-engrained habit of white Americans to privilege interpretive frames that masquerade as "objectivity" and "normalcy" but that systematically discount black testimony. White citizens must also prepare themselves for an event that is out of the American "order of nature":[92] the event of black citizens revealing white citizens to themselves. "Nobody else knows white Americans except black Americans," Baldwin insists:[93] "Whereas you never had to look at me, because you've sealed me away along with sin and hell and death and all the other things you didn't want to look at, including love, my life was in your hands, and I had to look at you. I know more about you, therefore, than you know about me."[94]

Cross-racial conversation will often be tough, for it must spurn false civility for honest expressions of anger, outrage, and resentment. This aspect of democratic conversation not only is cathartic but also advances political understanding by revealing the passion behind political positions. White citizens must accustom themselves to hearing blacks' imperative voice— modes of address resembling Baldwin's meditation on history in "The White Man's Guilt" (1965): "White man, hear me! History . . . is not merely something to be read. And it does not refer merely, or even principally, to the past. On the contrary, the great force of history comes from the fact that we carry it within us, are unconsciously controlled by it . . . and history is literally *present* in all that we do."[95] Facing themselves in the "disagreeable mirror" of black testimony,[96] white citizens must credit that testimony as they would the testimony of those they most trust.

Democratic reconstitution involves as much risk for black citizens as for white—for black citizens must love white citizens (once more) so that the latter can let their defenses down enough to hear black testimonies. Love is also essential to motivate black speakers' leap of faith—against the evidence of historical experience—that white listeners will hear their testimonies. Love inspirits the act of embracing the oppressor, and interpreting his stammering speech, his defensive posture, his grappling with guilt, as "a personal confession—a cry for help and healing."[97] The embrace will work only if white citizens acknowledge that they need black help to achieve self-understanding; acknowledging that need is predicated on even deeper acknowledgments of blacks' complex and equal humanity and whites' existential incompletion.

Here we arrive at one of the paradoxes of Baldwin's individualism: self-examination must be social, dialogical, for our perspectives on the world are partial, and our perspectives on ourselves are riddled with obscurity. Only through conversation can we arrive at a fuller picture of ourselves, a fuller sense of who we are. Democratic conversation delivers us to greater self-knowledge. Democratic citizens "must, like lovers, insist on, or create, the consciousness" of each other. Baldwin's dialogical model of self-examination reveals yet again how Baldwin's individualism is not atomistic but relational, not heroic but democratic.[98]

Speech and Self-Understanding

Baldwin's politics of reconstitution is tantalizing, for it has qualities we desperately desire in democratic politics: conversation, self-searching, passionate speech, collective reflection, honest assessment, new beginning. But is it so hopeful that it evades politics, as well as Baldwin's own diagnosis of the American condition? Baldwin runs into a classic problem of democratic reconstitution: reconstitution is necessary both to do justice to citizens and to create citizens capable of sustaining a just regime. But for citizens to recognize that reconstitution is necessary, they must be better than they presently are.[99] Reconstitution thus requires the improvement of citizens to the point where they will authorize reconstitution. If the present regime is corrupt, how will such improvement occur? Baldwin suggests an answer: through the assertive speech of dissident citizens.

In his classic lecture "In Search of a Majority" (1961), Baldwin argues that democratic majorities do not consist in "numerical strength" but rather in "moral influence."[100] Democratic majorities are those who set prevailing standards, the same way that the "aristocracies of Virginia and New England"—who did not have numerical strength—set the standards of seventeenth-, eighteenth-, and early nineteenth-century America.[101] Democratic transformation thus occurs when new majorities of influence emerge and reconstitute the standards by which the polity judges itself, as well as the polity's understanding of the gap between those standards and current reality. Insurgent political actors use rhetoric to create new majorities of influence: they appeal to prior commitments and show how true adherence to those commitments requires attitudinal and behavioral change.[102]

This calls to mind George Shulman's characterization of Baldwin's rhetoric as prophetic. "Prophecy," says Shulman, is "a performance to incite audiences to self-reflection and action." Prophecy "announces what is disavowed and unsayable"; it re-centers political discourse on "what (and who) we count as real"; it gives voice to "what we forget or refuse to see."[103] Shulman's characterization of Baldwin as a prophet par excellence is both powerful and accurate. But I would like to supplement his portrait by exploring the way Baldwinian prophecy presupposes an Emersonian individualist virtue: self-trust. This reveals not only an Emersonian element in Baldwinian prophecy but also Emersonian self-trust's political potential: the practice of self-trust by the politically marginalized enables vigorous contestation of what society counts as "real" and the democratic disturbance of prevailing ideology.

In "The American Scholar" (1837), Emerson argued that the scholar's duties "are such as become Man Thinking. They may all be comprised in self-trust. The office of the scholar is to cheer, to raise, to guide men by showing them facts amidst appearances. He plies the slow, unhonored, and unpaid task of observation."[104] Emerson's call for the scholar to "cheer" seems to oppose Baldwin's call for American citizens "to ask very hard questions and take very rude positions."[105] The contradiction, however, is only apparent. Emerson means "cheer" in the sense of "encourage," and asking "hard questions" and taking "very rude positions" requires courage. Emerson himself characterized truth as "rude."[106] He might as well have been describing Baldwin when he said, "Your goodness must have some edge to it,—else it is none."[107] Emerson, like Baldwin, knew that speaking the truth before the public could elicit antagonism, and like Baldwin, he believed that that antagonism could be ethically productive. Showing men "facts amidst appearances" can be a rude awakening. Learning "the slow, unhonored, and unpaid task of observation" means realizing that one was blind. For both Baldwin and Emerson, however, learning the art of observation, learning to see with one's own eyes, is essential to democratic freedom and citizenship. Only by seeing with one's own eyes, and staying true to one's own perception, can one ensure that one is not hostage to another's worldview, that one is not mentally enslaved to power and convention. Only by seeing with one's own eyes, and staying true to one's perception, can one hold political representatives and fellow citizens accountable, for the vision of dissidents acts as a check against both leaders and mobs trying to obscure public perception.

Emerson's emphasis on self-trust is well known, but Baldwin's is underrecognized. Speaking generally of the American character, Baldwin writes, "We are afraid to reveal ourselves because we trust ourselves so little."[108] Baldwin's most profound meditation on self-trust, however, is "My Dungeon Shook: Letter to My Nephew on the One Hundredth Anniversary of Emancipation," the opening of his best-known book, *The Fire Next Time*. In that letter, Baldwin writes to his nephew: "This innocent country set you down in a ghetto in which, in fact, it intended you to perish. . . . You were born where you were born and faced the future that you faced because you were black and *for no other reason.* . . . I know your countrymen do not agree with me about this, and I hear them saying, 'You exaggerate.' They do not know Harlem, and I do. Take no one's word for anything, including mine—but trust your experience."[109] Baldwin's deployment of the idea of self-trust in this context makes it politically insurgent: self-trust enables the oppressed to heed the evidence of their own senses against prevailing powers and ideologies that downplay their oppression. On the basis of this kind of self-trust, Baldwin is able to denounce the white assumption that blacks are just like any other "immigrant group" and need simply to imitate Europeans to be successful:[110]

> We've talked a great deal about immigrant groups here—that is, people who came to this country voluntarily and who managed, once they got here, to achieve a way of life and a whole attitude toward reality and toward themselves which they could not have achieved had they remained in Europe. In that sense it is perfectly true that the idea of rising expectations is part of the American experience: you leave the famine-ridden farm in Ireland, you come to America, you fit into the American scene, you rise, you become part of a new social structure. But that is only the European immigrants' experience. It is not the Black experience. I did not one day decide to leave my farm and come to America. I was brought here. I did not want to come. And when I got here, I did not, like the Irish and the Jews and the Russians and the Poles and the Czechs and the Italians, immediately find myself in a slum and then by hard work and saving my pennies rise out of the slum into a position of relative economic security so that my idea of reality changed. That is not the black experience in this country, and there is no point in pretending to ourselves whatever that it *is*. The black experience is entirely different. You find yourself in a slum and you realize at a certain point that no amount of labor, no amount of hard work, no amount of soap is going to get you out of that slum.[111]

Self-trust enables Baldwin to resist a classic American temptation: to fold black experience into a narrative of inexorable progress, to pretend that if black people simply become more like the Irish or the Jews (or just wait long enough) they will realize the American dream.[112] Self-trust also allows Baldwin to insist against conventional wisdom that the line between past and present is indistinct. Baldwin recognizes the longitudinal historicity of his own identity.[113] Thus he is able to say, "I was brought here. I did not want to come here," with confidence that he is philosophically intelligible: Baldwin's "I" is constituted not only by the uniqueness of James Baldwin but also by near and far-flung ancestors whose lives gave shape to his.[114]

One of the paradoxes of Baldwin's praise of self-trust is that it seems to uphold a principle white Americans can use to defend their innocence. When asked why he sees the world the way he does, the white innocent can respond that he is just adhering to his senses, just listening to his intuition. Baldwin, however, believes that white Americans' self-*dis*trust is the deeper cause of their innocence: "Something very sinister happens to the people of a country when they begin to distrust their own reactions as deeply as they do here. . . . It is this individual uncertainty on the part of white American men and women, this inability to renew themselves at the fountain of their own lives, that makes the discussion, let alone the elucidation, of any conundrum—that is, any reality—so supremely difficult. The person who distrusts himself has no touchstone for reality—for this touchstone can be only oneself."[115] Self-distrust drives the white individual to seek an "all-American" identity, to subsume the messy particulars of his experience under dominant narrative formulas, rather than attend to those particulars and interpret them into an authentic sense of self. Whites' recovery of self-trust, however, enables them to confront the truth of their experience, to recall those aspects of their past and trace those elements of their present that implicate them in others' suffering, and to reorder their relationships according to the principle of equality.

Baldwin keeps faith in an idea that Emerson originally suggested: self-trust leads the individual to dedicate himself to the principle of equality. Urging him to acknowledge his own inner wildness and internal contradictions, self-trust acquaints him with both individual infinitude and human fallibility. The lessons of infinitude, on the one hand, and fallibility, on the other, force the individual to recognize the miraculousness of every person's existence, the inexhaustibility of each individual's inner life, and the impossibility of ranking human beings. If each individual's infinitude does not by itself constitute a type of human equality, then it at least counsels us to accept equality as the most responsible operating assumption. Assuming otherwise might tempt us to grade human beings in ways that insult their infinitude.[116]

What most distinguishes Baldwin's idea of self-trust from Emerson's is the way Baldwin fuses it with the obligation to know the furthest reaches of one's history. "Know whence you came," Baldwin tells his nephew. "If you know whence you came, there is really no limit to where you can go."[117] In one of his final essays, "The Price of the Ticket" (1985), Baldwin reiterates the point. Linking the democratic obligation of self-examination to the black church tradition of "doing our first works over," he writes: "To do your first works over means to reexamine everything. Go back to where you started, or as far back as you can, examine all of it, travel your road again and tell the truth about it. Sing or shout or testify or keep it to yourself: but *know whence you came.*"[118] Self-examination requires historical investigation, and self-trust enables one to conduct that investigation and trust one's conclusions. Historical self-understanding, for Baldwin, becomes the basis for personal freedom: "In great pain and terror one begins to assess the history which has placed one where one is, and formed one's point of view. In great pain and terror because, thereafter, one enters into battle with that historical creation, Oneself, and attempts to re-create oneself according to a principle more humane and more liberating: one begins the attempt to achieve a level of personal maturity and freedom which robs history of its tyrannical power, and also changes history."[119] Baldwin transfigures the great American, the great Emersonian, idea of self-creation into a self-conscious struggle with historical inheritance, a battle to reduce history's power over the self through patient and forthright confrontation.[120] Out of that confrontation, the self moves closer to self-knowledge by becoming better able to distinguish those parts of the self that are historical inheritance from those parts that are creative energy capable of transforming historical inheritance into something new. This is why Baldwin insists on the term *self-creation,* rather than *self-invention.* Self-invention implies making a self out of thin air. Self-creation implies transforming given materials—the body and mind history has begotten—into a work of art: "The truth, forever, for everybody, is that one is a stranger to oneself, and that one must deal with this stranger day in and day out—that one, in fact, is forced to create, as distinct from invent, oneself. . . . One begins to discover, with great pain, and very much against one's will, that whatever it is you want, what you want, at bottom, must be to *become yourself:* there is nothing else to want."[121] Baldwin's democratic individualism exceeds Emerson's in the relentlessness with which it insists that self-knowledge requires social and historical inquiry. This does not imply that Baldwin's conception of the self is merely social or historical. He believed that each newborn baby contained a surplus of creative energy that formed the mainspring of his individuality: "One has to look on oneself as the custodian of a quantity and a quality—oneself—which is absolutely unique."[122] Self-understanding, however, requires a long, hard look at one's connections to others. This is true at both the personal and the political level. The quest for personal self-knowledge is thus implicated in the political closing of Baldwin's portrait of the desolation of Harlem: "Walk through the streets of Harlem and see what we, this nation, have become."[123] The streets of Harlem mirror the American polity and the individuals composing it. No citizen can walk honestly through the streets of Harlem without seeing himself in his surroundings. Insofar as we are democratic and responsible, we must interpret Harlem's impoverishment as our own, for it reflects our failure to live up to the promise implied by democratic citizenship: to uphold each other's freedom. The worst corners of democratic society reflect the souls of democratic citizens, for they measure their indifference.[124] Indifference, for Baldwin, is a sign of spiritual coma—of diminished capacity for humane connection, and diminished faith in the possibility of self- and social transformation. Yet Baldwin keeps faith in the possibility of American awakening.[125] The promise of awakening lies partly in the accumulated wisdom of black experience, which counsels "the acceptance, totally without rancor, of life as it is, and men as they are".[126] "White Americans appear to be under the compulsion to dream, whereas black Americans are under the compulsion to awaken."[127] Realizing the democratic America of Baldwin's dreams will require reconstitution, which will require collective authorization. The instigators of this authorization will be a numerical minority striving for a "majority of influence": they will be seers—both black and white—who acquire their vision through the hard work of self-understanding. Baldwin's politics of self-understanding occurs both at the site of the self and in the space between selves. We examine ourselves through both introspection and conversation. We cannot know ourselves except through community.

Calls for national conversations about race are stale and tiresome. Too often they take the place of political initiative. Too often they constitute an evasion of self-examination. Yet Baldwin's model of national conversation is not the same as those of contemporary leaders. First, it is citizen-initiated. Most leader-initiated calls for conversation are political smoke screens for preset agendas. Second, Baldwin's model of national conversation cannot occur at the mass level. It must occur at the interpersonal level; it cannot be mediated by television or the Internet; it requires face-to-face encounter and time sufficient for personal acquaintance. Third, it requires a willingness to entertain—even if skeptically—the possibility of national reconstitution. It requires us to heed the words, ironically, of the slaveholder

Jefferson, who warned against regarding constitutions "with sanctimonious reverence . . . too sacred to be touched."[128] Baldwinian conversation addresses more than the meaning of the Fourteenth Amendment, more than the meaning even of the Declaration: it addresses the possibility of founding a polity that will for the first time in history guarantee *everyone* equal effectual freedom. Such refounding will involve reconceiving freedom to absorb the lessons of the life and afterlife of slavery. It will thus involve redefining the very terms of both personal and national self-understanding. This is appropriate given that the political world, in Baldwin's eyes, turns on our use of words: how we use them to awaken to reality, or how we use them "to cover the sleeper."[129] By revisiting the meaning of the "keywords" of American democracy—freedom, equality, rights, individuality—we empower ourselves to re-create our political world.[130] "We have it in our power to begin the world over again," said Thomas Paine.[131] Baldwin's politics of self-understanding aims at that power's exercise.

Notes

An earlier version of this essay was published as "Democratic Reconstitution," in Jack Turner, *Awakening to Race: Individualism and Social Consciousness in America* (Chicago: University of Chicago Press, 2012). Reprinted by permission.

I have revised the chapter with the benefit of hindsight and in light of new scholarship. For help in thinking about Baldwin over the years, I thank Lawrie Balfour, Sean Butorac, Eddie Glaude, Denise James, Christopher Lebron, Shannon Mariotti, Annie Menzel, Susan McWilliams, Heather Pool, Melvin Rogers, Rachel Sanders, Joel Schlosser, George Shulman, Kirstine Taylor, and Cornel West.

1. James Baldwin, "Down at the Cross: Letter from a Region of My Mind," in *The Fire Next Time* (1963), in *Collected Essays*, ed. Toni Morrison (New York: Library of America, 1998), 339. Cf. George Shulman, *American Prophecy: Race and Redemption in American Political Culture* (Minneapolis: University of Minnesota Press, 2008), 145.

2. Molly Farneth, "James Baldwin, Simone de Beauvoir, and the 'New Vocabulary' of Existentialist Ethics," *Soundings* 96, no. 2 (2013): 183.

3. James Baldwin, "Nothing Personal" (1964), in *Collected Essays*, ed. Morrison, 701. Cf. George Kateb's interpretation of Emerson's conception of individual uniqueness: "The world is new to each of us, and each of us is new in it. Out of this encounter comes the ability to say or do what has never appeared before" (*Emerson and Self-Reliance*, new ed. [1995; Lanham, MD: Rowman and Littlefield, 2002], 167).

4. Nancy Rosenblum, "Thoreau's Democratic Individualism," in *A Political Companion to Henry David Thoreau*, ed. Jack Turner (Lexington: University Press of Kentucky, 2009), 15.

5. James Baldwin, "As Much Truth as One Can Bear" (1962), in *The Cross of Redemption: Uncollected Writings*, ed. Randall Kenan (New York: Pantheon, 2010), 34.

6. James Baldwin, "Notes of a Native Son," in *Notes of a Native Son* (1955), in *Collected Essays*, ed. Morrison, 84. My understanding of Baldwin is generally indebted to Lawrie Balfour, *The Evidence of Things Not Said: James Baldwin and the Promise of American Democracy* (Ithaca, NY: Cornell University Press, 2001); and Shulman, *American Prophecy*, chap. 4. See also Stephen H. Marshall's recent political reading of Baldwin, *The City on the Hill from Below: The Crisis of Prophetic Black Politics* (Philadelphia: Temple University Press, 2011), chap. 4. The pioneering study of Baldwin as a political theorist remains Wilson Carey McWilliams, *The Idea of Fraternity in America* (Berkeley: University of California Press, 1973), 610–17. Following both Balfour and Shulman, I focus on Baldwin's nonfiction. Yet I place greater emphasis than they do on the speeches and essays recently collected in *The Cross of Redemption*. For two important works integrating Baldwin's fiction into the study of him as a political theorist, see Wilson Carey McWilliams, "*Go Tell It on the Mountain*: James Baldwin and the Politics of Faith," in this volume (originally published in *Democracy's Literature: Politics and Fiction in America*, ed. Patrick J. Deneen and Joseph Romance [Lanham, MD: Rowman and Littlefield, 2005], 153–70); and Joel Alden Schlosser, "Socrates in a Different Key: James Baldwin and Race in America," in this volume (originally published in *Political Research Quarterly* 66, no. 3 [2012]: 487–99).

7. James Baldwin, *No Name in the Street* (1972), in *Collected Essays*, ed. Morrison, 357. This, of course, resembles Hannah Arendt's idea of "natality" (Arendt, *The Human Condition*, 2nd ed. [1958; Chicago: University of Chicago Press, 1998], 9, 247). Individuals' unprecedented quality makes them a force against repetition, which for both Baldwin and Arendt is the opposite of freedom.

8. Baldwin, *No Name in the Street*, in *Collected Essays*, ed. Morrison, 355.

9. See, for example, James Baldwin, "The Discovery of What It Means to Be an American," and "Nobody Knows My Name: A Letter from the South," in *Nobody Knows My Name: More Notes of a Native Son* (1961), in *Collected Essays*, ed. Morrison, 139, 199.

10. James Baldwin, "A Word from Writer Directly to Reader," in *Cross of Redemption*, ed. Kenan, 8.

11. Balfour, *Evidence of Things Not Said*, 52.

12. Baldwin, *No Name in the Street*, in *Collected Essays*, ed. Morrison, 393.

13. On the ethics of noncomplicity, see Jack Turner, "Self-Reliance and Com-

plicity: Emerson's Ethics of Citizenship," in *A Political Companion to Ralph Waldo Emerson*, ed. Alan M. Levine and Daniel S. Malachuk (Lexington: University Press of Kentucky, 2011), 125–51; and Eric Beerbohm, *In Our Name: The Ethics of Democracy* (Princeton, NJ: Princeton University Press, 2012), chap. 9.

14. Baldwin, *No Name in the Street*, in *Collected Essays*, ed. Morrison, 430.

15. This, of course, parallels Aristotle's idea of ruling and being ruled in turn (*Politics*, trans. C. D. C. Reeve [Indianapolis: Hackett, 1998], 1279a8–10). Rotating citizenship, however, applies specifically to the sphere of civic action (as opposed to office holding); it is also a model most apt for ongoing struggles against large-scale injustice.

16. See Shannon Mariotti, *Thoreau's Democratic Withdrawal: Alienation, Participation, and Modernity* (Madison: University of Wisconsin Press, 2010).

17. *The Autobiography of Martin Luther King, Jr.*, ed. Clayborne Carson (New York: Warner, 1998), 137.

18. Ibid.

19. McWilliams, *Idea of Fraternity in America*, 96.

20. Baldwin, "The Discovery of What It Means to Be an American," in *Collected Essays*, ed. Morrison, 142.

21. Balfour, *Evidence of Things Not Said*, 27.

22. Shulman, *American Prophecy*, 134. See also Schlosser, "Socrates in a Different Key"; Bruce Baum, "James Baldwin's 'Discovery of What It Means to Be an American,'" in *Racially Writing the Republic: Racists, Race Rebels, and Transformations of American Identity* (Durham, NC: Duke University Press, 2009), 263–80; and Jeff Frank, "Reconstructing Deweyan Growth: The Significance of James Baldwin's Moral Psychology," *Education and Culture* 29, no. 2 (2013): 123–28.

23. James Baldwin, "The Nigger We Invent" (1969), in *The Cross of Redemption*, ed. Kenan, 91–92.

24. For an illuminating discussion of Baldwin in relation to the white paternalism of mid-twentieth-century American liberalism, see Rebecca Aanerud, "Now More Than Ever: James Baldwin and the Critique of White Liberalism," in *James Baldwin Now*, ed. Dwight McBride (New York: New York University Press, 1999), 58–65. For an account of some of the origins of liberalism's missionary impulse, see Jack Turner, "John Locke, Christian Mission, and Colonial America," *Modern Intellectual History* 8, no. 2 (2011): 267–97.

25. James Baldwin, "Many Thousands Gone," in *Collected Essays*, ed. Morrison, 34.

26. Baldwin, *No Name in the Street*, in *Collected Essays*, ed. Morrison, 377.

27. James Baldwin, "Review of *A Man's Life: An Autobiography* by Roger Wilkins" (1982), in *Cross of Redemption*, ed. Kenan, 288.

28. See ibid., 288–89; James Baldwin, "We Can Change the Country" (1963),

in *Cross of Redemption,* ed. Kenan, 50; and James Baldwin, "What Price Freedom?" (1964), in *Cross of Redemption,* ed. Kenan, 68.

29. Baldwin, "Down at the Cross," in *Collected Essays,* ed. Morrison, 322.

30. Baldwin, *The Fire Next Time,* passim; Baldwin, "Notes of a Native Son," in *Collected Essays,* ed. Morrison, 84; Balfour, *Evidence of Things Not Said,* 18, 75.

31. In Balfour's eloquent words, Baldwin thought "sustaining the dream of democracy entails appreciation of the fact that it has never been attempted, much less realized, in this country" (*Evidence of Things Not Said,* 29).

32. Charles W. Mills brilliantly criticizes the tendency of liberal theorists to explain racial domination in liberal polities as historical "anomalies" (see "The Racial Polity," in *Blackness Visible: Essays on Philosophy and Race,* by Mills [Ithaca, NY: Cornell University Press, 1998], 119–37).

33. See James Baldwin, Nathan Glazer, Sidney Hook, and Gunnar Myrdal, "Liberalism and the Negro: A Round-Table Discussion," *Commentary* 3, no. 37 (1964): 35. Podhoretz moderated this discussion. Baldwin himself noted the transformation of 1960s liberals into 1980s neoconservatives in *The Evidence of Things Not Seen* (1985; New York: Owl, 1995), 79. Cf. Aanerud, "Now More Than Ever," 66.

34. Baldwin, "Many Thousands Gone," in *Collected Essays,* ed. Morrison, 34.

35. Cf. Balfour, *Evidence of Things Not Said,* 17, 33, 95; Shulman, *American Prophecy,* 167.

36. Baldwin, "Many Thousands Gone," in *Collected Essays,* ed. Morrison, 34.

37. For insightful analysis of Baldwin on the relationship between embodiment and moral life, see Shulman, *American Prophecy,* 132–34, 139, 145, 151.

38. Baldwin, "Many Thousands Gone," in *Collected Essays,* ed. Morrison, 34.

39. James Baldwin, "Fifth Avenue, Uptown: A Letter from Harlem," in *Nobody Knows My Name,* in *Collected Essays,* ed. Morrison, 177.

40. Cf. Balfour, *Evidence of Things Not Said,* 88.

41. James Baldwin, "The Uses of the Blues" (1964), in *Cross of Redemption,* ed. Kenan, 62.

42. Cf. Schlosser, "Socrates in a Different Key," in this volume.

43. For an academic elaboration of this point of view, see Stephan Thernstrom and Abigail Thernstrom, *America in Black and White: One Nation, Indivisible* (New York: Touchstone, 1997). For a devastating critique of it, see Michael C. Dawson, "Twisting History: *America in Black and White* by Stephan Thernstrom and Abigail Thernstrom," *CommonQuest* (Winter 1998): 54–57.

44. James Baldwin, "The American Dream and the American Negro" (1965), in *Collected Essays,* ed. Morrison, 716. Cf. Lisa A. Beard, "'Flesh of Their Flesh, Bone of Their Bone': James Baldwin's Racial Politics of Boundedness," *Contemporary Political Theory* 15, no. 4 (2016): 378–98.

45. James Baldwin, "Blacks and Jews" (1985), in *Cross of Redemption*, ed. Kenan, 147–48.

46. Eddie S. Glaude Jr. makes a compelling case for the substantive continuity of Baldwin's pre- and post-1965 political thought (*In a Shade of Blue: Pragmatism and the Politics of Black America* [Chicago: University of Chicago Press, 2007], 11–16). Cf. Nikhil Pal Singh, *Black Is a Country: Race and the Unfinished Struggle for Democracy* (Cambridge: Harvard University Press, 2004), 56, 185.

47. James Baldwin, "Fifth Avenue, Uptown," in *Collected Essays*, ed. Morrison, 177. Notwithstanding his sensitivity to sexuality, Baldwin was often guilty of masculinism (see Balfour, *Evidence of Things Not Said*, 50–55).

48. See Baldwin's late essays "Notes on the House of Bondage" (1980) and "The Price of the Ticket" (1985) in *Collected Essays*, ed. Morrison, 798–807, 830–42.

49. For the full context, see Amy Fox, "Battle in Black and White," *New York Times*, March 26, 2006; and Samuel Zipp, *The Rise and Fall of Urban Renewal in Cold War New York* (Oxford: Oxford University Press, 2010), 435n63.

50. Baldwin, "Fifth Avenue, Uptown," in *Collected Essays*, ed. Morrison, 175.

51. Ibid.

52. Ibid., 176.

53. Baldwin, "From *Nationalism, Colonialism, and the United States*," in *Cross of Redemption*, ed. Kenan, 14.

54. Cf. Baldwin, "Fifth Avenue, Uptown," in *Collected Essays*, ed. Morrison, 178–79; Baldwin, "Blacks and Jews," in *Cross of Redemption*, ed. Kenan, 149–50.

55. Balfour neatly summarizes Baldwin's critique of the ideal of inclusion: "The idea that moral progress involves the inclusion of black Americans in an ever-expanding circle of people deserving of respect or recognition leaves the center of the circle unexamined and preserves the assumption that the center contains some value worth having or emulating" (*Evidence of Things Not Said*, 127).

56. James Baldwin, "East River, Downtown: Postscript to a Letter from Harlem," in *Collected Essays*, ed. Morrison, 183; Baldwin, "Down at the Cross," in *Collected Essays*, ed. Morrison, 340.

57. Baldwin, "Down at the Cross," in *Collected Essays*, ed. Morrison, 342.

58. James Baldwin, *The Devil Finds Work: An Essay* (1976), in *Collected Essays*, ed. Morrison, 566–67.

59. James Baldwin, "Freaks and the American Ideal of Manhood" (1985), in *Collected Essays*, ed. Morrison, 815–16. Cf. Marc Lombardo, "James Baldwin's Philosophical Critique of Sexuality," *Journal of Speculative Philosophy* 23, no. 1 (2009): 45–49.

60. James Baldwin, "The White Problem" (1964), in *Cross of Redemption*, ed. Kenan, 77; Baldwin, "What Price Freedom?," in *Cross of Redemption*, ed. Kenan, 68.

61. James Baldwin, "An Open Letter to My Sister Angela Y. Davis" (1970), in *Cross of Redemption*, ed. Kenan, 210.

62. James Baldwin, "A Talk to Teachers" (1963), in *Collected Essays*, ed. Morrison, 679.

63. Thomas Jefferson to Samuel Kercheval, July 12, 1816, in *Jefferson: Political Writings*, ed. Joyce Appleby and Terence Ball (Cambridge: Cambridge University Press, 1999), 215–16. Cf. Jefferson to James Madison, September 6, 1789, ibid., 593–98.

64. Thomas Paine, *Common Sense and Related Writings*, ed. Thomas P. Slaughter (1776; Boston: Bedford/St. Martin's, 2001), 113. Cf. Paine, *Rights of Man*, ed. Eric Foner (1790; New York: Penguin, 1985), pt. 2, chap. 4.

65. James Baldwin, "A Question of Identity," in *Collected Essays*, ed. Morrison, 100.

66. Baldwin, "Down at the Cross," in *Collected Essays*, ed. Morrison, 314.

67. Baldwin, "Nobody Knows My Name," in *Collected Essays*, ed. Morrison, 208; Baldwin, "Down at the Cross," in *Collected Essays*, ed. Morrison, 347.

68. Baldwin, "Down at the Cross," in *Collected Essays*, ed. Morrison, 347.

69. Baldwin, "Talk to Teachers," in *Collected Essays*, ed. Morrison, 679.

70. On the democratic promise of political action by undocumented workers, see Victoria Hattam, *In the Shadow of Race: Jews, Latinos, and Immigrant Politics in the United States* (Chicago: University of Chicago Press, 2007), 160–68; and Cristina Beltrán, *The Trouble with Unity: Latino Politics and the Quest for Identity* (Oxford: Oxford University Press, 2010), chap. 5.

71. My model resembles Jefferson's "ward system," through which, he believed, periodic reconstitution would best occur (Letter to Samuel Kercheval, 216–17).

72. Balfour, *Evidence of Things Not Said*, 112.

73. James Baldwin, "Faulkner and Desegregation," in in *Collected Essays*, ed. Morrison, 209.

74. Put in a Lockean idiom, Baldwinian reconstitution entails not just the reconstitution of government but the reconstitution of *society*. In Locke's political theory, property is conceived as a natural institution that comes into existence prior to the constitution of either political society or government. Baldwin's radicalism exceeds Locke's in that he subjects the "natural institution" of property to political negotiation. This difference between Locke and Baldwin partly arises out of Locke's questionable assumption that any pauper could find untilled land and create property by mixing his labor with it. Locke could make this assumption because vast amounts of land were available for appropriation in England's North American colonies (albeit at the expense of Native Americans, whom Locke did not appropriately recognize). The citizens of Baldwin's Harlem could not "go west" and create wealth. From their perspective, politically insulated property rights

functioned to preserve a distribution of wealth that abridged their freedom and was the ill-begotten product of their ancestors' unpaid labor (Locke, *Two Treatises of Government*, ed. Peter Laslett, student ed. [1690; Cambridge: Cambridge University Press, 988], II: chap. 5). See also Jimmy Casas Klausen, "Room Enough: America, Natural Liberty, and Consent in Locke's *Second Treatise*," *Journal of Politics* 69, no. 3 (2007): 760–69.

75. Baldwin, "Letter to Angela Davis," in *Cross of Redemption*, ed. Kenan, 210; cf. Baldwin, "What Price Freedom?," in *Cross of Redemption*, ed. Kenan, 71.

76. James Baldwin, "A Letter to Prisoners" (1982), in *Cross of Redemption*, ed. Kenan, 213.

77. Cheryl I. Harris, "Whiteness as Property," *Harvard Law Review* 106, no. 8 (1993): 1736. C. B. Macpherson points out, however, that the right to exclude is essential to only one particular species of property: private property. Common property does not necessarily entail the right to exclude; in fact, it entails the right not to be excluded. Macpherson advocates the reconceptualization of property so that it entails both an exclusive right to "consumable property" and a civic right to "some minimum share in the means of life." I suspect that Baldwin would sympathize with Macpherson's reconceptualization. At the same time, I frame Baldwin's politics of redistribution as a form of proprietary divestment because this framing is more consistent with his language of "surrender" (Macpherson, "The Meaning of Property" and "Liberal-Democracy and Property," in *Property: Mainstream and Critical Positions*, ed. C. B. Macpherson [Toronto: University of Toronto Press, 1978], 1–13, 199–207).

78. Baldwin, "Letter to Angela Davis," in *Cross of Redemption*, ed. Kenan, 210.

79. Baldwin, "What Price Freedom?," in *Cross of Redemption*, ed. Kenan, 70.

80. Baldwin, "My Dungeon Shook," in *Collected Essays*, ed. Morrison, 294.

81. George Kateb, "Democratic Individuality and the Meaning of Rights," in *Liberalism and the Moral Life*, ed. Nancy Rosenblum (Cambridge: Harvard University Press, 1989), 188; Milan Kundera, *The Unbearable Lightness of Being*, trans. Michael Henry Heim (New York: Harper and Row, 1984).

82. Baldwin, "Down at the Cross," in *Collected Essays*, ed. Morrison, 336.

83. James Baldwin, "Black English: A Dishonest Argument" (1980), in *Cross of Redemption*, ed. Kenan, 128. See also Beard, "'Flesh of Their Flesh, Bone of Their Bone,'" 13.

84. See Judith Shklar, "Positive Liberty, Negative Liberty in the United States" (1980), trans. Stanley Hoffman, in *Redeeming American Political Thought*, ed. Hoffman and Dennis F. Thompson (Chicago: University of Chicago Press, 1998), 111–26.

85. On the idea of effectual freedom, see Amartya Sen, *The Idea of Justice* (Cambridge: Harvard University Press, 2009), 19, 225–38, 253–60, 270–71,

286–90, 295–309, 370–71; and Martha C. Nussbaum, *Creating Capabilities: The Human Development Approach* (Cambridge: Harvard University Press, 2011), chap. 2.

86. These two principles parallel the principles of "truth and tenderness" animating Emerson's ideal of friendship. For a discussion of this ideal's political significance, see Jason Scorza, "Liberal Citizenship and Civic Friendship," *Political Theory* 32, no. 1 (2004): 85–108.

87. Declaration of Independence (1776), in *Jefferson: Political Writings*, 102. Baldwin alludes to the Declaration in "Nobody Knows My Name," in *Collected Essays*, ed. Morrison, 208: "Any honest examination of the national life proves how far we are from the standard of human freedom with which we began. The recovery of that standard demands of everyone who loves this country a hard look at himself, for the greatest achievements must begin somewhere, and they always begin with the person."

88. Baldwin, "The White Problem," in *Cross of Redemption*, ed. Kenan, 72–79.

89. At the same time, as both Balfour and Baum point out, Baldwin thinks that America has an exceptional opportunity to realize multiracial democracy, which in his eyes would be a monumental historical achievement (Balfour, *Evidence of Things Not Said*, 136–37; Baum, "Baldwin's 'Discovery,'" 274–76).

90. As explained by Shulman in *American Prophecy*, 148–51.

91. Cf. Martin Luther King, Jr., "Letter from Birmingham Jail" (1963), in *Why We Can't Wait* (1964; New York: Signet Classic, 2000), 74: "Time itself is neutral; it can be used either destructively or constructively."

92. Baldwin, "My Dungeon Shook," in *Collected Essays*, ed. Morrison, 294.

93. Baldwin, "Black English," in *Cross of Redemption*, ed. Kenan, 129.

94. Baldwin, "From *Nationalism, Colonialism, and the United States*," 15. Cf. James Baldwin, "In Search of a Majority: An Address," in *Collected Essays*, ed. Morrison, 220–21.

95. Baldwin, "The White Man's Guilt" (1965), in *Collected Essays*, ed. Morrison, 722–23.

96. Ibid., 722. Cf. Balfour, *Evidence of Things Not Said*, chap. 2.

97. Baldwin, "The White Man's Guilt," in *Collected Essays*, ed. Morrison, 725.

98. Baldwin, "Down at the Cross," in *Collected Essays*, ed. Morrison, 346. For an extended analysis of Baldwin's figuration of citizens as lovers, see Marshall, *City on the Hill from Below*, chap. 4.

99. This is a variation of the paradox of republican founding addressed by Rousseau in his discussion of "the Legislator." See *On the Social Contract*, in *Jean-Jacques Rousseau: The Basic Political Writings*, trans. Donald A. Cress (Indianapolis: Hackett, 1987), bk. 2, chap. 7.

100. Baldwin, "In Search of a Majority," in *Collected Essays*, ed. Morrison,

215–16, 221. Cf. Balfour, *Evidence of Things Not Said*, 135–39; Baum, "Baldwin's 'Discovery,'" 269.

101. Baldwin, "In Search of a Majority," in *Collected Essays*, ed. Morrison, 216.

102. On rhetoric's essential role in democracy, see Danielle S. Allen, *Talking to Strangers: Anxieties of Citizenship since "Brown v. Board of Education"* (Chicago: University of Chicago Press, 2004), chap. 10; Bryan Garsten, *Saving Persuasion: A Defense of Rhetoric and Judgment* (Cambridge: Harvard University Press, 2006), esp. introduction and chap. 6; David Bromwich, "Moral Imagination," *Raritan* 27, no. 4 (2008): 4–33; and Melvin L. Rogers, "The People, Rhetoric, and Affect: On the Political Force of Du Bois's *The Souls of Black Folk*," *American Political Science Review* 106, no. 1 (2012): 188–203.

103. Shulman, *American Prophecy*, 6, 132, 30. See also George Shulman, "Thinking Authority Democratically: Prophetic Practices, White Supremacy, and Democratic Politics," *Political Theory* 36, no. 5 (2008): 708–34.

104. Ralph Waldo Emerson, "The American Scholar" (1837), in *Essays and Lectures*, ed. Joel Porte (New York: Library of America, 1983), 63.

105. James Baldwin, "The Artist's Struggle for Integrity" (1963), in *Cross of Redemption*, ed. Kenan, 47.

106. Emerson, "Self-Reliance," in *Essays: First Series* (1841), in *Essays and Lectures*, 262.

107. Ibid.

108. Baldwin, "Nothing Personal," in *Collected Essays*, ed. Morrison, 697.

109. Baldwin, "My Dungeon Shook," in *Collected Essays*, ed. Morrison, 293.

110. Baldwin et al., "Liberalism and the Negro," 35.

111. Ibid., 32.

112. As he said in "The White Man's Guilt," white Americans fall into the "stunning and intricate trap of believing that they deserve . . . their comparative safety and that black people, therefore, need only do as white people do to rise where white people now are" (in *Collected Essays*, ed. Morrison, 724).

113. Ibid., 723.

114. For another remarkable instance of Baldwin speaking in the voice of his ancestors, see "The American Dream and the American Negro," in *Collected Essays*, ed. Morrison, 715: "I am speaking very seriously, and this is not an overstatement: I picked cotton, I carried it to market, I built the railroads under someone else's whip for nothing. For nothing."

115. Baldwin, "Down at the Cross," in *Collected Essays*, ed. Morrison, 311–12.

116. I explain this idea of moral equality in "Self-Reliance and Complicity: Emerson's Ethics of Citizenship," 126–27.

117. Baldwin, "My Dungeon Shook," in *Collected Essays*, ed. Morrison, 293.

118. Baldwin, "The Price of the Ticket," in *Collected Essays*, ed. Morrison, 841.

119. Baldwin, "The White Man's Guilt," in *Collected Essays*, ed. Morrison, 722–23.

120. Cf. Shulman, *American Prophecy*, 148–51.

121. Baldwin, "The White Problem," in *Cross of Redemption*, ed. Kenan, 73.

122. Baldwin, "Nothing Personal," in *Collected Essays*, ed. Morrison, 701.

123. Baldwin, "Fifth Avenue, Uptown," in *Collected Essays*, ed. Morrison, 179.

124. See James Baldwin, Emile Capouya, Lorraine Hansberry, Nat Hentoff, Langston Hughes, and Alfred Kazin, "The Negro in American Culture," *Cross Currents* 11, no. 2 (1961): 205.

125. Baldwin, "My Dungeon Shook," in *Collected Essays*, ed. Morrison, 294: "We can make America what America must become."

126. Baldwin, "Notes of a Native Son," in *Collected Essays*, ed. Morrison, 84.

127. Baldwin, "Sidney Poitier," in *Cross of Redemption*, ed. Kenan, 183.

128. Jefferson, Letter to Samuel Kercheval, 215–16.

129. Baldwin, "As Much Truth as One Can Bear" (1962), in *Cross of Redemption*, ed. Kenan, 29.

130. On the ways certain "keywords" in American politics mediate conflict, see Daniel Rodgers, *Contested Truths: Keywords in American Politics since Independence* (Cambridge: Harvard University Press, 1987).

131. Paine, *Common Sense*, 113.

IV

Violence and Vision

12

James Baldwin on Violence and Disavowal

Lisa Beard

We are tired of forgiving people because they most assuredly *do* know what they do.

—Brittney Cooper, *In Defense of Black Rage*

It is fitting that in national discourse surrounding police killings and related Black Lives Matter protests, so many reporters and activists have turned to James Baldwin to interpret contemporary racial politics and summon people toward political action. Baldwin, so relentless at confronting "white innocence" in his time, offers a vocabulary about violence and disavowal that aligns with and enunciates Black Lives Matter interventions in important ways.

In Baldwin's account, white violence is not only monstrous but also denied, hidden behind national stories of civic virtue and myths of black criminality. The contemporary moment in US racial politics—from protests in the wake of Trayvon Martin's death to protests in Ferguson and Baltimore—has been described rightly by organizers and writers in the public press as a particularly Baldwinian moment: they call it "The Fire This Time."[1] With this language, they invoke Baldwin's 1963 best seller, *The Fire Next Time.*[2]

Baldwin's call in *Fire* is urgent and prophetic. His proposed political actors are small in number and linked across lines of race: they may be able to "end the racial nightmare" if they, "like lovers, insist on, or create, the consciousness of the others."[3] Baldwin's political actor is one who intimately struggles with and on behalf of society and shows society that which it has disowned.[4] Some of Baldwin's contemporaries were frustrated that his political provocations did not translate clearly into policy but such a critique misses Baldwin's choice to take direct aim at the myths and disavowals that animate certain racial ideologies.[5] Baldwin demands a reckoning with the historical scope of antiblack violence in the United States and a dismantling of whiteness itself.

Fifty years later, activists in the contemporary movement for black lives have in many ways taken up Baldwin's call. They have constructed and successfully circulated an interpretive framework that connects police killings to each other (they are not isolated events), connects them to other forms of antiblack violence, and connects them to histories of antiblack racism. The message "Black Lives Matter" was conceptualized and launched in 2013 by Alicia Garza, Patrisse Cullors, and Opal Tometi after Trayvon Martin's death and George Zimmerman's acquittal.[6] As Alicia Garza explains, the message and "movement project" was created as "an ideological and political intervention in a world where Black lives are systematically and intentionally targeted for demise."[7] Against legacies of antiblack racism, Black Lives Matter is a "love letter" to black people.[8] It is also, in Eddie Glaude's words, a "political provocation"—a call to action for black people and their allies, and a political demand aimed at those who are inured to and complicit in black disposability.[9] The message calls attention to its own negative corollary in US racial politics—what political theorist Melvin Rogers calls the "norm of Black devaluation," what political theorist Stephen Marshall calls "black fungibility," and what scholar-activist Ruth Wilson Gilmore calls "premature death."[10]

As the contemporary record attests, returning to Baldwin's political thought and the intimate style of his interventions is important at the current juncture. Baldwin helps illuminate the role of white disavowal in dominant accounts of racialized violence and reinvests white subjectivity with political responsibility. As George Shulman argues, it was Baldwin who introduced disavowal and acknowledgment as an "idiom" to analyze politics and its ethical dimension. For Baldwin, the problem is "not quite ignorance, but the 'innocence' of whites who do not want to know, or who disavow what they already know, about racial injustice, the conduct of the state acting in their name, the humanity of the other."[11] Disavowal is a denial of what one indeed knows, and is thus an avoidance of the ethical responsibilities that come with that knowledge. As a "fantastic system of evasions," innocence itself is the crime.[12] In a context of systemic state and civilian violence against black people, Baldwin shows that white people's active participation and/or silent innocence is thick, heavy with history, and willfully enacted in the present moment.[13]

Baldwin is also useful to contemporary racial politics because he insists on a historically rooted and multifaceted account of antiblack violence and assists in keeping this lens wide under the narrowing forces of political messaging. Baldwin not only attends to police violence but also reminds us how a focus on police and extralegal killings alone understates the degree to which black lives have been impacted by antiblack violence. In *Fire,* he bears witness to how his peers in Harlem are drinking and fighting in hallways or streets, are "ruined" in military service, or "carried off to jail." He describes the "incessant and gratuitous humiliation and danger one encountered every working day, all day long."[14] He accounts for young people's suicides, for street fights, and for "an indestructible aunt rewarded for years of hard labor by a slow, agonizing death in a terrible small room."[15] For Baldwin, gun violence, drugs, self-hate, and even hyperreligiosity are all manifestations of antiblack violence, and all of these are produced through American innocence.[16]

We can read Baldwin today for help in deciphering the underlying investments and disavowals in public discussions about racial violence. One of the things that becomes evident is the durability of a "violence versus nonviolence" framework between Baldwin's time and the current moment. This framework deeply structured dominant political discourse surrounding Black Power Mobilizations in 1963 and has surrounded mobilizations in Ferguson and Baltimore in 2014–2015, in both cases distorting the ongoing violence against black communities and the meanings of black political action. Baldwin's own interventions into this framework offer important theoretical resources. He disrupts the ways in which dominant conceptual frameworks portray black protests as unreasonable, violent, unprincipled, inappropriate, and deviant. He rejects white enactments of spatial, affective, and epistemological separation from black lives and black embodiment.

And he illuminates the boundaries of political action against racialized violence: the invitations to be in solidarity, the reinvestments in "innocence," and the violent disavowals.

In this chapter, I pair a CBS interview of James Baldwin just days after the Birmingham Children's Crusade in May 1963 with a CNN interview of community organizer Deray McKesson during the April 2015 Baltimore protests after the death of Freddie Gray Jr. In the 1963 interview, Baldwin refuses a paradigm in which black-led freedom struggles and violence against black people are imagined to be separate and distant from his white, Los Angeles–based television host. Baldwin rejects a framework in which black freedom struggles must bear the questions of "violence versus nonviolence" and in which the legitimacy of black people's political demands are jeopardized by these questions. In the second half of the chapter, I bring Baldwin's interventions to bear on the 2015 interview in order to illuminate how dominant American political discourse attempts to depoliticize race by shifting the site of violence from state practices to black communities themselves.

Basis of Solidarity

Baldwin and activists in the contemporary movement for black lives call into question the very identities and social systems in which black lives are conceptualized as disposable and interracial solidarity is foreclosed.[17] Their political lessons operate on both ethical and affective registers. Although their projects *do* summon nonblack people to identify with (and as I will discuss, actively support) the struggle, it is not to be out of pity, sympathy, or charity—but out of solidarity, a sense of shared freedom, and a concept I call boundness.

In his interventions into US racial politics in the 1960s, Baldwin calls for interracial solidarity by deploying a concept of boundness—a notion that people's lives are co-constituted and their freedom is bound together across racial lines. In Baldwin's work, white and black people—even though they have been subjected to centuries of racist laws, policies, ideologies, and other forms of violence that encourage each group to think of themselves as different and separate—are literally bound (by blood) and morally bound together. Using geographic, temporal, and kinship narratives, Baldwin invokes boundness as a political strategy to trouble forms of historical amnesia and to compel white people to see their own responsibility for ending antiblack racism. Baldwin refuses the contemporary language of "race relations" because he rejects corresponding notions of discrete groups and insists that the history of race-making in the United States is one of intimate violence and disavowal.[18] As such, Baldwin argues, confronting racism must be an intimate political endeavor.

Today, Black Lives Matter cofounders articulate a notion of boundness in their work. In her essay "A Herstory of the #BlackLivesMatter Movement," cofounder Alicia Garza invokes a related basis of identification and solidarity for nonblack people. She invokes ethical obligation through familial language, explaining that "when Black people cry out in defense of our lives, which are uniquely, systematically, and savagely targeted by the state, we are asking you, our family, to stand with us in affirming Black lives." Garza explains that "our collective futures" (across lines of race) depend on nonblack people's active and "unwavering" solidarities with black people "in defense of our humanity" and that black people's freedom is and will be transformational for everyone: that "when Black people get free, everybody gets free."[19]

Garza extends a profoundly generous invitation. And yet, dominant media coverage, public commentary, and silence are not the "active and unwavering" solidarity that Garza calls for. Instead, they tend to obscure, misinterpret, or ignore central messages from the movement. In the face of contemporary activism, many white people enact a spectacular disavowal of racial power and racialized violence and participate in the continued devaluation of black lives—for example, by sending money to police officer Darren Wilson, interpreting and condemning black political action as pathological, insisting that racism is "over," or tuning out.[20] There is a clear invitation in Garza's essay and elsewhere in the broader movement to understand one's freedom as deeply linked to the fight against racial injustice and to act accordingly. I understand Garza's "active solidarities" to mean ongoing political actions and political movements that work to fundamentally transform structures of power. Garza calls for solidarities that are not simply a pledge or an ethos but are deeply connected to structural and cultural transformation.

James Baldwin in 1963 on "Violence"

In early May 1963, just days after the Children's Crusade in Birmingham that culminated in police use of dogs and high-pressure water hoses against protesting youth, James Baldwin was interviewed on CBS news.[21] At this time, Baldwin was at the peak of his popularity. *The Fire Next Time* had been listed as a best seller since late January, bringing Baldwin national and international attention. That month, Baldwin had been traveling on the West Coast for the Congress of Racial Equality (CORE), warning white people of the price they would pay for not facing racial politics with honesty and urgency. In his speeches, Baldwin intervened in regional patterns of disavowal—that is, a narrative of northern or West Coast racial innocence—insisting that race dynamics in the North were *not* unrelated to those in Birmingham. Also that month, PBS filmed footage for the documentary *Take This Hammer,* in which Baldwin analyzes race politics in San Francisco, and on May 17, Baldwin's face appeared on the cover of *Time Magazine,* with the magazine's lead article on Birmingham followed by an article by Baldwin.[22] On May 24, Attorney General Robert F. Kennedy invited Baldwin to organize a "quiet, off-the-record" gathering of prominent black public intellectuals, organizers, and artists to discuss contemporary racial politics.[23] Although Baldwin understood himself as a witness, and not a spokesperson, he was in high demand as an authority on US race politics.

By this time, it had been eight years since the brutal murder of Emmett Till in Mississippi and the launching of the Montgomery Bus Boycott after years of black women's organizing against sexual assault of black women by white men.[24] This was two years since the first Freedom Riders sponsored by CORE and the Student Nonviolent Coordinating Committee (SNCC) were beaten and firebombed by mobs as they attempted to desegregate interstate travel. As civil rights organizers and activists escalated their direct action campaigns across the US South, activists were maimed, sexually assaulted, jailed, threatened, and murdered by law enforcement agents, civilians, and vigilante groups. Television and newspaper images of burning buses, white mobs, and attack dogs reached national audiences, and President Kennedy was being pulled in to engage civil rights issues under mounting political pressure. That spring marked Malcolm X's foray into the national civil rights arena, and mainstream press presented Martin Luther King Jr.'s nonviolent strategies contra a "new" and militant black politic in northern urban centers.[25] At the time of Baldwin's interview, national attention was pivoted toward Birmingham, where King had been jailed three weeks earlier during antisegregation protests and where the May 2–5 Children's Crusade was met with fire hoses, police dogs, and almost three thousand arrests. It is in this context that we must read Baldwin's account of racial violence.

In the interview, the white interviewer opens by referencing Martin Luther King Jr. as dedicated to nonviolence as a "tactic and a principle." He then asks Baldwin: "Do you think nonviolence will be the pattern, or are we likely to have violence?" Baldwin answers by rejecting the framework in which black freedom struggles must bear the questions of violence and nonviolence and in which the legitimacy of black people's political demands is jeopardized by those questions. In other words, Baldwin rejects a framework in which black political action is imagined as the site where violence may or may not occur. Baldwin asks how many people the reporter knows "who are, really, nonviolent? How many children do you know who are nonviolent?" After provoking the reporter to scan his own white life world for people totally committed to nonviolence (a task in which the reporter, if he is honest, will largely fail), Baldwin moves to a wider frame. He continues: "The history of the civilization that you want me to imitate is a history of violence, of bloodshed. Whether it becomes violent or nonviolent, I repeat, depends on you."

"The civilization" Baldwin invokes—what he in other speeches calls "the Western world"—is defined by violence. In "On Being White . . . and Other Lies," Baldwin writes that "white men—from Norway, for example, where they were 'Norwegians'—became white by slaughtering the cattle, poisoning the wells, torching the houses, massacring Native Americans, raping Black women."[26] The Western world and white racial identity are irrevocably tied to oppression—in that they are *defined by* and *generated through* violence. That civilization projects its own violence onto black people, indigenous people, immigrants—and onto antiracist freedom struggles.[27] Baldwin's interviewer obscures both the long-term and intensely acute, deadly, sexualized and racialized violence faced by civil rights organizers and black communities. Baldwin returns the question of violence and nonviolence to "the Western world," giving back the responsibility for violence to that civilization. Baldwin's refusal to act as native informant brings into relief how white liberals in the civil rights and post–civil rights era need black people to mediate and articulate anxiety about their own identity and about black political action.

Part of what is at stake in the interview is the location of the question of violence versus nonviolence. In the first part of the interview, when the interviewer asks Baldwin whether *Baldwin* thinks black political action will be "nonviolent" or "violent," he positions Baldwin as a representative of black people. In this framework, the questions of "violence versus nonviolence" are black people's responsibility to answer. The interviewer invites Baldwin to align with whiteness by criticizing black "violence." Baldwin intervenes: white people actually produced this violence; it is their fault and their responsibility. White people across the country are responsible for the fact that white people have killed children in Birmingham, and they are responsible for producing the conditions to which black freedom struggles respond. Black political action—what the host calls "violence"—is not gratuitous. It aims to change political conditions and end white supremacy. Violence, Baldwin says, defines this civilization, and whether or not black political struggle becomes "violent or nonviolent" depends on white people because that struggle would not be necessary if racial justice were realized. In this move, Baldwin reinvests the interviewer with responsibility and animates him as a political actor who is completely implicated in the unfolding struggles for racial justice. In Baldwin's reframing, the interviewer and the civilization he represents face a choice to change the conditions and meet the demands of civil rights and Black Power activists.

The reporter fails to follow Baldwin into a different framework. Instead, he presses forward in his own framework, asking Baldwin to be representative and predictive. The reviewer reveals his underlying assumption: that Baldwin is fixated on a future of "violence," organized by black political leaders. He summarizes: "I take it that you are convinced in your mind that what is termed generally the 'new militant Negro' that kind of leadership will dominate rather than the . . . if you will . . ." As the reporter trails off, Baldwin rejects the paradigm a second time:

Let's take [that question] out of that extraordinary vacuum where we've had it all these years. It is not a matter of a militant Negro leadership. It is a matter of changing the attitudes of this country. Martin Luther King is a great and heroic man, but he cannot do for you what only you can do; it is your country too. What is happening to Martin, for example, what is happening to all those children in Birmingham is being done in your name. You have no right, *no right* not to know that. And you have no right to pretend that Birmingham is in another country. It is not, it is right here in Los Angeles, it is in New York, it is in Detroit. *This is THE* national problem, it has never been a regional problem.

In this exchange, Baldwin refuses the paradigm that black-led freedom struggles and violence against black people are somehow apart from, outside of, or merely observable by the television host. In Baldwin's account, as black freedom struggles unfold, white liberals think they are just "watching" something that is out of control (out of *their* control), and out of their sphere. It is as if they are "innocent" spectators, in danger and at the whim of black political choices. They fail to take responsibility for black death and obscure the ways in which black political action is seriously circumscribed by state power.

When Baldwin invokes King here, he references the host's own deployment of King at the start of the interview. Whereas the interviewer used King as an authority figure to invest nonviolent black political action with moral authority over "violence," Baldwin says that King cannot save white people from their unique responsibility to address and change racism in the United States. In doing so, Baldwin pulls the interviewer and white people out from behind the image of King or the notion of black militancy and into the political arena.

Baldwin flatly refuses a paradigm in which the host's world in Los Angeles is at all separate from violence in Birmingham. He implicates the host as being equally and deeply a part of the very issues that Baldwin has been asked to represent. In doing so, Baldwin articulates a particular way of understanding the relationship between people across lines of race (black/white) and racialized region (the US West Coast/the US South). He rejects the interviewer's performed distance from Birmingham, and the concomitant notion that West Coast and northern spaces are innocent. Whereas white liberal racism relies on a concept of regional (and also temporal) distance to disavow racism and responsibility, Baldwin rejects the notion that Birmingham is some unimaginably distant place where all the violence against black people and black political action exist and the notion that Los Angeles is free of both. Baldwin asserts that the reporter *does* know his own boundness to white and black people in Birmingham—he says the reporter "has no right to pretend that Birmingham is in another country." *Pretending* not to know implies an underlying and disavowed knowledge instead of an actual lack of knowledge.

To be clear, Baldwin is not arguing that white and black people in different regions have *separate* issues that are linked or connected. Instead, white people's lives in Los Angeles and violence against black children in Birmingham are co-constituted and bound together. Baldwin underscores that the violence done to black people is being done *in the name of* and quite literally for, white people. Police and extralegal violence against communities of color have historically protected white communities and white power structures. White people's lives and the social and political world they inhabit are simultaneously produced and protected by deadly violence against black people, against other people of color, and against indigenous people. Baldwin insists that it is morally impermissible for white people to "not know" that the violence is done in their name.

The Fire This Time

Fifty years later, police killings of black people and related protests are in many ways the "Fire Next Time" that Baldwin warned of in 1963. Activists today inherit a project charted by Baldwin and other forebears to confront and undo white disavowal: white disavowal of racial power and racialized violence, white disavowal of what is in fact the nonnegotiable value of black lives, white people's disavowal of their responsibility for black experiences of violence and responsibility to black people. On one level, public actions within the contemporary movement for black lives form a series of public ruptures, profound breaks in the normalization of black death. Alongside embodied public demonstrations around the country, the repetition/proliferation of images in social media—as in the posting and reposting of videos of Walter Scott's death in Charleston or of the police officer attack of Dajerria Becton in McKinney, Texas—functions as evidence. These are strategic deployments against white disavowal.

Within these ruptures, activists teach ethics. They demand not only knowledge of, but also care and concern for, people whose lives are endangered or lost. Activists "orient us appropriately"—as Glaude puts it—demonstrating appropriate responses to black death. By "appropriate responses," I mean responses to patterns of death and destruction that reflect a deep caring and concern for people who are endangered or killed by racialized state violence and for those who have lost family members to that violence. Appropriate affective responses would be grief, pain, and anger, as opposed to disregard or a fixation on "property damage"—as in the news anchors' fixation on a burned CVS building and vehicle fires during their coverage of Freddie Gray's death.

On April 12, 2015, twenty-five-year-old Freddie Gray was arrested for alleged possession of an illegal switchblade and sustained what would be fatal spinal injuries from the Baltimore Police Department.[28] Over the previous ten months, organizers had lifted up police killings of Eric Garner, Michael Brown, and Tamir Rice as connected incidents, demanding attention to the ways in which police violence in black communities is epidemic, structural, and deeply rooted in histories of antiblack violence. The contemporary social movement responds to an increasingly militarized police force and their inherited "broken windows" and "quality of life" policies; the accelerating expansion and fatal reach of the prison system since the War on Drugs, justified through racially coded "get tough on crime" measures; and the cumulative effects of neoliberal social divestment atop 1960s and 1970s urban "renewal" policies.[29] By April 2015, activists had successfully circulated an interpretive framework to understand Freddie Gray's death as a part of a larger epidemic in racialized police killings. Interventions by #SayHerName addressing the erasure of black women and girls from national discourses on police violence were on the horizon.

On April 28, the day after Gray's funeral and in the midst of heightened protests and a citywide state of emergency, CNN news reporter Wolf Blitzer interviewed community organizer Deray McKesson. I am reading Blitzer not as a lone or unique voice but as participating in and, for my purposes, representative of a larger discourse of liberal exceptionalism and racial progress.

Blitzer had already reported on Baltimore events during the days prior to the interview. From the television studio on April 27, Blitzer commented on live footage of people entering and exiting a CVS store and a check-cashing business, narrating a story of "stealing," "looting," and "running." Blitzer concluded: "I don't know what's going on over there, but I don't remember seeing anything like this in the United States of America in a long time."[30] In fact, just four months earlier, Blitzer had expressed the same kind of disbelief when reporting on Ferguson, declaring: "It's hard for me to believe that in this day and age, 2014, so many years after Dr. Martin Luther King and the civil rights movement—we're seeing National Guard troops on the street to prevent this kind of violence. In this day and age, it's something I didn't think we'd be seeing again."[31] Here, we see not only a disavowal of the contemporary conditions of racial injustice and racial violence itself but also the use of civil rights struggles of the 1960s to delegitimize contemporary activism. Although Blitzer's teleology of racial progress and performed temporal distance from racism is part of the postracial ideology discussed at length by other scholars, what especially concerns me in the Baltimore interview is Blitzer's performance of spatial, epistemological, and affective distance from black embodiment and his construction of black political action as violent.[32]

In his April 28 interview with McKesson, Blitzer sits in the newsroom studio, and McKesson stands outside on a street in Baltimore in front of a metal barricade and several police vehicles.[33] Blitzer introduces McKesson as being in Baltimore as a part of a *"peaceful* protest" and begins by asking about McKesson's objectives in Baltimore. McKesson answers that he and others are there supporting protestors "on the ground" and are "continuing the movement." Despite protests over the previous months, police killings have continued, he explains, and thus the organizing has continued. McKesson links the Baltimore protests to a larger body of contemporary political struggle across the country. Protestors are confronting a corrupt system.

Blitzer then invokes a conceptual framework of "violence versus nonviolence" that structures each of his questions throughout the remainder of the interview. He interrupts McKesson's first answer about police violence, social movements, and corrupt systems with the qualifying question, "But you want peaceful protests, right?" He hides himself as the arbitrator and poses his question as if "peaceful versus violent" is an agreed-upon framework. Blitzer's frame of valid "peaceful protests" sets up an implied opposite—illegitimate "violent protests." Blitzer thus attempts to render the legitimacy of the movement and its demands contingent on activists conforming to his definition of "peaceful protests." Blitzer's move is also discursively coercive: He sets up a framework in which the validity of McKesson's entire account is contingent on McKesson's complicity with the frame of "peaceful protests."

Responding to the confinement of Blitzer's narrow question, McKesson agrees briefly—"Yes, for sure"—before inverting Blitzer's frame. In a move reminiscent of Baldwin's, McKesson upends the imagined site of violence and returns it to Blitzer. He emphasizes that the people who have been violent are the police: "We think about the three hundred people that have been killed this year alone—*that* is violence." But even as he intervenes, McKesson's answer nonetheless reveals how he is constrained by the framework of "violent versus nonviolent" protests. He explains that there has, unfortunately, been property damage and reminds Blitzer that there have been "many days of peaceful protests" in Baltimore and around the country.

Blitzer then lists statistics that include fifteen police injuries, two hundred arrests, and property damage ("144 vehicle fires" and "fifteen structure fires") as a reply to McKesson's reminder that three hundred people have been killed by the police since January 2015.[34] After listing these statistics, Blitzer presses McKesson with moralizing language, saying, "There's no excuse for that kind of violence, right?"

Blitzer's list contains a deadly logic. By invoking a list of police injuries, arrests, and vehicle and structure fires in this moment, he proposes a series of equivalences that we should understand as being rooted in the transatlantic slave trade and chattel slavery. In what Saidiya Hartman calls "the afterlife of slavery," the equation of lost property with lost lives evokes the status of black people as property, as comparable in value to material resources.[35] That "144 vehicle fires and fifteen structure fires" are more distressing to Blitzer than the deaths of black people underscores the ways in which white racial identity makes such a comparison even conceivable. McKesson has to explain that black lives are *lives*, and that human lives are not, under any circumstances, equivalent to material property. The deployment of fifteen police injuries in this exchange communicates that injury to representatives of the state are equally or more important than the life and death of Freddie Gray.

What I want to emphasize here is that Blitzer's project is not simply about pressuring McKesson to condemn the property damage; it is about trying to corral the meanings of black political action and grievances into a specific conceptual framework. Blitzer needs McKesson to endorse a framework in which black life—human life—is measured in terms of property. McKesson responds by rejecting this framework in which black lives are weighed against vehicles: "There's no excuse for the seven people that the Baltimore City Police Department has killed in the past year either, right?" At this point, Blitzer invokes what Baldwin calls racial innocence to disavow responsibility for devaluing black lives: "We're not making comparisons. Obviously we don't want anybody hurt." The membership in

Blitzer's first-person plural pronoun "we" is notably ambiguous, diverting personal accountability by summoning a group-level innocence, agreement, and good intention. In the context of the interview, Blitzer's "we" can mean Blitzer and the Baltimore cops, or himself and white America, or himself and McKesson. The ambiguity allows Blitzer to invoke different sources of authority in different moments. Blitzer's language of "hurt" distorts McKesson's statistics of police killings as if they were cases of minor and reparable injury rather than death, implying again that injury to police officers is comparable to the seven killings by the Baltimore City Police Department that year.

Blitzer continues: "I just want to hear you say that there should be peaceful protests, not violent protests, in the tradition of Dr. Martin Luther King." Blitzer now spells out explicit instructions, pushing McKesson to endorse "peaceful protests" and reject "violent protests" in order to solidify the framework. Just as the Los Angeles television host did with James Baldwin, Blitzer invokes Martin Luther King Jr. to authorize his project.[36] In this remarkable but also common move, Blitzer uses King to name and condemn many of the protests in Baltimore. He hides his investments in white supremacy behind an image of King. McKesson intervenes and refuses Blitzer's earlier statistics: "You *are* making a comparison. You are suggesting this idea that broken windows are worse than broken spines." Here, the metaphor of broken windows evokes James Q. Wilson's "broken windows theory" and the urban policing policies that it has generated since the 1980s. "Broken windows" also represents "property damage" in political action, and "broken spines" evokes the conditions of Freddie Gray's death, as well as other deaths at the hands of the police.[37] These paired metaphors appear twice more in the interview. It is as if McKesson has to teach Blitzer what death is—its permanence and significance, reminiscent of Baldwin's account that whiteness makes every effort to avoid facing mortality.[38] When Blitzer weighs lost black lives against vehicle fires, McKesson must intervene into this haunted arithmetic and clarify that black lives lost are *lost lives,* not lost property.

Blitzer ignores McKesson's response and invokes President Obama: "You agree, I assume, with President Obama who said just a few moments ago, 'There's no excuse for the violence that erupted yesterday. There's no excuse for the stealing. No excuse for the arson.' You agree with the President." (Here, Blitzer represents Obama's words as if they are a direct quote, although he is paraphrasing.) In his invocations of King and Obama, Blitzer removes authority and social questions from a multisite, multivocal social movement and public discourse and relocates them in finite figures who seem to be unquestionable authorities—here, introduced with titles of "Dr." and "President" and invoked commonly in "postracial" discourse. Further-more, in this kind of move, black people are imagined as a homogeneous group for whom a single member can serve as spokesperson.

McKesson explains to Blitzer that he understands that "pain manifests in different ways." He rereads what Blitzer calls "property damage" as em-bodied manifestations of "grieving" and "mourning."[39] McKesson retrieves public political action from the framework of "violence versus nonviolence" and opens a conversation about the magnitude of the pain that comes from losing people to police killings as well as losing loved ones to what Brian Klopotek, Brenda Lintinger, and John Barbry call "ordinary trauma"—the grinding and ongoing traumas of racism or colonialism over long periods of time.[40] McKesson, while in some ways positioning himself in this interview as a "peaceful protester," does claim a way of knowing and understanding multiple forms of political action and emotion. By "understanding," I mean relating to the pain itself, and recognizing emotions like pain and grief as both embodied and political. In the interview, Blitzer's failure to demon-strate grief for Freddie Gray is put into sharp relief. McKesson's account of other people's grief is instructive for Blitzer as a lesson in ethics and political emotions. However, Blitzer makes no indication that he is affected.

In his final comment, Blitzer invokes President Obama again, togeth-er with the family of Freddie Gray: "The president also said—President Obama—he said the violence *distracted* from the peaceful protests and distracted from the mourning that the family of Freddie Gray was seeking yesterday." Here, just as political theorist Michelle-Renée Smith observes in the aftermath of Michael Brown's death, loss itself becomes a private and individualized matter, and mourning is a process that belongs to Freddie Gray's family alone.[41] Only certain sites of grief are authorized, and state-sanctioned murder becomes a private matter to be mourned by surviving relatives. When the site of grief is a nuclear family instead of the public, the remedy is to console the family instead of changing society.

McKesson flips Blitzer's concept of "distraction," countering that dis-traction is not public protest; it is "when city officials get on T.V. and call black people in pain 'thugs.'" He says, "I think the 'unrest,' 'the uprising,' whatever you call it, is again a cry for justice here and a cry for justice across the country." By bracketing Blitzer's vocabulary ("the 'unrest,' the 'uprising,' whatever you call it") McKesson reveals the unsettledness of that vocabulary and renarrates the protests as a "cry for justice."

What is so stark in this interview is the enormous cognitive and affective gap between the two people. Blitzer maintains a location where he thinks he is far away from black people, black pain, and black death. He is nonetheless quite invested in how black pain and black death are read and interpreted. There is lot at stake: As Baldwin argues, a whole system of seeing and knowing—that is, ideas of black criminality, white innocence, and postracial ideology—would be at risk if white America were to genuinely face the violence and loss. Thus Blitzer's persistence, his repeated and nearly unchanging statements across the entire interview. He wants to interpret protests in Baltimore and elsewhere as unreasonable and violent, to locate the violence within black communities themselves. His anxiety represents a broader anxiety in US political culture and is underlined by a disavowed knowledge of his connection to the violence.

Even as Blitzer performs distance from black experiences and black pain, he also performs a careful intimacy with certain black people. Liberal white racial identity depends on the performance of both distance/separation from *and* intimacy with blackness. Just as Baldwin's interviewer needed Martin Luther King Jr. or Baldwin himself, Blitzer needs President Obama, Freddie Gray's family, King, and activists like McKesson to disavow enduring investments in white supremacist ideology and state violence. Blitzer is not actually interacting with Deray McKesson; he is interacting with a concept of McKesson. Perhaps even more so, he is interacting with his concept of what stands on the other side of McKesson: his imagination of black "violence" in Baltimore. McKesson is positioned here in a space between native informant (if he plays Blitzer's game, he legitimates the white liberal framework) and getting lumped in with the "thugs" causing the unrest (if he rejects the framework, refusing the "lesson" signified by King and Obama, then he is discredited). It is impossible to have an authentic conversation in these conditions: conditions of aggressive apathy, profound misreading, and coercive exchange.

McKesson ends his final statement by foregrounding the source of the pain—that "the police continue to terrorize people"—and another explication about the severity: "The terrorizing is actually deadly. Broken windows are not broken spines." McKesson ends by conveying a message for President Obama (and thus bypassing any further conversation with Blitzer): he hopes the president will "understan[d] the conditions that created the unrest and that continue the unrest." He ends with the finitude of death: that Freddie Gray, Tamir Rice, Aiyana Jones, or Mike Brown will "never see another day."

Intelligibility, Distance, and the Site of Violence

Although they are fifty years apart, the two interviews have striking parallels. Both interviews occurred in the midst of heightened discourse in US racial politics due to highly publicized direct action campaigns, in the midst of a rupture in the insular sheen of white consciousness. Just a week before Baldwin's interview, the protesting youth in Birmingham were met with attack dogs and high-pressure fire hoses from the Birmingham Police Department. National and international attention was turned toward race politics in the South, and with the rise of Black Power organizing in northern and western urban areas came heated debates about militancy versus nonviolent civil disobedience tactics in black freedom struggles. The April 2015 interview took place at the height of Baltimore protests, connected in social movement organizing and in public imagination to earlier police and extralegal killings in Charleston, Ferguson, Staten Island, and Sanford.

In both interviews, the *intelligibility* of black political action is at stake. The reasons for black political action in 1963—and white people's responsibility for those conditions—are concealed by the interviewer's questions about violence and nonviolence. When Baldwin inverts the questions, he challenges the interviewer and audience to recognize black political action as a response to racism and state violence. Questions of intelligibility also structure McKesson and Blitzer's encounter. Despite McKesson's interventions, Blitzer's constrained terms of engagement prevent addressing historical legacies and contemporary forms of racism (manifest in cultural, social, economic, and political dimensions). If the conceptual "site" of violence is understood as rooted in antiblack racism, then embodied engagements in the streets of Ferguson or Baltimore could be understood not as regrettable expressions of legitimate grief and pain—they could be politically legible.[42] That is, they could be interpreted and understood as legitimate action that "makes sense" and is informed by valuable knowledge.[43] In this framework, unauthorized black political actions in Birmingham in 1963 or in Ferguson and Baltimore in 2014–2015 are valid expressions of appropriate affective and political responses to police killings, broader police violence, urban divestment, a rapidly shrinking welfare state, and other forms of cultural, political, and economic expressions of antiblack racism.[44]

In both interviews, the white reporter imagines black embodiment, black death, and black political action as absolutely separate from his own life. The reporters try to use their interviewees to represent and connect them to "black issues." The way they ask Baldwin and McKesson to answer their "questions" obscures their own chosen distance and their investment in what Charles Mills calls an "epistemology of ignorance"—a system of cognitive dysfunctions (which are psychologically and socially functional) in which white people misunderstand, evade, and self-deceive in matters related to race.[45] As Mills explains, part of what is required to "achieve Whiteness" is an agreement to misinterpret the world. A closer look at the interviews reveals the mechanics through which the white interviewers attempt (unsuccessfully) to corral the meaning of black experience, black political action, and black death into something disconnected from their own lives. In contrast, Baldwin theorizes a basis of connection that links his Los Angeles interviewer to black youth and white cops in Birmingham. He insists that their lives are co-constituted, and that white people geographically far away from the imagined hub of racial conflict—Birmingham and the US South more generally—are in fact utterly tied to and responsible for the fire hoses and attack dogs. In these moves, he suggests an intimate way of understanding racial politics, and he holds white people accountable for historical and contemporary forms of racism. McKesson's own inversions of his interviewer's framework are more constrained. He does, however, make a bid for Blitzer to attend to the gravity of the police killings and to honestly inhabit and face the violence and the loss. Although Blitzer himself does not appear to be affected, McKesson's interventions hold and protect important ground. His steady responses call attention to Blitzer's contortions away from solidarity or care, maneuvers that are both effortful and grotesque.

Taken together, the interviews also raise important temporal questions about what Jacquelyn Dowd Hall calls the "uses of the past" in racial politics, and the relationship between racial violence and white innocence in the 1960s and the present. In many places in his work, Baldwin collapses time in order to underscore the durability and continuity of white innocence, and to underscore the way that historical racial violence not only haunts but constitutes the present both materially and ideologically. Baldwin is known for demanding attention to the ways in which "we carry [history] within us," as when he tells William Buckley in their 1968 Oxford debate: "I am stating very seriously, and this is not an overstatement: *I* picked the cotton, *I* carried it to the market, and *I* built the railroads under someone else's whip for nothing."[46] Baldwin's preface anticipates those who would render his claims a fantastic exaggeration; he closes any historical gap where white liberal fantasies of temporal distance rest. If Baldwin picked the cotton, then his contemporaries cannot evade demands for racial justice by relegating the violence to the past. And yet, though the conditions of the 1960s are bound to the past, they also are different, and Baldwin also attends to this other sense of time. He exposes the ways in which white people have, across generations, continued to commit acts of violence, reinvested in innocence, and, when confronted, offered stalling excuses under a twentieth-century banner of liberal racial progress.

In the contemporary moment, liberal and conservative discourses pull on the 1960s in many ways—especially in claiming civil rights history for a celebratory, redemptive postracial narrative. Blitzer illuminates how the 1960s are used to interpret contemporary politics. When he says that civil unrest is "something I didn't think we'd be seeing again" "so many years after Dr. Martin Luther King and the civil rights movement," he asserts that issues of racial domination and racial justice were settled, and that a half century should safely secure such concerns in the past. In this framework represented by Blitzer, the concerns and demands raised by contemporary black activists are interpreted as obsolete and, as Tiffany Willoughby-Herard explains, their political consciousness is figured as outmoded and pre-political.[47] Blitzer's comment suggests that the activists and their concerns are outdated, and therefore groundless, even uneducated, frenzied, and pathological. When Baldwin insists that *he* picked the cotton, he refuses these temporal evasions of white liberal exceptionalism.

In each of the two interviews, the white reporter fixates on a conceptual and rhetorical framework of "violence versus nonviolence." This framework structures all of their questions. Both reporters try to persuade their respondent to speak within this structure and thereby authorize it and all the work it does. In doing so, each of the white reporters makes an attempt to transfer the site and origin of violence as being in blackness. The repetition of this racial representation in American history is telling; it is worth noting that a full century ago, journalist Ida B. Wells intervened in this very logic. In her activism, journalism, and theoretical work, Wells worked to lift the meanings of sexual menace off of black bodies and foregrounded the sexual and physical violence enacted by white men and enabled by white women.[48] In Wells's time, in 1963, and in 2015, "violence" is attached to black bodies to obscure violence by white people and the state. To intervene in this historical process of signification, Baldwin refuses and inverts his interviewer's questions about militancy and nonviolence. When the interviewer asks whether leadership of the "new militant Negro" will dominate, Baldwin responds, "Let's take that question out of the vacuum where we've had it all these years," gesturing to the history of white fixation on concepts of black violence. Baldwin in the 1960s and Garza, McKesson, and other contemporary activists contest the very frameworks used to interpret black political action, claiming their white interlocutors as utterly linked and deeply responsible for an unfolding political history.

Notes

Many thanks go to Lawrie Balfour, Daniel Martinez HoSang, Joseph Lowndes, Ernesto Javier Martínez, Susan McWilliams, Alaí Reyes-Santos, Courtney Thorsson, Tiffany Willoughby-Herard, and Priscilla Yamin for their valuable comments.

Epigraph: Brittney Cooper, "In Defense of Black Rage: Michael Brown, Police, and the American Dream" *Salon,* August 12, 2014, www.salon.com/2014/08/12/in_defense_of_black_rage_ michael_brown_police_and_the_american_dream/.

1. For example, at UC Berkeley, a large art piece used text from *The Fire Next Time* as a background, overlaid by fifty names of victims of police violence (Cathy Cockrell, "Reflections on #BlackLivesMatter, from Ferguson to Sproul," *Berkeley News,* February 10, 2015, http://news.berkeley.edu/2015/02/10/reflections-on-blacklivesmatter-from-ferguson-to-sproul/).

2. James Baldwin, *The Fire Next Time* (1963; New York: Vintage International, 1993).

3. Ibid., 105–6.

4. Stephen H. Marshall, *The City on the Hill from Below: The Crisis of Prophetic Black Politics* (Philadelphia: Temple University Press, 2011), 24, 142–61; George Shulman, *American Prophecy: Race and Redemption in American Political Culture* (Minneapolis: University of Minnesota Press, 2008), 136–40; Lisa Beard, "'Flesh of Their Flesh, Bone of Their Bone': James Baldwin's Racial Politics of Boundness," *Contemporary Political Theory* 15, no. 4 (2016): 378–98.

5. "Hillary Clinton's Meeting with Black Lives Matter Activists," *Democracy Now*, August 19, 2015, www.democracynow.org/blog/2015/8/19/watch_full_video_of_hillary_clintons.

6. In fall 2014, the organization facilitated movement building for protests in Ferguson, Missouri, after white police office Darren Wilson killed fifteen-year-old Mike Brown.

7. Alicia Garza, "A Herstory of the #BlackLivesMatter Movement," *Feminist Wire*, October 7, 2014, www.thefeministwire.com/2014/10/blacklivesmatter-2/; Black Lives Matter, "Demands," *Black Lives Matter*, http://blacklivesmatter.com/about/.

8. Alicia Garza, in "#BlackLivesMatter Founders on Immigration & the Fight for 'Safety beyond Policing,'" *Democracy Now*, Pacifica Radio, June 24, 2015, www.democracynow.org/2015/7/24/part_2_blacklivesmatter_founders_on_immigration.

9. Eddie Glaude Jr., "James Baldwin and Black Lives Matter," in this volume, 361.

10. Melvin L. Rogers, "Introduction: Disposable Lives," *Theory & Event* 17, no. 3 (2014); Ruth Wilson Gilmore, *Golden Gulag: Prisons, Surplus, Crisis, and Opposition in Globalizing California* (Berkeley: University of California Press, 2007), 37; Stephen Marshall, "The Political Life of Fungibility," *Theory & Event* 15, no. 3 (2012); Tiffany Willoughby-Herard, "South Africa's Poor Whites and Whiteness Studies: Afrikaner Ethnicity, Scientific Racism and White Misery," *New Political Science* 29, no. 4 (2007): 480n4.

11. George Shulman, "Acknowledgment and Disavowal as an Idiom for Theorizing Politics," *Theory & Event* 14, no. 1 (2011).

12. James Baldwin, *The Cross of Redemption: Uncollected Writings* (New York: Pantheon, 2010), 95.

13. More money was raised for Darren Wilson, the police officer who killed Mike Brown, than for the family of Mike Brown (see Dora Apel, "'Hands Up, Don't Shoot': Surrendering to Liberal Illusions," *Theory & Event* 17, no. 3 [2014]).

14. Baldwin, *The Fire Next Time*, 19.

15. Ibid., 20.

16. I thank Lawrie Balfour for drawing my attention to this point.

17. On interracial solidarity, see Juliet Hooker, *Race and the Politics of Solidarity* (New York: Oxford University Press, 2009).

18. Beard, "Flesh of Their Flesh."

19. Garza, "A Herstory," 3.

20. Apel, "Hands Up, Don't Shoot," 2.

21. "CBS-JB 1963 Interview" and "RFK," both from Moving Images and Sound Division, Schomburg Center for Research in Black Culture.

22. David Leeming, *James Baldwin: A Biography* (New York: Knopf, 1994), 220–21.

23. Clarence Jones and Joel Engel, *What Would Martin Say?* (New York: Harper, 2008).

24. Danielle L. McGuire, "'It Was Like All of Us Had Been Raped': Sexual Violence, Community Mobilization, and the African American Freedom Struggle," *Journal of American History* 91, no. 3 (2004): 906–31.

25. Peniel Joseph, *Dark Days, Bright Nights: From Black Power to Barack Obama* (New York: Basic Civitas, 2010), 66.

26. Baldwin, *Cross of Redemption*, 136.

27. Michael Rogin, *Ronald Reagan, the Movie and Other Episodes in Political Demonology* (Berkeley: University of California Press, 1987).

28. Gray passed away on April 19, 2015, in a coma. Protests began at this time and increased in intensity and participation over the next ten days, with mainstream national news coverage paying special attention to buildings and vehicles set on fire. Baltimore city government closed public schools, libraries, and other facilities and mandated a citywide curfew. Baltimore city and Maryland state government declared a state of emergency on April 27 and called upon the National Guard.

29. Michelle Alexander, *The New Jim Crow: Mass Incarceration in the Age of Colorblindness* (New York: New Press, 2010); Lisa Duggan *The Twilight of Equality? Neoliberalism, Cultural Politics, and the Attack on Democracy* (Boston: Beacon, 2003); George Lipsitz, "The Possessive Investment in Whiteness: Racialized Social Democracy and the "White" Problem in American Studies," *American Quarterly* 47, no. 3 (1995): 369–87.

30. On the ways in which dominant media interpret black versus white embodied action, see Lisa Marie Cacho, *Social Death: Racialized Rightlessness and the Criminalization of the Unprotected* (New York: New York University Press, 2012), 1–3. Relatedly, in a 1968 interview with *Esquire*, James Baldwin refuses his interviewer's question about "looting," explaining: "I object to the term 'looters' because I wonder who is looting whom, baby. . . . The mass media-television and all the major news agencies endlessly use that word 'looter.' On television you always see black hands reaching in" ("How Can We Get Black People to Cool It?," *Esquire* 70, no. 1 [July 1968]: 49–53). This distortion and displacement is, as Joseph Lowndes explains, the phenomena by which "those who are victims of state aggression can be made to seem the aggressors" ("Fear and Fantasy in Ferguson," *New West*, November 26, 2014, https://thewpsa.wordpress.com/2014/11/26/fear-and-fantasy-in-ferguson/).

31. CNN, November 26, 2014.

32. Jacquelyn Dowd Hall, "The Long Civil Rights Movement and the Political Uses of the Past," *Journal of American History* 91, no. 4 (March 2005): 1233–63; Jodi Melamed, "The Spirit of Neoliberalism: From Racial Liberalism to Neoliberal Multiculturalism," *Social Text* 89, no. 4 (Winter 2006): 1–24.

33. "Wolf Blitzer Interviews Deray McKesson about Violence in Baltimore," www.youtube.com/watch?v=NyYdKD0af78.

34. Blitzer invokes "two hundred arrests" as evidence of the unnamed black people's "violence" instead of as evidence of police action.

35. Saidiya Hartman, *Lose Your Mother: A Journey along the Atlantic Slave Route* (New York: Farrar, Straus and Giroux, 2007), 6.

36. Dowd Hall, "The Long Civil Rights Movement," 1234.

37. In the United States, the concept of "property" itself cannot be understood apart from its historical meanings in chattel slavery (see Saidiya Hartman, *Scenes of Subjection: Terror, Slavery and Self-Making in Nineteenth-Century America* [New York: Oxford University Press, 1997]). In the system of chattel slavery, black death is conceptualized as "lost property."

38. Baldwin, *The Fire Next Time*, 92.

39. On the politics of emotions, see Deborah Gould, *Moving Politics: Emotion and ACT UP's Fight against AIDS* (Chicago: University of Chicago Press, 2009); Sara Ahmed, *The Cultural Politics of Emotions* (New York: Routledge, 2004); and Audre Lorde, "Uses of Anger: Women Responding to Racism," in *Sister Outsider: Essays and Speeches* (New York: Ten Speed, 2007).

40. Brian Klopotek, Brenda Lintinger, and John Barbry, "Ordinary and Extraordinary Trauma: Race, Indigeneity, and Hurricane Katrina in Tunica-Biloxi History," *American Indian Culture and Research Journal* 32, no. 2 (2008): 55–77.

41. As Smith observes, within Sharpton's framework, only Brown's family is allowed to express pain or anger about Brown's death (see "Affect and Respectability Politics," *Theory & Event* 17, no. 3 [2014]).

42. Cooper, "In Defense of Black Rage."

43. Ernesto Javier Martínez, *On Making Sense: Queer Race Narratives of Intelligibility* (Red Wood City, CA: Stanford University Press, 2013), 14. Martínez cites the philosopher Miranda Fricker to define "epistemic injustice" as injustice that affects people in their capacity as knowers and as community members worthy of being known.

44. In the wake of Michael Brown's death, Michelle-Renée Smith observes a failure to attend to the *lost lives*, the marked brutality, or the historical haunting. Instead, she notes a fixation on questions of "riots" or "looting." Were people to profoundly attend to the lost lives, she theorizes that perhaps they could "acknowledge the destruction and violence following Brown's murder as politically salient instead of seeing it as simple hooliganism"—as "legitimate black rage at irrational police violence." Many critiques of political action in Ferguson or Baltimore reveal an inability to perceive young black activists as political actors, or their actions as legitimate means for progress (Smith, "Affect and Respectability Politics").

45. Charles Mills, *The Racial Contract* (Ithaca, NY: Cornell University Press, 1997), 18–19.

46. James Baldwin, "White Man's Guilt" in *The Price of the Ticket: Collected Nonfiction, 1948–1985* (New York: St. Martin's, 1985), 410; James Baldwin and William Buckley, "James Baldwin Debates William F. Buckley (1965)," www .youtube.com/watch?v=oFeoS41xe7w.

47. Tiffany Willoughby-Herard, "More Expendable than Slaves? Racial Justice and the After-life of Slavery," *Politics, Groups, and Identities* 2, no. 3 (2014): 507.

48. Ida B. Wells-Barnett and J. J. Royster, *Southern Horrors and Other Writings: The Anti-Lynching Campaign of Ida B. Wells, 1892–1900* (Boston: Bedford, 1997).

13

James Baldwin and Black Lives Matter

Eddie S. Glaude Jr.

I found myself the other day—and upon reflection this was an astonishing thing to say, no less think—wishing my son were seven years old again. He was adorable at seven. The vexations of the teenage years were far off, and he still liked me. But I said this not because I find having an empty nest unbearable, although at times I do, or that I long to raise a teenager again—and eventually he would be a maddening teenager again. I just thought—felt, even—that he would be safer at home, with us.

Now my son attends Brown University. But that doesn't matter. He is subject to a kind of precarity that comes with being a black person in this country even when a black man, perhaps especially because a black man, occupies the White House. At any moment, someone or some police officer could see him as a threat and, because of the value or, I should say, the lack of value accorded his body, he could easily suffer premature death (that feature of black life that makes it, among other things, so distinctive).[1]

I want to think about Black Lives Matter in a different register, one that connects this complex movement with the extraordinary insights of James Baldwin. My reflections were triggered by citations of Baldwin by protesters (and serve as kind of run-up to a more extensive engagement with his disturbing book on the Atlanta child murders, *The Evidence of*

Things Not Seen).[2] To put it bluntly, Jimmy is everywhere. People, especially young people, seem to be reaching for him as way of accounting for the latest disaster—the latest national panic around race—that has defined this country since its beginnings. In fact, when I think about the protests and the damning precarity of black life in this country, Baldwin's words come to mind: "America sometimes resembles . . . an exceedingly monotonous minstrel show; the same dances, same music, same jokes. One has done (or been) the show so long that one can do it in one's sleep."[3] To be sure, there is something familiar and wholly unprecedented in our current moment. No wonder activists are reaching for Baldwin.

My thoughts are preliminary; they are inchoate. They reflect my efforts to think about Baldwin as a kind of exemplar of a perfectionist tradition that takes shape under the conditions of domination. I want to suggest that Black Lives Matter refracts this tradition in particularly interesting ways. Of course, against the backdrop of events in Ferguson and Baltimore and the deaths of so many black women and men at the hands of the police, the assertion that black lives matter takes on added significance. We utter the words in the context of life-and-death circumstances—at least some of us do—circumstances that seem to be a constant feature of what it means to be black in this country.

Black Lives Matter emerged as a heartfelt rallying cry in the aftermath of Trayvon Martin's death and the acquittal of George Zimmerman in 2012. Alicia Garza, Patrisse Cullors, and Opal Tometi came up with the hashtag #BlackLivesMatter to express their outrage and to forcefully assert, especially given the contrary evidence, that black people matter. The organization puts it this way: "#BlackLivesMatter is working for a world where Black lives are no longer systematically and intentionally targeted for demise. We affirm our contributions to this society, our humanity, and our resilience in the face of deadly oppression. We have put our sweat equity and love for Black people into creating a political project—taking the hashtag off of social media and into the streets. The call for Black lives to matter is a rallying cry for ALL Black lives striving for liberation."[4] The hashtag #BlackLivesMatter works on a number of registers. It is a mobilizing/organizing tool in this particular moment; it is also a form of political critique and an evocative imagining of what Sheldon Wolin calls the political. (I don't have the space to vindicate this last claim, but I think it is important.)

To think of the hashtag only as an assertion of the value of black lives limits its aims and purposes.

Even in the previous description, Garcia, Cullors, and Tometi "affirm our contributions to society, our humanity, and our resilience in the face of deadly oppression." They aren't arguing for black humanity. And beyond their specific purposes, when we see people in the streets chanting "Black lives matter," the slogan works in the context of political action, like an incantation that challenges not only forms of policing that terrorize particular communities but also indicts current social, political, and economic arrangements that cut short the life chances of black people—practices and arrangements that lead to premature death. This isn't about asserting the value of black life. That is already known. The price of that ticket, to echo Baldwin echoing Dostoevsky, has already been paid.

The hashtag #BlackLivesMatter registers the unseemly belief, and it is a belief baked into the DNA of this country, that white lives are more valued than others. And this, I maintain, is at the heart of white supremacy. White supremacy is more than bad people in hooded robes burning crosses and screaming the word "nigger." These people are easily condemnable. White supremacy involves the way a society organizes itself, and what and whom it chooses to value. It determines where you live, which schools you attend, what jobs are available to you, and reminds you daily of your status and station in life. And, to my mind, this is white supremacy in a nutshell: a set of practices informed by the fundamental belief that white people are valued more than others. This is what I call elsewhere the *value gap*.[5]

In no way do we live in a society like apartheid South Africa (that would be an example at the extreme), but we do live in a country where black people confront every day the damning reality that we are less valued; it is experienced, as Clarissa Hayward argues, in the very built environment of this nation—in our neighborhoods, where we go to school, and the places we work.[6] The data are crystal clear. African Americans suffer chronic double-digit unemployment. We lead the nation in rates of heart disease and HIV/AIDS. African Americans make up nearly 1 million of the 2.4 million Americans in prison. When we think about the differences between whites and blacks in high school graduation rates, among those with college degrees, mortality rates, in access to health care, in levels of wealth, differences in salaries with the same level of education, in the percentage of children in poverty, we can see, independent of individual acts of racism, that white Americans, particularly those with money, matter more than others.[7]

We ought to understand the Black Lives Matter movement as a rejection of this belief. More to the point, we ought to understand it as a rejection of the belief that white lives are presumed more valuable than black lives. Because, it is that belief—the view that animates so much of the mess that has undermined democratic life in this country—that limits our ability to reach for higher excellences (and I mean this for both black and white Americans).

I use the language of excellences purposefully. I want to think about the Black Lives Matter movement in the tradition of what I call black democratic perfectionism: that is, a radical cultivation of democratic individuality in the service of racial justice. Within the Black Lives Matter movement, we find an insistence on the expansiveness of black life—at the forefront of the protests are black members of the LGTBQ community, the working black poor, and others challenging the state as well as narrow conceptions of black political leadership and action—all in the name of a robust form of black individuality (and I don't mean some facile bourgeois idea of individualism consistent with the political rationality of neoliberalism—although it is certainly susceptible to it).[8]

My model for this view is James Baldwin. In his essay "The Uses of the Blues," Baldwin clearly states what he takes to be the "Negro Problem":

> I'm talking about what happens to you if, having barely escaped suicide, or death, or madness, or yourself, you watch your children growing up and no matter what you do, no matter *what* you do, you are powerless, you are *really* powerless, against the force of the world that is out to tell your child that he has no right to be alive. And no amount of liberal jargon, and no amount of talk about how well and how far we have progressed, does anything to soften or to point out any solution to this dilemma. In every generation, ever since Negroes have been here, every Negro mother and father has had to face that child and try to create in that child some way of surviving this particular world, some way to make the child who will be despised not despise himself. I don't know what the "the Negro Problem" means to white people, but this is what it means to Negroes.[9]

Here Baldwin foregrounds the idea of white supremacy that I put forward earlier: that the fact of growing up, of coming of age, in a place that denies you standing distorts one's sense of self and disfigures one's character. It arrests one's capacities, and, in that light, it is with great effort and risk that one takes up the task of self-creation in such a world.

This is what Baldwin tries to convey to William Buckley and the young students at Cambridge in 1965. Here Baldwin insists on a sense of perspective: how the question of who we are gets handled, managed, and pursued under adverse conditions matters. It matters if one bears the brunt of the police baton and if one does not, if one is a descendant of slaves or of slaveholders. Both may be inheritors of Ralph Waldo Emerson's call upon us, but the difference matters greatly. As Baldwin writes, "To persuade black boys and girls, as we have for so many generations, that their lives are worth less than other lives, and that they can live only on terms dictated to them by other people, by people who despise them, is worse than a crime; it is the sin against the Holy Ghost."[10] This is, and it must be said without concern for hurt feelings or guilt, undeniably white supremacy.

Baldwin makes explicit the primal scene of instruction: it is a context in which black people are seen as disposable. This scene, in all of its messiness, casts in relief what Stanley Cavell calls Emersonian perfectionism.[11] For Emerson, we have the task before us to ascend to higher forms of excellences. But this task isn't rooted in some fixed destination or some final resting place of perfection (the spiral stairs going upward—taking each step and leaving others behind). That final resting place, however, differs for each person. Life's journey consists of better and more excellent versions of who we take ourselves to be. Each experience of significance calls us to a higher sense of ourselves and requires the abandonment of older versions. Jeffrey Stout puts it best: "The higher self congeals out of the highest intimations of excellence you can intuit from where you stand. Excellence and sacred value are the kinds of goodness that matter most for living well."[12]

But the daunting challenge of seeking a higher self in a world that denies one standing gives new meaning to W. E. B. Du Bois's cry of "two unreconciled strivings."[13] For African Americans, as Langston Hughes said, life ain't been no crystal stair.[14] To embrace perfectionism across the proverbial tracks, then, requires something more fundamental; it requires a confrontation with what Baldwin calls *reality*. For Baldwin, reality is a denotative term for whatever happens in experience: the doings and sufferings of people transacting with environments that result in joys and suffering, even though white people are seen as more valuable than others.[15]

Baldwin asserts a form of perfectionism in such an environment, and that assertion requires an unflinching encounter with the ugliness of who we are and a rejection of comforting illusions that hide the lie and all of the rot underneath the American Idea. Here our moral and ethical senses are profoundly distorted, and any robust idea of the public good is obscured. As Baldwin put it: "What is most terrible is that American white men are not prepared to believe my version of the story, to believe that it happened. In order to avoid believing that, they have set up in themselves a fantastic system of evasions, denials, and justifications, which system is about to destroy their grasp of reality, which is another way of saying their moral sense."[16] This adds another layer of complexity to the context of the black democratic perfectionism he commends. It is not just white supremacy—the fact that life as it is in this country says over and over again to the black child of fifteen and to the black woman of forty that you are less then (and it says this in every possible way)—it is also the maddening fact that the country denies what it has done and continues to do to black people, a kind of willful ignorance. As if Baltimore or Ferguson is somehow a surprise just as Harlem and Watts and Detroit were shocking some fifty years ago. That innocence is the crime, as Baldwin noted, and it corroborates what he mercilessly described as the monstrous quality of this place: "There is something monstrous about never having been hurt, never having been made to bleed, never having lost anything, never having gained anything because life is beautiful, and in order to keep it beautiful you're going to stay just the way you are and you're not going to test your theory against all the possibilities outside. America is like that. The failure on our part to accept the reality of pain, of anguish, of ambiguity, of death has turned us into a very peculiar and sometimes monstrous people."[17] The reality of white supremacy and its repeated evasion or outright denial makes the idea of abandoning older versions of ourselves damn near impossible. We seem to be comfortable right where we are—permanently docked in the station.

But for black folk, especially those who languish in the shadows of America's ghettos, to stay right where we are means to surrender to death. So, Baldwin's insistence on reaching for higher forms of excellence under captive conditions demands an unflinching encounter with the uses and abuses of the past. As he says in "The White Man's Guilt":

History, as nearly no one seems to know, is not merely something to be read. And it does not refer merely, or even principally, to the past.

> On the contrary, the great force of history comes from the fact that we carry it within us, are unconsciously controlled by it in many ways, and history is literally present in all that we do. It could scarcely be otherwise, since it is to history that we owe our frames of reference, our identities, and our aspirations. And it is with great pain and terror that one begins to realize this. In great pain and terror one begins to assess the history which has placed one where one is, and formed one's point of view. In great pain and terror because, thereafter, one enters into battle with that historical creation, Oneself, and attempts to recreate oneself according to a principle more human and more liberating.[18]

Such an approach to history requires a black self, in particular, that isn't reducible to sociology as Ralph Ellison and Albert Murray described it—the flat statistics and stereotypes that trap Americans in the farce that is race relations.

I am not talking about the version of the story that trades in the Willie Hortons, Bigger Thomases, the welfare queens, the thugs of the world—those black people who are natively criminal or, because of their woeful circumstances, destined to be criminal. I am not talking about that. Instead, black democratic perfectionism requires a self with a rich and complex interiority, what William James refers to in *The Varieties of Religious Experience* as a two-storied self—an interior that has been, whether we want to admit it or not, terribly wounded by the inescapability of what Toni Morrison describes as a nastiness that will dirty you on the inside.[19]

Perhaps I can bring this home by way of example. The internationally acclaimed Ghanaian artist El Anatsui, known for his amazing sculptures and metal sheets made of discarded bottle caps, created a series of clay pots called *The Broken Pots.* Here Anatsui revealed his predilection for the found object. Fragments or shards of broken pots, given depth and form by the trace of his hands, reveal something about the form of black perfectionism that I am reaching for with my reading of Baldwin.

Anatsui insists on the importance of clay: its permanence and transience, its fragility and resilience. As Oli Oguibe noted: "The transfiguration of clay from the state of malleability to one of rigidity invokes natural processes of formation and maturation. Yet the susceptibility of the rigid form to reductive transformation also denotes the absence of finality and the presence of infinite possibility."[20] Think about the references to John Jones in Du Bois's "Of the Coming of John": "For a long time the clay seemed unfit for any sort of molding."[21] Here Du Bois registers how the context of America denies black people the possibility of an existence otherwise; the clay is unfit—permanence and rigidity are its primary features.

But Anatsui helps us see otherwise. The clay pot should be seen as a metaphor for the fragility of existence and the delicate nature of life. The broken pot, in his hands, comes to represent not a permanent state of brokenness. Its transformation (from one state to another, from that relegated to the trash bin to that which is beautiful) reflects what Oguibe sees as "a will to overcome" or what I am suggesting as a reconstructed perfectionism: "Leak as we may, we nevertheless continue to mend. We are reminded of Beckett. Try. Fail. Never mind. Try Harder. Fail better."[22]

Oguibe explains: "A broken pot may never regain its wholeness in terms of its original form, but at the point of its fracture appears a new objectivity, a new entity. And since no form is absolute nor any condition final, no state is primary."[23] Fate loses its sting. Life ain't been no crystal stair, but we keep climbing! What we find in Anatsui's work is "the indelible trace of that which survives in spite of," and that trace, marking brokenness and wound as the ground upon which we stand, provides a foundation for the continuous work for higher excellences, for better selves.

This is what I am referring to as Baldwin's black democratic perfectionism. It begins with brokenness and doesn't have as its aspiration wholeness, but a sense of what's *more,* what's possible without the comfort of metaphysical guarantees.

Baldwin commends perfectionism in the context of a system of domination that denies black selves any standing. He also insists on a vibrant and complex black interiority in a world that reduces us to flat, predictable characters and narrates its history to corroborate such descriptions. Both are bound up, constrained by, an idea of history that corroborates the lie that some people matter more than others. But, again, this is not some bourgeois preoccupation, some private affair with no public consequence. Black democratic perfectionism has radical implication for the order of things. As Baldwin puts it, "When a black man, whose destiny and identity have always been controlled by others, decides and states that he will control his own destiny and rejects the identity given to him by others, he is talking revolution."[24]

Baldwin's witness entailed aspirational claims about what kind of society we hoped to live in and what kind of persons we aspired to be as well as claims, rooted in care, about the historical depth of where we now stand (that is, about the enduring legacy of white supremacy that deforms self-formation and about the history of struggle that constitutes the backdrop of current efforts). His democratic perfectionism is situated in the histories of black life in particular and American life more generally—stories that narrate the litany of events and the chorus of black voices struggling for freedom and resisting the arbitrary use of power. These histories carry with them an *ethical ought:* that the struggle and sacrifices of so many require of those who are its immediate beneficiaries a commitment to treating one's fellows justly and to ensuring a society where all can flourish—a society in which all of us can reach for higher excellences.

Invocations of that history can spur or constrain; they can serve as "wind beneath our wings" in the context of creative engagement with the present, or they can limit the range of actions to a stale, ossified set of practices that purportedly best represent our efforts. Baldwin's democratic perfectionism commends the former. He insists that we look the facts of our experience squarely in the face and challenge directly the idea that white people matter more and upend a world comfortable with the senseless death of black people.[25]

To my mind, Black Lives Matter, at its best, works in this register. Young people all around the country are challenging the underlying assumptions of white supremacy. They are putting their bodies on the line, disturbing the peace, and "asking hard questions and taking very rude positions." This is what our moment requires. Turning our backs on the status quo and demanding a revolution of value. But it also requires that we abandon older versions of ourselves. That we break loose from stale models of black political engagement and confining ideas of black community and obligation. We can no longer suffer from what I want to call *catalepsis:* that political condition characterized by rigidity and fixity of posture; it is that which arrests the perfectionist impulse; it paralyzes us, keeps us where we currently are, allows for a black political class to exploit that fixed position in the name of progress, and desensitizes us to the pain and terror of what it means to be black in this country. We remain trapped.

But these young folk are daring to break free (with all of the complications that daring and risk entail). They are asserting the uniqueness and distinctiveness of their own voices. In short, they are daring to *be*—and that, if I understand Baldwin, is a revolutionary act in this country. As he put the point in a short piece written in 1959 titled "A Word from Writer Directly to Reader": "What the times demand, and in an unprecedented fashion, is that one be—not seem—outrageous, independent, anarchical. That one be thoroughly disciplined—as a means of being spontaneous. That one resist at whatever cost the fearful pressures placed on one to lie about one's experience."[26] To my mind, Black Lives Matter, at its best, enacts this formulation courageously and, to take a phrase from Henry James, "at the pitch of passion."[27]

Notes

1. One could think about the fact of premature death as one way of cashing out what we mean by the condition of black living. Think about it this way: Du Bois answered the question about the meaning race in *Dusk of Dawn* by pointing our attention to the back of a Jim Crow car. But that was only one manifestation of the fact of black living in this country (see *Dusk of Dawn: An Essay toward an Autobiography of a Race Concept* [New York: Oxford University Press, 2007]). The underlying reality is that we are all exposed to the possibility of premature death. So if you want to know the meaning of race, let's look at the rate of death. . . .

2. James Baldwin, *The Evidence of Things Not Seen* (New York: Holt, Reinhart, 1985).

3. James Baldwin, "Black Power," in *The Cross of Redemption: Uncollected Writings*, ed. Randall Kenan (New York: Pantheon, 2010), 81.

4. See www.blacklivesmatter.com/about.

5. Eddie Glaude, *Democracy in Black: How Race Still Enslaves the American Soul* (New York: Crown, 2016).

6. Clarissa Rile Hayward, *How Americans Make Race: Stories, Institutions, Spaces* (New York: Cambridge University Press, 2013).

7. I am mindful of arguments like William Buckley's and other conservatives that attribute much of this state of affairs to the pathologies of black people. In his debate with James Baldwin at Cambridge in 1965, Buckley mobilizes this argument in response to Baldwin by citing Nathan Glazer. Here Buckley shifts the blame, after citing the progress that Baldwin himself represents, onto shoulders of black people. Baldwin's eyes were ablaze upon hearing this "nonsense." But Baldwin answers this argument clearly in his essay "The Uses of the Blues" (which first appeared in *Playboy* in January 1964).

The fact that Harry Belafonte makes as much money as, let's say, Frank

Sinatra, doesn't really mean anything in this context. Frank can still get a house anywhere, and Harry can't. . . . [W]hen we talk about what we call "the negro problem" we are simply evolving means of avoiding the facts of this life. Because in order to face the facts of a life like Billie's [Holiday] or, for that matter, a life like mine, one has got to—the white American has got to—accept the fact that what he thinks he is, he is not. He has to give up, he has to surrender his image of himself and apparently this is the last thing white Americans are prepared to do.

See "The Uses of the Blues," in *The Cross of Redemption,* ed. Kenan, 60–61. Well, Buckley is clear about this. In fact, he says if it comes down to America's precious ideals, then they "will fight the issue."

8. Wendy Brown, *Undoing the Demos: Neoliberalism's Stealth Revolution* (New York: Zone, 2015).

9. Baldwin, *The Cross of Redemption,* ed. Kenan, 60.

10. Ibid., 84.

11. See Stanley Cavell's *Conditions Handsome and Unhandsome* (Chicago: University of Chicago Press, 1991).

12. Jeffrey Stout and Ron Kuipers, "Excellence and the Emersonian Perfectionist: An Interview with Jeffrey Stout, Part 1," in *The Other Journal: An Intersection of Theology and Culture* (September 1, 2009), http://theotherjournal.com/2009/09/01/excellence-and-the-emersonian-perfectionist-an-interview-with-jeffrey-stout-part-i/.

13. W. E. B. Du Bois, *The Souls of Black Folk* (New York: Simon and Schuster, 2014), 7.

14. Langston Hughes, "Mother to Son," in *The Collected Works of Langston Hughes: Works for Children and Young Adults: Poetry, Fiction, and Other Writing,* ed. Dianne Johnson (Columbia: University of Missouri Press, 2003), 81.

15. The connection to Emerson is strong. In the beginning of "As Much Truth as One Can Bear" (1962), Baldwin strikes an Emersonian note, recalling the beginning of *Nature,* as he seeks to open space for young writers who write in the shadow of Hemingway, Fitzgerald, Dos Passos, and Faulkner. I was particular struck by this formulation. It gives one a sense of the different stakes in Baldwin's perfectionism: "We live in a country in which words are mostly used to cover the sleeper, not to wake him up; and therefore, it seems to me, the adulation so cruelly proffered our elders has nothing to do with their achievement—which I repeat was mighty—but has to do with our impulse to look back on what we now imagine to have been a happier time. It is an adulation which has panic at the root" (*The Cross of Redemption,* ed. Kenan, 29).

16. Ibid., 77.

17. Ibid., 64.

18. James Baldwin, "The White Man's Guilt," in *James Baldwin: The Collected Essays: Volume 2* (New York: Library of America, 1998), 722–23. This echoes Baldwin's point about God in *The Fire Next Time* (New York: Vintage, 1962). If the concept doesn't make us larger, freer, and more loving—in short, more humane and more liberating—then it's time we got rid of him.

19. William James, *The Varieties of Religious Experience: A Study in Human Nature* (New York: Modern Library, 1902).

20. Olu Oguibe, "El Anatsui: Beyond Death and Nothingness," *African Arts* (Winter 1998): 48

21. Du Bois, *Souls of Black Folk*, 222.

22. Oguibe, "El Anatsui," 52.

23. Ibid., 53.

24. Baldwin, *The Cross of Redemption*, ed. Kenan, 81. How might we think of Philip Petit's notion of freedom as nondomination in light of Baldwin's position? Petit argues that freedom ought to be understood "as the absence of subjection to the will of others." He limits this, however, to social, political, and economic questions/concerns. But subjection can happen, and Baldwin insists on this point, at the level of historical memory—how our refusal to confront the past or willingness to disremember that past can do the work of domination much more efficiently, or at least less brutally, than the coercive arm of the state. That refusal to remember, as you recall, results in a startling fact: that white folks are as unfree, if not more so, than black folks. They're stuck.

25. This is the connective tissue of the tradition I am trying to outline here. As Ms. Ella Baker said so powerfully, "Until the killing of black men, black mothers' sons, becomes as important to the rest of the country as the killing of a white mother's son, we who believe in freedom cannot rest." This is the direct challenge to white supremacy as I have defined it. It is the ground upon which Black Lives Matter acquires meaning. So it is not about asserting our value; it is about rejecting the belief that snuffs out the ability of others to reach for higher selves.

26. Baldwin, *The Cross of Redemption*, ed. Kenan, 8.

27. Henry James, *The Art of Criticism: Henry James on the Theory and Practice of Fiction*, ed. William Veeder and Susan M. Griffin (Chicago: University of Chicago Press, 1986), 235. In *The Cross of Redemption*, Baldwin writes, "I am aiming at what Henry James called 'perception at the pitch of passion'" (49).

14

"Tell Him I'm Gone"

On the Margins in High-Tech City

Rachel Brahinsky

Wandering through San Francisco with a public television crew in 1963, writer James Baldwin commented on the crumbling geographies of liberally inclined cities like this one. At the time, the politics of racism smoldered across the nation. Shuttled by the TV crew from one end of the city to the next, Baldwin listened as young Black teens expressed their frustrations and anger at a city that enjoyed a progressive reputation, even as these youth and their neighbors struggled to survive the premature deaths of unemployment and urban renewal, which were rippling through the city at the time.

A half century later the TV documentary on Baldwin's visit emerged from the archives and saw a revival in the city in which it was filmed. This was a very different San Francisco in many ways, and yet the spatial politics of race and capital were again at the forefront, with marginalized communities and their haunts facing daily losses. Like the youth in Baldwin's time, people on the socioeconomic fringe in twenty-first-century San Francisco struggled to reconcile the progressive reputation of their city with the facts of their own lives, as they and their communities weathered a new era of race-class urban removal.

Like the narrator in the traditional Black labor ballad "Take This Hammer," after which Baldwin's documentary was named, the contemporary city was also breeding fugitives from urban life. Poor and working-class San Franciscans were being forced from their homes by a rising tide of rents, in an era in which privatization of all things had become so normalized that it was hard for many to imagine another way.

> *Take this hammer, carry it to the captain*
> *Take this hammer, carry it to the captain*
> *Take this hammer, carry it to the captain,*
> *Tell him I'm gone, boys*
> *Tell him I'm gone.*[1]

The ebb and flow of populations is part of urbanness; this has long been understood. Just as separation—of ethnic groups or land use types like industrial or residential spaces—marks the shape of cities, so have relocation and im/migration defined the shape of our metropoles. The evolution of place in these ways can be fascinating, exciting, and beautiful. But it is the *why* of urban migrations and containments that defines urban justice. It is the power behind such motion and containment that matters, and too often that power has been guided by race-class exclusion.[2] Whether it is containment through racial segregation, or displacement through evictions, rent hikes, or demolitions, power-laden patterns of racialized urbanism bring deep social disruption at multiple scales.

San Francisco has long played host to many rounds of such disruption and containment. Even so, there has always been a subaltern struggle in the city, a creative resistance to capitalist urbanization, often led by racial castaways whose life stories undercut the well-hewn narrative of San Francisco as a haven for marginalized people.[3] These stories of struggle are also narratives of resilience in which marginalization is redefined.

This chapter draws lessons from linked historical moments of such struggle, using James Baldwin's commentary on 1960s San Francisco to consider racial capitalism's urban consequences years later. Using a mixed-method approach, I look at the KQED film as a primary sociopolitical text and incorporate historical-geographic research on racial politics in the city to develop a context for conversations about race-making.[4] I argue that urban space plays a key role in shaping the bounds of racial justice, both in Baldwin's time and beyond. By foregrounding the politics of place, I seek clues toward a broader urban justice.

In the next section of this chapter, we encounter San Francisco through the KQED film narrative, exploring the spatial politics of race—and the meaning of race itself—as it played out in two of San Francisco's two largely African American neighborhoods. Throughout, the chapter reflects on how urban policy has intersected with the everyday Black geographies that Baldwin investigated, with a call for a revisioning of those same geographies. Through reseeing place, I argue, we may also reimagine racial marginalization in our cities.

The rhythm of the song "Take This Hammer" permeates this chapter, as I seek to illuminate the role of what geographer Clyde Woods called the "blues epistemology" in shaping knowledge and power in racialized cities.[5] Woods conceived of this as a way to understand the role of underground music-makers and creative forces as "sociologists, reporters, counselors, advocates, preservers of language and customs, and summoners of life."[6]

These life-affirming practices, for Woods, played a key role in keeping alive social critique and even policy alternatives through times in which such alternatives were crushed by the spatial pressures of urban change—like urban renewal and its offspring—pressures that still threaten to extinguish everyday life in Black communities.

Multiple Marginalities: "We Don't Even Have a Country"

The film begins with a drive into San Francisco, streaming west over the San Francisco–Oakland Bay Bridge. The city lights burn through the dark night, and Baldwin's voice narrates the view, speaking of the paradox of San Francisco. Though it seemed to beam a message of social progress, he reflected, San Francisco remained problematic in many of the quotidian realms of urban American exclusion: chiefly, through its legacies of race-class segregation.

Then: Pan to the grassy hillside, to the sight of a young girl chasing a ball on a classically Californian slope. The hill is brown with summer grass that shimmers like the hips of some giant golden bear. It's summertime, and the living here is typically quite dry.

Soon, images of other kids walking and talking offer glimpses of the city's two largely African American neighborhoods. The documentary, conceived and created by Richard O. Moore for KQED public television, paired

novelist and sharp-tongued social commentator Baldwin with Orville Luster, a community advocate known for his work with Black youth from the
city's southeastern corner.[7] Baldwin's national and international profile was
rising. A scathing essay on religion, race, and sexuality—later published as
The Fire Next Time—had just come out, following the publication of his
boundary-pushing novel *Another Country* in 1962. In much of his work, as
in these texts, Baldwin took race, sexuality, and religion head on, often with
the trans-Atlantic perspective for which he was to become known. Even so,
his critique of American racism stood at the center of his work, with his position as a member of a triply marginalized group—having been born poor,
Black, and gay—shaping his literary voice.[8]

Hunter's Point Hill, where many of Luster's teens lived, sits adjacent to
San Francisco's Naval Shipyard, an institution that both built and destroyed
the neighborhood around it. Having long been a shipbuilding center, the
place was acquired by the US Navy to serve as a key node in the World War
II Pacific theater. The activity there through the 1940s and 1950s drew
migrants from across the country for shipbuilding, atomic-weapons process-
ing, and administration of the war effort.[9] At the time of Baldwin's visit,
the Hill was largely an African American space, with Blacks representing
about 80 percent of residents. The places they occupied included dilapi-
dated housing, which had been assembled as temporary shelter for shipyard
workers during the war, and which was largely left to crumble after conversion into federally managed public housing in the postwar period.[10]

Though the Hill boasted incredible views of the San Francisco Bay
and the city itself, it had begun its urban life as a fringe industrial place one
hundred years earlier—and had long struggled to shake off its marginal
status. Nearby urban landscapes had included outlaw Chinese shrimpers,
the city's Butcher's Reservation, electric power plants, sewers, and all manner of industrial workshops. By the late 1940s the African American community called it home. The Hill was a key geographic feature of the larger
neighborhood of Bayview–Hunter's Point, which was undergoing a racial
and economic transition as working- and middle-class white-ethnics packed
out of the city.[11] Swept up in the federal housing programs that enabled
their upward mobility, whites sought a more suburban existence down the
San Francisco Peninsula to the south, in synch with others quite a bit like
them across the country.[12]

As the *white pull*[13] of federal housing programs generated what urbanists tend to call white flight, Bayview–Hunter's Point filled with Black families fleeing the urban demolitions of the Western Addition, known also as the Fillmore.[14] At the same time, the labor opportunities of the shipyard were disappearing, lingering in short supply through the Cold War, soon to vanish entirely. In that context, the young people of Hunter's Point Hill, who were generally the poorest Black youth in a struggling Black neighborhood, sought extralegal employment and tangled with the white San Francisco power structure. Orville Luster was focused on the young men of the Hill, working largely with those whose lives were dangerously veering away from stability, if they had ever experienced it at all.[15]

By 1963 the urban renewal program that later made the city infamous for bulldozer politics was long under way in the Fillmore, and Luster's youth were well aware of it. Displacees from the central city were appearing in the southeastern corner of the city week by week, in search of work, stability—and home. This was a community that had already been in shock, having fled the Jim Crow South just a short generation earlier, and not too many generations after their ancestors had endured American slavery. Now they were making home out of the San Francisco hills, having sought "the warmth of other suns," though that warmth now seemed fleeting.[16]

In many ways this story was a classic California experience lived by cultures of all kinds: a people, drawn west by desperation and aching hopes, sought the many golds of the Left Coast, from mining to jobs to cultural freedoms. Upon arrival they found that the mythos of western success was warped by race, class, and time. Attention to these dynamics, to the ways that racial politics shaped western cities, and the way that "space-time" shapes the bounds of urban justice, helps explain the predicaments of Black San Franciscans in the 1960s.[17] It was capital that drew African Americans to the West during the World War II period; it was race that defined their spatial freedoms, or lack thereof. And it was time that shaped the intersection between race, place, and capital, such that Luster's youth found themselves surviving the city with a steady thrump of fear that their rickety owner-neglected homes were about to disappear under yet another state-mandated bulldozer. The experiences of Black urbanism were fluid, sometimes dangerously so.

Now: the kids are surrounding Baldwin, saying that they can't get jobs; there are none to be found if one is Black, they say. Baldwin responds, acknowledging the invisibility of their situation: "This is the San Francisco

Americans pretend does not exist. They think I'm making it up." They clamor to be seen by Baldwin, to air the complaints of the unheard. Baldwin says, in mentoring tones: "I want *you* to think about *this*. There will be a Negro president of this country. But it will not *be* the country we're sitting in now. It will be someplace else." The young people respond, calling out over each other in the crowd: "We have no flag. We don't even have a country. Do we have a country?"[18]

The film has its imperfections. On the one hand, the public television camera is obsessed with the figure of Baldwin. Baldwin's words and flair, as he smokes and takes in the sights, dominate the screen, eclipsing the voices of the youth. From Baldwin's perspective, this was problematic; he had apparently hoped that the youth would be prominent in the final cut.[19] Meanwhile, some of Baldwin's observations about Black life were strangely objectifying of the people who are offered, nameless, as universal representatives of Black people and culture. These points weaken the narrative and its political force. Even so, the documentary offers a text through which to see the refractions of racialization as life-affirming rather than centralized around death or violence.

Now: a girl skipping along the street, running, to the sounds of gospel music. Baldwin's voice is overlaid, talking about the inner life of Black people, and the ways that they are misunderstood, by whites, by others, and by each other. For Baldwin, some of this was wrapped up in what he called "the God shops"—the storefront churches that peddled religion in its various forms. Having grown up as the son of a Baptist minister and having trained in the clergy himself as a young man, Baldwin later saw those operations as preying on the weak, the poor. Religion was a social force that thrived on the ongoing search among the disaffected for belonging and safety. He had long linked religion and the notion of racial progress to experiences of belonging and home in his writing.[20]

Luster confirmed this sense of dislocation, the ongoing existential experience of the Diaspora: "The negro in San Francisco, he doesn't really know his place. He's trying to find his place. That's one of the problems: *What place is there for me?*," suggesting that for Black San Franciscans, "You came out here to escape."[21]

> *If he ask you, was I running*
> *If he ask you, was I running*

If he ask you, was I running,
Tell him I'm flyin', boys
Tell him I'm flyin'[22]

"Oh, They Talk about the South! The South Ain't Half as Bad as San Francisco!"

The KQED documentary came together because Baldwin was flying in to give a talk in the Bay Area, on the themes he explored in *The Fire Next Time*. Moore, who is white, recalls thinking, "Let's get him to come here and look behind the veneer in San Francisco of the cosmopolitan liberal city." Asked why he was drawn to the topic, Moore explained: "Don't you think it would have become my responsibility to become interested in the black experience at that time?" To refuse attention to the subject, he reflected, would have been "immoral."[23]

It was mostly filmed out of the windows of a Chevrolet Corvair station wagon—with the engine in the rear. Moore's camera crew took off the hood of the car and fit a camera in the windshield. The rear of the wagon was packed with batteries and a sound recorder, with just enough space for one cameraman to lie on his stomach to train the camera on the landscape while Baldwin spoke.[24]

For those who know Baldwin's work as centered on sexuality and gender, such topics and their intersections with race may seem like a strange omission in the film. Any read of Baldwin is richer with attention to his work on intersectional politics, and in many other texts Baldwin spoke about love and sex and belonging and race as interwoven problems, often suggesting that his position in the society as Black and gay pushed him to the edges in a way that he used to develop his power as a writer. It was a place from which he could look back at the rest of us with unique perspective and critique. Even so, not much of his analysis of gender or sexuality comes through in the film. Perhaps that wasn't Moore's mission.

It's also worth noting that though San Francisco is known for its openness to sexual fluidity, Baldwin didn't seem to have deep connections there. One might guess that San Francisco would appear prominently in Baldwin's work or life. In a survey of Baldwin's talks and writings, however, including his plays, essays, novels, and other film commentary, it's hard to find much reference to the city by the bay. Baldwin's cartography circulated transnationally between the orbits of New York and Paris for much of his life, with key visits to Turkey and Eastern Europe. The racial exclusions of San Francisco—perhaps in its queer communities as well—could have been at play here.

Though San Francisco may not have been that significant for Baldwin, however, Baldwin was ultimately very meaningful for residents of San Francisco. This wasn't true right away. With its stark commentary on racism and exclusion in the city, Baldwin's visit and the documentary record that it left behind could have gashed open the sparkling image of San Francisco progressivism. The city had long enjoyed a reputation as a bastion of liberal sociopolitics, and yet the African Americans who had most recently migrated here found that this reputation did not extend to racial liberalism.[25]

Baldwin's visit exposed this alternative, often bitter view of the city, focusing on the young people who felt cast away by the mainstream and who viewed their social and geographic place in the city largely through the lens of race and racism. As one young man says to Baldwin, in a challenge to the progressive ideal: "Oh, they talk about the South! The South ain't half as bad as San Francisco! You want me to tell you about San Francisco? I'll tell you about San Francisco. The white man he's not taking advantage of you out in public the way they do in Birmingham, but he's killing you with that pencil and paper, brother, oh he's killing you."[26]

It was this quote that would be aired over and over upon the film's revival. But in 1963 it remained relatively unheard. It aired on public television, probably just once; following that, the film went largely unnoticed in the press. Moore commented years later that he felt that the work was sidelined because the critique was too strong and the depiction of angry Black youth was seen as untenable material for the general public; ultimately, to his disappointment, Moore believed that "nobody paid attention."[27] Indeed, if city leaders or media producers were worried about volatile tensions, they would not have been so far off. It was barely five years later that a white police officer killed Black seventeen-year-old Matthew Johnson on Hunter's Point Hill. The uprising that ensued captured the city for five days.[28]

The Black radical politics that may have terrified the KQED higherups are not often associated with San Francisco but rather with Oakland. The Black Panther Party was strongest in Oakland, building power even as San Francisco's urban process pushed new Black families into the Oakland fray, having radicalized many of them via displacement. Where San Francisco's Black exodus began as early as 1970, Oakland's African American population continued to rise through the late 1980s.[29] With that growing population, the symbiosis between the urban politics of postwar neighborhood clearance with the political development of radical Black politics was broadly evident in Oakland.[30]

Still, the everyday material conditions of life for Black people in San Francisco produced theorists out of young minds. The issue of housing, for example, for the KQED youngsters was no distant policy concern. Rather, it was the heart of their quotidian existence. They needed no imported theoretical lens to see that. As one young man put it: "They tryin' to tear down our homes, brother! When the white man try to tear down your homes, what are you gonna do?" He went on, framing jobs and labor as fundamentally linked: "You know what kinda job they gonna give us? They gonna let us tear down our own homes, here in Hunter's Point." In that light, Black San Francisco's role in its own displacement would then be complete. "It's a job, temporarily, and then what you gonna do? Where you gonna live?"[31]

One of the only girls quoted in the film offered the same clarity, suggesting that the displacement of urban renewal would arrive with the erasure of more than just housing but would entail a more thorough eradication of *home,* with its deep sense of place. This place, she told Baldwin, "ain't gonna be no place, when they get through. We gonna be living out on the streets."[32]

Now: Baldwin, Luster, and the film crew pack into the Chevy, with cameras poised in multiple directions as they drive. Passing public housing in the Western Addition, Baldwin talks about the dangers of living in what he calls the ghetto. He says that being forced to live among danger at all times is deeply unsettling in long-term ways. The children here, he says, are exposed to "a million forces that appear, when a people are despised."[33]

Images of a weed-filled yard with wilting cars take over the screen. Although the camera moves along streets that served as the city center after the Great Quake and Fire of 1906, signs of demolition and abandonment surround Baldwin and Luster. Where urban renewal had first staked its claims, tearing through Victorian homes, there now were empty lots, awaiting development. Some of those spaces would fill quickly, with a new hospital and union-backed affordable housing. Many blocks would fester for decades, leaving the community with a visible reminder of the gaping wound that urban renewal's displacements had wrought in the city.[34] Baldwin speaks: "There is no moral distance, that is to say—no distance—between the facts of life in San Francisco and the facts of life in Birmingham."[35]

This was the year that the March on Washington was to take place, the same year that Martin Luther King Jr.'s "Letter from Birmingham Jail" pled for dialogue and action on race-class inequality.[36] Later that year four Birmingham girls would be murdered by a Ku Klux Klan bomb. But then, soon after, the Civil Rights Act would be passed by the US Congress, marking a new level of mainstream acceptance of the shifting times.

On the precipice of all of this political change, Baldwin and Luster paused in front of the Eichler crane near Laguna and Geary Streets in San Francisco. With the camera running, they mused on the state of reconstruction of the city streets and the ways that it might serve the working-class Black community that had been removed to make way. City officials would later feature this redevelopment site as a sign of hope and progress for the area. The public-private partnership between Eichler Homes and the SF Redevelopment Agency was lauded for its new-modernist dwellings suited for the masses, which would replace the old Victorians. This was in the era before preservationism gained traction, and the 1880s structures made of California redwood were not yet valued by the real estate industry. Conversely, it was construction projects like Eichler Homes that had inspired community members to turn out en masse to public meetings in the years prior, some with guns in hand, in defense both of their right to stay and of their need for a piece of the economic pie represented by symbols like the Eichler crane.[37]

In front of that symbol, Baldwin turns to Luster: "I don't know what I could say to those kids that would make any sense. Because in fact, it does not make any sense."[38]

The hopelessness of that moment did not tell the whole story. The 1960s closed with Fillmore residents and others across the city developing tactics of participation that reshaped the redevelopment schemes in favor of affordable housing and increased community retention.[39] In Bayview–Hunter's Point, women leaders would further develop this activism to ensure that an entire hillside would be populated with subsidized housing, creating a bulwark for Black residential stability for decades.[40]

At the same time, the processes that Baldwin witnessed kicked into gear a long, slow march out of the city as African American San Franciscans began to leave for the East Bay and beyond, often returning only on Sundays to attend church services in the Fillmore. By the mid-2000s, "Black flight" was understood as a crisis with public policy implications, but years later there were still no clear programs to stem the tide.[41]

If he ask you, was I laughing
If he ask you, was I laughing
If he ask you, was I laughing
Tell him I'm cryin', boys
Tell him I'm cryin'[42]

By 2015 the geographic center of the Internet-tech economy had expanded substantially from Silicon Valley into San Francisco, rattling the demography and landscape of the city, with striking impacts on Black San Francisco. With the spread of tech firms—from information storage services to web-based startups to biotech expansions—came a boom in demand for housing that drew out the toughest tendencies of urbanism. Residential evictions, small-business displacement, and rising rents marked the days and filled the newspapers. Having counted as about 14 percent of the city in 1970, Black people now comprised less than 6 percent of the booming population, and key Black cultural institutions were shuttered by the steep heights of the real estate market.[43]

Black people who remained in the city talked of feeling isolated and abandoned. A group of Black artists formed a collective museum show titled "Hiraeth," telling stories of home and drawing on narratives of gentrification-driven expulsion, which they connected to the historic Black Diaspora. Hiraeth is a Welsh word that suggests longing or homesickness, as the collective expressed it: "a longing for a far-off home—one that may not even exist, now changed by time or idealized memory."[44] The art in the show centered on dreams of belonging and rootedness and the strong desire for a sense of place and home. Some pieces evoked the particular ways that this longing played out for Black San Franciscans at a time when the Black Lives Matter movement was growing across the country.

The connections weren't hard to make. Black Lives Matter emerged around national concerns, appearing on social media after the nonindictment of Trayvon Martin's killer. The movement itself was spearheaded in part by a woman who had developed her political organizing skills working around Hunter's Point Hill, fighting the city's redevelopment plan for the naval shipyard.[45]

"As Long as You Think You're White, There's No Hope for You"

There's a second version of the KQED documentary with extended discussions on race and religion. These conversations push the edges of white comfort even further than the original cut. This version was released in 2014, after *Take This Hammer* had already been reintroduced to the general public and was starting to make the rounds among San Franciscans. Moore later reflected—in yet another film, this one was about the making of the original—that after a day of interviewing youth, Baldwin was exhausted. After a bubble bath and some scotch, Moore said, Baldwin appeared in the filmmaker's living room ready to reflect on the day.[46] With cameras rolling one more time, he delivered a forty-five-minute monologue, concluding with a classic Baldwin commentary on racial formation, which could have been aimed at the presumptive white KQED viewership or editorial staff: "I've always known that I'm not a nigger. But if I am not . . . [then] who is? . . . I am not the victim here. But *you* still think, I gather, that the negro is necessary. Well he's unnecessary to me, so he must be necessary to you. So: I give you my problem back. You're the nigger, baby, not me."[47]

With that provocative stance Baldwin raised one of the key lessons of *Take This Hammer*, and perhaps of his larger legacy as a writer and thinker: to reverse the conversation about race, to turn it toward white people and whiteness itself as a site of political and literary analysis. This was one of Baldwin's signature theoretical moves, echoing the work of W. E. B. Du Bois, Frantz Fanon, Toni Morrison, and many other Black intellectuals who recognized that race and racialization were above all defined by ways that power defined biology, not the other way around.[48]

One of Baldwin's characters in the 1964 play *Blues for Mr. Charlie* elaborates on this idea. The trouble with blackness, he argues, is in fact not blackness but whiteness. He puts it this way: "It's up to you—as long as you think you're white, there's no hope for you, because as long as you think you're white, then I'm black."[49] This is a complicated but important theoretical turn. On the one hand, Baldwin gives the power of racialization to white people in this formulation, which could be seen as removing agency from Black people and others. A closer read shows that the point of the comment is to degrade whiteness as a hopeless category that relies on demonizing others. Beyond that, the comment clarifies the ways that race is a dynamic and relational category. Race is created through relationships between people and places.

Much later, in the scathing 1985 essay "The Price of the Ticket," which was also developed as a film, Baldwin again describes whiteness as a yoke or a burden. He suggests that the notion of blackness as a solid category is perpetuated by whites to hold on to their elite status, and that they cling to whiteness as a status symbol reflecting class mobility and power.[50] Fanon had suggested the same in the 1950s when he explored the meaning of the color line and the power relations embedded there. As he put it, "What is called the black soul is a construction by white folk."[51]

This attention to the relationality of race also positioned Baldwin alongside critical-race scholars who have argued that racialization is a process of "othering" through political, social, legal, and spatial systems.[52] Consistently, Baldwin argued in his writing and lectures that black positionality—that is, experiencing the world as a person understood to be Black, and being treated in the ways that follow in a racist society—allows one to understand the broader social structure of the United States in particularly useful ways. He argued that the experience offered a lens through which to see events like the end of legal slavery in the nineteenth century and of formal segregation in the twentieth as the result of geopolitical pressures rather than goodness of heart among the white majority.[53]

Baldwin thus exposed the fallacy of what Audre Lorde described as the white "mythical norm," or what Adrienne Rich would call "white solipsism," in which she suggested that white people narrowly believe that whiteness is the baseline from which to measure the world.[54] Like Baldwin's work, these interventions sought to reclaim master narratives—retelling stories of people and places through the eyes of the ignored.

This wasn't just for the telling. It mattered beyond that. Similar experiences emerged over the years in the work of Black intellectuals, who described seeing themselves split in two, living out the "double consciousness" that Du Bois had named at the turn of the century: "Between me and the other world there is ever an unasked question: unasked by some through feelings of delicacy; by others through the difficulty of rightly framing it. All, nevertheless, flutter round it. They approach me in a half-hesitant sort of way, eye me curiously or compassionately, and then instead of saying directly, How does it feel to be a problem? they say, I know an excellent colored man in my town. . . . To the real question, how does it feel to be a problem? I answer seldom a word."[55]

With blackness embedded deep in the American psyche as a foil to mainstream white purity, Baldwin followed Du Bois in insisting that the un-freedoms of the nation at large could be resolved and corrected only when the boundedness of Black life was finally cleared. This was the same position that would be adopted by the Black Lives Matter movement, making the claim that Black life still served as the proverbial canary in the coal mine of human exclusion. That's why they've recoiled when people quickly declare that "all lives matter," noting that the inability to make Black life, in particular, matter is revelatory.

Toni Morrison wrote about the process of retaking the master narrative as an act of what she called "literary cartography," situating place-making as a way of simultaneously redefining both identity and freedom. In her essay "Black Matters," she explained the radical impulse to reshape the world cartographically: "I want to draw a map, so to speak, of a critical geography, and use that map to open as much space for discovery, intellectual adventure, and close exploration as did the original charting of the New World—without the mandate for conquest. I intend to outline an attractive fruitful and provocative critical project, unencumbered by dreams of subversion or rallying gestures at fortress walls."[56]

Morrison explored the polarity of race that Baldwin and Du Bois highlighted, insisting that it was the un-freedom of Black slavery—which was a geographically defined labor- and social-relationship—that bolstered the broader notion of American Freedom. The traits ascribed to Blackness over time became the traits of the un-free. As she wrote: "Black slavery enriched the country's creative possibilities. For in that construction of blackness and enslavement could be found not only the not-free but also, with the dramatic polarity created by skin color, the projection of the not-me. The result was a playground for the imagination. What rose up out of collective needs to allay internal fears and to rationalize external exploitation was an American Africanism—a fabricated brew of darkness, otherness, alarm and desire that is uniquely American."[57]

Race, ever since, acts as "a metaphor so necessary to the construction of Americanness that it rivals the old pseudo-scientific and class-informed racisms whose dynamics we are more used to deciphering. . . . Deep within the word 'American' is its association with race."[58] It is this Americanness of race and racism that Baldwin raised as he wandered San Francisco—charging that liberal/progressive places contained the same poisons as the South.

The contemporary videos of police killings that spurred the Black Lives Matter call has drawn from this same intellectual well, both revealing still-seated racisms and working to retell the story of America from the margins. The act of video-making has both raised awareness of a long-existing problem (police impunity) and quite literally turned the lens on an institution with a long antiblack legacy. The cell-phone videos brought names like Oakland's Oscar Grant, Ferguson's Mike Brown, Sandra Bland in Texas, and others every day of the year into the public eye and shed light on what it's like to live on the very dangerous margins.[59]

I don't want these, your cold iron shackles
I don't want these, your cold iron shackles
I don't want these, your cold iron shackles
Around my leg, boys
Around my leg[60]

Calling All Summoners of Life

Just a few blocks away from the sites that Baldwin visited, the Baldwin documentary was screened in celebration of its fiftieth anniversary. It was 2014, and the film had been restored and revived by public archivists from San Francisco State University, and it had been shown around town a few times. This was a special screening, held at the Bayview Opera House, which is a historic Victorian-era building that serves as a Black cultural community center for Bayview–Hunter's Point. Bayview was still home to a third of the city's quickly dispersing Black population.

Though decades had passed since Baldwin's visit, many of the telling statistics about the place remained intact in troubling ways. Unemployment was much worse, now twice the rate of the rest of the city. Foreclosures, which were relatively uncommon in San Francisco compared with the rest of California, were a key part of the neighborhood landscape. Black youth struggled to find legitimate employment and faced ongoing racial profiling.[61] At the same time, there was a renewed energy in the community, with community organizers working to draw people together.

Perhaps that's part of why, when local activists pulled together the screening, the Opera House was packed and buzzing with hundreds who had gathered to watch. A community restaurant served plates of pulled pork in the back. The place hummed with a sense of purpose and importance. The screening was marred by technical glitches; even so, it was a time in which local community members came together to witness the evolution of their own history.

In his work, Baldwin often called for an activist mode of social observation, which represented a refusal to simply watch the disintegration of Black people and Black places. By doing so he was part of a larger tradition of staking a claim against white-dominated notions of academic or journalistic objectivity, which presuppose that activism and observation cannot be entwined.

Geographer and urban planner Clyde Woods once commented that he had spent his life witnessing the death of African Americans and their communities—through environmental disease, through the force of the development bulldozer, and through what could be called a *designed neglect* of urban communities. Woods wrote about the ways that mainstream social science, in its attempt to rigidly follow rules of objective observation, ignores so much about how these disappearances take place. Questioning his own role in documenting the death of communities and people, he wrote, "Have we become academic coroners? . . . Have the tools of theory, method, instruction, and social responsibility become so rusted that they can only be used for autopsies? Does our research in any way reflect the experiences, viewpoints, and needs of the residents of these dying communities? On the other hand, is the patient really dead? What role are scholars playing in this social triage?"[62]

Like Woods, critical-race scholars including Kimberlé Crenshaw have long insisted that the task at hand in documenting stories of racism and exclusion—through all social mechanisms, including housing, employment and legal formations—is not "simply to understand the vexed bond between law and racial power, but to change it."[63] Crenshaw's words could be reframed to reflect the links between urban history and racial power, in which the "premature deaths" of police violence, urban demolitions, and poverty itself are enacted through race.[64]

To the extent to which researching race is about *doing race*,[65] our research and observational paradigms weigh heavily on the production of the social facts of racism and inequality. That is, in the ways that we focus on social problems, we may reproduce them. If the purpose of deep observation is to change the social conditions that we are explaining, then we may need to reframe the very meaning of observation. Black feminist theorists and feminist geographers argue for this in a variety of ways—all urging for reordering analytical visions to reflect the view of the subaltern or the counterpublics that persist beyond the white gaze.[66]

With that in mind, a few observations about the facts on the ground in San Francisco are necessary. In 1963 the "asset stripping" of gains that had been made by African American midcentury migrants, many of whom had purchased homes and planted roots in the city with their high wartime wages, had already begun.[67] In 2015 these processes continued in formal and informal ways, most prominently through market-capitalism's authority over the real estate market, and the dominance of that market over other realms of everyday life. The corporate tech economy, which is plagued with race and gender exclusions, has flooded San Francisco with a tech-centered nouveau riche who have crowded out Black culture and people, among many other aspects of this onetime hub of creativity. This has accelerated the stringency of the housing market, squeezing out the oldest Black bookstore on the West Coast, along with many other cultural institutions.[68]

There is more to tell about the ways in which the tech economy has tipped the economic balance in San Francisco. But this work is largely accomplished elsewhere, and Baldwin's work called for attention to the beauty and inspiration that grows out of the cracks of so-called ghetto sidewalks. Clyde Woods described the process as excavating cultural rebellions from subterranean places, noting that "Brilliance often flashes brightly, just as suddenly disappears, and then reappears decades later. . . . The reader will have to explore the subterranean caverns that shelter the wellsprings of dreams during the seasons when hope can't be found. . . . Expertise in the arts of social, economic, political, cultural, and spiritual reconstruction is required.[69] Geographer Katherine McKittrick builds on Woods's work, calling for a reframing of the body counts of the past through creativity. Using the poem "Inventory" by Dionne Brand to explore poetic reimagining of the effects of racism, McKittrick writes:

The body count that frames much of "Inventory"—800 every month for the last year, 120 in four days—is thus also about survival and human life, or a new math-space, where the calculus of human actions and cooperative human efforts encounter poetry to reinvent the unambiguous dead-end culmination that is so often coupled with analyses of violence. . . . Here, we envision a life on the edge, a geography that demands you stay alive yet threatens your physiology, a spatial politics of living just enough, just enough for the city: this is a political location that fosters more humanly workable, and alterable, geographic practices.[70]

In McKittrick's vision, the inventory of deaths and urban racial injustices can be rewoven through the words of creative acts. In these ways, the spaces of racism and injustice may be reexperienced as spaces of radical empowerment.

> *Take this hammer, carry it to the captain*
> *Take this hammer, carry it to the captain*
> *Take this hammer, carry it to the captain*
> *Tell him I'm gone, boys*
> *Tell him I'm gone*[71]

Transforming Geographies of Racism

Aug. 15, 2014. Field notes. On the BART train tonight the kids in the front of the car retook the place for themselves. They were about sixteen or seventeen years old, Black and Asian American boys. They were lanky and angular, wearing saggy skinny jeans, their bodies covered in tattoos. Leaping through the subway doors as they closed, one boy pressed "play" on a small gray box, and his friends began to dance as music tinned through the metal train car. They were amazing: body-popping, yoga-hip-hop-acro-blending, using the poles of the train to flip and bend in incredible ways.

It was hard to simply enjoy the beauty of their performance. The crowd seemed to watch them display their double-jointed prowess while watching each other for tension. We were traveling under the San Francisco Bay on the same train line on which Oscar Grant had died, shot dead by transit cops on New Year's Eve three years earlier, the first high-profile event in the wave of cell-phone-captured police killings that has persisted since.[72]

The train was packed. Most people were nose-down in their smart phones as usual. A small group turned to watch the show, which pushed so many boundaries at once—stretching notions of dance and gender and race and public space, all at once. Then one older white man piped up, angry about the loud music and the kids' dominance of the space. He demanded that they leave with the authority of someone who was used to being heard. The tension rose.

At the next exit, the boys bowed and leapt off the train, deftly; they seemed to have been here before. "We out! We out!" they hollered. They taunted the man through the train windows, but the doors were closing, and we pulled off through downtown Oakland and into the night.[73]

"That's, I Suppose, All That Saved My Life"

James Baldwin read the landscape through race. He saw the spaces of cities and the shape of human experience as deeply linked. Driving through urban renewal zones in San Francisco, for him, was revelatory not of new experiences but of the universal processes that Black communities faced at the time—even in progressive places like San Francisco, or in the open landscapes of the American West. His visit and his words sought to challenge the liberal-minded city, pushing on the meaning of race and racism. Racism wasn't just an unfortunate social problem that limited the lives of Black people; it was not just something that affected the young men in Orville Luster's programs on the Hill. It was, Baldwin showed, a rot inherent to American society that prevented the society from living up to its founding liberal ideals of freedom and equality.

It would be wrong to say that nothing has changed since Baldwin passed through San Francisco in the early 1960s. The dynamics of race itself are different, and real changes in the demography of power have shifted rights and access in many realms. Still, the concrete gains of civil rights have been undercut by economics. The "roll out" of neoliberal policies over the last thirty years has reinscribed the problems of racial inequality in new ways.[74] Black representation in the prison population is beyond disproportionate and continues to boom.[75] Segregation is more pronounced now than it was in the 1980s.[76] These dynamics play out across the country, and the increase in global inequality is sharply pronounced in historically progressive San Francisco.

This new civil rights era, a time in which communities are networking across the country to develop a broad response to racialized inequality, comes as there has been a revival of interest in Baldwin's oeuvre. A barrage of papers, symposia, and events appeared around the globe in the last few years—revealing the ongoing relevance of Baldwin's analysis for people in these times.

He was central to the Black radical intellectual tradition, though he was sometimes sidelined because of his sexuality. In the end, as a writer and intellectual force, he left us with the notion that to survive the materiality of marginalization requires both creativity and love, those summoners of life. As he said in one of many interviews about surviving racism: "I think the trick is to say yes to life. . . . Love comes in very strange packages. I've loved a few men. I've loved a few women. A few people loved me—and that's, I suppose, all that saved my life."[77]

Notes

I want to thank and acknowledge Alex Cherian, the archivist at the San Francisco State University Library who made both the original and director's cut of *Take This Hammer* available to the public, who also filmed the 2013 interview with director Richard O. Moore, and who is thus largely responsible for getting the film and its history back into the public eye. My sincere thanks goes to volume editor Susan McWilliams and to the two anonymous reviewers who offered incredibly detailed readings that significantly reshaped this chapter. My thanks also go to colleagues at the 2015 Association of American Geographers meeting in Chicago for their comments, and to the University of San Francisco College of Arts and Sciences writing retreat for the time and space to write. Any mistakes are my own.

1. Odetta Holmes, "Take This Hammer," on *At the Gate of Horn*, LP (Tradition Records, 1957). These lyrics come from the traditional Black Gospel song "Take This Hammer," which has been recorded, revised, and reinterpreted by Mississippi John Hurt, Odetta, Johnny Cash, a Spanish hard-core band, and many others over the decades. The song is central to the soundtrack of the KQED documentary. The lyrics quoted throughout this chapter are excerpted from the version recorded by Odetta. I encourage readers to find the song online or elsewhere and listen so you have a sense of the melody.

2. Rachel Brahinsky, "Race and the Making of Southeast San Francisco: Towards a Theory of Race-Class," *Antipode* 46, no. 5 (November 1, 2014): 1258–76.

3. Albert S. Broussard, *Black San Francisco: The Struggle for Racial Equality in the West, 1900–1954* (Lawrence: University Press of Kansas, 1993); Nayan Shah, *Contagious Divides: Epidemics and Race in San Francisco's Chinatown* (Berkeley: University of California Press, 2001).

4. Rachel Brahinsky, "The Making and Unmaking of Southeast San Francisco" (PhD diss., University of California, Berkeley, 2012).

5. Clyde Adrian Woods, *Development Arrested: The Blues and Plantation Power in the Mississippi Delta* (London: Verso, 1998).

6. Ibid., 17.

7. Ibid.

8. James Baldwin, *Another Country* (New York: Dial, 1962); James Baldwin, *The Fire Next Time* (New York: Dial, 1963); James Baldwin, *The Cross of Redemption: Uncollected Writings* (New York: Pantheon, 2010).

9. Lindsey Dillon, "Waste, Race and Space: Urban Redevelopment and Environmental Justice in Southeast San Francisco" (PhD diss., Department of Geography, University of California at Berkeley, 2014).

10. Brahinsky, "The Making and Unmaking of Southeast San Francisco."

11. Ibid.

12. Eric Avila, *Popular Culture in the Age of White Flight: Fear and Fantasy in Suburban Los Angeles* (Berkeley: University of California Press, 2006); Kevin Michael Kruse, *White Flight: Atlanta and the Making of Modern Conservatism* (Princeton, NJ: Princeton University Press, 2005).

13. Rachel Brahinsky, "Race and the City: The (Re)development of Urban Identity," *Geography Compass* 5, no. 3 (2011): 144–53.

14. Rachel Brahinsky, "'Hush Puppies,' Communalist Politics, and Demolition Governance: The Rise and Fall of the Black Fillmore," in *Ten Years That Shook the City: San Francisco 1968–1978*, ed. Chris Carlsson (San Francisco: City Lights Books, 2011), 141–53; Elizabeth Pepin and Lewis Watts, *Harlem of the West: The San Francisco Fillmore Jazz Era* (San Francisco: Chronicle, 2005).

15. Christopher Agee, *The Streets of San Francisco* (Chicago: University of Chicago Press, 2014).

16. Isabel Wilkerson, *The Warmth of Other Suns: The Epic Story of America's Great Migration* (New York: Random House, 2010).

17. Clyde Adrian. Woods, "'Sittin' on Top of the World': The Challenge of Blues and Hip Hop Geography," in *Black Geographies and the Politics of Place*, ed. Katherine McKittrick and Clyde Adrian Woods (Toronto: Between the Lines, 2007), 46–81.

18. Moore, *Take This Hammer*; italics added by author to reflect spoken cadence.

19. Alex Cherian, *The Making of "Take This Hammer,"* Bay Area Television

Archive, 2013, https://diva.sfsu.edu/collections/sfbatv/bundles/210522. There was a divide between what Baldwin wanted out of the documentary and what director Moore produced, and Moore later reflected that he believed that Baldwin never forgave him for not living up to his vision for the project.

20. James Baldwin, *Go Tell It on the Mountain* (New York: Knopf, 1953); Baldwin, *Another Country*; Baldwin, *Blues for Mister Charlie: A Play* (London: M. Joseph, 1965); Baldwin, *The Price of the Ticket: Collected Nonfiction, 1948–1985* (New York: St. Martin's/Marek, 1985).

21. Moore, *Take This Hammer.*

22. Holmes, "Take This Hammer," on *At the Gate of Horn.*

23. Cherian, *The Making of "Take This Hammer."*

24. Ibid.

25. Broussard, *Black San Francisco;* Daniel Crowe, *Prophets of Rage: The Black Freedom Struggle in San Francisco, 1945–1969* (New York: Garland, 2000).

26. Moore, *Take This Hammer.*

27. Cherian, *The Making of "Take This Hammer."*

28. Ford E. Long et al., *128 Hours: A Report of the Civil Disturbance in the City & County of San Francisco* (San Francisco: San Francisco Police Department, Planning and Research Bureau, 1966).

29. US Bureau of the Census, "Census 1960" (Washington, DC: US Department of Commerce, 1960); US Bureau of the Census, "Census 1970" (Washington, DC: US Department of Commerce, 1970); US Bureau of the Census, "Census 1980" (Washington, DC: US Department of Commerce, 1980); US Bureau of the Census, "Census 1990," http://factfinder.census.gov.

30. Robert O. Self, *American Babylon: Race and the Struggle for Postwar Oakland* (Princeton: Princeton University Press, 2003); James A. Tyner, "Urban Revolutions and the Spaces of Black Radicalism," in *Black Geographies and the Politics of Place*, ed. McKittrick and Woods, 218–32.

31. Moore, *Take This Hammer.*

32. Ibid.

33. Ibid.

34. Brahinsky, "Race and the City," 144–53; Clement Lai, "The Racial Triangulation of Space: The Case of Urban Renewal in San Francisco's Fillmore District," *Annals of the Association of American Geographers* 102, no. 1 (2012): 151–70.

35. Moore, *Take This Hammer.*

36. Martin Luther King, *Letter from Birmingham Jail* (Stamford, CT: Overbrook, 1968).

37. Brahinsky, "Race and the City," 144–53

38. Moore, *Take This Hammer.*

39. Calvin Welch, "The Fight to Stay: The Creation of the Community Housing

Movement in San Francisco, 1968-1978," in *Ten Years That Shook the City*, ed. Carlsson, 154–69.

40. Brahinsky, "The Making and Unmaking of Southeast San Francisco."

41. S. A. Ginwright and A. Akom, "African American Out-Migration: Initial Scan of National and Local Trends in Migration and Research on African Americans" (San Francisco: Mayors Office of Community Development Task Force on African American Out-Migration, 2008); US Bureau of the Census, "Census 1970"; US Bureau of the Census, "Census 2010."

42. Holmes, "Take This Hammer," on *At the Gate of Horn*.

43. Rebecca Bowe, "Marcus Books of San Francisco Evicted," *San Francisco Bay Guardian*, May 8, 2014, www.sfbg.com/politics/2014/05/08/marcus-books-san-francisco-evicted; Ian S. Port, "Coda: The End of Yoshi's SF," *SF Weekly*, June 18, 2014, www.sfweekly.com/sanfrancisco/coda-the-end-of-yoshis-sf/.

44. Aaron Chavez, "Hiraeth: The 3.9 Collective Searches for Home," University of San Francisco, November 16, 2015, www.usfca.edu/thacher-gallery/gallery-hstory/previous-shows/hiraeth. Chavez quotes from the description of the show by the 3.9 Collective.

45. Alicia Garza, who co-birthed the #BlackLivesMatter movement with Opal Tometi and Patrisse Cullors in 2013, was a community organizer in Bayview–Hunter's Point in the early 2000s.

46. Cherian, *The Making of "Take This Hammer."*

47. Richard O. Moore, *Take This Hammer—Director's Cut* (KQED Inc., 1963), https://diva.sfsu.edu/collections/sfbatv/bundles/187041.

48. W. E. B. Du Bois, *The Souls of Black Folk* (Oxford: Oxford University Press, 2007); Frantz Fanon, *Black Skin, White Masks* (New York: Grove, 2008); Toni Morrison, *Playing in the Dark: Whiteness and the Literary Imagination* (Cambridge: Harvard University Press, 1992),

49. Baldwin, *Another Country*, 51.

50. Baldwin, *The Price of the Ticket*.

51. Fanon, *Black Skin, White Masks*, xviii.

52. Kimberlé Crenshaw et al., eds., *Critical Race Theory: The Key Writings That Formed the Movement* (New York: New Press, 1995); Michael Omi and Howard Winant, *Racial Formation in the United States: From the 1960s to the 1990s* (New York: Routledge, 1994); George Lipsitz, *How Racism Takes Place* (Philadelphia: Temple University Press, 2011).

53. Baldwin, *The Fire Next Time*.

54. Audre Lorde, *Sister Outsider: Essays and Speeches*, Crossing Press Feminist Series (Trumansburg, NY: Crossing Press, 1984); Adrienne Rich qtd. in Ula Y. Taylor, "Making Waves: The Theory and Practice of Black Feminism," *Black Scholar* 28, no. 2 (July 1, 1998): 18–28.

55. Du Bois, *The Souls of Black Folk*, 1.

56. Morrison, *Playing in the Dark: Whiteness and the Literary Imagination*, 3.

57. Ibid., 38.

58. Ibid., 47.

59. There are political and research boundaries that limit our knowledge of the totality of such killings. One widely cited statistic comes from a 2012 report by the Malcolm X Grassroots movement, which found that every twenty-eight hours during that year a Black person was killed by a security guard, police officer, or vigilante (see Arlene Eisen, "Operation Ghetto Storm: 2012 Annual Report on the Extrajudicial Killing of 313 Black People [updated in 2013]," Malcolm X Grassroots Movement, October 2013, https://mxgm.org/wp-content/uploads/2013/04/operation_ghetto_storm_updated_october_2013.pdf.

60. Holmes, "Take This Hammer," on *At the Gate of Horn*.

61. In March 2015, a news report uncovered a police sweep of a youth hip-hop rehearsal, turning a musical recording event into a crime (cf. Jonah Owen Lamb, "Hunter's Point Rap Video Shoot Interrupted by Police, Two Arrested," *San Francisco Examiner*, March 13, 2015, www.sfexaminer.com/sanfrancisco/hunters-point-rap-video-shoot-interrupted-by-police-two-arrested/). This is not presented as quotidian but as one of many examples of similar challenges.

62. Clyde Woods, "Life after Death," *Professional Geographer* 54, no. 1 (2002): 62–66, 63.

63. Crenshaw et al., *Critical Race Theory*, xii.

64. Ruth Wilson Gilmore, *Golden Gulag: Prisons, Surplus, Crisis, and Opposition in Globalizing California* (Berkeley: University of California Press, 2007).

65. See Jackson John L., Jr., *Harlemworld: Doing Race and Class in Contemporary Black America* (Chicago: University of Chicago Press, 2001).

66. Patricia Hill Collins, "Learning from the Outsider Within: The Sociological Significance of Black Feminist Thought," *Social Problems* 33, no. 6 (1986): S14–S32 ; Donna Haraway, "Situated Knowledges: The Science Question in Feminism and the Privilege of Partial Perspective," *Feminist Studies* 14, no. 3 (Autumn 1988): 575–99; G. Rose, "Situating Knowledges: Positionality, Reflexivities and Other Tactics," *Progress in Human Geography* 21, no. 3 (September 1, 1997): 305–20; E. Schoenberger, "Interdisciplinarity and Social Power," *Progress in Human Geography* 25, no. 3 (September 1, 2001): 365–82; Taylor, "Making Waves: The Theory and Practice of Black Feminism."

67. Clyde Adrian Woods, "Katrina's World: Blues, Bourbon, and the Return to the Source," *American Quarterly* 61, no. 3 (2009): 427–53.

68. Rachel Brahinsky, "The Death of the City? Reports of San Francisco's Demise Have Been Greatly Exaggerated," *Boom: A Journal of California* 4, no. 2 (June 2014): 43–54.

69. Woods, "Katrina's World: Blues, Bourbon, and the Return to the Source," 430.

70. Katherine McKittrick, "Plantation Futures," *Small Axe* 17, no. 3 (November 1, 2013): 1–15.

71. Holmes, "Take This Hammer," on *At the Gate of Horn*.

72. Grant's killing was the subject of the 2013 film *Fruitvale Station* (Ryan Coogler, Significant Productions).

73. Adapted from author's research field notes, August 14, 2014, Oakland, CA.

74. Jamie Peck and Adam Tickell, "Neoliberalizing Space," in *Spaces of Neoliberalism: Urban Restructuring in North America and Western Europe*, ed. Neil Brenner and Nikolas Theodore (Malden, MA: Blackwell, 2002).

75. Gilmore, *Golden Gulag*; Michelle Alexander, *The New Jim Crow: Mass Incarceration in the Age of Colorblindness* (New York: New Press, 2012).

76. John Logan and Brian Stults, "Racial and Ethnic Separation in the Neighborhoods: Progress at a Standstill," American Communities Project, Russell Sage Foundation, December 14, 2010, www.s4.brown.edu/us2010/Data/Report/report1 .pdf.

77. Karen Thorsen, *James Baldwin: The Price of the Ticket* (Films Media Group, 1990).

Acknowledgments

I owe a great debt of gratitude to Pomona College for supporting and sustaining my work on this volume. I am particularly grateful to my colleagues Lorn Foster and Evelyn Khalili, who in different ways enabled this book to come into being.

At Pomona, my students Cameron Cook, Amaryllis Rodriguez, and Matthew Wolfson provided top-notch editorial assistance, each at a distinct stage in the book's development. Without their contributions and insights, this would be a much impoverished volume.

I also owe great thanks to my students Joaquin Banuelos, Matthew Dahl, Casey Goodwin, Peter Mason, Sean McCoy, and Kevin Tidmarsh for their invaluable work in helping this book get to press. Their careful attentions were a gift to this project.

There are few better gifts in life than getting to work with such caring and thoughtful people.

S. J. M.

Selected Bibliography

Works by James Baldwin

The Amen Corner. New York: Dial, 1968.

Another Country. New York: Dial, 1962.

Black Anti-Semitism and Jewish Racism. By James Baldwin et al. New York: Richard W. Baron, 1969.

Blues for Mister Charlie. New York: Dial, 1964.

The Cross of Redemption: Uncollected Writings. Edited by Randall Kenan. New York: Vintage, 2011.

The Devil Finds Work. New York: Dial, 1976.

A Dialogue. By James Baldwin and Nikki Giovanni. Philadelphia: Lippincott, 1973.

The Evidence of Things Not Seen. New York: Holt, Rinehart and Winston, 1985.

The Fire Next Time. New York: Dial, 1963.

Giovanni's Room. New York: Dell, 1956.

Go Tell It on the Mountain. New York: Knopf, 1953.

Going to Meet the Man. New York: Dial, 1965.

If Beale Street Could Talk. New York: Dial, 1974.

James Baldwin: The Last Interview and Other Conversations. Brooklyn: Melville House, 2014.

Jimmy's Blues: Selected Poems. London: Michael Joseph, 1983.

Just above My Head. New York: Dial, 1979.

Little Man Little Man: A Story of Childhood. By James Baldwin and Yoran Cazac. New York: Dial, 1976.

Native Sons. By James Baldwin and Sol Stein. New York: One World/Ballantine, 2004.

No Name in the Street. New York: Dial, 1972.

Nobody Knows My Name: More Notes of a Native Son. New York: Dell, 1961.

Notes of a Native Son. Boston: Beacon, 1955.

Nothing Personal. By James Baldwin and Richard Avedon. New York: Atheneum, 1964.

One Day When I Was Lost: A Scenario Based on "The Autobiography of Malcolm X." London: Michael Joseph, 1972.

The Price of the Ticket: Collected Nonfiction, 1948–1985. New York: St. Martin's, 1985.

A Rap on Race. By James Baldwin and Margaret Mead. Philadelphia: Lippincott, 1971.

Tell Me How Long the Train's Been Gone. New York: Dial, 1968.

Biographies

Boyd, Herb. *Baldwin's Harlem: A Biography of James Baldwin.* New York: Atria, 2008.

Campbell, James. *Talking at the Gates: A Life of James Baldwin.* Berkeley: University of California Press, 1991.

Eckman, Fern Marja. *The Furious Passage of James Baldwin.* New York: Evans, 1966.

Field, Douglas. *All Those Strangers: The Art and Life of James Baldwin.* Oxford: Oxford University Press, 2015.

Leeming, David. *James Baldwin: A Biography.* New York: Knopf, 1994.

Weatherby, W. J. *James Baldwin: Artist on Fire.* New York: Dell, 1989.

Interpretive Works

Achebe, Chinua, et al. *A Tribute to James Baldwin: Black Writers Redefine the Struggle.* Amherst: University of Massachusetts Press, 1989.

Balfour, Lawrie. *The Evidence of Things Not Said: James Baldwin and the Promise of American Life.* Ithaca, NY: Cornell University Press, 2001.

Beckley, Ralph, ed. *James Baldwin, in Memoriam: Proceedings of the Annual Conference of the Middle Atlantic Writers' Association, 1989.* Baltimore: Middle Atlantic Writers' Association Press, 1992.

Bloom, Harold, ed. *James Baldwin.* New York: Chelsea House, 1986.

Bobia, Rosa. *The Critical Reception of James Baldwin in France.* New York: Peter Lang, 1997.

Brim, Matt. *James Baldwin and the Queer Imagination.* Ann Arbor: University of Michigan Press, 2014.

Dickstein, Morris, ed. *James Baldwin: Critical Insights.* Pasadena, CA: Salem, 2011.

Elam, Michele, ed. *The Cambridge Companion to James Baldwin.* New York: Cambridge University Press, 2015.

Field, Douglas. *James Baldwin.* Devon: Northcote House, 2011.

———, ed. *A Historical Guide to James Baldwin.* Oxford: Oxford University Press, 2009.

Francis, Conseula. *The Critical Reception of James Baldwin, 1963–2010: "An Honest Man and a Good Writer."* Rochester: Camden House, 2014.

Hardy, Clarence E., III. *James Baldwin's God: Sex, Hope, and Crisis in Black Holiness Culture.* Knoxville: University of Tennessee Press, 2003.

Harris, Trudier. *Black Women in the Fiction of James Baldwin.* Knoxville: University of Tennessee Press, 1985.

———, ed. *New Essays on "Go Tell It on the Mountain."* Cambridge: Cambridge University Press, 1996.

Henderson, A. Scott, and P. L. Thomas, eds. *James Baldwin: Challenging Authors.* Rotterdam: Sense, 2014.

Henderson, Carol E., ed. *James Baldwin's "Go Tell It on the Mountain": Historical and Critical Essays.* New York: Peter Lang, 2004.

Kinnamon, Keneth, ed. *James Baldwin: A Collection of Critical Essays.* Englewood Cliffs, NJ: Prentice-Hall, 1974.

Köllhofer, Jakob, ed. *James Baldwin: His Place in American Literary History and His Reception in Europe.* New York: Peter Lang, 1991.

Kornegay, E. L., Jr. *A Queering of Black Theology: James Baldwin's Blues Project and Gospel Prose.* New York: Palgrave Macmillan, 2013.

Lee, A. Robert. *James Baldwin: Climbing to the Light.* New York: St. Martin's, 1991.

Macebuh, Stanley. *James Baldwin: A Critical Study.* New York: Third Press, 1972.

McBride, Dwight A., ed. *James Baldwin Now.* New York: New York University Press, 1999.

Miller, D. Quentin. *A Criminal Power: James Baldwin and the Law.* Columbus: Ohio State University Press, 2012.

————, ed. *Re-viewing James Baldwin: Things Not Seen.* Philadelphia: Temple University Press, 2000.

O'Daniel, Therman B., ed. *James Baldwin: A Critical Evaluation.* Washington, DC: Howard University Press, 1977.

Pavlić, Ed. *Who Can Afford to Improvise? James Baldwin and Black Music, the Lyric and the Listeners.* New York: Fordham University Press, 2016.

Porter, Horace. *Stealing the Fire: The Art and Protest of James Baldwin.* Middletown, CT: Wesleyan University Press, 1989.

Pratt, Louise H. *James Baldwin.* Boston: Twayne, 1978.

Schwarz, Bill, and Cora Kaplan. *James Baldwin: America and Beyond.* Ann Arbor: University of Michigan Press, 2011.

Scott, Lynn Orilla. *Baldwin's Later Fiction: Witness to the Journey.* East Lansing: Michigan State University Press, 2002.

Standley, Fred L., and Nancy V. Burt, eds. *Critical Essays on James Baldwin.* Boston: G. K. Hall, 1988.

Standley, Fred L., and Louis H. Pratt. *Conversations with James Baldwin.* Jackson: University Press of Mississippi, 1989.

Standley, Fred L., and Nancy V. Standley. *James Baldwin: A Reference Guide.* Boston: G. K. Hall, 1980.

Sylvander, Carolyn Wedin. *James Baldwin.* New York: Frederick Ungar, 1980.

Troupe, Quincy, ed. *James Baldwin: The Legacy.* New York: Simon and Schuster, 1989.

Young, Josiah Ulysses III. *James Baldwin's Understanding of God: Overwhelming Desire and Joy.* New York: Palgrave Macmillan, 2014.

Zaborowska, Magdalena J. *James Baldwin's Turkish Decade: Erotics of Exile.* Durham, NC: Duke University Press, 2009.

Contributors

Lawrie Balfour is professor of politics at the University of Virginia and currently serves as editor of *Political Theory*. She is the author of *Democracy's Reconstruction: Thinking Politically with W. E. B. Du Bois* and *The Evidence of Things Not Said: James Baldwin and the Promise of American Democracy*. Her research and teaching focus on race, democracy, feminist theory, and politics and literature.

Lisa Beard is a Chancellor's Postdoctoral Fellow in political science at the University of California, Riverside, with a research focus in racial politics and political thought. Beard has published an article on James Baldwin in *Contemporary Political Theory* and is currently working on a book on identification and intimate political appeal in racial politics.

Rachel Brahinsky is a geographer and assistant professor at the University of San Francisco, where she directs the graduate program in Urban & Public Affairs. Her scholarship focuses on race and justice in cities, particularly in California. Her current work, on the historical geography of race and urban development in San Francisco, situates these histories in the context of broader contemporary urban transformations like gentrification.

P. J. Brendese is assistant professor of political science and codirector of the Racism, Immigration, and Citizenship program at Johns Hopkins University. His recent work addresses issues of racial inequality, memory politics, and temporality. He is the author of *The Power of Memory in Democratic Politics*, and his essays have appeared in *Theory & Event*, *Contemporary Political Theory*, *Politics, Groups and Identities*, *Polity*, and edited anthologies. He is currently completing a book on race and segregated time that advances a theoretical account of the accelerated temporality of neoliberalism as tied to the proliferation of disposable populations. The study explores how racial inequalities are often experienced as impositions on human time and resistance to racial injustices are frequently figured in temporal terms.

Nicholas Buccola is professor of political science and the founding director of the Frederick Douglass Forum on Law, Rights, and Justice at Linfield College. He is the author of *The Political Thought of Frederick Douglass* and the editor of

The Essential Douglass and *Abraham Lincoln and Liberal Democracy*. His essays have been published in scholarly journals including the *Review of Politics* and the *Journal of Social Philosophy* as well as popular outlets including *Salon*, *Dissent*, and the *Claremont Review of Books*.

Eddie S. Glaude Jr. is the William S. Tod Professor of Religion and African American Studies and chair of the Center for African American Studies at Princeton University. He is the author of *Democracy in Black*; *African-American Religion: A Very Short Introduction*; *In a Shade of Blue: Pragmatism and the Politics of Black America*; and *Exodus! Religion, Race, and Nation in Early Nineteenth-Century Black America*. Glaude also edited *Is It Nation Time? Contemporary Essays on Black Power and Black Nationalism* and coedited *African-American Religious Thought: An Anthology* with Cornel West. Glaude's research interests include American pragmatism, specifically the work of John Dewey, and African American religious history and its place in American public life.

Vincent Lloyd is associate professor of theology and religious studies at Villanova University. His most recent books are *Black Natural Law* and a coedited volume, *Race and Secularism in America*. Lloyd coedits the journal *Political Theology*.

Susan McWilliams is associate professor of politics at Pomona College, where she has twice received the Wig Distinguished Professor Award for Excellence in Teaching. She is the author of *Traveling Back: Toward a Global Political Theory* and the coeditor of four other books, most recently (with John Seery) *The Best Kind of College: An Insiders' Guide to America's Small Liberal Arts Colleges*. Her writing has appeared in journals including *Commonweal*, the *Los Angeles Review of Books*, *The Nation*, and *Review of Politics*. McWilliams has won the Graves Award in the Humanities and a National Endowment for the Humanities Fellowship.

Wilson Carey McWilliams (1933–2005) was professor of political science at Rutgers University. In addition to his influential *The Idea of Fraternity in America*, he was the author of many essays, including those on American elections collected as *The Politics of Disappointment* and *Beyond the Politics of Disappointment*. His work has also been collected in two more recent volumes, *The Democratic Soul* and *Redeeming Democracy in America*.

Brian Norman is professor of English and associate vice president for academic affairs and dean of faculty affairs and diversity at Loyola University Maryland. He is the author of *Dead Women Talking: Figures of Injustice in American Literature*; *Neo-Segregation Narratives: Jim Crow in Post–Civil Rights American Literature*; and *The American Protest Essay and National Belonging*. Norman also coedited a collection with Piper Kendrix Williams entitled *Representing Segregation*. He serves on the editorial board of the *James Baldwin Review*.

Joel Alden Schlosser is assistant professor of political science at Bryn Mawr College. He previously held the Julian Steward Chair in the Social Sciences at Deep Springs College and taught political theory and constitutional law at Carleton College. He is the author of *What Would Socrates Do?* as well as numerous articles on ancient political thought, politics and literature, and democratic theory.

Ulf Schulenberg is visiting professor of American studies at the University of Erlangen-Nuremberg, Germany. He is the author of *Zwischen Realismus und Avantgarde: Drei Paradigmen für die Aporien des Entweder-Oder; Lovers and Knowers: Moments of the American Cultural Left*; and *Romanticism and Pragmatism: Richard Rorty and the Idea of a Poeticized Culture*. He is also the coeditor of *Americanization-Globalization-Education* and a forthcoming work on American rock journalism. His current book project focuses on the relationship between pragmatism and Marxism.

George Shulman teaches political theory and American studies at the Gallatin School of New York University. He is the author of *Radicalism and Reverence: Gerrard Winstanley and the English Revolution* and *American Prophecy: Race and Redemption in American Political Culture*. His most recent book, *American Prophecy*, was awarded the David Easton Prize in political theory.

Jack Turner is associate professor of political science at the University of Washington and director of the Washington Institute for the Study of Inequality and Race (WISIR). He specializes in American political thought, race in American politics, critical race theory, and democratic theory. He is the author of *Awakening to Race: Individualism and Social Consciousness in America* and the editor of *A Political Companion to Henry David Thoreau*. His most recent article is "Thinking Historically," published in *Theory & Event*.

Index

Political Companions to Great American Authors

Series Editor
Patrick J. Deneen, University of Notre Dame

Books in the Series

A Political Companion to Philip Roth
Edited by Claudia Franziska Brühwiler and Lee Trepanier

A Political Companion to Saul Bellow
Edited by Gloria L. Cronin and Lee Trepanier

A Political Companion to Flannery O'Connor
Edited by Henry T. Edmondson III

A Political Companion to Herman Melville
Edited by Jason Frank

A Political Companion to Walker Percy
Edited by Peter Augustine Lawler and Brian A. Smith

A Political Companion to Ralph Waldo Emerson
Edited by Alan M. Levine and Daniel S. Malachuk

A Political Companion to Marilynne Robinson
Edited by Shannon L. Mariotti and Joseph H. Lane Jr.

A Political Companion to James Baldwin
Edited by Susan J. McWilliams

A Political Companion to Walt Whitman
Edited by John E. Seery

A Political Companion to Henry Adams
Edited by Natalie Fuehrer Taylor

A Political Companion to Henry David Thoreau
Edited by Jack Turner

A Political Companion to John Steinbeck
Edited by Cyrus Ernesto Zirakzadeh and Simon Stow